Wissenschaftliche Untersuchungen
zum Neuen Testament · 2. Reihe

Herausgeber / Editor
Jörg Frey (Zürich)

Mitherausgeber / Associate Editors
Friedrich Avemarie (Marburg)
Markus Bockmuehl (Oxford)
James A. Kelhoffer (Uppsala)
Hans-Josef Klauck (Chicago, IL)

314

Ben C. Blackwell

Christosis

Pauline Soteriology in Light of Deification
in Irenaeus and Cyril of Alexandria

Mohr Siebeck

Ben C. Blackwell, born 1974; 2010 PhD from Durham University (England); 2008–2010 Research Assistant to N. T. Wright; currently Assistant Professor of Christianity at Houston Baptist University.

ISBN 978-3-16-151672-6
ISSN 0340-9570 (Wissenschaftliche Untersuchungen zum Neuen Testament, 2. Reihe)

Die Deutsche Nationalbibliothek lists this publication in the Deutsche Nationalbibliographie; detailed bibliographic data are available on the Internet at *http://dnb.d-nb.de*.

The book was printed by Laupp & Göbel in Nehren on non-aging paper and bound by Buchbinderei Nädele in Nehren.

Printed in Germany.

For Heather, Elam and Silas

Preface

This monograph is a slightly altered form of my doctoral thesis submitted to Durham University in 2010. I would like to thank Professor Jörg Frey and the editors for accepting this work as a part of the WUNT II series and the editorial staff at Mohr Siebeck who were so helpful in completing the project. In addition to the response from Professor Markus Bockmuehl, the feedback from Professors Lewis Ayres and John Riches at my viva improved this final output.

When I told my brother Dan Blackwell that I was writing about theosis, his first question was 'Can you die from that?' His joke indicates the general lack of awareness in the West of alternate soteriological models that the Eastern church has found fundamental to their understanding of scripture and theology for centuries. Some might argue that ascribing deification to Paul is foolish. We have his words recorded in Acts 14.15 in which he and Barnabas explicitly deny being gods. At the same time, Herod accepted the acclamation of the crowds that he was a god, and, in fact, he did die from it (Acts 12.20-23). You'll see that my argument about embodying Christ's narrative does entail dying but his life is also shared through that experience.

One of the most gratifying aspects of this project is the opportunity to reflect on the many people who have contributed to its completion. I am first indebted to those who helped me get to Durham and made our time there better. My academic career began at Ouachita Baptist University, where Scott Duvall, Danny Hays, and Terry Carter, among others, spurred my interest in the Bible, history, and theology at an academic level. I was later introduced to deification and patristic theology by Jeff Bingham and Scott Horrell at Dallas Theological Seminary. We have many friends from churches along the way that have encouraged me along this path, but the community at Carrville Methodist Church in Durham stands above them all as a source of love and encouragement.

My experience at Durham was better than I could ask for. Since doctoral studies demand much individual work, they are often noted as a lonely affair, but the support from friends and family kept it from being anything but lonely. All my fellow researchers in the 37 N. Bailey offices served as insightful conversation partners, especially Nijay Gupta and John

Goodrich for all things Pauline and Kevin Hill for all things patristic. In addition to their insight, I am especially appreciative for the time colleagues took out of their busy schedules to respond to sections of the thesis: Mark Mathews, Jason Maston, Ben Dunson, Francis Watson, Mike Gorman, and especially Kevin Hill who read the whole thesis. Also, as much as any other David Litwa has spurred me to think more broadly and write more precisely through our conversations and emails.

I am very grateful for Professor John Barclay's supervision of this project. His insights into the project greatly improved this final output, as well as my own intellectual and professional development. Importantly, he models not only top scholarship but also graciousness and friendliness, along with the rest of his family. I cannot thank John enough for his help overall and for the time he gave to this project during his sabbatical.

Along with John, Loren Stuckenbruck as my secondary supervisor and Tom Wright contributed significantly. Loren offered much more time and input than was expected in this secondary role, for which I am most appreciative. During my time in Durham, I had the pleasure of working with Tom Wright as his research assistant for two years. My studies were definitely enriched though this work and by our various discussions. I must also give a note of gratitude for the extra time he allowed me in the last stages just before submission.

In addition to their input in the project, I want to thank the faculty of the Department for their support throughout and for helping me secure the Durham University Doctoral Fellowship.

My family has walked alongside me throughout my academic studies. Above all, my parents Mack and Brenda Blackwell helped spark my love of study and have been generous with love and encouragement throughout. At the same time, Bill and Patt Elam, Norm and Alice MacDonald, and Rob and Sue Mills, my wife's family, have treated me like I was their own and have generously supported us, each in their own way.

And finally, my studies in England were most enriched by my immediate family: Heather, Elam, and Silas. We all embarked on this journey together and enjoyed almost every minute of it. Elam and Silas are two of the best kids a dad could ever ask for. As my wife, Heather has always shown her love and encouragement, and she even put up with NFL nights every Sunday in Durham. She, like no other, has helped me keep going when I didn't want to and celebrated the victories with me along the way.

Thanks to you all!

September 2011   Ben C. Blackwell

Table of Contents

List of Tables

List of Illustrations

Abbreviations

Abbreviations and citation conventions for ancient literature and modern scholarship SBL (1999) are followed wherever possible. In addition, the following abbreviations are used for key patristic texts:

AH	*Against Heresies*, Irenaeus
De Incarn.	*On the Incarnation*, Athanasius
Dem.	*The Demonstration of Apostolic Preaching*, Irenaeus
In Jo.	*Commentary on John*, Cyril of Alexandria
In Luc.	*Homilies on Luke*, Cyril of Alexandria
Life	*Life of Moses*, Gregory of Nyssa
Quod	*On the Unity of Christ*, Cyril of Alexandria
Thes.	*Thesaurus*, Cyril of Alexandria
Dial. Trin.	*Dialogues on the Trinity*, Cyril of Alexandria

I. Setting the Stage

1. Introduction

1. The Question

With the rise in ecumenical dialog in recent years, the Eastern Orthodox doctrine of theosis, or deification, is gaining popularity as a soteriological category for Westerners. Most of the discussion about becoming like God or even becoming 'gods' has occurred on the theological level (e.g., with the Finnish Interpretation of Luther[1]), but more attention is beginning to be placed on biblical texts. In fact, Kärkkäinen notes a need for work in biblical studies to develop the level of discussion.[2] There is clear interest in 2 Pet 1.4,[3] but Pauline texts, which stand at the heart of Western theology, are becoming a centre of focus.[4] While a few essays have been devoted to the topic, the question of the relationship of theosis to Paul's theology has yet to be thoroughly explored. Accordingly, the aim of this monograph is to explore whether and to what extent theosis helpfully captures Paul's presentation of the anthropological dimension of soteriology. That is, does this admittedly later, and thus anachronistic, notion help us to read Paul in a way that draws out and connects aspects of his theology that Western readers have routinely missed or underplayed?

---

[1] E.g., Veli-Matti Kärkkäinen, *One with God: Salvation as Deification and Justification* (Collegeville, MN: Liturgical Press, 2004); B. Marshall, 'Justification as Declaration and Deification', *IJST* 4 (2002): 3–28.

[2] Kärkkäinen, *One with God*, 121–23.

[3] Stephen Finlan, 'Second Peter's Notion of Divine Participation' in *Theosis: Deification in Christian Theology,* eds. Stephen Finlan and Vladimir Kharlamov (Eugene, OR: Pickwick, 2006), 32–50; James Starr, 'Does 2 Peter 1:4 Speak of Deification?' in *Partakers of the Divine Nature: The History and Development of Deification in the Christian Traditions,* eds. Michael J. Christensen and Jeffery A. Wittung (Grand Rapids: Baker, 2008), 81–92.

[4] Stephen Finlan, 'Can We Speak of *Theosis* in Paul?' in *Partakers of the Divine Nature: The History and Development of Deification in the Christian Traditions,* eds. Michael J. Christensen and Jeffery A. Wittung (Grand Rapids: Baker, 2008), 68–80; M. David Litwa, '2 Corinthians 3:18 and Its Implications for *Theosis*', *JTI* 2 (2008): 117–133; Michael J. Gorman, *Inhabiting the Cruciform God: Kenosis, Justification, and Theosis in Paul's Narrative Soteriology* (Grand Rapids: Eerdmans, 2009); idem., 'Romans: The First Christian Treatise on Theosis', *JTI* 5 (2011), 13–34.

Two qualifications regarding this study are important to note. First, if
we are going to make any statements about the helpfulness of theosis in
our understanding of Paul, we must be clear about what the terminology
means. This is even more pressing because of the unfamiliarity with the
concept in Western traditions. Therefore, since the explicit terminology of
deification is absent from Paul's letters, a significant goal of Part II of this
book is to define deification more narrowly for comparison with Paul.

For purposes of our preliminary discussion, I offer a brief background
of the concept here. Drawing from Greco-Roman concepts, a variety of
terms has been used throughout history to describe the Christian version of
this soteriology.[5] The first terminology was just the appellation of 'gods'
(θεοί, *dii*) applied to believers, but by the third century numerous verbs
were used for the process of becoming or being made gods, e.g., θεοποιέω,
ἐκθεόω, and ἐκθειάζω. In fact, theopoiesis (θεοποίησις) is probably the
best term to generally capture earlier and less synthetic views of deification. Though most popular today because of wide use in the Byzantine
period, the term θέωσις was not coined by Gregory of Nazianzus until the
fourth century (although the verb θεόω, from which it comes, was in use
from the early third century). Deification and divinisation are just the
Latin-based translations for theosis/theopoiesis,[6] and I use Greek and Latin
forms interchangeably for Paul. However, using the Latin forms, of which
I prefer deification, is preferable when speaking of Greek patristic writers
if we are not using cognates of the actual Greek terminology so earlier and
later notions are not confused. Just as the terminology changed over time
and in various contexts, the meaning ascribed to the terminology changed
as well. However, Russell argues that likeness (*homoiosis*) to God and
participation (*methexis*) in God stand as twin pillars upon which notions of
deification stand.[7] This general definition of deification as likeness to and
participation in God will guide our discussion until Part II where we will
clarify this further.

The second qualification to our study is our focus upon the *anthropological* dimension of soteriology. Deification naturally intersects with a
variety of other theological themes, such as the nature of God, Christology,
anthropology, atonement, and conceptions of protology and eschatology.
To maintain a manageable scope for this project, I have restricted the study

---

[5] For more detail on the historical development of the terminology, see Norman
Russell, *The Doctrine of Deification in the Greek Patristic Tradition* (Oxford: Oxford
University Press, 2004); Jules Gross, *The Divinization of the Christian According to the
Greek Fathers* (trans. Paul A. Onica; Anaheim: A&C Press, 2002).

[6] Though outside the scope of this project, Ittai Gradel (*Emperor Worship and Roman
Religion* [Oxford: OUP, 2002], 63–66) outlines the ancient Roman distinctions between
deus and *divus*, and how these changed with the deification of the emperors.

[7] Russell, *Deification*, 1–2.

to the anthropological dimension of this soteriology. That is, our focus will be on the transformation of the human condition believers experience, rather than the process of atonement that procured that change. These, of course, cannot be easily disconnected, but addressing questions of monotheism and atonement would make the project unwieldy.

With these preliminary qualifications in mind, a survey of the landscape of previous scholarship on the issue would now be helpful to situate this project.

2. Review of Literature

A number of NT interpreters have made comments for or against deification in Paul, but few offer any detailed discussion of the topic. For example, Bousset raises the possibility that Paul interacts with Greek ideas of deification, but he argues that Paul's soteriological focus is primarily upon redemption from sin and condemnation rather than deifying immortality.[8] However, he later briefly notes how the use of glory and immortality language brings Paul into this sphere of discussion.[9] Schweitzer and Käsemann capture the two main sentiments against deification in Paul, though only through brief comments. Schweitzer strongly argues for union with Christ as central to Paul but denies this could be a *Hellenistic* form of deification.[10] Later, Käsemann associates the hope of deification with a theology of glory, which is antithetical to Paul's theology of the cross.[11] Of those that address the issue in more depth, we will first examine the two works that provide a history of deification: Jules Gross and Norman Russell. Afterwards, we will then attend to Pauline exegetes who address the issue of deification: Morna Hooker, Stephen Finlan, David Litwa, and Michael Gorman.

---

[8] Wilhelm Bousset, *Kyrios Christos* (trans. John E. Seely; Nashville: Abingdon, 1970), 164–67, 194, 210.

[9] Ibid., 227–28, esp. n.68.

[10] Albert Schweitzer, *The Mysticism of Paul the Apostle* (trans. William Montgomery; Baltimore: Johns Hopkins, 1998), 15–16.

[11] Ernst Käsemann, 'The Saving Significance of the Death of Jesus in Paul' in *Perspectives on Paul,* (London: SCM, 1971), 32–59, at 59; idem., 'The Cry for Liberty in the Worship of the Church' in *Perspectives on Paul,* (London: SCM, 1971), 122–37, at 134.

2.1 Histories of Deification

2.1.1 Jules Gross

Responding to negative assessments of deification near the turn of the 19th century,[12] Gross provided one of the first large-scale studies of the history of deification, in which he briefly discusses the biblical foundations.[13] He is quite positive about the role of deification in the Pauline letters when he writes: 'The revelation of the mystery of deification owes its most decisive progress to Saint Paul .... And the most personal element of Pauline soteriology is a mysticism of deification of which the glorious Christ is the center'.[14] In his discussion of Paul's soteriology, Gross points to the Adam-Christ association and new creation as fundamental. In addition, union with Christ, as expressed with the phrase ἐν Χριστῷ and effected through baptism, is the basis of an objective and mystical transformation. However, the true culmination of deification in Paul is 'the participation in the specifically divine attribute of blessed incorruptibility'.[15] Gross summarises Paul's contribution: 'Deification ... is obtained by a mystical assimilation to the death and resurrection of the God-Savior – a conformity that is definitely produced by baptism'.[16] Following Pauline scholarship from the time, Gross surmises that Paul may have utilised language used by the Mystery Religions but he did not directly borrow from them.[17]

Gross' discussion of Pauline soteriology is necessarily short because his purpose is to describe deification in the Greek fathers, but he highlights key themes that influence later writers. Implicit within Gross' argument is that Paul's theology is directly equivalent to later notions of deification, which Gross has explored in his work. To be sure, Pauline terminology and concepts were a primary source for later theological developments but implicit affirmations regarding their equivalence do not provide adequate evidence for scholarly conclusions.

2.1.2 Norman Russell

In his monumental work on the history of deification in the Greek patristic tradition, Russell offers a section on Paul in which he explores 'participatory union with Christ' as a fundamental theme, in which his dependence

---

[12] E.g., Adolf Harnack, *History of Dogma* (trans. Neil Buchanan; 7 vols.; New York: Dover, 1961), 2:318.

[13] Gross, *Divinization*, 82–88.

[14] Ibid., 82.

[15] Ibid., 86.

[16] Ibid.

[17] Ibid., 87–88.

upon E.P. Sanders is evident.[18] As part of this theme, Russell mentions the Pauline themes of Adam and Christ, Abraham and Christ, being sons of God, and the present/future pneumatic experience of believers, with Romans 8 and 1 Corinthians 15 regarded as central passages. Although noting the strong reality of participation based upon Sanders' reading of Paul and the Pauline basis for much of the later development regarding deification, Russell remains hesitant about finding a place for deification in Paul's writings. He offers three arguments for this position:

First, Christ is not called 'God' unequivocally before the second century. Until that step is taken, union with Christ is not the same as union with God. Secondly, Paul did not isolate 'participation' for special consideration. He did not have fixed technical term for participatory union with Christ, the various expressions which he uses – 'in Christ', 'with Christ', 'Christ in us', 'sons of God' and so on – reflecting different aspects of that union or being utilized in different contexts. Thirdly, we should not forget that these expressions are metaphorical images. 'Deification' as a theological term only emerges when the Pauline metaphors are re-expressed in metaphysical language. Paul simply gives us a hint of what is to come in the writings of Clement, Origen, and their successors.[19]

Regarding the first objection, this study will not explore the question of Jesus' divinity since the issue is secondary to our focus on the anthropological dimension of Paul's soteriology; however, the issue about human participation in divine attributes through Christ will be an area for us to explore. The second and third objections are closely related. Russell rightly raises the question about the nature of Pauline metaphors, but having other priorities Russell does not explore this in depth. In fact, he describes deification as a metaphor in the early church, but 'by the sixth century the metaphorical sense was fading'.[20] However, this does not make the reality of the concept any less real in those writers before the sixth century. In the same way, the metaphorical use of participatory language in Paul does not minimise the possibility of its reality.[21] Thus, an aspect of our study will be the analysis of this language and what it represents.

2.2 Morna Hooker

In a series of essays, Morna Hooker explored the various 'interchange' passages in the Pauline letters.[22] She argues that participation in Christ is

---

[18] Russell, *Deification*, 79–85.

[19] Ibid., 85.

[20] Ibid., 1.

[21] All theological language is at one level or another metaphorical, so the question is not is this 'only' metaphorical, but does this metaphor helpfully explore the grammar of Paul's theology? Cf. George Lindbeck, *The Nature of Doctrine: Religion and Theology in a Postliberal Age* (London: SPCK, 1984), 84.

[22] Morna D. Hooker, *From Adam to Christ* (Eugene, OR: Wipf & Stock, 2008), 13–69.

central to Pauline theology and that these interchange passages capture the essence of this participation. In summary she writes: 'It is *not* that Christ and the believer change places, but rather that Christ, by his involvement in the human situation, is able to transfer believers from one mode of existence to another'.[23] The implicit association with deification comes with her argument that Irenaeus' famous exchange statement ('he became what we are so that we could become what he is') in *Against Heresies* 5.Pr.1 aptly sums up the theology captured in these interchange statements, which in turn captures the whole of Paul's theology. Irenaeus' statement does not explicitly affirm deification, but it stands as an important step in the trajectory of Athanasius' slight modification: 'he became human that we might become gods' (*De Incarn.* 54).

Later, however, Hooker qualifies her assessment since the correspondence between Paul and Irenaeus appears to relate to form and not content. Although Paul's interchange idea is virtually equivalent to Irenaeus' statement, Paul's 'understanding of this statement would have remained Hebraic; he would not have interpreted it, as happened later, in terms of Greek philosophy'.[24] She does not explicitly clarify what this distinction between Hebraic and Greek entails, but the prior context discussed how Christ restores believers, making them 'truly human', which may be an implicit rebuttal of deification as a Greek idea where people become more than human. But we must ask: do Irenaeus and other patristic writers understand deification as making believers more than human?

Methodologically, this use of a later interpreter to clarify Paul's language is intriguing. In some ways she gestures towards the use of Irenaeus to help understand Paul, but at the same time discounts the meaning that Irenaeus gives to the language. Her brief qualification about the fundamental differences leaves the reader wanting more explanation. Ultimately, Hooker at most gives a nod to deification in Paul by her comparison with Irenaeus, but she leaves much room further clarification regarding the distinction between the two.

2.3 Stephen Finlan

Stephen Finlan is one of the first Pauline exegetes to focus directly on the association of Pauline theology and theosis in recent times.[25] He notes that various definitions may be offered for theosis, and Paul's theology would only fit some of them, an issue I will address presently. Finlan first focuses upon Paul's promise of 'a spiritual and glorious body, which theo-

---

[23] Ibid., 5, emphasis original.

[24] Ibid., 22.

[25] Finlan, *'Theosis* in Paul?'.

logically constitutes divinization'.[26] Drawing from 1 Corinthians 15, 2 Corinthians 3, Romans 8, and Philippians 3, Finlan highlights Paul's use of the terminology of transformation and conformation to characterise this process of theosis. He later concludes: One must recognise

> the believer's necessary participation in the Savior's cruciform life so that one may also share in his *anastasiform* living. Since the *anastasiform* benefits begin already in this lifetime, an exclusive focus on sin and deliverance would suppress a crucial aspect of Paul's teaching: gaining an ability to discern the will of God, and being transformed into Christlikeness, which can truly be called *theosis*. Thus, *theosis* in Paul always involves both cruciform and *anastasiform* living, but points to a thoroughly *anastasiform* destiny, when the believer will 'be with Christ' (Phil 1.23).[27]

He then ends with a statement that this process could also be called Christification, 'not ... becoming Christ, but rather Christlike in substance and character'.[28] This is a three-stage process – 1) dying to sin, 2) reflecting righteousness and light, and 3) receiving a glorious body – with each aspect modelled by Christ.[29] Implicit within Finlan's argument is that becoming like Christ – christification – is equivalent to becoming like God – deification.

The difficulty comes when Finlan calls this theosis. He notes that several notions of deification exist (and this variety is exemplified by the other essays in the same volume in which his essay occurs), but he never clarifies what theosis actually entails. According to him, Paul's version of theosis includes the cruciform and anastasiform existence, but what makes this theosis? Though an essay format does not allow space for all issues, without such clarity about what theosis means, arguing that this is what Paul's soteriology represents becomes difficult. Thus, his essay raises the hermeneutical question: In what sense can one claim that when Paul says 'x' he really means 'y', in which 'y' is different language of a different era?

2.4 M. David Litwa

In distinction to the previous works that tried to analyse Paul's soteriology as a whole with regard to theosis, Litwa limits his discussion to 2 Cor 3.18 and its immediate context.[30] By focusing on a particular text, Litwa avoids

---

[26] Ibid., 68. Finlan finds the specific nature of this new embodiment important, and spends several pages rebutting N.T. Wright's view of the resurrection body. In response, Finlan argues: the '"spiritual body" is neither physical body nor a disembodied spirit' but something different altogether (71).

[27] Ibid., 78.

[28] Ibid., 79.

[29] Ibid., 73. Gorman (*Inhabiting*, 6) abstracts these, labelling them '(1) dying to sin, (2) moral transformation, and (3) eschatological transformation'.

[30] Litwa, '2 Corinthians 3:18'.

debating 'whether Paul had a "doctrine" or "theory" or "idea" of deification. Rather the question is whether an aspect of Paul's soteriology can be called "deification," by which I mean "sharing in God's reality through Christ"'.[31] In this article, he is primarily responding to Scott Hafemann who says that becoming the same image means that believers become only the same human (i.e., anthropological) reality as Christ, and not the same divine (i.e., theological) reality.[32] Litwa first argues that the 'same image' (3.18) is the image of Christ (4.4). Thus, when humans are transformed into 'the same image' they are deified, becoming like Christ in his divinity. That is, when believers are transformed into that image, they share in Christ's theological (divine) and anthropological (human) reality. In his words: 'the eschatological image of the church will share in the divinity of the Christological image'.[33] To support his interpretation of 'image' Litwa also focuses on other passages that use this language, in particular 1 Cor 11.1–7 and 1 Cor 15.42–29. Litwa secondly argues that this participation in the humanly divine and divinely human image 'is not an ontological state – let alone a mystical one – but consists (at least in this life) in a mode of being that is manifested in concrete ethical acts'.[34] At this point in his article, Litwa leans heavily upon the parallel use of μεταμορφόω in Rom 12.2 and then discusses the problem of deification and the continuing struggle with sin.

Litwa determined that the lexical parallels of 'image' in 1 Corinthians 11 and 15 and 'transform' in Romans 12 were formative for understanding 2 Cor 3.18.[35] Unfortunately, the concept of 'image' that was so important to the first argument plays little role in the second, and so the connection between the two feels strained. However, Litwa's fundamental argument that being transformed into the 'same image' cannot be separated from Christ as the image of God must not be ignored. Like Finlan, Litwa makes explicit the notion that identifying with Christ has key implications for one's relationship to the divine, but he takes a step beyond Finlan by situating Christ's divine status in one particular text. Litwa also provides a definition of what he understands deification to be ('sharing in God's reality through Christ'), which, based on personal correspondence, he understands as ontological and moral but with a focus on the moral here. This interesting but highly focused argument whets one's appetite but leaves us

---

[31] Ibid. 117.

[32] Scott J. Hafemann, *Paul, Moses, and the History of Israel: The Letter/Spirit Contrast and the Argument from Scripture in 2 Corinthians 3* (Peabody, MA: Hendrickson, 1996).

[33] Ibid. 120.

[34] Ibid. 129.

[35] Litwa (117n.1) intentionally leaves aside the epistolary context of 2 Cor 3–4.

desiring a further discussion of other texts and contexts. However, the language of 'reality' and the discussion of how ethical acts relate to ontological transformation leave room for more specificity. Fortunately, as of this printing Litwa is finalising a monograph about deification in Paul, which I am eagerly anticipating.

2.5 Michael Gorman

To date, Gorman's discussion in his monograph provides the largest and most in-depth exploration of the topic of theosis in the Pauline letters. He has recently followed this up with an essay about theosis and the letter to the Romans.[36] The core of Gorman's argument in his monograph is this: 'that Paul's experience of Christ was precisely an experience of God *in se*, and that we must either invent or borrow theological language to express that as fully and appropriately as possible'.[37] The term that Gorman argues that best describes Paul's soteriology is theosis. Gorman defines theosis in Paul as this: 'Theosis is transformative participation in the kenotic, cruciform character and life of God through Spirit-enabled conformity to the incarnate, crucified, and resurrected/glorified Christ, who is the image of God'.[38] Ultimately, Gorman concludes that with Paul's emphasis on cruciformity, the best description of his soteriology is 'cruciform theosis'.[39] As with the writers above, Gorman does a good job of exploring the contours of Pauline soteriology and then affirms that this is equivalent to theosis. In fact, Gorman argues that not to use the term theosis 'would mean seriously misrepresenting what is perhaps at the core of Paul's theology'.[40]

In his essay on Philippians 2 his primary argument is that Christ reveals the divine identity and that his action, particularly that of death and resurrection, is that of God himself (cf. 1 Cor 1.18–25). As the basis of this argument he focuses particularly on the language of Phil 2.6 with its although [x], not [y], but [z] formula.[41] Based upon his analysis, he contends that inherent in the 'although' is a 'because'. Christ acts in a kenotic and cruciform manner because he is divine. Consequently, when believers are drawn up into the pattern of death and resurrection through participation and conformation, they are living in a divine way. Gorman then applies this conceptuality more widely when he explores the method of participation in this divine cruciformity in terms of justification by co-crucifixion and in terms of holiness. The primary emphasis of Gorman's

---

[36] Gorman, 'Romans'.
[37] Gorman, *Inhabiting*, 4.
[38] Ibid., 7.
[39] Ibid., 162.
[40] Ibid., 8.
[41] Ibid., 16–25.

work is on the moral embodiment of Christ's life, but he notes there are
other aspects as well.[42] In particular, he mentions other items need to be
addressed: 'Among the themes that will deserve subsequent attention are
adoption of God's children, life in the Spirit, the body of Christ, Adam
typology, interchange/exchange, and the resurrection of the body and the
nature of eternal life'.[43]

Gorman also addresses theosis in his chapter on holiness as he generally
associates Paul's call for believers to act in a holy manner like God. However, the strongest chapter in his argument about theosis is the one based
on Philippians 2 because it derives from a close reading of a particular text
rather than a thematic summary of different texts. His affirmation of theosis in that passage is based upon the human embodiment of Christ's divine
activity. As with Litwa's analysis of 2 Cor 3.18, this argument holds together on its own, but its plausibility would be strengthened by situating
this reading within an historical context. That is, do other writers of any
era agree that theosis is about embodying Christ's death? This leaves the
reader wanting more explanation why theosis is the best way to describe
this pattern, where this term comes from, and what connotations it carries.

With Gorman's recent article on Romans, he expands his discussion of
theosis by addressing the soteriology of the letter. His thesis is that 'Paul's
soteriology [in Romans] of human *dikaiosunē* and *doxa* means participation in the divine *dikaiosunē* and *doxa* by participation in the death and
resurrection of the Messiah Jesus, God's righteous and now glorified Son',
and that this corresponds directly to his earlier definition of theosis in Paul
(as quoted above).[44] In addition to a defintion of Paul's theosis, Gorman
now gives a broader definition of theosis ('becoming like God by participation in the life of God'), such that it when Christ and the Spirit mediate
'certain divine attributes' to believers this is theosis.[45] An important aspect
of Gorman's argument in this article is that he explicitly places himself in
a stream of confessional interpretation, in which historical Christian,
namely Eastern and patristic, readings serve as aids, but his argument is no
less exegetical since the particularities of *dikaiosunē* and *doxa* are his emphasis. We'll address his argument more specifically later in the monograph, but we may note that there is still room to further clarify how a
'*cruciform* theosis' fits within the larger Christian tradition which he situates himself.[46]

---

[42] Ibid., 6.

[43] Ibid., 8n.22.

[44] Gorman, 'Romans', 15.

[45] Ibid., 17.

[46] Ibid., 19, emphasis original.

2.6 Issues and Questions

While progressing beyond the mere assertions that characterised earlier treatments, these contributions by patristic and NT scholars raise as many questions as they answer. In particular, the essay length treatment that each provides allows them to advance the dialogue related to deification in the Pauline letters but without the space to explore lengthier matters of justification, methodology, and definition. This by itself shows the need for a longer treatment, but two primary questions are clear from these previous discussions.

The first question relates to the matter of definition: what do we mean by deification? Key topics of discussion included conformation and transformation, image, glory, and immortality language, and the deity of Christ. Of these recent NT interpreters who have been optimistic about reading deification in Paul, Finlan focused more on the ontological or physical aspects of this transformation, whereas Litwa and Gorman highlighted moral aspects. In addition, Litwa and Gorman based their soteriological arguments upon the theological and narrative evidence for the deity of Christ in particular passages. Thus, becoming like Christ entails deification. While these readings attend to the contours of the Pauline text, they are not situated within a historical context, with the exception of Gorman's article on Romans. That is, these three NT have offered readings of Paul that are not explicitly supported by contemporary Jewish or Greco-Roman ideas (within a history of religions context) nor associated with later patristic and medieval interpretations (within a history of interpretation context). They implicitly place their discussion within a reception historical stream (particularly due to the use of 'theosis' rather than merely 'deification'), but none of the three appeals to this. Since notions of deification developed over time, which traditions or streams are they drawing from? As a result, a primary task in this study will be clarifying a definition of deification and situating the use of this language within a particular context.

The second question arises from this dependence upon conceptualities derived centuries after the Pauline letters were written. The explicit language of theosis is absent in Paul, so we must ask: in what sense can one claim that when Paul says 'x' he really means 'y', in which 'y' is different language of a different era? Paul's letters were employed in the development of patristic ideas of deification, so there is a connection that may be explored. However, this does not resolve the challenge of anachronism. To answer this question, we must first determine how this study will approach the question – from a history of religions or a history of interpretation perspective.

3. Route of Study: History of Interpretation

3.1 Two Paths

As this is a relatively new area of inquiry, there are at least two equally valid paths to assess the helpfulness of deification for understanding Paul: 1) history of religions or 2) history of interpretation. For the former, one could try to find models of deification antecedent to or contemporary with Paul and then compare these to Paul's soteriological construction. Potential candidates include Jewish mystical traditions, imperial apotheosis, or the Greek mystery religions. However, two significant problems exposed in earlier history of religions studies exist with this route which make it less helpful for this initial project. First, as interpreters compare Paul's writings to these different backgrounds, the temptation is to construct an artificial structure from the various pieces of data that appear separately but never all together. In particular, the Gnostic redeemer myth, which is now soundly rejected, stands as an example, though careful scholarship regularly avoids this type of problem.[47] The second problem is that of pinning down the determinative background for Paul within all the different traditions since so many have been offered but no consensus has yet been reached. These problems are not insurmountable, but they give us reason to consider approaching our question in this initial study from a different angle – that of history of interpretation.

With a reception-historical study any number of interpreters might serve as our basis – patristic, Byzantine/medieval, or modern – though patristic interpreters would be the best place to start due to their proximity. Richard Hays argues for this when he writes:

E.P. Sanders has rightly emphasized that participatory soteriology stands at the center of Paul's thought ..., and he confesses himself unable to explain what Paul means by this 'real participation in Christ'. My own guess is that Sanders's insights would be supported and clarified by a careful study of participation motifs in patristic theology, particularly the thought of the Eastern Fathers.[48]

Since deification arose primarily in the Greek patristic tradition, analysing writers from this tradition would best serve as the basis of our discussion. These theologians provide early models as benchmarks against which we can compare Paul. Thus, the previous problem of artificial constructions becomes moot. With regard to the topic of deification we can move from the (to some degree) clearer – patristic – to the unclear – Paul – rather than from the more unclear – backgrounds – to the unclear – Paul. This is not

---

[47] Cf. R.M. Grant, *Gnosticism: An Anthology* (London: Collins, 1961), 18.

[48] Richard B. Hays, *The Faith of Jesus Christ: The Narrative Substructure of Galatians 3:1–4:11* (2nd ed.; Grand Rapids: Eerdmans, 2002), xxxii.

the usual route taken in NT studies, so we must ask how such a move can be supported. This avenue has its own problems, and primary among these is the issue of anachronism, or making Paul parrot views from later centuries.[49] We will address this issue and others as we discuss the hermeneutical justification and methodology.

3.2 Hermeneutical Justification and Methodology

The recent decades have marked an evident growth in interest in the history of interpretation of NT texts. Following the impulse of Hans-Georg Gadamer, Ulrich Luz is notable in his incorporation of the history of interpretation, and the larger category of *Wirkungsgeschichte* under which it falls for help in interpreting the text.[50] Following on his heels, others promoted the usefulness of *Wirkungsgeschichte* in the interpretation of NT texts,[51] seminar groups on the Use and Influence of the NT (BNTC) and Romans through the Centuries (SBL) were added to prominent conferences, and several commentary series arose that focus specifically upon the history of interpretation.[52] This shows the growing popularity of *Wirkungsgeschichte* but there is no consensus about how to use this material. Some argue that it can show the influence of the Bible in culture but not determine interpretations,[53] whereas others see some place for getting at the meaning of texts.[54] With this lack of clarity, we should return again to

---

[49] Since we are looking at Paul's letters, we do not face the complex issues related to allegory and the like, thus making our use of patristic writers more straight-forward, although their use of Paul is decidedly theological.

[50] Ulrich Luz, *Das Evangelium nach Matthäus* (EKK 1; 3 vols.; Zürich: Benzinger, 1985). See also, idem., *Matthew 1–7: A Commentary* (trans. Wilhelm Linss; Minneapolis: Augsburg, 1989), 95–99; idem., *Matthew in History: Interpretation, Influence, and Effects* (Minneapolis: Fortress, 1994). Cf. Anthony C. Thiselton, *The First Epistle to the Corinthians* (NIGTC; Cambridge: Eerdmans, 2000).

[51] Heikki Räisänen, 'The Effective "History" of the Bible : A Challenge to Biblical Scholarship?', *SJT* 45 (1992): 303–324; Markus Bockmuehl, 'A Commentator's Approach to the "Effective History" of Philippians', *JSNT* 60 (1995): 57–88; Wayne A. Meeks, 'Why Study the New Testament', *NTS* 51 (2005): 155–70, at 165; Markus Bockmuehl, *Seeing the Word: Refocusing New Testament Study* (Studies in Theological Interpretation; Grand Rapids: Baker, 2006). Thiselton also discusses Gadamer's help for NT interpretation: Anthony C. Thiselton, *The Two Horizons: New Testament Hermeneutics and Philosophical Description* (Exeter: Paternoster, 1980), 293–326.

[52] E.g., The Blackwell Bible Commentary Series (Blackwell), The Church's Bible (Eerdmans), the Ancient Christian Commentary Series (IVP), and the Ancient Christian Texts Series (IVP).

[53] Räisänen, 'Effective "History"'.

[54] Rachel Nicholls, *Walking on the Water: Reading Mt. 14:22–33 in the Light of Its Wirkungsgeschichte* (Biblical Interpretation 90; Leiden: Brill, 2008), 1–25; Luz, *Matthew 1–7*, 96.

primary theoreticians, Gadamer, his student Hans Robert Jauss, and Mikhail M. Bakhtin, to see what help they can provide for a project like this.

Although there had been steps to recognise the historical assumptions and prejudices of interpreters in the mid-20th century, most sought an objective perspective on the NT texts by following historical-critical methods.[55] Gadamer, on the other hand, in his magnum opus *Wahrheit und Methode* eschewed as unrealistic the enlightenment preoccupation with objectivity and its consequent repulsion of tradition's influence.[56] He argued that as much as we would like to distance ourselves from our own historical situation and to reach back into the historical situation of the original setting, we cannot escape our own historicality any more than the writers of the original texts.[57] Our understanding of texts is not in spite of our historical situation, but rather by means of it. This understanding is determined by 'horizons', always changing perspectives on the world, which are formed by the very *Wirkungsgeschichte* (or 'history of influence'/'effective history') of the texts that interpreters are trying to engage.[58] Accordingly, to recognise the influence of their own historical situation, interpreters must have an effective-historical consciousness.[59] Hence, his emphasis on the *Wirkungsgeschichte* of a text is not for the sake of understanding the effective-history in itself nor even primarily to interpret the text, but it is a means to understanding better one's own historical context.

When it comes to interpreting texts, Gadamer describes the process as including first a projection of the historical horizon of the text, in which the interpreter situates the text's argument in its original context. Then, the interpreter must have a fusion of horizons. He explains:

The projecting of the historical horizon, then, is only a phase in the process of understanding, and does not become solidified in the process of self-alienation of a past consciousness, but is overtaken by our present horizon of understanding. In the process of understanding there takes place a real fusing of horizons, which means that as the historical horizon is projected, it is simultaneously removed.[60]

---

[55] For instance, Bultmann argues that interpreters always have presuppositions, but that these should not be determinative of exegetical readings: Rudolf Bultmann, 'Is Exegesis Without Presuppositions Possible?' in *New Testament and Mythology and Other Basic Theological Writings*, (trans. Schubert M. Ogden; Philadelphia: Fortress, 1984), 145–53.

[56] Hans-Georg Gadamer, *Wahrheit und Methode: Grundzüge einer philosophischen Hermeneutik* (2nd ed.; Tübingen: JCB Mohr, 1975).

[57] idem., *Truth and Method* (trans. J. Weinsheimer and D.G. Marshall; 2nd rev. ed.; London: Sheed & Ward, 1989), 262–64.

[58] Ibid., 302.

[59] Ibid., 305.

[60] Ibid., 273.

He then clarifies that the historicality of the text and interpreter is not lost in this fusion:

> Every encounter with tradition that takes place within historical consciousness involves the experience of the tension between the text and the present. The hermeneutical task consists in not covering up this tension by attempting a naive assimilation but consciously bringing it out. That is why it is part of the hermeneutical approach to project an historical horizon that is different from the horizon of the present.[61]

Although the horizons of the interpreter and text are fused, the tension remains because Gadamer sees the whole process as one of dialogue between the I and Thou of question and answer.[62]

Gadamer does not speak to our question directly because his emphasis is upon traditions that presently inform the horizon of contemporary interpreters. Our question about deification is one that is outside the effective-historical tradition of most Western interpreters. However, his emphasis on the dialogue between text, tradition, and the interpreter is crucial for our own conversation, because he reminds us that we are not objective observers of the Pauline texts. Our horizon of understanding is highly influenced by our tradition in which we stand. At the same time, a dialogue with texts and historically-effected traditions that arise from it help us to understand not only our position but also the texts themselves. Jauss, his student, develops this further.

Building upon Gadamer's thought, Hans Robert Jauss discusses the aesthetics of reception and how this influences understanding.[63] He argues that when one encounters a text, the reader is predisposed to the text by a 'horizon of expectation', which has been previously determined by other works and one's understanding about genre, literary form, etc.[64] When encountering a text, the horizon of expectation may be satisfied or challenged by the text. In the former case, where the distance between what is expected and what is received is short, the closer 'the work comes to the sphere of "culinary" or entertainment art' because the text fits neatly in the box prepared for it.[65] In the case of the latter, contact with the text re-

---

[61] Ibid.

[62] Ibid., 321–41.

[63] Works central to our discussion include Hans Robert Jauss, 'Literary History as a Challenge to Literary Theory' in *Toward an Aesthetic of Reception*; trans. Timothy Bahti (Minneapolis: University of Minnesota Press, 1982), 3–45; idem., 'Horizon Structure and Dialogicity' in *Question and Answer: Forms of Dialogic Understanding*; trans. Michael Hays (Minneapolis: University of Minnesota Press, 1989), 197–231.

[64] Jauss, 'Literary History', 20–24.

[65] Ibid., 25. He also writes: 'This latter work can be characterized by an aesthetics of reception as not demanding any horizontal change, but rather as precisely fulfilling the expectations prescribed by a ruling standard of taste, in that it satisfies the desire for the reproduction of the familiarly beautiful; confirms familiar sentiments; sanctions wishful

shapes one's horizon of expectation. Thus, when one next encounters a
text, the process of challenge or satisfaction occurs again but with this
modified horizon of expectation. For 'masterworks' (what we might term
'classics') our expectations so govern our understanding of these texts that
it becomes difficult for them to challenge us. According to Jauss, for these
masterworks

> their beautiful form ... has become self-evident, and their seemingly unquestionable
> 'eternal meaning' bring them, according to an aesthetics of reception, dangerously close
> to the irresistibly convincing and enjoyable 'culinary' [or entertainment] art, so that it
> requires a special effort to read them 'against the grain' of the accustomed experience to
> catch sight of their artistic character once again.[66]

Thus, finding avenues for fresh readings of these classics can open up
these texts again. In his terms, this starts a fresh *dialogue* between readers
and texts because new answers arise for new questions.

In a later work Jauss sees his dialogic understanding of texts as in continuity with that of Mikhail M. Bakhtin, but the continued dependence
upon Gadamer is evident.[67] The question-answer dialogue that forms the
conversation is central:

> Literary understanding first becomes dialogic when the alterity of the text is sought out
> and acknowledged before the horizon of one's own expectations – with the result that
> instead of attempting a naive fusion of horizons, one's own expectations will be cor-
> rected and expanded through the experience of the other.[68]

The search for meaning in the text does not ignore the text by preferring
the meaning the reader provides it. Rather, the text is held in a position of
honour as the other with its own voice in the conversation.

Jauss shows us that our reading of Paul is informed by our horizon of
expectation, which has been formed by previous readings of Paul and by
the Western tradition. Since Paul's letters are well known, they have become, in some ways, an 'entertainment art' because they are 'masterworks'. We might, therefore, have difficulty reading him again with fresh
eyes, against the grain. However, by holding a conversation between Paul
and his Greek patristic interpreters, we have the opportunity for our understanding to be challenged so we can reshape our horizon of expectation.

Bakhtin, while not addressing the issue of *Wirkungsgeschichte*, per se,
also promotes a dialogic method of interpreting texts. He argues that
'great works' draw from the depths of culture and thus speak beyond their
own present situation, and they are thus understood in 'great time', that is,

---

notions; makes unusual experiences enjoyable as "sensations"; or even raises moral problems, but only to "solve" them in an edifying manner as predecided questions' (25).

[66] Jauss, 'Literary History', 25–26.

[67] Idem., 'Question and Answer', 207–9, 214–18.

[68] Ibid., 207–8.

in epochs beyond their own. As those in later epochs engage these works they continually find new semantic depth. But is this not merely reading meaning into a text instead of out of it? Using Shakespeare's works as an example, Bakhtin responds:

> But do we then attribute to Shakespeare's works something that was not there, do we modernize and distort them? ... [Shakespeare] has grown because of that which actually has been and continues to be found in his works, but which neither he himself nor his contemporaries could consciously perceive and evaluate in the context of the culture of their epoch. Semantic phenomena can exist in concealed form, potentially, and be revealed only in semantic cultural contexts of subsequent epochs that are favorable for such disclosure.[69]

Bakhtin points us to the meaning potential within texts that is uncovered through later engagement. Readings of Paul using, of course, a later conceptuality may not simply alter or misconstrue his text but draw out the meaning potential in a way that he did not, and could not, himself articulate. The writer's own historical situation cannot be ignored because the writing arose specifically within a historical situation; however, it cannot be left there because 'its fullness is revealed only in *great time*', that is throughout later engagement.[70]

When he later discusses how to get at that semantic depth, Bakhtin then proposes the balance of emic and etic dialogue. However, an external point of view allows a holistic analysis that those within a culture cannot achieve.[71] In a later essay, he explores this concept of dialogue further and writes: 'The text lives only by coming into contact with another text (with context). Only at the point of this contact between texts does a light flash, illuminating both the posterior and anterior, joining a given text to a dialogue'.[72] As a result, Paul's later interpreters can serve as the context which contacts his letters and thus sparks new light, aiding new understanding of his letters.

Drawing closer to modern biblical hermeneutics, Stephen Fowl expresses the excess of meaning potential which Gadamer, Jauss, and Bakhtin point towards. Showing the weaknesses of determined (historical-critical) and undetermined (postmodernist deconstruction) views of scripture, Stephen Fowl proposes that we view these texts as underdetermined.[73]

---

[69] Mikhail M. Bakhtin, 'Response to a Question from the *Novy Mir* Editorial Staff' in *Speech Genres and Other Late Essays,* eds. Caryl Emerson and Michael Holquist (trans. Vern W. McGee; Austin: University of Texas Press, 1986), 1–9, at 4–5.

[70] Ibid., 5, emphasis original.

[71] Ibid., 6–7.

[72] Idem., 'Toward a Methodology for the Human Sciences' in *Speech Genres and Other Late Essays,* eds. Caryl Emerson and Michael Holquist; trans. Vern W. McGee (Austin: University of Texas Press, 1986), 159–72, at 162.

[73] Stephen Fowl, *Engaging Scripture* (Oxford: Blackwell, 1998).

The texts open doors to a variety of readings.[74] Within each of his letters and especially the corpus as a whole, a level of 'underdetermined' ambiguity remains and thus invites discussion between his interpreters as how to understand the interrelationships between his different motifs. Thus, by allowing new voices in the conversation of Pauline interpretation, the meaning potential of the text can plumbed more deeply. Based upon the work of Gadamer, Jauss, and Bakhtin, I thus propose that we hold a conversation between Paul and his Greek patristic interpreters regarding the issue of deification.

This project may be construed in many ways, but based on the nature of contemporary debates I have chosen to focus on deification as a theological construct and not on patristic interpretation, per se. This distinction will become clearer in chapter 4 (§2.2), but it means our focus will be on key Pauline passages where he most fully presents his soteriology rather than an analysis of all the primary texts utilised by these patristic writers. By allowing Paul to speak for himself through these passages, this mitigates the problems raised by Skinner, which I discuss below.

Since Paul's texts are our primary focus, we will allow the Greek patristic writers to serve a heuristic role in our reading of Paul concerning the subject of deification. These later interpreters are thus not seen as a series of misreadings of Paul and developments away from him but as an aid to our study. In some sense, this is just an expansion of a traditional methodology. All good studies are aware of previous thought on an issue, and this is just an attempt to include more interpreters in the review of literature than just those from the past 25 years.[75]

At the same time, Gadamer and Jauss encourage a dialogic study in which the members of our conversation have their own voice. It is important to note that Gadamer and Jauss are not against historical study but rather historicism, that is, an over-optimistic expectation of objectivity. If we are to hold a dialogic conversation between Paul and his later interpreters regarding the topic of deification, we should allow them to have their own voice through historical investigation. To this end, we will first analyse the patristic writers to determine how they develop deification themes and what aspects of Pauline theology were helpful, even necessary, for

---

[74] Augustine notes this ambiguity in readings of Genesis (*Confessions* 12.27): The meaning of the text is like a spring being fed through a small pipe that comes out with great force. Although it is channelled through limited words, the meaning is not limited by these words.

[75] That is, this methodology rejects the enlightenment prejudice for the recent. Bockmuehl (*Seeing*, 66) rightly notes that this type of project helps us better understand our own situation and not just that of Paul, when he writes: 'Critically applied, *Wirkungsgeschichte* offers a hermeneutically sensitive and powerful instrument for interpreting both the reader and his or her text'.

supporting their notions of deification. Second, we will then read Paul with fresh questions and insights regarding how motifs might relate to one another. Possible outcomes may be that the Pauline texts are ambiguous, being generative of both traditional Western readings and readings supportive of deification, or that the texts explicitly affirm or deny the patristic constructions.

As Rachel Nicholls makes clear in her innovative use of *Wirkungsgeschichte* to explore biblical texts, this reception-historical methodology should not be viewed as exclusive of other methods, whether literary, historical-critical, or ideological:

While *Wirkungsgeschichte* draws attention to the unexamined preconceptions which sometimes unduly influence traditional critical results, this is in order to redeem and supplement insights which are based on earlier critical investigations. *Wirkungsgeschichte* is not an independent and rival method but a useful insight into the task of interpreting historical texts. It is an insight which has given birth to a procedure; and this procedure could usefully combine with a number of different critical methods.[76]

Accordingly, this study attempts to incorporate insights from the reception history of his letters with a study of the letters themselves using traditional methods which focus on the Paul's contemporary and antecedent contexts.

While the conversation between Paul and his later interpreters may shine light on Paul's theology, some may respond that the focus upon later terminology, in our case, deification, robs Paul of his voice. That is, it forces Paul to address topics and questions that were not relevant to his situation.[77] David Yeago helpfully addresses this issue when he discusses the relationship of the NT to later creedal constructions.[78] While later formulations sometimes use different terminology, particularly at key points, this change does not necessarily entail a difference in meaning. He bases this upon a distinction between judgments and concepts. Yeago writes:

We cannot concretely perform an act of judgement without employing some particular, contingent verbal and conceptual resources; judgement-making is an operation performed with words and concepts. At the same time, however, the same judgement can be rendered in a variety of conceptual terms, all of which may be informative about a particular judgement's force and implications. The possibility of valid alternative verbal/conceptual

---

[76] Nicholls, *Walking on Water*, 191.

[77] For example, see Morna D. Hooker for an explanation about how Chalcedonian emphases are different from the NT and how care should be taken when reading the NT in light of these: Morna D. Hooker, 'Chalcedon and the New Testament' in *The Making and Remaking of Christian Doctrine: Essays in Honour of Maurice Wiles,* eds. Sarah Coakley and David A. Pailin (Oxford: Clarendon Press, 1993), 73–93.

[78] David S. Yeago, 'The New Testament and the Nicene Dogma: A Contribution to the Recovery of Theological Exegesis', *ProEccl* 3 (1994): 152–64.

renderings of the identical judgement accounts for the fact that we ourselves often do not realize the full implications of the judgements we pass: only some of their implications are ever unpacked in the particular renderings we have given them.[79]

Different language and 'concepts' are employed by different writers at different times, but this does not mean that they are making different 'judgments' about the subject matter.[80] Yeago provides three aspects related to comparing the judgments of different writers:

We must ask 1) about the logical subjects of which predicates are affirmed and denied, 2) about the logical type of the particular predicates affirmed or denied within the conceptual idioms they employ, and 3) about the point or function of their affirmations or denials within their respective contexts of discourse.[81]

When the conceptual language of two or more writers can determined as making the same affirmations in each of these three areas, we can determine that they are making the same judgments. Our study relates to a comparison of the nature and structure of Pauline and patristic soteriology with regard to the later patristic concept of deification. This analysis is not limited to the concept of 'deification', though the language of deification will drive our study of the patristic authors. Thus, we will return to these criteria in our conclusion as we address the similarity of the soteriological constructions between Paul and his patristic interpreters regarding deification.

Yeago's structure gives a method for comparison, but Quentin Skinner's critique of the 'mythology of doctrines' is especially relevant for studies such as this which are diachronic and concerned with the history of ideas.[82] He argues that these studies often promote anachronisms because they ignore the settings out of which the texts arise. Thus, in our comparison we must remember the different contexts, genres, and goals of the writers and seek to understand how these influence their constructions. Gadamer and Jauss are acutely aware of this issue, and they remind us to be aware of the historical context of authors and texts because writers are always attempting to answer particular questions.[83] In our discussion of deification, our

---

[79] Ibid., 159.

[80] Accordingly, chastising patristic writers for not parroting biblical language seems to be misdirected, examples of which are numerous.

[81] Ibid., 160.

[82] Quentin Skinner, 'Meaning and understanding in the history of ideas' in *Visions of Politics. Volume I: Regarding Method,* (Cambridge: Cambridge University Press, 2002), 57–89. Kaufman explores Skinner's critique regarding the study of deification in relation to Irenaeus: John Kaufman, 'Becoming Divine, Becoming Human: Deification Themes in Irenaeus of Lyons' (Ph.D. diss., MF Norwegian School of Theology, 2009), 25–33.

[83] See Gadamer, *Truth and Method,* 333–41. Cf. Hans Robert Jauss, 'Goethe's and Valéry's *Faust*: On the Hermeneutics of Question and Answer' in *Toward an Aesthetic of*

goal is not to abstract the subject matter in these various texts from the historical contexts from which it arises. Rather, it is through the particularity of the historical situation that the subject matter becomes most clear. Approaching this question from a history of interpretation approach does not, thus, abandon historical inquiry. As we address the Pauline letters, the historical situation cannot be and is not ignored. However, the focus will not be a search for origins of Paul's thought but rather a comparison of Paul's thought within his context with theological constructions, albeit later, that wrestle with similar topics within their own contexts.

Within Paul's context of Judaism and the early church, certain questions remained unanswered, to which he offered answers through his letters. In turn, as our patristic interpreters read Paul and other scriptural texts, they attempted to answer those questions which arose from their own contexts. As a response to those questions, these later writers provide a synthetic account of theology; however, they use particular texts to build that theology. Accordingly, Simonetti writes: 'the history of doctrine is the history of exegesis, in that the whole development of catholic doctrine is based on the interpretation of a certain number of passages in Scripture in light of particular needs ...'.[84] The biblical texts, and especially the Pauline letters, are integral to the development of patristic theology. Being aware of the context of which the texts arose, then, is integral. As a result, in the concluding chapter we will highlight not only the similarities but also the differences, which are highly dependent upon the different contexts out of which these writings arose.

As with the discussion of the historical context of the different writers in our conversation, my own historical situation cannot be ignored. Even though reading Paul in light of his patristic interpreters gives fresh eyes to view Paul, this does not allow me, or any of us, to somehow escape the historical tradition through which I interpret these past writings. I cannot escape the Protestant tradition which has influenced me, any less than Paul and his later interpreters could escape their own contexts. Thus, as I give my interpretation of Paul, I use language like 'Paul argues ...', but this is just shorthand for 'Based upon my reading of the text, Paul argues ...'.[85] While not claiming to be an objective interpreter of texts, my intension is

---

Reception (trans. Timothy Bahti; Minneapolis: University of Minnesota Press, 1982), 110–38.

[84] Manlio Simonetti, *Biblical Interpretation in the Early Church: An Historical Introduction to Patristic Exegesis* (trans. John A. Hughes; Edinburgh: T&T Clark, 1994), 1. Cf. Lewis Ayres, *Nicaea and Its Legacy: An Approach to Fourth-Century Trinitarian Theology* (Oxford: Oxford University Press, 2006), 31–40.

[85] Accordingly, I am attempting to foster a conversation between Paul and his later interpreters, but since I am the only one orchestrating the conversation, the study might also be characterised as a comparison.

to incorporate the historical and literary data in a manner that provides a simple and coherent reading.[86] In that way, the contours of the theology of Paul and his interpreters can shine through, while not ignoring my own influence. The test of this reading of is not whether or not it corresponds to the patristic writers, but how well it corresponds to the data within the Pauline letters themselves.

Although this conversation could naturally fit within the realm of theological interpretation, this project is intentionally not that type of study.[87] We are after the subject matter of the text as Barth proposes,[88] but with theological interpretation confessional and canonical concerns exert a greater hermeneutical control over the process. While I am not opposed to this methodology, the difference in our study will be seen in the fact that patristic comments not are brought into play when we are looking at the Pauline texts themselves.

3.3 Conclusion

In contemporary discussions about biblical notions of deification, a need for hermeneutical clarity has been exposed. We have the option to choose one of two equally valid (and even compatible) paths: history of religions or history of interpretation. In order to argue from the more concrete to the less concrete for this particular question, we have chosen the path of reading Paul in light of his interpreters. Our community of interpretation has not been substantively influenced by notions of deification, so analysing the effective history through the Greek tradition allows us to view Paul from a different vantage point. Thus, we will hold a conversation between

---

[86] Cf. N.T. Wright, *The New Testament and the People of God* (Minneapolis: Fortress, 1992), 98–104.

[87] Louth, while not in the centre of theological interpretation debates, makes a strong case for the use of patristic interpretation: Andrew Louth, *Discerning the Mystery: An Essay on the Nature of Theology* (Oxford: Oxford University Press, 1983). One primary example of the use of patristic interpretation is seen in Davis' and Hays' recent work. They give nine theses about theological interpretation and the seventh reads: 'The saints of the church provide guidance in how to interpret and perform Scripture' (Ellen F. Davis and Richard B. Hays, eds. 'Nine Theses on the Interpretation of Scripture' in *The Art of Reading Scripture* [Grand Rapids: Eerdmans, 2003], 1–8, at 4). Cf. David C. Steinmetz, 'Uncovering a Second Narrative: Detective Fiction and the Construction of Historical Method' in *The Art of Reading Scripture,* eds. Ellen F. Davis and Richard B. Hays (Grand Rapids: Eerdmans, 2003), 54–68.

[88] Following Karl Barth ('The Preface to the Second Edition' in *The Epistle to the Romans* [trans. Edwyn C. Hoskyns; London: Oxford University Press, 1933], 7), theological interpretation attempts to hold a 'conversation between the original record and the reader [which] moves round the subject-matter, until a distinction between yesterday and to-day becomes impossible'. Nicholls (*Walking*, 8–9) is right to distinguish this from Gadamer's fusion of horizons.

Paul and his Greek interpreters as we consider the topic of deification. By following this path our hope is that we can better understand Paul's soteriology in light of the notion of deification as advanced by these Greek interpreters.

4. Selection of Patristic Theologians

In order to hold this conversation between Paul and his later interpreters, we need to decide who the partners should be. A number of writers in the Greek patristic tradition would be worthy partners, but in order to have a manageable project two writers will give us enough variety for an interesting conversation. The following criteria, therefore, will be the basis for selecting the two writers.

4.1 Criteria For Selection

1. Deification Themes
Since our study is about deification, we clearly need to engage authors who employ, and even develop, deification themes. Russell and Gross are helpful in this regard because they survey the growth of deification themes through the Greek patristic writers.[89]

2. Pauline Interpreter
With the primary aim being a better understanding of the contours of Paul's theology, investigating writers that significantly utilise Pauline texts to develop their notions of deification is necessary. Obviously, Paul is not the only NT writer who influenced later notions of deification, but we should focus upon writers who use the Pauline letters more often when developing and explaining their views on deification.

3. Representative of Broader Traditions
Space limitations allow for study of no more than two early Christian authors, so the implications of the study can be enhanced by analysing authors whose thought is representative of broader traditions. Since this is a preliminary study on this topic, those traditions that were of limited influence are interesting but less helpful for this project.

4. Pre-Chalcedonian Writer
As with most theological doctrines, the idea of deification developed with time. A tension exists in that those interpreters closer to Paul's cultural setting have less defined views of deification whereas those who are later

---

[89] Russell, *Deification*; Gross, *Divinization*.

have more defined views but are at a greater distance from Paul. As a result, choosing multiple interpreters over different time periods will help mitigate this issue. With deification's relation to Christology, we should be aware of current christological debates that influence the discussion of deification in relevant authors. The council of Chalcedon (AD 451) and its Definition served as a watershed, not only in christological debates, but because they precipitated ecclesial divisions not previously experienced. The decisive nature of the council, thus, makes it a useful boundary marker for study of early notions of deification.[90] Understanding that the doctrine developed over time, I have chosen to study two writers before Chalcedon – one early (c. 150–300) and one later (c. 300–451). Based on our desire to have two writers as conversation partners, we will now discuss the selection of each.

4.2 Selection of Irenaeus as the Early Writer

Our sample of writers in the second and third centuries is not large, but we do have a variety of different perspectives and traditions represented (see Table 1.1). Although Gnostic traditions represented by Nag Hammadi texts would be interesting to study as Pauline interpreters because of their distinct ideas regarding divine-human interaction, their limited influence on historical developments of deification restricts their usefulness for this project. This leaves Irenaeus and Origen as those who both discuss deification and significantly engage the Pauline letters.[91] Origen's commentary on Romans stands as direct evidence of his interaction with Paul, but his

---

[90] After Chalcedon, Denys, Maximus, and John of Damascus provide some of the most sustained and more systematic treatments of deification. In particular, Denys is the first to give a direct definition of deification: 'theosis is the attaining of likeness to God and union with him so far as possible' (*Ecclesiastical Hierarchies* 1.3 in Russell, *Deification*, 248). Cf. Pseudo Dionysius, *The Complete Works* (Classics of Western Spirituality; trans. Colm Luibheid; New York: Paulist, 1987). We cannot speak of a systematic and fully refined system of deification until Maximus the Confessor (cf. Russell, *Deification*, 1).

[91] Clement of Alexandria does play an important role, but it is important to note that the major study on Clement's idea of deification situates him against several backgrounds – heterodox Christian, Hellenistic Jewish, and academic Middle Platonist – but not against a New Testament (or specifically, Pauline) background: Arkadi Choufrine, *Gnosis, Theophany, Theosis: Studies in Clement of Alexandria's Appropriation of his Background* (Patristic Studies 5; New York: Peter Lang, 2002). Thus, while Clement would be an interesting and early witness to early ideas about deification from within a mystical tradition, his explicit integration of Hellenistic philosophical ideas and his requisite de-emphasis on Pauline texts (relative to other interpreters) in explicating his theology make him less fruitful for an initial study on how the reception history helps us better understand the Pauline texts.

use of 'mystical philosophy' and his controversial status in later centuries makes his work less representative.[92]

Table 1.1: Earlier Greek Writers (c. 150–300)

Writer/Text	Deification Themes	Pauline Interpreter
Marcion (c. 85–160)		√
Justin Martyr (c. 100–165)	√	
Nag Hammadi Texts (1st–4th cent)	√	√
Irenaeus (c. 130–200)	√	√
Clement of Alexandria (c. 150–215)	√	
Hippolytus (c. 170–236)	√	
Origen (c. 185–254)	√	√

The role of Pauline texts in Irenaeus' writings is debated,[93] but Irenaeus, particularly in *Against Heresies*, is noted for his dependence upon Pauline texts to support his arguments.[94] In fact, it is the constructive use of Pauline texts that make him interesting for this project. Irenaeus' employment of Ps 82.6 (81.6 LXX) helps shape later development of the language with regard to immortality and adoption, which appear in later interpretive streams. In fact, Gross argues that 'almost all subsequent [soteriological] development will follow paths shown by him'.[95] While Irenaeus' constructions are highly representative of later traditions, his specific influence is debatable, which is evidenced by the fact that four out of his five books in *Against Heresies* are only fully extant in Latin.[96] Nevertheless, Irenaeus fits best as our early writer.[97]

---

[92] Andrew Louth, *The Origins of the Christian Mystical Tradition: From Plato to Denys* (2nd ed.; Oxford: Oxford University Press, 2007), 110.

[93] See Chp 2 §1 for further discussion.

[94] In his comprehensive study of Irenaeus' use of Paul, Noormann shows the variety of ways Irenaeus employs Pauline texts: Rolf Noormann, *Irenäus als Paulusinterpret: zur Rezeption und Wirkung der paulinischen und deuteropaulinischen Briefe im Werk des Irenäus von Lyon* (WUNT 2/66; Tübingen: Mohr Siebeck, 1994). See also my 'Paul and Irenaeus', in *Paul in the Second Century*, Michael F. Bird and Joseph R. Dodson, eds., (LNTS 412; London: T&T Clark, 2011), 190–206.

[95] Gross, *Divinization*, 266.

[96] On Irenaeus' influence on Athanasius, for example, see Khaled Anatolios, 'The Influence of Irenaeus on Athanasius' in *Studia Patristica: XXXVI*, eds. M.F. Wiles and E.J. Yarnold (Leuven: Peeters, 2001), 463–76. However, Anatolios overstates the relationship because Athanasius appears to make no direct quotations of Irenaeus.

[97] This fits well with Bockmuehl's (*Seeing*, 169, emphasis original) proposal 'to privilege the *earlier* over the more remote effects for a historical understanding of Christian-

4.3 Selection of Cyril of Alexandria as the Later Writer

In distinction to the limited number of writers in the second and third centuries, we have a number of texts and traditions to consider from the fourth and fifth centuries (see Table 1.2).

Table 1.2: Later Greek Writers (c. 300–451)

Writer/Text	Deification Themes	Pauline Interpreter
Eusebius of Caesarea (c. 263–339)		
Athanasius (c. 293–373)	√	√
Cyril of Jerusalem (c. 313–386)		
Basil of Caesarea (330–379)		
Gregory Nazianzus (c. 330–389)	√	
Gregory of Nyssa (c. 335–395)		
Didymus the Blind (c. 313–398)	√	√
John Chrysostom (c. 347–407)		√
Macarian Writings (c. 380s)	√	
Theodore of Mopsuestia (c. 350–428)		√
Cyril of Alexandria (375–444)	√	√
Theodoret of Cyrus (c. 393–457)		√

Gregory Nazianzus stands out as the writer who most utilises and develops deification within the Christian tradition. In fact, he coins the term θέωσις (*Orations* 4.71).[98] Were he to have used Pauline material more consistently, he would have been our top choice as a conversation partner. This leaves Athanasius, Didymus the Blind, and Cyril of Alexandria. All three stand within the Alexandrian tradition and thus represent similar points of view regarding deification. However, with Cyril being the latest of the three, we are able to capture the full development of thought since he draws from the previous two.[99] Also, of these three, Cyril stands out as the most significant exegete. For instance, approximately 70% of the extant

---

ity's texts, persons, and events' due to proximity and shared contexts. Bockmuehl (*Seeing*, 178–80) argues that Irenaeus stands in the third generation of leaders from Christ. He thus may provide unique knowledge, but must still be treated with caution.

[98] Russell, *Deification*, 214–15.

[99] Gross writes: 'With Cyril of Alexandria the doctrine of divinization indeed appears as the sum total of all that the previous fathers have written on this theme'. Gross, *Divinization*, 233.

writings we have of Cyril are exegetical works. With regard to Pauline texts in particular, Russell writes: 'Cyril's perspective is profoundly Pauline as well as Johannine .... Cyril's approach to deification is not mystical in a speculative sense but deeply theological, drawing on Paul, John, Irenaeus, and Athanasius for its leading ideas'.[100] Cyril thus fits best as our later writer.[101]

4.4 Formulations of Deification

While our study has necessarily limited its scope to Irenaeus and Cyril, we should recognise that these two writers do not represent the full scope of views on deification in the Greek tradition. For instance, Irenaeus and Cyril are often associated with a 'physical theory' of Christ's work[102] or 'realistic' views of deification[103] due to an emphasis on the incarnation in their theology. Their accounts of deification balance between the body and the soul differently than other traditions. For example, other schools of thought place the accent on different areas, in particular the 'mystical tradition' which emphasises the soul.[104] Greek writers that are generally characterised as mystical are Clement of Alexandria, Origen, Evagrius, Gregory of Nyssa, Dionysius (or Denys) the Areopagite, and Maximus the Confessor.[105] These writers regularly focus upon the ascent of the soul towards God and incorporate Platonic and Neoplatonic categories. Although those in the mystical tradition readily use Greek philosophical categories most also maintain key Christian emphases, such as a personal view of God and creation *ex nihilo*.[106]

Gregory of Nyssa's *Life of Moses* provides a good example of this tradition.[107] In this text Gregory focuses primarily on the ascent of the soul towards the transcendent and infinite God. Though Gregory emphasises knowledge in the ascent of the soul, God is ultimately unknowable in his

---

[100] Russell, *Deification*, 197.

[101] Bilaniuk writes: 'St. Cyril of Alexandria, who probably represents the pinnacle in the development of teaching on *theosis*'. Petro B.T. Bilaniuk, 'The Mystery of Theosis or Divinization' in *The Heritage of the Early Church*, eds. David Neiman and Margaret Schatkin (Rome: Pont. Institutum Studiorum Orientalium, 1973), 337–359, at 351.

[102] Gross, *Divinization*, 124–26, 223–25.

[103] Russell, *Deification*, 1–3, 105–10, 191.

[104] Cf. Donald Fairbairn, 'Patristic Soteriology: Three Trajectories', *JETS* 50 (2007): 289–310.

[105] Cf. Louth, *Origins*.

[106] Ibid., 186–99. Origen and Evagrius are notable exceptions, in that they focus on the ability to know God and the divine source of the soul, though Origen's formulations are foundational for all who follow later. idem., *Origins*, 71–2.

[107] Gregory of Nyssa, *The Life of Moses* (trans. Abraham J. Malherbe and Everett Ferguson; New York: Paulist, 1978).

nature because he is infinite. Thus, after initial stages of knowledge, believers must transcend knowledge at the highest level. Believers meet God
in the stages of light, cloud, and finally darkness. As part of this process,
purification of the soul based upon dying with Christ and synergistic coop-
eration through ascetic struggle are explicit aspects of spiritual growth.[108]

Some of these themes are reflected in the works of Irenaeus and Cyril,
but not with the emphasis of the mystical tradition. As a result, the conversation we are holding between Irenaeus, Cyril, and Paul is just one of
many that could be held between Paul and later theologians. We also must
recognise that the genre of the different works we will analyse will also
determine which aspects are emphasised and deemphasised,[109] and so we
must be cautious not to overstate the results. With these cautions in mind,
we can still have a robust and fruitful conversation between these three
writers that will illumine our study regarding deification in Paul.

In this conversation between Paul and his later interpreters regarding
deification, Keating helpfully notes the issues related to studying the history of an idea.[110] He writes:

> It is crucial, however, to recognize a distinction between the content of the doctrine of
> deification and its characteristic vocabulary. On the one hand the content of deification
> may be present in the absence of the technical vocabulary, while on the other the vocabu-
> lary may be used with only some marginal aspect of the doctrine in view. The terminol-
> ogy is significant, and it does signal to us that an author has some concept of deification
> in view, but it is not required for us to recognize the content of the doctrine. In other
> words, we cannot simply follow a terminological trail in order to discover what the con-
> tent of this doctrine is.[111]

Keating thus reflects concerns similar to Yeago's, which we discussed
above.[112] Our study of patristic authors will focus heavily on their use of
key terminology, but we will see that the shape of thought they associate
with deification reflects their soteriology as a whole. A necessary caution
in comparative studies like these has been noted by Hallonsten.[113] He
rightly critiques the over-reliance on terminology to make unsubstantiated

---

[108] Cf. *Life*, 2.183, 187, 274.

[109] For instance, while Gregory is known for his more mystical writings such as *Life
of Moses* with its focus on the soul, we cannot ignore his other writings that present a
more balanced emphasis on soul and body, such as his *On the Making of Man*.

[110] In this he resembles Barr's caution about the history of a *word* versus the history
of a *concept*. James Barr, *The Semantics of Biblical Language* (London: Oxford
University Press, 1961).

[111] Daniel A. Keating, *Deification and Grace* (Naples, FL: Sapientia, 2007), 8–9.

[112] See pages 21–22.

[113] Gösta Hallonsten, '*Theosis* in Recent Research: A Renewal of Interest and a Need
for Clarity' in *Partakers of the Divine Nature: The History and Development of
Deification in the Christian Traditions,* eds. Michael J. Christensen and Jeffery A.
Wittung (Grand Rapids: Baker, 2008), 281–93.

claims about some western writers and argues that we should distinguish between 'themes' of deification and a 'doctrine' of deification. Those who use deification 'themes' make use of some of the terminology but do not embed deification within their larger theological construct. On the other hand, those with a 'doctrine' of deification build their theological structure around the concept. As a result, we will analyse both the terminology and theological structures as we hold this conversation.

5. Conclusion

In our study about the possible contribution the notion of deification makes in our understanding of Paul, we have chosen to address the question through a history of interpretation route so that we can attempt to see Pauline texts in a new light. The monograph is thus divided into three parts. In Part II, Patristic Views of Deification, we analyse how Irenaeus (chapter 2) and Cyril of Alexandria (chapter 3) develop their ideas of deification and how they utilise Pauline texts and themes to support their views of deification. With a short concluding chapter (chapter 4), we summarise the salient points drawn from Irenaeus and Cyril and address questions for the Pauline texts based on this reading. It is at this point that we determine the Pauline texts that are most pertinent for our present study. In Part III, Pauline Soteriology, we focus on two primary Pauline passages. The first is Romans 8 (chapter 5) with an excursus on Colossians 2 and Galatians 3–4, and the second is 2 Corinthians 3–5 (chapter 6) with excursus on 1 Corinthians 15 and Philippians 2–3. A short concluding chapter (chapter 7) summarises the key points drawn from these Pauline texts. In Part IV, we conclude the monograph with a comparison of the soteriological systems and with an assessment whether and to what extent theosis helpfully captures Paul's presentation of the anthropological dimension of soteriology.

II. Patristic Views of Deification

2. Deification in Irenaeus

'But where the Spirit of the Father is, there is a living man,
... adopting the quality of the Spirit, being made conformable to the Word of God'. *AH* 5.9.3.

1. Introduction

With our desire to understand Paul's theology in relation to deification, we
have selected Irenaeus (AD c.130–c.202) as an early interpreter to help us.
Irenaeus arose to the bishopric in Lugdunum (Lyons) around AD 177, and
during the last two decades of the second century he authored his most
well known writings.[1] These writings include the five books of *The Detection and Refutation of So-called Knowledge*, also known as *Against Heresies* or *Adversus Haereses* (hereafter, *AH*).[2] This work provides his summary and refutation of 'Gnostic', Marcionite, and Ebionite teachings as he
sees them.[3] Other than *AH*, the *Demonstration of Apostolic Preaching*
(hereafter, *Dem.*) is the only significant work that remains extant, though

---

[1] Eric F. Osborn, *Irenaeus of Lyons* (Cambridge: Cambridge University Press, 2001),
2.

[2] For critical editions of the extant Latin and Greek texts along with a French translation, see the following: Irenaeus, *Contre les hérésies, Livre I* (eds. A. Rousseau and L.
Doutreleau; SC 263, 264; 2 vols.; Paris: Cerf, 1979); idem., *Contre les hérésies, Livre II*
(eds. A. Rousseau and L. Doutreleau; SC 293, 294; 2 vols.; Paris: Cerf, 1982); idem.,
Contre les hérésies, Livre III (eds. A. Rousseau and L. Doutreleau; SC 210, 211; 2 vols.;
Paris: Cerf, 1974); idem., *Contre les hérésies, Livre IV* (ed. A. Rousseau; SC 100.1,
100.2; 2 vols.; Paris: Cerf, 1965); idem., *Contre les hérésies, Livre V* (eds. A. Rousseau,
et al.; SC 152, 153; 2 vols.; Paris: Cerf, 1969). Unless noted otherwise, the English
translation in the ANF collection is used: idem., "Against Heresies, Books 1–5 and
Fragments," in *The Ante-Nicene Fathers. Vol. 1, The Apostolic Fathers with Justin
Martyr and Irenaeus* (Edinburgh: T&T Clark, 1885–1887).

[3] Williams offers a critique of the term 'gnosticism' and proposes instead 'biblical
demiurgical traditions': Michael Allen Williams, *Rethinking "Gnosticism"* (Princeton:
Princeton University Press, 1996), 51, passim. While his criticisms are weighty, I continue to use Gnosticism for simplicity's sake, especially since any interaction I have with
Gnosticism in this essay is concerned only with Irenaeus' interpretation and not historical
reality, per se.

only in a sixth century Armenian translation.[4] The *Dem.* is primarily an apologetic work 'proving' the consistency of the Old and New Testaments, with an emphasis on the New fulfilling the Old.

In these works, soteriology plays an important role. Importantly, Irenaeus is often noted as the patristic writer who lays the foundation for deification in the eastern tradition, which leads some to apply liberally the term deification to the whole of Irenaeus' soteriology.[5] John Kaufman has recently argued that deification is not the best term for Irenaeus' soteriology, and that we should be suspicious of its use at all.[6] While Kaufman rightly cautions us against uncritical use of terminology, we will see below that Irenaeus advances the use of deification themes and integrates these within his larger theological discourse.

Paul is not the only biblical writer that Irenaeus uses, but he is one of the most central.[7] Werner notes that about a third of the approximately 1000 NT citations are Pauline.[8] A variety of opinions exists regarding the nature of Irenaeus' use of Paul. An older perspective argued that Irenaeus used Pauline texts almost grudgingly, merely for the sake of polemical purposes.[9] More recent studies on Irenaeus' use of Pauline texts have shown that he utilises these texts in a variety of contexts, which demonstrates dependence outside of polemical contexts.[10] Still recognising many

---

[4] Unless noted otherwise, the English translation of the *Demonstration* is from Irenaeus, *On the Apostolic Preaching* (trans. John Behr; Crestwood, NY: St. Vladimir's Seminary Press, 1997).

[5] E.g., Gross, *Divinization*, 120–31; Jeffrey Finch, 'Irenaeus on the Christological Basis of Human Divinization' in *Theosis: Deification in Christian Theology*, eds. Stephen Finlan and Vladimir Kharlamov (Eugene, OR: Pickwick, 2006), 86–103.

[6] Kaufman, 'Becoming'.

[7] Dassmann offers the thought that Irenaeus' theology binds together the Johannine incarnation theology with the frame of Paul's picture of salvation history. Ernst Dassmann, *Der Stachel im Fleisch: Paulus in der frühchristlichen Literatur bis Irenäus* (Münster: Aschendorff, 1979), 311–2.

[8] Johannes Werner, *Der Paulinismus des Irenaeus* (TU 6.2; Leipzig: J.C. Hinrichs, 1889), 7–8. Based on *Biblia Patristica*, there are more than 700 allusions and quotations of Pauline texts in *AH* and the *Dem.* Jean Allenbach, *Des origines à Clément d'Alexandrie et Turtullien* (BiPa; vol. 1: CNRS, 1975–), 428–519. Irenaeus attributed all 13 letters to Paul and clearly did not make the modern distinction between undisputed and disputed Pauline letters. In addition to the wide use of Paul within his argumentation, Irenaeus also expounds several Pauline passages in 5.1–14 where Irenaeus defends the resurrection of the body based upon a large range of Pauline texts (e.g., 2 Cor 12.7–9; 1 Cor 3.1–3; 15.42–50).

[9] E.g., Werner, *Der Paulinismus*; Harnack, *History of Dogma*, 250–53; Wilhelm Schneemelcher, 'Paulus in der griechischen Kirche des zweiten Jahrhunderts', *ZKG* 75 (1964): 1–20, at 18–19; Roetzel, 'Paul in the Second Century'.

[10] Andreas Lindemann, *Paulus im ältesten Christentum: Das Bild des Apostels und die Rezeption der paulinischen Theologie in der frühchristlichen Literatur bis Marcion*

expansions and changes, Noormann's analysis of Irenaeus' interpretation of 1 Corinthians 15 seems to apply more widely: 'Die irenäische Gegen-interpretation des Texts [ist], obgleich die Argumentation im einzelnen durchaus nicht immer zu überzeugen vermag, im ganzen als eine Weiter-führung der paulinischen Aussageabsicht zu verstehen'.[11] Since Paul and Irenaeus wrote to different audiences for different purposes – pastoral let-ters versus theological treatises – we should expect differences in formula-tions, even if the theological vision might have been similar.

As we consider Irenaeus' use of Pauline texts to support and construct his soteriology, we should be aware of his interpretive method.[12] He is often characterised as a harmoniser, who draws out (or even imposes) agreement between the different biblical writers and the rule of truth. However, recent study has noted two factors that speak against this more simplistic analysis. First, scholars have pointed out his use of exegetical tools drawn from the ancient grammarians, particularly with his key theo-logical terms: hypothesis, *oikonomia*, and recapitulation. As a result, his interest in reading the part in light of the whole in not merely an attempt to bring theological harmony; rather, it is a practice promoted by some read-ers in his ancient context. Second, when addressing particular texts Irenaeus does not use the rule of truth as argumentative evidence for his reading. Rather, 'the rule of truth appears to be principally a tool to argue against theological outcomes rather than exegetical particularities – that is, mainly a tool to make a general point about coherence rather than as a means for interpreting a specific text'.[13] This is not to say that Irenaeus is somehow impartial or uninfluenced by his theological perspective. How-ever, this picture presents a more complex interplay between the text, his theological perspective, and his use of the grammarian's exegetical method.

Our purpose is not to evaluate Irenaeus' interpretations, but rather to explore how Irenaeus elaborates his themes of deification and how he uses Pauline texts to develop these. In that way we allow him his own voice in our dialogue, as Gadamer, Jauss, and Bakhtin encourage. Since our focus is upon the anthropological dimension of soteriology, the emphasis of this chapter is upon the anthropological impact and result of salvation rather

---

(BHT 58; Tübingen: Mohr Siebeck, 1979); Dassmann, *Der Stachel im Fleisch*, 292–315; Richard A. Norris, 'Irenaeus' Use of Paul in his Polemic against the Gnostics' in *Paul and the Legacies of Paul,* ed. William S. Babcock (Dallas: Southern Methodist University Press, 1990), 79–98; David L. Balás, 'The Use and Interpretation of Paul in Irenaeus's Five Books *Adversus haereses*', *SecCent* 9 (1992): 27–39; Noormann, *Irenäus*; Osborn, *Irenaeus*; Blackwell, 'Paul and Irenaeus'.

[11] Noormann, *Irenäus*, 529.

[12] For a more detailed analysis see my 'Paul and Irenaeus', esp. 196-99.

[13] Ibid., 199.

than its procurement, though they cannot be easily separated. In order to situate our discussion, we will first briefly look at Irenaeus' understanding of the relationship between God and humanity (§2). Then, after exploring his larger theological programme, we will look more specifically at the anthropological dimension of Irenaeus' soteriology. This will include a discussion of passages where Irenaeus calls believers 'gods' (§3.1 and §3.2) and then a discussion of larger themes which intersect with deification language (§3.3 and §3.4).

2. God and Humanity

Irenaeus' theology, though not based upon a reaction to the Gnostics, served to refute their dualistic cosmology. In distinction to the Gnostic tendency to posit divisions between various divine agents (1.1.1–1.2.6), between Jesus and Christ (1.24.4; 1.26.1), or between different types of humans (1.8.3), Irenaeus argued for a theology of unity. This unity is captured in the common 'faith' of the church, in which he describes first the triune God and then the 'economies' or 'dispensations' of God's work (1.10.1). Taking our direction from Irenaeus we will first look at Irenaeus' understanding of God (§2.1) and then at creation and humanity (§2.2) as the expression of God's plan, or economy, and finally at the divine action in salvation through Christ and the Spirit (§2.3).

2.1 The Creator and His Two Hands

While Irenaeus only explicitly ascribes deity to the Father and Son, the Spirit is also placed alongside the Son as one of the hands of God. In *Dem.* 5–6 Irenaeus presents his 'rule of faith', the unified work of God the Father along with the Word and the Spirit as his two agents for interacting with creation. The unity of God's work is evident from Irenaeus' idea of *oikonomia* (οἰκονομία, *dispositio*) by which all things cohere. Through this Irenaeus emphasises God's overarching control and intention regarding creation and salvation.[14] Osborn argues that

oikonomia can be taken as the ruling metaphor which holds Irenaeus' theology together .... In Irenaeus, *oikonomia* becomes central, unifying creation and recapitulation. In the singular, it refers chiefly to the incarnation and in the plural to the old testament [*sic*] manifestations of the word.[15]

Thus, while we see different agents, the work of God stands together.

---

[14] Cf. Jan Tjeerd Nielsen, *Adam and Christ in the Theology of Irenaeus of Lyons* (Assen, Netherlands: Van Gorcum, 1968), 56–7.

[15] Osborn, *Irenaeus*, 78.

Maintaining the unity between Father, Son and Spirit, Irenaeus denies the divine multiplicity offered by the Gnostics (e.g., 1.1.1–1.2.6) or by Marcion (3.12.12). God himself is the Creator through his two hands – the Word and Wisdom (or Spirit) – and not a duality or multiplicity of agents as with Irenaeus' opponents. By affirming the work of the Word and the Spirit, Irenaeus is able to deny the work of intermediaries, even angels, in the act of creation (cf. 4.20.1). Being so sensitive to the issue of divine multiplicity, Irenaeus even explains away Paul's description of the 'god of this age' (2 Cor 4.4) as the true God (3.7.1–2). Surprisingly, this interpretation follows a passage where Irenaeus applies the appellation of 'gods' to believers (3.6.1–3), which shows his commitment to deification language. Irenaeus clearly understands a difference between God and humanity, which we will now discuss, but he is also willing to associate these two closely.

2.2 Humanity: The Created

That Irenaeus holds to a fundamental distinction between humanity and God as the created and the Creator is clear when he writes:

In this respect God differs from man, that God indeed makes, but man is made; and truly, he who makes is always the same; but that which is made must receive both beginning, and middle, and addition, and increase. (4.11.2)

God remains the same, whereas humanity always changes and grows. Maintaining this dissimilarity between God and humans, he highlights their similarity through the concepts of image and likeness, which serve as the centrepiece of his anthropology.[16] In *Dem.* 11 Irenaeus develops the idea that humanity was created to be like God in formation and inspiration, corresponding to the Word and Spirit. In particular, the Word serves as the

---

[16] Regarding image and likeness, Ysabel de Andia (*Homo vivens: incorruptibilité et divinisation de l'homme selon Irénée de Lyon* [Paris: Études Augustiniennes, 1986], 68) writes: 'Le terme εἰκών ou *imago* semble toujours garder la note d'extériorité ou de visibilité chez Irénée, à l'inverse de la ressemblance (ὁμοίωσις – similitudo) qui implique, comme nous le verrons, un élément dynamique, nécessairement requis pour une assimilation spirituelle'. Several contemporary authors note a distinction in the way Irenaeus uses the term 'likeness' (*similitudo*). They posit that Irenaeus used two different terms – 'similitude' (ὁμοιότης) with regard to rationality and free will and 'likeness' (ὁμοίωσις) with regard to spiritual transformation. See Jacques Fantino, *L'homme image de Dieu: Chez Saint Irénée de Lyon* (Paris: Cerf, 1986), 135; Mary Ann Donovan, 'Alive to the Glory of God: A Key Insight in St Irenaeus', *TS* 49 (1988): 283–97, at 293–4; John Behr, *Asceticism and Anthropology in Irenaeus and Clement* (Oxford: Oxford University Press, 2000), 90–1. However, without the Greek texts this lexical distinction cannot be proven. For further discussion see Hans Boersma, 'Accommodation to What? Univocity of Being, Pure Nature, and the Anthropology of St Irenaeus', *IJST* 8 (2006): 266–93, at 286–292, esp. 288n.82.

basis of the image in humanity. For example, Irenaeus writes: 'For in times long past, it was said that man was created after the image of God, but this was not shown; for the Word was as yet invisible, after whose image man was created' (5.16.2; cf. esp. *Dem.* 22).[17] The Word shows both the original intent for humanity but also restores humanity towards that goal (e.g., 3.18.1).

With regard to human composition, in Book 5 Irenaeus uses image and likeness language to explain the relative place of the body, soul, and spirit. Particularly, in 5.3–13 he presents an extended argument about humanity's natural state and the effects of salvation, emphasising the Spirit (cf. 3.17.3).[18] He offers here a focused discussion of his anthropology:[19]

Now God shall be glorified in his handiwork, fitting it so as to be conformable to, and modelled after, his own Son. For by the hands of the Father, that is, by the Son and the Holy Spirit, man, and not [merely] a part of man, was made in the likeness of God. Now the soul and the spirit are certainly a part of the man, but certainly not the man; for the perfect man consists in the commingling and the union of the soul receiving the spirit of the Father, and the admixture of that fleshly nature which was moulded after the image of God. (5.6.1)

This combination of image and likeness thus serves both as the model for original humanity and as the goal to which they will return. Importantly, this is intimately linked to the Son and Spirit. In 5.6.1 those that are 'carnal' and 'imperfect' consist of only a body and soul, and they possess the image of God but not his likeness. In contrast, those who are 'spiritual' and 'perfect' 'partake in the Spirit of God', have God's Spirit in addition to the body and soul, and therefore are in the image and likeness of God (cf. 3.22.1). This distinction of image and likeness, however, is not found throughout *AH* and occurs primarily in sections of Book 5.[20] In earlier instances the two serve as a hendiadys.

Since his debates with the 'Gnostics' often relate to readings of Genesis, Irenaeus regularly discussed Adam to express his anthropology. As the original human, Adam was created in a state of infancy and childlike understanding, with only the capacity for perfection if he grew into it.[21] Thus, rationality and free will play a central role in Irenaeus' anthropol-

---

[17] Also, see 3.22.1; 3.23.1; 4.33.4.

[18] Cf. James G.M. Purves, 'The Spirit and the Imago Dei: Reviewing the Anthropology of Irenaeus of Lyons', *EvQ* 68 (1996): 99–120.

[19] See 1.5.5–1.7.5 for the anthropology that Irenaeus is refuting. In the background of Irenaeus' argument in this section of Book 5 are the interpretations of texts like 1 Cor 2–3 that discuss people in categories of 'spiritual,' 'natural,' and 'carnal,' as well as interpretations of 1 Cor 15.50.

[20] Kaufman, 'Becoming', 196, 211.

[21] Cf. *Dem.* 11, 14; *AH* 4.38.1

ogy, which also enable humans to be like God.[22] However, Adam was dis-
obedient due to ignorance, seeking immortality quickly, and introduced sin
as the heritage of all humanity. Irenaeus speaks of the results of sin in
various ways: death/mortality,[23] a break in fellowship/communion with
God,[24] facing judgment,[25] being in bondage/captivity,[26] being debtors to
God[27] and debtors to death.[28] Humanity's problem, then, is primarily described by death and alienation from God.[29] According to Irenaeus' anthropology, the body and soul were always mortal by nature (2.34.4;
3.20.1), and only immortal by participating in the life of God. When separated from God by sin, the body is thus shown to be mortal: Sin shows a
human is 'an infirm being and mortal by nature, but that God is immortal
and powerful' (5.3.1).[30] By God's will, however, the soul participates in
the breath of life (5.4.1; 5.7.1; 5.13.3), which means it will not die as the
body does. The spirit is immortal (5.13.3) 'and is itself the life of those
who receive it' (5.7.1). In other words, it is the very Spirit of God and the
foundation of all life as 5.6–13 explores. Thus, even before the fall humanity's experience has always been that of being created and experiencing life by participation in the life of God.

2.3 The Work of Christ and the Spirit

With the variegated imagery related to the problem of sin, Irenaeus presents an equally comprehensive description of the work of God through
Christ and the Spirit to effect salvation for believers. Integrating the image
of God theme, salvation might be well summarised: He 'furnished us ...
with salvation; so that what we had lost in Adam – namely, to be according
to the image and likeness of God – that we might recover in Christ Jesus'
(3.18.1).[31] The primary terminology to describe this view of Christ's work

---

[22] Cf. 4.4.3; 4.6.3–7; 5.15.2; 4.29; 4.37.2–7; 4.38.4; 4.39.3–4; 5.27.1–5.28.1. See
Gustaf Wingren, *Man and the Incarnation: A Study in the Biblical Theology of Irenaeus*
(Edinburgh: Oliver & Boyd, 1959), 35–38.

[23] Irenaeus speaks regularly of mortality as resulting from the fall: Humans were 'cast
off from immortality' (3.20.2). Satan 'wrought death in them' (3.23.1). Instead of giving Adam and Eve access to the tree of life, God 'interpos[ed] death, and thus caus[ed]
sin to cease' (3.23.6). See also 5.12.1.

[24] 5.14.3, 5.17.1; 5.27.2

[25] 4.20.1.

[26] 3.23.1–2; 5.21.3.

[27] 5.16.3; 5.17.1, and especially 5.17.3

[28] 3.18.7; 3.19.1; 5.23.2.

[29] Gustaf Aulén, *Christus Victor: An Historical Study of the Three Main Types of the
Idea of the Atonement* (trans. A.G. Hebert; London: SPCK, 1931), 22–25.

[30] Cf. de Andia, *Homo vivens*, 125.

[31] Cf. 5.16.2.

is 'recapitulation' (ἀνακεφαλαίωσις) (e.g., 5.14.2–3; 5.21.2).[32]   Christ comes as a man – the second Adam – to restore obedience and sanctify humanity by his participation in their state.[33]   Accordingly, he is the mediator between God and humanity. The summary of benefits from Christ's work may be noted, among other things, as remission of sin/debts,[34] reconciliation of enemies,[35] release from captivity,[36] and, most often, the grant of immortality.[37]

In the process of restoring divine likeness, Irenaeus regularly employs his exchange formula: Christ became human so humans could become like him.[38] Some interpret this as an ascription to the saving significance of the incarnation itself in distinction to the cross and resurrection. The cross, while lacking the strong emphasis of Paul, still plays an important role for Irenaeus. We see this specifically in one central section where Irenaeus twice uses a version of the exchange formula (3.18.3–3.19.3). After using the exchange formula, he then mentions the death of Christ, showing that they are not separated. Since mortality is the central problem of fallen creation, as Christ partakes of true humanity, he partakes of human mortality.   The cross is the supreme act of obedience that undoes the disobedience of Adam. Irenaeus at times uses it by itself metonymically to refer to the totality of Christ's saving work. In addition, in *Dem.* 34, Irenaeus notes the whole creation is marked with a cross. Harnack rightfully points out the two main ways Irenaeus speaks of Christ's work in Irenaeus: *'filius dei filius hominis factus est propter nos'* and also *'filius dei passus est propter nos'*.[39] As a result, the incarnation cannot be neatly separated from Christ's death and resurrection, but they stand together. At the same time, we should note that Paul's repeated emphasis upon the cruciform life for believers does not appear to be as significant for Irenaeus.[40]

---

[32] See especially 3.18.1–7; 5.12–14; and 5.20–21. Osborn (Osborn, *Irenaeus*, 97–98) writes: 'The complexity of the concept [of recapitulation] is formidable. At least eleven ideas – unification, repetition, redemption, perfection, inauguration and consummation, totality, the triumph of Christus Victor, ontology, epistemology, and ethics – are combined in different permutations'.

[33] Irenaeus describes the basis for the efficacy of recapitulation when speaking of Eve and Mary in 3.22.4.

[34] E.g., 4.27.1–4; 5.2.2; 5.16.3; 5.17.1; 5.17.3.

[35] E.g., 5.14.3; 5.17.1

[36] E.g., 5.21.3

[37] E.g., 3.18.7; 5.3.3, 5.12.1–6, 5.13.3, 5.21.3, 5.23.1, 5.29.1. This corresponds to defeating the power of death. Wingren, *Man*, 114. Cf. 3.19.5–6; 5.21.

[38] Cf. 3.10.2; 3.16.3; 3.18.7; 3.19.1; 3.20.2; 4.33.4; 5.*Pr.* 1.

[39] Harnack, *History of Dogma*, 2:288–90. Cf. Michael Abineau, 'Incorruptibilité et Divinisation selon Saint Irénée', *RSR* 44 (1956): 25–52, at 39–40.

[40] Cf. my 'Paul and Irenaeus', 199–200, 204.

God's work is not limited to Christ. Through Christ and the Spirit God created humans according to the divine image and likeness. Christ unites believers to the Spirit (5.20.1), who vivifies believers, imparting the immortality that Christ has won (5.6–13) and restoring the creature to be in the image and likeness of God (*Dem.* 97). In his united economy, God also restores the world through Christ and the Spirit with the goal that humanity will again be formed according to this original intent of divine likeness. Thus, we again see the unity of God's work through his two hands in the activity of creation and re-creation.

3. Humanity and God

In light of the preceding discussion of Irenaeus' soteriology in general terms, we may now look at his language regarding deification, which stems from his exposition of Psalm 82 (81 LXX). We will first explore the four passages where Irenaeus identifies believers as 'gods' based on Psalm 82 (§3.1) and also how he treats the Genesis 2–3 association of knowlege making humans 'like gods' (§3.2). In these texts, we discover that Irenaeus develops deification in terms of relational models: adoption, vision, and union (§3.3). We afterwards discuss the restoration of the divine image and likeness resulting from this divine-human relationship (§3.4).

3.1 Believers as 'Gods' and Psalm 82

That the psalmist's pronouncement "I said you are gods (θεοί) and sons of the Most High" (Ps 82.6) plays a central role in Greek Patristic views of deification goes without dispute.[41] Irenaeus was not the first theologian to interpret Psalm 82 as describing Christian deification, but the grid he uses to explain the Psalm served as the basis of several later writers. Before Irenaeus, Justin Martyr (AD c.100–c.165) in *Dialogue with Trypho* 124 uses Psalm 82 in a polemical situation arguing that Christians are the true people of God.[42] He contends that being 'gods' means all people 'were made like God, free from suffering and death, provided that they kept his commandments, and were deemed deserving of the name of his sons', but

---

[41] Psalm 81.6–7 (LXX) reads: ⁶ἐγὼ εἶπα θεοί ἐστε καὶ υἱοὶ ὑψίστου πάντες ⁷ὑμεῖς δὲ ὡς ἄνθρωποι ἀποθνήσκετε καὶ ὡς εἷς τῶν ἀρχόντων πίπτετε.

[42] Cf. Carl Mosser, 'The Earliest Patristic Interpretations of Psalm 82, Jewish Antecedents, and the Origin of Christian Deification', *JTSns* 56 (2005): 30–74, at 40–1. Nispel persuasively argues that the use of Psalm 82 arose out of the use of *testimonia* that were used to promote the divinity of Christ from the OT, and this appears to be supported by Irenaeus' first two uses of the psalm: Mark D. Nispel, 'Christian Deification and the Early *Testimonia*', *VC* 53 (1999): 289–304.

they fell like Adam and Eve and now experience death and judgement.[43] Justin interprets the passage in light of creation and the fall in Genesis 2–3, but he does not go much beyond the specific details of the Genesis passage in his interpretation. Irenaeus makes similar use of death and sonship, but he expands the discussion to present not only what humanity lost but also what humanity can and should regain. In the four passages where he addresses Psalm 82, Irenaeus does not refer to Jesus' use of this OT passage in John 10:34, but rather interprets it exclusively with texts found in Paul's letters, especially Gal 4.4–7, Rom 8.15, and 1 Cor 15.53–54.

3.1.1 'Gods' and Divine Adoption (3.6.1–3)

In 3.6.1 Irenaeus begins a new section of Book 3, in which he defends the singular God in distinction to those who might use biblical texts to argue for divine multiplicity.[44] He briefly addresses several biblical passages that contain a plurality of divine names (Ps 110.1; Gen 19.24; Ps 45.6). For each, he draws a distinction between the Father and the Son as the reason for the language. He then addresses a group of three passages that use the term 'gods' (θεοί, *dii*): Ps 82.1; 50.1; and 82.6. The Father and Son were the focus of previous exegesis, but when he explains these texts, he expands the discussion to include believers in Ps 82.1 (81.1 LXX). With regard to the θεοί (*dii*), he writes: 'He refers [here] to the Father and the Son, and those who have received the adoption; but these are the church. For she is the congregation of God ...' (3.6.1). Irenaeus then directly turns to Ps 50.1, 3 (49.1, 3 LXX) where he addresses the phrase 'God of gods'. Based on the repetition of 'God' in verse three, Irenaeus affirms that 'God' is 'the Son, who came manifested to men' while identifying the 'gods' as believers.

Returning to Psalm 82, Irenaeus states that the gods in Ps 82.6 are 'those, no doubt, who have received the grace of adoption (*adoptionis gratia*), through which we cry "Abba, Father"' (3.6.1). Since the phrase 'sons of the Most High' parallels 'You are gods', Irenaeus feels free to use sonship by adoption to define further who the gods are. Consequently, when explaining both Ps 82.1 and 82.6, he mentions adoption, and in the second reference he directly refers to Rom 8.15 and its "Abba, Father" cry (cf. Gal 4.6) which is the cry of adopted sons in the Rom 8.13–30 context.[45] While Irenaeus does not explicitly relate the adoption of sons to Christ as the Son, the focus of his characterisation of Christ throughout this passage is Christ's sonship. The adoption imagery allows believers to

---

[43] *Dialogue with Trypho* 124 (*ANF* 1:262).

[44] Balás, 'Use and Interpretation', 32–33.

[45] Noormann, *Irenäus*, 117–8. Irenaeus exchanges 'Spirit of adoption' from Rom 8.15 with 'grace of adoption' (cf. 3.19.1), though he later uses 'Spirit of adoption' in 4.1.1.

parallel this filial relationship, but it also marks these children out as distinct from the natural Son.

In 3.6.2 Irenaeus continues to explain and clarify other instances where 'gods' is used in Scripture, such as Ps 96.5; 81.9 and Jer 10.11. In this context he writes: 'When, however, the Scripture terms them [gods] which are no gods, it does not, as I have already remarked, declare them as gods in every sense, but with a certain addition and signification, by which they are shown to be no gods at all' (3.6.3). Carl Mosser understands Irenaeus as applying this to believers, who are labelled gods but are to be distinguished from God.[46] Irenaeus does in fact make that distinction, but Mosser incorrectly reads that meaning here. The gods mentioned here (i.e., Ps 96.5; 81.9 and Jer 10.11) are false gods. For these false gods, 'he (Esaias) removes them from [the category of] gods, but he makes use of the word alone ...' (3.6.3). Thus, in distinction to these that are gods in name alone, believers are implicitly gods in reality.

This text (cf. 3.6.1–3) does not give any direction about what Irenaeus means by the identification of believers as gods beyond the qualifying statement from Romans regarding adoption. This language provides a ground of similarity between believers and God whilst preserving distinction, such that believers and God share the same title and are familially related, but believers are only adopted to this position. Thus, Irenaeus only identifies the status of believers rather than teasing out the implications of that new status. In the next passage dealing with Psalm 82 he offers a deeper treatment.

3.1.2 'Gods', Adoption, and Immortality (3.19.1–2)

The next discussion of Psalm 82 fits within Irenaeus' extended argument about the nature of Christ as Son of God incarnate, who recapitulates the whole of humanity (3.16–23).[47] Irenaeus affirms the reality of the incarnation by challenging those who argue that Christ did not take on a fully human nature or only temporarily indwelled the man Jesus (3.16–18). He responds that the Word's full humanity is necessary for complete salvation.[48] In 3.19.1–3 he rebuts the opposite challenge from the Ebionites that Jesus was only human, born from Joseph. Irenaeus responds that Christ is divine and became human. He describes the state of those who deny this truth:

---

[46] Mosser ('Psalm 82', 46) writes, 'Irenaeus acknowledges that one can in a certain sense legitimately refer to glorified human beings as gods, but he insists that these are not the same kind of being as the one God'.

[47] Balás, 'Use and Interpretation', 32–33.

[48] *AH* 3.18.7 stands as one of the best summaries of Irenaeus' soteriology as a whole.

Being ignorant of him who from the Virgin is Emmanuel, they are deprived of his gift, which is eternal life; and not receiving the incorruptible Word, they remain in mortal flesh, and are debtors to death, not obtaining the antidote of life. To whom the Word says, mentioning his own gift of grace: 'I said, You are gods and all the sons of the most High;[49] but you die[50] like men'. He speaks undoubtedly these words to those who have not received the gift of adoption, but who despise the incarnation of the pure generation of the Word of God, depriving man of his ascension to God,[51] and prove themselves ungrateful to the Word of God, who became flesh for them. For it was for this end that the Word of God was made man, and he who was the Son of God became the Son of man, that man, having been taken into the Word and receiving the adoption, might become the son of God. For by no other means could we have attained to incorruptibility (*incorruptela*) and immortality (*immortalitas*), unless we had been united to incorruptibility and immortality. But how could we be joined to incorruptibility and immortality, unless, first, incorruptibility and immortality had become that which we also are, so that the corruptible might be swallowed up by incorruptibility, and the mortal by immortality, that they might receive the adoption of sons (*filiorum adoptio*)? (3.19.1)

Whereas in 3.16–18 Irenaeus has argued for the humanity of the saviour, he now grounds the argument in the divinity of the saviour and draws the fate of believers into that divinity. The fate of those who reject the true and full divinity of Christ is that they are no longer gods: they have not been adopted, and, therefore, they experience mortality as Ps 82.7 points out. Therefore, those who have been adopted and experience immortality should rightfully be called gods. Importantly, we see allusions to Galatians 4 and 1 Corinthians 15 as the basis of this argument. By introducing Ps 82.7 into the discussion, he now associates gods with immortality and humans with mortality. Since the antithesis between humans and gods in the ancient Mediterranean is central, I offer a brief excursus to situate this relationship.

Excursus: Immortality and the Gods in the Ancient Mediterranean

In the Greek tradition the term θεός is not limited to one individual God; rather, it can refer to a multiplicity of subjects. Thus it can be used for the gods of the myths and the cults as well as for people such as for deified emperors.[52] Two primary characteristics that characterised the gods are that of immoratlity and power to bring order out of chaos.

---

[49] I have amended the *ANF* to follow the critical text of SC (211: 372), which follows the traditional LXX reading.

[50] Following the critical text of SC (211: 372), I translate this as a present tense verb.

[51] The *ANF* translation reads 'defraud human nature of promotion into God'. I follow Grant's translation (Irenaeus, *Against Heresies: On the Detection and Refutation of the Knowledge Falsely So Called* [trans. Robert McQueen Grant; New York: Routledge, 1997]), which reduces ambiguities and better reflects the Latin: 'fraudantes hominem ab ea ascensione quae est ad Deum' (SC 211: 372).

[52] S.R.F. Price, 'Gods and Emperors: The Greek Language of The Roman Imperial Cult', *JHS* 104 (1984): 79–95.

With regard to immortality, Kleinknecht writes: 'To the Gk. ἀθάνατος is synon. with θεός. The gods are called the immortals (ἀθάνατοι, Hom. Il., 1,503; Od., 1,31 etc.). This does not mean eternal pre-existence. It means only that they have no end, that they are not subject to death'.[53] For example, this divine cosmology is attested by Plato, who wrote in the *Timaeus* (41d) that immortality is the defining mark of the gods in distinction to mortal humans.[54] Other philosophers make this clear as well, e.g., Cicero, *De Natura Deorum* 1.3, 1.14, 2.17, 2.153. Since the immortality of the gods is so entrenched in the cultural grammar, Josephus is able to shine the irony on Agrippa who is called a god but then is shown to be all too mortal and dies: 'I, a god in your eyes, ... who was called immortal by you, am now under sentence of death' (*Antiquities* 19.347).[55]

However, divine immortality does not necessarily entail a corresponding ontology as Kleinknecht argues because immortality could be social as well as ontological. For instance, Jaeger notes that when early Greek poetry honoured its heroes, this 'immortality' had nothing to do with ontology.[56] Similarly, Wisdom argues that the righteous will be immortal because they are remembered by the community (Wis 3-4, esp. 4.1, 7-9, 18-19). As such, social immortality mediated through honour, fame, and remembrance continued to play a role in the Hellenstic honour-shame culture.

When we consider the imperial cult, the second characteristic related to deity comes to the fore. Gradel maintains that the cult had little to do with affirmations about ontology; rather, the ascribed divinity was more about relative status that stemmed from their power.[57] The cult thus immortalised the emperors by recognising their power. Friesen in particular, notes that this is a recognition of their ability to bring order out of chaos by referencing Aristides (Or. 26.32; 26.103–105, 107).[58] At the same time, this ability to bring order out of chaos is also represented in the gods' role in

---

[53] H. Kleinknecht, TDNT, 'θεός', 3:70. For further discussion of the synonymy between 'god' and 'immortal', see Mosser, 'Psalm 82', 38n.22; Kaufman, 'Becoming', 146–49.

[54] Theophilus of Antioch hints towards this in *To Autolycus* 2.24. See Kaufman, 'Becoming', 142.

[55] Josephus, *Antiquities*. (Louis H. Feldman, trans.; LCL; Cambridge, Mass: Harvard University Press, 1989).

[56] Werner Jaeger 'The Greek Ideas of Immortality: The Ingersoll Lecture for 1958', *HTR* 52 (1959): 135–147, at 135–39. Children were also a source of immortality: E.M. Griffiths, 'Euripides' *Heracles* and the Pursuit of Immortality', *Mnemosyne* 56 (2002): 641–56.

[57] Gradel, *Emperor Worship and Roman Religion*, 25–32, 72, 305. Cf. S.R.F. Price, 'Gods and Emperors', 95.

[58] Steven J. Friesen, *Twice Neokoros: Ephesus, Asia and the Cult of the Flavian Imperial Family* (Leiden: Brill, 1993), 151–52.

creation the *Timaeus* 90d. Thus, immortality and power together formed ancient conceptions of deity.[59]

Irenaeus appears to draw from this conceptuality of immortality and power as characterising deity. For instance, with his quotation of Wis 6.19 in 4.38.3 ('Incorruption brings one near to God; ἀφθαρσία δὲ ἐγγὺς εἶναι ποιεῖ θεοῦ)', he makes his association between incorruption/immortality and divinty clear. At the same time, in 4.11.2 we remember how Irenaeus distinguishes between God and humanity: God makes, humanity is made. Thus, with his use of immortality language Irenaeus shows that believers are drawn into a divine manner of being, but the difference from creation shows the difference between humanity and the divine. Returning to 3.19.1, his identification of believers as 'gods' due to their experience of immortality indicates he is probably working with this Greek taxonomy in mind.

In 3.19.1 since unbelievers reject the *descent* of the divine Word into the flesh, they will not experience the *ascent* to God as union to incorruptibility. This shows the necessity of the incarnation, and it allows Irenaeus to introduce a version of his famous exchange formula: 'the Son of God became the Son of man, that man, having been taken into the Word and receiving the adoption, might become the son of God'.[60] This has clear parallels to Galatians 4 where Paul explains that God sent his Son 'born of a woman, born under the law, in order to redeem those who were under the law, that we might receive adoption as sons' (Gal 4.4–5). Thus, Christ's sonship is the basis for the sonship of believers. Noormann, thus, rightly states: 'Irenäus übernimmt von Paulus nicht nur den Begriff der υἱοθεσία, sondern auch die Grundstruktur von Gal 4,4f'.[61] Irenaeus' pithy statement about the results of the incarnation does not limit the incarnation to just becoming human. In the next paragraph, Irenaeus clarifies that this incarnation included liability to suffering and even death (3.19.2), though Christ's humanity was later raised up (3.19.3). In the bare exchange statement in 3.19.1, Irenaeus thus sums up this narrative of death and life poetically in a manner like that of Paul in Galatians 4.

The effect of this sonship becomes clear through the intertextual connection to 1 Cor 15.53–54 and its mortality-immortality dialectic. Employing 1 Cor 15.53–54 with Gal 4.4, 'die beiden Finalsätze interpretieren

---

[59] Speaking of Pindar (*Nemean Odes* VI, lines 1-10), John Passmore (*The Perfectibility of Man* [London: Duckworth, 1970], 30) writes: 'If in comparison with the gods man is "as nothing", this is only because he lacks their power, and the security which derives from their immortality'.

[60] Cf. 5.*Pr*.1: 'The Word of God ... became what we are, that he might bring us to be even what he is' (*Verbum Dei ... factus est quod sumus nos, uti nos perficeret esse quod est ipse*).

[61] Noormann, *Irenäus*, 149.

sich wechselseitig: Empfang der υἱοθεσία und Verwandlung zur Unvergänglichkeit bezeichnen denselben Vorgang'.[62] Thus, for Irenaeus adoption and incorruption are mutually constitutive. This incorruption appears to be primarily focused on the body based upon the implicit contrast with 'mortal flesh', but Irenaeus does not develop the contrast here. Accordingly, 1 Corinthians 15 and Galatians 4 stand as the basis of Irenaeus' exposition of Ps 82.

With the correlation of adoption and incorruption/immortality as the conclusion of the paragraph, we see the importance of this connection. In addition to adoption, though, we must note the use of union language: believers are 'united to incorruptibility and immortality' and 'ascend to God'. This language is not explored in depth here, but it connects deification to Irenaeus' larger soteriological discussion of union with God, which we will explore in more detail below.

Later, in 3.19.2 Irenaeus further clarifies the identity of Christ as divine in a way that distinguishes him from the elevated status of believers. He is

the Son of man, ... the Christ, the Son of the living God, [and] no one of the sons of Adam is as to everything, and absolutely, called God, or named Lord. But that he is himself in his own right, beyond all men who ever lived, God, and Lord, and King Eternal, and the Incarnate Word ... may be seen by all who have attained to even a small portion of the truth. (3.19.2)

Hence, believers may be called 'gods', but they cannot be called God in the way that Christ is called God. The fact that believers are adopted means that they are children by grace because it is a 'gift of adoption' and a 'gift of grace'. They have a changed status where Christ as God does not change in that fashion.

This discussion of Psalm 82 in terms of incarnation, adoption and incorruption presents a development over 3.6.1ff., where adoption alone was the central concept. Here, the incarnation of the Son is explicitly necessary for believers to become sons themselves through adoption which results in immortality and incorruption. de Andia thus writes: 'L'adoption filiale n'est pas autre chose que la divinisation'.[63] Something more than a new identity is established; a real anthropological change takes place since they take on immortality. In addition to these key themes, communion language also becomes more prominent with the descent of God to humanity and the ascent of humanity to God. Ultimately, this speaks of deification as a relational process through adoption and communion that culminates in the resurrection life of incorruption and immortality. Irenaeus primarily bases his argument upon the Pauline texts of Galatians 4 and 1 Corinthians 15. By juxtaposing these two texts Irenaeus is able to explain the ex-

---

[62] Ibid., 150. Cf. de Andia, *Homo vivens*, 177.
[63] de Andia, *Homo vivens*, 176.

change between the incorrupt Word, the Son of God, who came to make humans adopted sons of God and give them immortality.

3.1.3 The Adopted as 'Gods' (4.Pr.4; 4.1.1)

In 4.Pr.4–4.1.1 Irenaeus again uses similar language with regard to believers being gods, along with adoption as the basis of their status. Summarising his work which we just discussed in Book 3, he writes: I 'have shown that there is none other called God by the Scriptures except the Father of all, and the Son, and those who possess the adoption' (4.Pr.4). In the next paragraph (4.1.1), he then rephrases his affirmation with an explicit focus upon the work of the Spirit in adoption:

No other God or Lord was announced by the Spirit [in the Old Testament], except him who, as God, rules over all, together with his Word, and those who receive the Spirit of adoption, that is, those who believe in the one and true God, and in Jesus Christ the Son of God. (4.1.1)

It is quite interesting that the Father, Son, *and Spirit* are not called God, but only the Father, Son *and those who are adopted.*

While these are brief statements, several points can be drawn from 4.Pr.4 and 4.1.1. First, Irenaeus explicitly introduces the Spirit into his discussion of adoption. With 'Spirit of adoption' he specifically refers to Rom 8.15 (as in 3.6.1), rather than Gal 4.4–7 (as in 3.19.1). Second, within 4.Pr.4, the immediately preceding context refers to the salvation of the flesh. By implication, this is the benefit for those who are adopted, which would parallel the association between immortality of the flesh and adoption in 3.19.1.[64] While not providing a deeper discussion than prior treatments (besides making inclusion of the Spirit explicit), the repetition of Pauline adoption texts shows how Irenaeus integrated deification language and adoption in his thought.

3.1.4 'Gods' but Not Perfect From the Beginning (4.38.1–4; 4.39.1–3)

Irenaeus next discusses Psalm 82 in Book 4 as he focuses on anthropology and explains that human destiny is determined by free will and not by nature (4.37–49). He argues that God designed humans for growth and progress towards God, but those who turn away from this goal experience judgment.[65] In 4.38 Irenaeus discusses why humanity was not perfect from

---

[64] Irenaeus adds an appositional phrase to clarify that those who are adopted are 'those who believe in the one and true God and in Jesus Christ the Son of God'. For Irenaeus *belief* is one of the most regularly repeated descriptions of one in a correct relationship with God.

[65] Jeff Vogel ('The Haste of Sin, the Slowness of Salvation: An Interpretation of Irenaeus on the Fall and Redemption', *AThR* 89 [2007]: 443–59, at 450) writes: 'While

the beginning: God created humans in the state of infancy, beginning with
Adam, and they only have the capacity to grow towards perfection
(4.38.1–2). In 4.38.3 Irenaeus focuses on the process of attaining that perfection by 'making progress day by day, and ascending towards the perfect, that is, approximating to the uncreated one'. By the work of Father,
Son, and Spirit, being rendered 'after the image and likeness of the uncreated God (κατ' εἰκόνα καὶ ὁμοίωσιν ... τοῦ ἀγενήτου Θεοῦ)' is then described as a process of being created, receiving growth, being strengthened, abounding, recovering, being glorified, and, finally, seeing the Lord
(ἰδεῖν τὸν ἑαυτοῦ Δεσπότην). Thus, a vision of God (ὅρασις Θεοῦ) is the
climax of the soteriological event.

After positively presenting his point of view regarding the growth of
humans, Irenaeus turns to challenge directly his interlocutors, who argue
either that God is like humankind or that humans are already like God.
Within this discourse, he addresses Psalm 82:

> For we cast blame upon him, because we have not been made gods from the beginning,
> but at first merely men, then at length gods; although God has adopted this course out of
> his pure benevolence, that no one may impute to him invidiousness or grudgingness. He
> declares, 'I have said, You are gods; and you are all sons of the Most High'.[66] But since
> we could not sustain the power of divinity (*divinitas*), he adds, 'But you die like men',
> setting forth both truths – the kindness of his free gift, and our weakness, and also that
> we were possessed of power over ourselves. For after his great kindness he graciously
> conferred good [upon us], and made men like to himself, [that is] in their own power;
> while at the same time by his prescience he knew the infirmity of human beings, and the
> consequences which would flow from it; but through [his] love and power, he shall over-
> come the substance of created nature. For it was necessary, at first, that nature should be
> exhibited; then, after that, that what was mortal should be conquered and swallowed up
> by immortality, and the corruptible by incorruptibility, and that man should be made after
> the image and likeness of God, having received the knowledge of good and evil. (4.38.4)

The quote of Ps 82.6 allows Irenaeus to point out that the ultimate goal of
this progress is for believers to become gods, and the quote of Ps 82.7
highlights the current mortal limitations on humanity. The fact that humanity is limited by virtue of being a creature rather than the Creator is
central to his argument. Thus, the capacity to be 'like God' is always held
in tension with the fundamental limitation inherent in being a creature.
Rhe role of the fall in revealing that limitation is implicit in his distinction
since the mortality of the nature is a result of the fact that humans 'could
not sustain the power of divinity' (4.38.4).

Even though humanity faces limitation and experiences the fall, God's
original design for humans is that they would be like God. In particular,

---

every human being is created with the ability to grow into the life of God, no one has an
immediate kinship with the divine nature'.

[66] The previous comments about the translation of 3.19.1 also apply here.

by their experience of immortality and incorruption they are made after the image and likeness of God (cf. Gen 1.26) and receive the knowledge of good and evil (cf. Gen 3.5, 22). This ties the initial goal to its culmination, which again is explained by recourse to 1 Cor 15.53–54,[67] with its mortality-immortality/corruptibility-incorruptibility dialectic.[68]　Since gods are immortal, believers' hope of overcoming mortality corresponds to the identification of believers as gods. However, Irenaeus surprisingly does not mention adoption in this setting as he has done in the prior three deification passages. It appears that the Creator-created relationship is the determining context for his discussion rather than Father-sons as before.

While physical immortality continues to stand at the centre of Irenaeus' discussion of deification, he now makes explicit the importance of moral progress. Believers must grow in their ability to choose the good and act in obedience. This growth in maturity is not merely a restoration of the original state of Adam, because Adam was originally created in immaturity. Rather, believers grow in obedience through faith and gratitude, and thus they are able to grow towards perfection. This growth corresponds to the growth in knowledge, particularly the knowledge of good and evil. According to the serpent's promise in Gen 3.5 (LXX) this knowledge would make Adam and Eve 'like gods'. As a result in §3.2 we will explore this relationship between knowledge of good and evil and being 'like gods'.

One aspect of the human person that he notes explicitly as being like God is self-determination (*potestas*).[69] Irenaeus goes on to explain in 4.39 that this freedom of will is displayed as people know good and evil and obey God by choosing good. Through experience of evil one is able better to distinguish the good. Before turning to an exhortation to obedience, Irenaeus summarises his previous argument in a series of rhetorical questions:

How, then, shall he be a god, who has not as yet been made a man? Or how can he be perfect who was but lately created? How, again, can he be immortal, who in his mortal nature did not obey his Maker? For it must be that you, at the outset, should hold the rank of man, and then afterwards partake of the glory of God. For you did not make God, but God you. (4.39.2)

---

[67] Cf. 2 Cor 5.4

[68] We should also note the use of 'image' in the same context (1 Cor 15.49).

[69] This is also similar to his affirmation that 'man is possessed of free will from the beginning, and God is possessed of free will, in whose likeness man was created' (4.37.4; cf. 4.4.3). Irenaeus also speaks of liberation from powers, such as from the law (4.13.1–4) or from Satan (3.23.1–2; 5.21.3). However, his emphasis on self-determination is explicit where it is found only implicitly, if at all, in Paul.

In this, we see that Irenaeus uses the terms and phrases 'god' (*deus*), 'perfect' (*perfectus*), 'immortal' (*immortalis*), and 'partake of the glory of God' (*participare gloriae dei*) synonymously (cf. 5.35.1). He concludes by arguing that since God is the maker, believers should allow themselves to be moulded by him by offering him a soft heart. Accordingly, Behr writes: 'To become truly human, to become a god, man must allow God to fashion him'.[70] The Creator-created relationship is not transcended, but the created does become like the Creator in perfection, glory and immortality.

Irenaeus leaves behind discussion of adoption, but incorruption and immortality still stands central to his discussion. However, beyond this apparently physical phenomenon, Irenaeus makes explicit that the life of faith as moral and intellectual progress are associated with the process of deification. In fact, we will see below that progress serves to characterise all human existence. Importantly, Irenaeus again ties this deification process into his theology of image and likeness.

Now that we have considered his treatment of these passages, we have seen that this identification of believers as gods based on Psalm 82 occurs in four very different settings. The first is within a setting about the nature of God, and Irenaeus explores who can be rightly termed 'God' or 'gods' (3.6.1). Of the options throughout the Old and New Testaments, only the Father, Son, and believers who are adopted children are worthy of that appellation. The second occurs in the midst of Irenaeus' argument for the divinity of Christ (3.19.1). Those who believe that the divine Word became a true human are those who experience adoption and immortality. While not mentioning Psalm 82 directly, Irenaeus confirms with the third passage his affirmations of believers as those who are worthy of the appellation gods but only by the adoption of the Spirit (4.Pr.4; 4.1.1). Then, finally, in the midst of one of his central anthropological sections, Irenaeus confirms that humans were designed to progress towards ethical maturity and to share in divine immortality and incorruption in fulfilment of God's image and likeness (4.38.4). Therefore, within the contexts of theological exposition about the nature of God, Christ, and humanity, Irenaeus uses Psalm 82 to explain and clarify the divine-human relationship, showing that deification is relevant to each.

Though Ps 82.6–7 is the basis of his discussion, in each passage Irenaeus reads Psalm 82 in light of Pauline texts and concepts. Though he follows the pattern of applying the name 'gods' to humans, as in John 10.34, Irenaeus does not refer to John in any of his explanations. When employing the theme of adoption in the first three passages, Irenaeus refers directly to both Romans 8 and Galatians 4. In conjunction with those ref-

---

[70] Behr, *Asceticism*, 116.

erences, Irenaeus regularly refers to 1 Corinthians 15, and possibly 2 Corinthians 5, as he utilises incorruption/immortality and image restoration
themes. Importantly, Irenaeus read the Pauline adoption and immortality
texts in tandem so that adoption and immortality are mutually constitutive.
Paul, to be sure, is not the only NT authority for Irenaeus, but it is telling
that for his exposition of this OT passage Paul is the primary one he uses.

With this direct affirmation of believers as 'gods', Irenaeus shows his
elevated expectations for humanity: that they would become like God
through the Son and the Holy Spirit. However, similarity between believers and God can only be correctly understood in light of the distinctions
Irenaeus also highlights. While the Father and the Son are uncreated, immortal, unchanging, and divine, humans are created, initially mortal, progressing, and only become divine by adoption. In each exposition of
Psalm 82, Irenaeus mentions that this is a gift or by grace, so becoming
divine is not something humans experience by nature (as the Gnostics), but
it is in conformity to God's original plan. Thus, Irenaeus balances his
strong language about believers being gods with a consistent distinction
between the Creator and the created.

Several themes and motifs arise out of these passages to explain this divine-human relationship. A central relational theme in these passages is
that of adoption (3.6.1; 3.19.1; 4.Pr.4; 4.1.1), but he also introduces communion with God (3.19.1) and vision of God language (4.38.3). Alongside
these ways of relating to God, Irenaeus highlights immortality/incorruption
(3.19.1; 4.38.4; 4.39.2) and the concept of progress (4.38–39) as the culmination of the divine-human interaction. In §3.3 we will explore how
believers relate to God as described by these relational models – adoption,
vision, and communion – and then in §3.4 we will address how the salvific
benefits of life expressed as immortality and incorruption (§3.4.1) through
progress towards God (§3.4.2) are applied to the believer, which culminates in a restoration in the image and likeness of God (§3.4.3). However,
before exploring these aspects of Irenaeus' soteriology that arise out of his
discussion of deification, the issue of knowing good and evil and its relationship to being 'like gods' in Genesis 2–3 should be addressed.

3.2 Being 'Like Gods' and Knowing Good and Evil

In Irenaeus' discussion in 4.38.4 we noted the connection with the text of
Genesis 2–3 where humans gain a knowledge of good and evil, and importantly in Genesis this knowledge associated with humans becoming 'like
gods' (Gen 3.4–5) or 'like us [God]' (Gen 3.22). Earlier in *AH* Irenaeus
recounts how some of his opponents positively characterised Adam and

Eve's acquisition of this knowledge in Gen 2–3,[71] as it was seen as a step towards liberation from from the creator God (1.28.5–7, 15). In 1.29.3 he then tells of Gnostics who see the tree of knowledge of good and evil as 'Gnosis itself'. Accordingly, Irenaeus' treatment of these Genesis passages is important, but they have yet to be discussed by modern interpreters in light of the topic of deification. He mentions knowing good and evil in three passages in *AH*: 3.20–23; 4.38–39; and 5.20–23.

3.2.1 Against Heresies 3.20–23

AH 3.20–23 fits in a larger discussion of how the unified divinity and humanity of Christ is necessary for the salvation of humanity. In 3.20 Irenaeus sets up his key emphases: Salvation is characterised by immortality that only comes through God, so proper human knowledge is founded upon humility and gratitude. Satan however deceived Adam into judging himself equal to God. The resulting experience of death and the later experience of deliverance through Christ helps believers to 'understand' more properly their own position and his.

In 3.21.4 Irenaeus, discussing Isaiah 7.14–16, asserts that knowledge of good and evil characterises someone who is mature, and that small children do not have this knowledge. He later alludes to knowledge of evil when he speaks of Adam and Eve's sewing of the fig leaves in 3.23.4. The knowledge of evil is associated with lustful propensities of the flesh and the resulting loss of their childlike mind.[72]

As he discusses Adam's salvation in 3.23 through Christ's recapitulation, Irenaeus responds to those like Tatian who do not expect Adam to be saved by walking through Genesis 3–4. He thus writes:

> For at the first Adam became a vessel in [the serpent's] possession, being held under his power, that is, by bringing sin on Adam iniquitously, and under colour of immortality entailing death upon him. For, while promising that they should be as gods, which was in no way possible for him,[73] he wrought death in them. (3.23.1)

Satan enticed them with immortal life, but he brought them death. Knowledge is not discussed, but their attempt to be like gods is characterised as the desire to become immortal. Irenaeus returns again to this idea in *AH*

---

[71] M.C. Steenberg, *Irenaeus on Creation: The Cosmic Christ and the Saga of Redemption* (SuppVC 91; Leiden: Brill, 2008), 177–79.

[72] Steenberg (*Irenaeus on Creation*, 192) writes: 'Humanity's knowledge of God comes directly from the source in Eden, in a manner that it does not in the economy outside paradise. The expulsion thus involves a certain distancing from direct knowledge of the divine ...'.

[73] I removed 'to be' at the end of this phrase from ANF since it is not in the Latin. It the Latin it is clearly speaking of the impossibility of Satan to give immortality, not in Adam's ability to possess it. Cf. *AH* 4.Pr.4.

3.23.5 where he explains that they had 'been beguiled by another under the pretext of immortality'. Since knowledge is not discussed there is no explicit connection drawn between knowledge and immortality.

In this larger section, Irenaeus thus associates a knowledge of good and evil with a loss of innocence, and being like gods as seeking immortality, but he does not relate the two.

3.2.2 Against Heresies 4.38–39

We earlier discussed this passage where Irenaeus offers his well-known argument for the gradual growth of believers which culminates in a vision of God. In 4.38.4 and 4.39.1, Irenaeus situates this growth in a discussion about Psalm 82 and the knowledge of good and evil. Being like God is not what is condemned by Irenaeus; it is wanting to be like God from the beginning, not properly recognising one's created position. Though humans are created, they can become immortal 'gods', but he importantly sets this in connection with being in the image and likeness of God and receiving the knowledge of good and evil. This knowledge is gained from the experience of obedience and disobedience, as he discusses further in 4.39.1:

> Since God, therefore, gave this mental power, man knew both the good of obedience and the evil of disobedience, that the eye of the mind, receiving experience of both, may with judgment make choice of the better things .... But if anyone shuns the knowledge of both these kinds of things, and the twofold perception of knowledge, he unwittingly divests himself of the character of a human being.

This essential character of humans is that they know good and evil through the experience of obedience and disobedience. The Creator-created duality serves as the ultimate distinction between God and humanity. Humans were created in weakness with the purpose of growing into perfection, and the act of sin misdirected that path, but God still uses that misdiretion to lead humans towards their original goal since the negative effects of evil and death highlight the good as much as the good itself does. This not only motivates one's acts of obedience, it reinforces the fact that humans are not perfect in and of themselves. 'Death', de Andia writes, 'is not only the consequence of disobedience, but precisely "the experience" or the knowledge of the nature of man without God, that is to say of man outside of this relation of obedience of the creature to the Creator'.[74] This distinction comes through in 5.20–23, our last passage.

---

[74] de Andia, *Homo vivens*, 125.

3.2.3 Against Heresies 5.20–23

In 5.20.2 Irenaeus uses Gen 2.16–17 as an allegory, reading scripture as the fruit of the garden and the heresy of the Gnostics as the forbidden fruit because the Gnostics

eat with an uplifted mind ... [and] profess that they themselves have the knowledge of good and evil; and they set their own impious minds above the God who made them. They therefore form opinions on what is beyond the limits of the understanding. (*AH* 5.20.2)

Their attempt to know something beyond the limits God has placed is really ignorance since humans can't know beyond the divine limits. Repeating an emphasis we saw in 3.20–23, he argues that they do not live in humility and gratitude, founded upon a true knowledge that does not come from humans but from Christ and the Spirit.

In 5.21 he spells out the battle between Christ as the woman's seed and Satan as foretold in Gen 3.15. Humans died because of their disobedience enticed by Satan (5.21.1), but Christ defeats Satan's pride with humility, Satan's disobedience with obedience (to the law) in the wilderness temptation (5.21.3). In their salvation thus accomplished, a believer 'learn[s] by actual proof that he receives incorruptibility not of himself, but by the free gift of God' (5.21.3). The importance is that humans gain true knowledge of their place in the cosmos: God is the creator and humanity, the created.[75] In fact 5.22.2 explores the pride of the devil who forgets 'creation is not subjected to his power, since indeed he is himself but one among created things'.

Along with pride, lying is one of the devil's great faults. In 5.23 Irenaeus defends God's truthfulness against the devil's deceitfulness, particularly with regard to the promise of death for eating the fruit in our key verse Gen 2.16–17. The focus is upon humanity's original disobedience which led to death and Christ's obedience rather than the knowledge of good and evil. However, in their experience of death as God promised they learned that God is true and that the devil is a liar. And when they experience deliverance, it is so that each one 'might learn by actual proof that he receives incorruptibility not of himself, but by the free gift of God' (5.21.3). Thus, rather than thinking that they have power like God to make themselves immortal, they are his creation and only receive incorruption by participation in God, not of themselves.

---

[75] Canlis demonstrates effectively that 'creating' is a divine attribute held by God alone: Julie Canlis, 'Being Made Human: The Significance of Creation for Irenaeus' Doctrine Of Participation', *SJT* 58(2005): 434–454.

3.2.4 Deification and Knowing Good and Evil

The knowledge of evil is fundamentally bound to disobedience and the death which it brings. Thus, he associates 'knowledge of good and evil' with a loss of childlike innocence (3.20–23). This twofold knowledge characterises humanity, and while negative, it can have a positive function, helping believers to follow the good (4.38–39). The primary function seems to be that death gives an experiential knowledge that highlights the Creator-created distinction. Therefore, when believers experience immortality, they know that it comes from a participation in God's immortality and not from themselves (3.20–23; 4.38–39; 5.20–23).

It is precisely this participation in immortality that makes them like God. Irenaeus does not say this directly in his discussion of Genesis 2–3, but Adam and Eve were enticed by the serpent to gain 'immortality' by eating the fruit, so the clear implication is becoming immortal is the goal of becoming like gods in the Genesis text.

What then does knowledge of good and evil have to do with being like gods? If he had not associated knowing good and evil with 'being made after the image and likeness of God' in 4.38.4, one might expect that knowing good and evil would be antithetical to being like God, or becoming immortal, since it is fundamentally tied up with disobedience and therefore death. However, the commandment which distinguishes good from evil was given to reinforce the Creator-created distinction. So, those who live most fully in light of that distinction will be those who are most obedient. With or without sin humans would have to follow this path of growth from innocence to maturity to be fully in the image and likeness of God, attaining immortality.

It is clear that the acquisition of this knowledge was negative but could be redeemed. However, what makes this reading significant is its place in the second-century context. Obviously the issue of knowledge was important for Irenaeus' Gnostic opponents. Irenaeus only explicitly places his discussion of the tree of knowledge in opposition to the Gnostics in 5.20.2, where he described their heresy as eating the fruit in disobedience. His other treatments of these Genesis texts are in opposition to Gnostic readings but not explicitly. With knowledge such a central issue, it is a little surprising that Irenaeus does not address two texts that support their argumentation. For instance, he never mentions directly Gen 3.22 which says that 'man has become like one of us, knowing good and evil' or Gen 3.7 which speaks of their eyes being opened and their knowledge of their nakedness. Steenberg notes that the latter text was utilized by his Gnostic opponents.[76] Rather than addressing these texts and their readings that

---

[76] Steenberg, *Irenaeus on Creation*, 177-79. However, Steenberg does note the possible connection between knowledge of nakedness and procreation.

seem more amenable to his opponents as he does with 1 Cor 15.50 (cf. AH 5.9.14), Irenaeus leaves several of these texts untouched even though he disagrees with their readings.

Since the Creator-created distinction is so fundamental to Irenaeus' theology, it is striking that he readily accepts the gods language for believers. He never condemns their desire to be like gods. Rather their problem was seeking to achieve it independently of God, in disobedience by following Satan's path. As Vogel states, 'According to Irenaeus, the fall is a mistake about means more than ends'.[77]

In Irenaeus' view of deification there is no hint of absorption here or loss of humanity, as some might naively think, but rather the opposite. Humans become most like God, participating in the divine likeness of immortality and glory, when they recognize most fully their distinction from him. He does not have a merely 'physical' view of salvation, since we have seen how maturity is a learning process, a noetic transformation, if you will. However, when he speaks of 'knowing good and evil', Irenaeus situates this within the sphere of immortality, interpreting knowledge of good and evil as a metonymy, representing immortality and mortality as the results from each. As a result, while this Genesis passage might lead Irenaeus to emphasise noetic aspects of soteriology, he primarily situates soteriology as the somatic experience of immortality when speaking about the interface of humans with deity.

3.3 Relational Models

While Irenaeus only uses direct deification language (i.e., believers as gods) in the passages related to Psalm 82, the key themes that he associates with this language resound throughout his works. Thus, we will see that deification is not the primary terminology that Irenaeus uses, but deification language is one means of explaining his overall soteriology. As we have noted, Irenaeus expresses his understanding of soteriology through three primary models that describe the relationship between God and the believer: adoption as children of God (§3.3.1), the vision of God (§3.3.2), and union with God (§3.3.3). We turn first to adoption.

3.3.1 Adoption as Children of God

The term adoption (*adoptio*, υἱοθεσία) arises some twenty times in the five books of *AH*, with most occurring in Books 3 and 4. The occurrences of adoption in Book 3 are found in Irenaeus' discussion about the nature of Christ and his incarnation (3.16–23), and this was exemplified in our discussion of the exchange formula in 3.19.1 (cf. esp. 3.16.3). While hemost

---

[77] Jeff Vogel, 'Haste of Sin', 443.

often associates adoption with Christ in this section, at other times the Spirit is more directly the focus of his discussion.[78] Romans 8 and Galatians 4 both include the work of Christ and the Spirit, and this provides the basis for his inclusion of them both. Associating inheritance and the promises to Abraham with sonship, this inheritance can be described as a future kingdom or an inheritance to land (cf. Galatians 4),[79] but it can also be more anthropologically focused with inheritance being described as immortality and eternal life (cf. Romans 8). In 4.41.2–3 Irenaeus explains in depth that only those who are obedient to God are God's true sons and thus inherit immortality.[80]

Adoption provides a useful metaphor that incorporates the fact that people who were once separate from God are now joined to him in a subordinate role as child to father. With his strong emphasis on Christ as the Son, Irenaeus focuses on how the Son establishes and models this filial relationship of believers to the Father. The result of adoption is that it allows believers to partake of the inheritance promised in the scriptures, namely a restored creation and immortality and incorruption of the body.

3.3.2 The Vision of God

Another relational model used by Irenaeus is that of the vision of God. This serves as the culmination of the human-divine relationship and as a way to express intimate knowledge. According to 4.38.3 the vision of God is the *telos* of the divine experience which produces immortality and brings one near to God. These themes show up primarily in Books 4 and 5, with a specific focus on the topic in 4.20, where Irenaeus addresses the knowledge and revelation of God through Christ and the Spirit.[81] The Spirit gave the prophets a glimpse of the vision of God (4.20.10), but the Son truly makes the Father visible (3.11.5; 4.6.5–6; 4.20.5). With such a repeated emphasis on knowledge and revelation, Loewe defines Irenaeus' soteriology as primarily 'noetic'.[82] Importantly, believers are still not able to know God in his 'greatness' (4.20.1).

---

[78] E.g., 4.1.1; 5.9.1,3; 5.12.2; 5.18.2; *Dem.* 5.

[79] See especially 5.30–36 and also 4.7.2; 4.8.1; 4.9.1; 4.21.1,3; 4.26.1; 4.30.4.

[80] Cf. 2.11.1; 3.5.3; 4.11.1; 4.41.3; 5.1.3; 5.8.1; 5.9.4. Related to the discussion of inheritance is Irenaeus' interpretation of 1 Cor 15.53 about whether flesh and blood can inherit the kingdom of God (5.9–14). He focuses specifically on the moral meaning of flesh in distinction to the works of the Spirit, and ultimately argues that Spirit is not an inheritance of flesh, but the physical flesh is an inheritance of the Spirit. Thus, this too is an inheritance of a bodily incorruptibility.

[81] Some of Irenaeus' opponents considered Bythus, as ineffable and unseen even by the emanations (4.19.1; cf. 1.2.1; 1.19.1–2).

[82] William P. Loewe, 'Irenaeus' Soteriology: *Christus Victor* Revisited', *AThR* 67 (1985): 1–15.

One important result of the vision of God is immortality and eternal life, as 4.20.5–8 repeatedly affirms (cf. 4.38.1, 3; 5.7.2). Irenaeus writes: 'Therefore men will see God in order to live, becoming immortal by the vision and attaining to God' (4.20.6). The vision is not just seeing something external, but a participation in the divine glory and light (4.20.2, 5). The vision of God, including sharing in divine glory and light, culminates in the personal experience of immortality and in the relational experience of knowing God. An oft-quoted summary of Irenaeus' thought is the following: 'The glory of God is a living man; and the life of man consists in beholding God' (4.20.7). Just as Christ's humanity aided the reflection of his divinity, so our humanity is not limited in its participation of divinity through vision and glory.[83]

Irenaeus affirms that believers grow in their ability to see God and become more accustomed to grasp him (3.20.2). This is most evident in 5.35.1, where Irenaeus writes: 'the righteous shall reign in the earth, waxing stronger by the sight of the Lord: and through him they shall become accustomed to partake in the glory of God the Father'. Reflecting Paul's eschatological hope in 1 Cor 13.12, he mentions several times the eschatological relationship with God where believers interact 'face to face' with him (4.9.2; 4.11.1, 5.7.2; 5.8.1), and even eschatologically there is growth in knowledge for believers.

Irenaeus does not spend much time explaining how to attain this vision of God;[84] rather, his emphasis is on the revelatory work of Christ and the Spirit. The vision of God is an experience in knowing God through his self-revelation of love, evidenced by following and serving God, which results in sharing in glory and life (4.14.1). This vision is not therefore just a personal change or an experience of life but an intimate relationship, characterised by a growing knowledge of God.

3.3.3 Union, Communion, and Participation

One of the other common models for describing the relationship between humanity and God is that of union (*adunitio*, ἕνωσις) and communion (*communio*, κοινωνία).[85] Irenaeus presents this union as a multifaceted relationship when he writes:

---

[83] Cf. Denis Minns, *Irenaeus* (Washington, DC: Georgetown University Press, 1994), 41; Donovan, 'Alive', 288–9.

[84] However, de Andia (*Homo vivens*, 342) highlights the role of our loving God based on 4.13.13 as she notes: 'il y a une proportionalité entre le don de la grâce, l'amour et la gloire ...'.

[85] As with other aspects of his theology, the concept of union and communion can be seen as in contrast with that of his Gnostic opponents. Irenaeus stands in contrast to the Gnostics who describe the creation of this evil world as a result of Sophia wanting to

The Lord thus has redeemed us through his own blood, giving his soul for our souls, and his flesh for our flesh, and has also poured out the Spirit of the Father for the union and communion of God and man, imparting indeed God to men by means of the Spirit, and, on the other hand, attaching man to God by his own incarnation, and bestowing upon us at his coming immortality durably and truly, by means of communion with God. (5.1.1)

Union then captures the heart of the salvific relationship of God and humanity, and it reflects the work of Christ and the Spirit.

The union of divine and human in Christ makes possible the union between God and humanity.[86] In 3.18.7 Irenaeus writes: 'He caused man (human nature) to cleave to and to become one (ἐνόω) with God', leading to a reciprocal unity between God and humans. Christ recapitulates the union of humanity and Spirit, which allows believers to experience the same union (5.20.2). Irenaeus draws out the Spirit-believer relationship in some detail in 5.6–13, where he argues that the Spirit of God joined to believers vivifies them. This relationship is described in terms of commingling (*commixtio*) and union (5.6.1), possession (5.8.2; 5.9.2), indwelling (5.8.2; 5.9.2), and communion (5.9.4; 5.11.1; 5.12.2). The union of the Spirit with the believer is so close that the Spirit of God can also be termed the spirit of man, which allows the believer to experience resurrection and return to the likeness of God (5.6.1).

Important to concepts of union and communion is the language of participation (μετέχω, *participo*). Irenaeus commonly mentions that believers participate in life, immortality, and glory,[87] and also more directly in God, Christ or the Spirit.[88] Believers do not merely share in divine attributes; rather, they share in God himself, particularly through the Spirit. Though participation bespeaks an intimate unity, it also presupposes a type of separation, which for Irenaeus is the separation between Creator and creation.[89] The ultimate expression of union, communion, and participation is becoming like God by means of Christ and the Spirit. Believers partake in life and incorruptibility through the close relationship with God but remain distinct from him.

---

know Bythus and also have communion and union with Theletus (1.2.2; 1.29.4; 2.12.3; 2.18.7; 3.11.1).

[86] Cf. 3.16.6; 3.18.1; 4.20.4; 4.31.2; 4.33.11; 5.14.3.

[87] 2.34.4; 3.18.7; 3.21.1; 4.14.1; 4.18.5; 4.20.5; 4.39.2; 5.3.3; 5.4.2; 5.5.1; 5.7.2; 5.35.1. Cf. 3.19.1

[88] In God: 4.28.2; in Christ: 3.17.2; in the Spirit; 3.24.1; 5.6.1; 5.9.2; 5.13.4. In 3.18.2 and 5.2.2 Irenaeus speaks of communion of the body and of the blood of Christ (cf. 5.1.3), and in 4.18.5 when the believers receive the Eucharist, their 'bodies [are] no longer corruptible, having the hope of resurrection to eternity'. Also, the importance of church in Irenaeus' thought regarding union and communion is not insignificant (cf. 3.24.1). However, his anthropology is the centre of our discussion.

[89] Cf. Canlis, 'Being Made Human'.

Adoption, vision, and union are three main ways Irenaeus speaks about the divine-human relationship, and we see that they are deeply interconnected. As adopted children (sons) of God based upon the work of the Son, believers are now called gods by the Spirit. Through the revelatory vision of God believers share in the divine glory. Believers are then united to God by participation and become one with him. These models are based thoroughly on the work of Christ and the Spirit and express the means for individual transformation into the likeness of God, resulting in the experience of immortality and incorruption as they gradually progress towards him. Put simply: 'the friendship of God imparts immortality to those who embrace it' (4.13.4).

3.4 Anthropological Effects

Humanity's restoration comes through a restored relationship with God through Christ and the Spirit. The anthropological effect arising from this restored relationship will now be our focus. The primary soteriological effects are an experience of immortality/incorruption (§3.4.1) and progression (§3.4.2). These climax in a restoration of the divine image and likeness (§3.4.3).

3.4.1 Immortality and Incorruption

In Irenaeus' anthropology the primary problem that humans face is mortality as the result of sin and separation from God. As a result, he presents sharing in divine immortality through the work of Christ and the Spirit as the primary anthropological effect of salvation. The importance of this effect for Irenaeus is evident due to its repetition in multiple contexts. Whether Irenaeus speaks of recapitulation, adoption, vision of God, or union with God, immortality (*immortalitas*, ἀθανασία) and incorruptibility (*incorruptela*, ἀφθαρσία) are always a primary result of these salvific encounters.[90] Regarding deification, Irenaeus makes clear that he sees immortality as central to the status of being gods, and that mortality separates one from divinity (3.19.1; 4.38.4). The experience of immortality and incorruption is captured in the experience of the resurrection of the body, of mortal flesh.[91] In fact, Irenaeus goes to some lengths to explain how the flesh itself experiences resurrection because Christ took flesh upon himself (5.10–15). However, he also notes that the soul is only immortal by means

---

[90] de Andia (*Homo vivens*, 25) notes a distinction between immortality as referring to the soul or a person, and incorruptibility as referring to the body.

[91] Abineau ('Incorruptibilité et Divinisation', 26–30, 35–36) importantly notes how this stands in distinction to 'Gnostic' notions of immortality.

of participation in God (2.34.4). Importantly, Irenaeus identifies the experience of immortality with glorification (4.20; 4.38.3–4).

3.4.2 Progress

Central to Irenaeus' anthropology is also the concept of progression from infancy to maturity, which culminates in, among other things, incorruption. One particular concept which highlights Irenaeus' view of anthropological development is that of being accustomed (*assuescere* or *adsuescere*, ἐθίζω) to grow in some capacity to take hold of (*capere*, χωρεῖν) God. God has situated the divine economy to accustom God to humans and humans to God.[92] In all these things believers grow in knowledge through experience and come closer to God relationally. Growth into God will not end because humans are ever changing, even into the eschaton. He describes the growth of the believer even after the resurrection in the millennial kingdom: 'the just will reign on earth, growing because of the vision of the Lord. Thanks to him, they will grow accustomed to contain the glory of God the Father and will receive life with the holy angels and communion and unity with spiritual realities in the kingdom' (5.35.1).[93] Progression into the divine glory then is the eternal state of believers.

In addition to a relational knowledge, a progression in moral faithfulness also plays a role for Irenaeus. We noted in §3.1.4 and §3.2 how the experience of evil aided humanity's moral progression (4.38–39). As believers express free will according to rationality, they become like God and grow to maturity (4.4.3; 4.36–41). Believers then fulfil the duty of obedience that humans owe God (4.14.1; 4.20.1; 4.39.2). While very little of Irenaeus' extant work is parenetic in nature, a gentle stream flows through his books encouraging the moral life of the believer.[94] His encouragement to life in the Spirit in 5.6–13 directly relates to a life of faithfulness and obedience.

This view of progression always serves as the background of the divine-human relationship. This then profoundly influences the nature of the realisation of salvation within humans and makes clear the distinction between God and humans. Irenaeus writes:

And in this respect God differs from man, that God indeed makes, but man is made; and truly, he who makes is always the same; but that which is made must receive both beginning, and middle, and addition, and increase .... God also is truly perfect in all things, himself equal and similar to himself, as he is all light, and all mind, and all substance, and the fount of all good; but man receives advancement and increase towards God. For

---

[92] 3.17.1; 3.20.2; 4.5.4; 4.14.2; 4.21.3; 4.38.1; 5.8.1; 5.32.1; 5.35.1.

[93] Cf. 5.35.2

[94] For example, key passages including moral encouragement include 4.12.1; 4.16.4; 4.20.8; 4.28.2; 5.1.1; 5.6.1; and 5.11.2.

as God is always the same, so also man, when found in God, shall always go on towards God. For neither does God at any time cease to confer benefits upon, or to enrich man; nor does man ever cease from receiving the benefits, and being enriched by God. (4.11.2)

If Irenaeus makes seemingly unqualified statements about believers being gods or having union with God, the distinction between the unchanging Creator and the ever-progressing creation serves as the context for understanding these correctly. Wingren thus writes: 'Irenaeus never depicts a future condition in which God's giving and man's receiving will have come to an end. Man continues to become to the end'.[95] The perfect person has the Spirit in such a way that the believer can be described as being comprised of a body, soul, and spirit (5.6.1); however, the vivification of the body by the Spirit will not be culminated until the resurrection. The consummation is not simply a return to Eden. Rather, 'Christ completes creation', Wingren argues, 'making it into something better and richer than it had ever been from the beginning'.[96]

3.4.3 Image and Likeness

Describing the work of Christ and the *telos* of humanity, Irenaeus' conclusion of Book 5 summarises his theology:

For there is one Son who achieved the will of the Father, and one human race, in which are achieved the mysteries of God, mysteries that 'angels desired to see', but they could not investigate the Wisdom of God, through which his work was shaped and made concorporate with the Son. For God wanted his firstborn Word to descend into his creation and be held by it, and in turn for the creation to hold the Word and ascend to him, thus surpassing the angels and coming to be in the image and likeness of God. (5.36.3)

His final statement affirms that believers, surpassing angels, 'come to be in the image and likeness of God'. We addressed this issue above in §2.2, but it is important to emphasise the place of 'image and likeness' in Irenaeus' soteriology.[97] These terms, which come from the creation of humanity in Gen 1.26, describe not only humanity's beginning but also its end.[98] Just as God created humans in the beginning according to the image of the Word, this also serves as their *telos*. In each of the areas above restoration of likeness was expressed in the context of the soteriological benefits: being called gods (4.38.4), receiving adoption (4.33.4), having a vi-

---

[95] Wingren, *Man*, 209n.78.

[96] Ibid., 26.

[97] While likeness may be distinguishable from image in some passages (e.g., 5.6.1), Irenaeus also uses them together as a hendiadys of the *telos* of humanity. Cf. Finch, 'Irenaeus', 88. See note 16 above which details the debate about a possible distinction between 'image' and 'likeness'.

[98] Osborn (*Irenaeus*, 132) notes: 'Deification moves from the image and likeness, by means of the Trinitarian economy, to the vision of God which gives incorruptibility'.

sion of God (4.37.7; 4.38.3), and attaining union with God (5.1.4; 5.6.1). In addition, incorruption and progress in the moral life are integrated with the culmination of image and likeness by the Spirit (5.6–13). Thus, the anthropological culmination of salvation is a restoration of the image and likeness of God in humanity.

4. Conclusion

4.1 Irenaeus' Soteriology

With regard to Irenaeus' soteriology, he presents the restored relationship between believers and God through his relational models of adoption, vision, and union. In particular, as Christ recapitulates humanity he restores the communion between humans, God, and his life-giving Spirit. This relational restoration allows believers to overcome their problems of corruption and immaturity as they experience incorruption and moral progression. Thus, restoration of inter-personal relationships between God and humanity allows for intra-personal restoration from sin and death. While moral progression is central to Irenaeus' anthropology, the ontological experience of immortality and incorruption is ubiquitous. Since the spirit and soul remain immortal through the presence of the life of God, the primary locus of noticeable soteriological change is that of the body, the flesh. As a result, much of Irenaeus' language focuses upon the future eschatological experience, rather than the current age. In distinction, the growing relationship with God that allows believers to morally progress relates to the current and eschatological ages.

This anthropological transformation is subsumed under the umbrella of the image and likeness of God.[99] With image and likeness as both the creational intent and the *telos* of humanity, God's saving work does not return believers to Adam's created *state* of moral and intellectual infancy but to the original divine *intention* that they will progress towards perfection and experience incorruption. The goal of humanity is not to transcend that distinction of Creator and creature but to fulfil it by God becoming reproduced in them, as a portrait reproduces the person. Therefore, the *telos* of humanity is believers growing towards God in Christ and by the Spirit through an intimate divine-human relationship. This likeness is revealed through the divine attributes of life, glory, and perfection.

---

[99] This corresponds to Fairburn's ('Patristic Soteriology', 294–7) argument that Irenaeus portrays a 'personal' or relational form of deification. Cf. Trevor A. Hart, 'Irenaeus, Recapitulation and Physical Redemption' in *Christ in Our Place,* eds. Trevor A. Hart and Daniel P. Thimell (Allison Park: Pickwick, 1989), 152–181, at 165–66, 180.

4.2 Deification in Irenaeus

Within this larger soteriological structure, Irenaeus employs deification language to capture the significance of the inter-personal and intra-personal aspects. While deification is perhaps not the most comprehensive term that would describe Irenaeus' soteriology (as if any one term could), he related the appellation of 'gods' to all of his central soteriological concepts – both the means and the effects. The importance of deification becomes evident when we consider his polemical context. Irenaeus wants to separate the genetic link between humans and the divine maintained by the Gnostics. Irenaeus, however, does not shy away from this language, which seems to blur the categories he wants to keep separate.[100] Thus, he takes the more difficult path and uses the same term for God and humans, thus elevating humans. The constantly affirmed distinction between the created and Creator allows such strong language.

Irenaeus employs this language in a variety of contexts, in passages discussing the nature of God, Christ, and humanity. Along with glory and perfection, Irenaeus focuses particularly upon incorruption (1 Cor 15.53–54; 2 Cor 5.4), adoption (Rom 8.15; Gal 4.4–6), and union with God through Christ's exchange (Gal 4.4–6) to build his model of deification. Specifically, believers stand as adopted sons and gods based upon Christ's work as the divine Son and his uniting exchange.[101] At the same time, this adoption is not only relational but it is actually identified with the experience of incorruption. Nevertheless, believers experience the presence of the Spirit and the proleptic experience of life before physical resurrection, and this allows Irenaeus to call believers gods presently. Deification then is the process of restoration of the image and likeness through a restored relationship with God experienced primarily through incorruption and a growth in maturity. This form of deification is 'realistic' according to Russell's taxonomy, in that it is focused on the personal transformation from corruption to incorruption.[102] With only four references to believers as gods, we should thus heed Kaufman's caution against uncritical use of

---

[100] The application of 'gods' language to humans probably arose more easily in a Greek context where θεός and ἀθάνατος are used synonymously.

[101] Athanasius did not make a leap when he made the exchange formula more explicit: 'He was made man that we might become gods' (*De Incarn.* 54). Regarding the exhange formula that Irenaeus uses and draws from Pauline language, Noormann (*Irenäus*, 527) writes: 'Begibt sich das Wort Gottes in die Gleichheit der von der Sünde beherrschten menschlichen Sarx, so wird der Mensch aufgerufen, seinerseits dem Wort Gottes in einem Prozeß allmählicher Angleichung gleich zu werden'.

[102] Russell, *Deification*, 1–3, 105–10. Gross (*Divinization*, 125) labels this 'physical' or 'mystical'.

the term, but we also note that other major Irenaean themes intersect with this language.

Based upon our analysis, we can now evaluate Kaufman's study on the topic. He addresses three primary deification themes in order to evaluate the place of deification in Irenaeus' theology: being called gods, becoming like God, and participation in God. Regarding these themes, he draws the following conclusions.[103] 1) He notes the limited use of the gods terminology for believers and the explicit lack of 'deification' language (that is, θεοποιέω and/or θέωσις).[104] 2) The use of image of God language is central for describing the starting point and goal of humanity, but this is particularly modelled after the *human* aspect of Christ. 3) Irenaeus makes significant use of language related to participation in God, which is a clear deification theme. Kaufman concludes that 'the three deification themes we have been studying do not fit into an overall doctrine of deification, but rather, into an overall understanding of the *telos* of man as becoming "fully human"'.[105]

While Kaufman is right to question deification as the comprehensive appellation for Irenaeus' soteriology, he unnecessarily bifurcates deification from other aspects of Irenaeus' theology. He himself notes that these three categories cannot be neatly separated in Irenaeus' theology, which reduces the strength of his critique.[106] The most telling weakness, though, is his unnecessary separation between becoming 'gods' and becoming fully human. For instance, he writes: 'If this passage [4.39.2] were to end here, we might be justified in concluding that Irenaeus is here speaking of deification, in the sense that man is to stop being human and become something more than human – a god'.[107] Kaufman works from the premise that to be a god and to be a human are necessarily distinct, despite his earlier discussion about the plasticity of the term θεός.[108] However, he appears to be importing a taxonomy into the discussion that Irenaeus does not use. For Irenaeus, being a god, at least when used of humans, relates to experiencing certain characteristics: immortality, perfection, and participating in divine glory. While this is an elevation of humanity, it does not necessitate becoming 'more than human'. In using this taxonomy, Kaufman wants to differentiate Irenaeus from the Gnostics who denigrated the body.

---

[103] Kaufman, 'Becoming', 247–48.

[104] His argument that Irenaeus lacks 'the technical terminology of deification' overly limits the category of 'the technical terminology of deification'. Surely, the use of 'gods' as an appellation for believers is unique and striking. It is clearly not a dead metaphor and, thus, should not be segregated.

[105] Kaufman, 'Becoming', 250.

[106] Ibid., 248–49.

[107] Ibid., 231.

[108] Ibid., 146–49.

By arguing that Irenaeus argues for a 'full humanity', Kaufman is thus able to emphasise the embodied aspect of Irenaeus' anthropology. However, Kaufman implicitly allows the categories of the Gnostics to determine his analysis of Irenaeus.[109] Thus, I agree with the content of Kaufman's argument but not the taxonomy that forces him to separate being a god and being fully human. In fact, by becoming human, Christ shows that divinity and humanity are not at odds but are, in fact, able to commune with one another and that humanity can thus experience the divine attributes of incorruption, perfection, and glory according to God's original intention.

4.3 Irenaeus and Paul

When employing Psalm 82, Irenaeus regularly makes use of two primary concepts: immortality and adoption. With regard to immortality and incorruption, he draws directly from 1 Cor 15.54 which parallels 2 Cor 5.4. This employment of immortality language allows him to draw together the appellation of gods and the mortality language in Ps 82.6–7, but it also reflects his repeated emphasis upon the reality of bodily resurrection in 1 Corinthians 15, to which he alludes almost twice as much as any other Pauline chapter.[110] At the same time, in three of the four passages Irenaeus also draws in the concept of adoption from Gal 4.4–6 and Rom 8.14–16 in order to explain how gods are 'sons of the Most High' (Ps 82.6). In fact, this association between being gods, immortality, and adoption leads Irenaeus to identify being adopted as receiving immortality. Irenaeus not only employs the adoption metaphor from the Galatians passage, but also the exchange formula. He focuses upon the Christ's and believers' sonship, but it is important to note that he makes no mention of the law, which is central to the argument of that passage.

In addition to these passages central to his explanation of deification, Irenaeus employs Pauline passages widely in the broader models and themes we explored. Within the larger Adam-Christ dialectic, Irenaeus makes much use of image language. However, he actually does not make much direct use of any one Pauline text that talks of being conformed to the image of Christ, though some fall in central Pauline passages.[111] Rather, he depends on a variety of texts, especially those from Genesis, to develop his theology of image and likeness. While Irenaeus regularly employs language of seeing God and sharing in his glory, of which the latter is common in Pauline texts, no individual Pauline text seems to gain pride of place because Irenaeus draws from a variety of sources. Preferring

---

[109] Ibid., 232–33.

[110] Cf. Allenbach, *Des origines*, 428–519.

[111] E.g., 1 Cor 15.49: 5.9.3; 5.11.2; 2 Cor 3.18: not used; Rom 8.29–30: 4.20.8; 4.37.7; Phil 3.21: 5.13.3.

more direct language, Irenaeus does not depend on the ubiquitous 'in Christ' language that Paul uses to describe the divine-human relationship. This employment of Pauline texts begins to raise several questions, but we will not develop these until after we explore deification in Cyril of Alexandria in the next chapter.

3. Deification in Cyril of Alexandria

The image of the Son of God 'was impressed on us, making
us the same form as himself and engraving the illumination
which is through his own Spirit as a divine image upon those
who believe in him, that they too may now be called both
gods and sons of God as he is'. *In Jo.* 1.9, 1:80 [1:103]

1. Introduction

In our analysis of patristic views of deification, we move from Irenaeus
who wrote in the late second century to Cyril of Alexandria (AD 378–444),
two centuries later. Following his uncle Theophilus, Cyril rose to the position of archbishop of Alexandria in AD 412 and is best known for his role
in the so-called Nestorian controversy. The two centuries after Irenaeus
experienced much debate, particularly over the divinity of the Son and the
Spirit, and spawned several ecclesial councils, of which two are considered
ecumenical: Nicaea (AD 325) and Constantinople (AD 381). Through the
work of Athanasius and the Cappadocians, the language of deification also
developed, reflecting the refinements from these Trinitarian debates.
Cyril's discourse reflects these theological clarifications and expansions;
however, he also provides new avenues of discussion regarding deification.
To further our study we will examine how Cyril presents deification in his
writings and analyse how Pauline texts and themes fit within his soteriological discourse.

Cyril has a wide variety of extant works – treatises, homilies, letters,
and commentaries – with the majority being biblical commentaries.[1] In
fact, seven out of the ten volumes of Cyril's works in PG are commentaries. While often polemical in nature, his commentaries provide a comprehensive image of his theological reflection, so I have chosen to focus upon
these. In an attempt to draw from a representative sample, I have chosen
works representing his earlier and later writings, with the start of the Nestorian controversy in 428 as the dividing line. For the former group, Cyril

---

[1] For a full listing of Cyril's works see M. Geerard and F. Glorie eds. *Clavis Patrum
Graecorum* (vol. III; Turnhout: Brepols, 1979), 5200–5438.

has commentaries on three Pauline letters which remain untranslated,[2] so I have chosen his lengthy *Commentary on the Gospel of John*.[3] From his later writings, I have chosen his *Homilies on Luke*[4] and his theological treatise *On the Unity of Christ* (*Quod Unus Sit Christus*, hereafter *Quod*),[5] which gives a focused exposition of his Christology in light of the Nestorian controversy. Rather than treating the works individually, I examine his thought as a whole, assuming a consistency throughout, which others have shown and the analysis below also reflects.[6]

As with Irenaeus, Cyril's confessional and polemical concerns are not far from his mind as he writes. For instance, in his *Commentary on John* he intertwines commentary on the gospel with a polemic against 'Arian' Christology and has been described as 'dogmatic exegesis'.[7] However, as

---

[2] These sizable, though fragmentary, commentaries on Romans, 1 Corinthians and 2 Corinthians have never been translated into any modern language. As translation of these would be a substantial endeavour in itself, for reasons of time this work has had to wait until after our current study, and I hope to take this up in the future.

[3] When citing the commentary, I note the verse reference in John, the page number of Pusey's/Randell's translations, and then the numbers of Pusey's critical Greek edition in square brackets. I utilise the LFC translations, with emendation where necessary: Cyril of Alexandria, *Commentary on the Gospel According to St. John (I–VIII)* (Library of the Fathers of the Church 43; trans. P.E. Pusey; Oxford: James Parker, 1874); idem., *Commentary on the Gospel According to St. John (IX–XXI)* (Library of the Fathers of the Church 48; trans. T. Randell; Oxford: Walter Smith, 1885). For the critical text, see: idem., *Sancti Patris Nostri Cyrilli Archiepiscopi Alexandrini in D. Joannis Evangelium* (ed. P.E. Pusey; 3 vols.; Bruxelles: Culture et Civilisation, 1965 [1872]).

[4] The full extant manuscripts are only in Syriac, so I follow Smith's translation: Cyril of Alexandria, *A Commentary Upon the Gospel According to St. Luke by St. Cyril* (trans. R. Payne Smith; 2 vols.; Oxford: Oxford University Press, 1859).

[5] idem., *On the Unity of Christ* (trans. John McGuckin; Crestwood, NY: St. Vladimir's Seminary Press, 1995). For the critical text, see: idem., *Deux Dialogues Christologiques* (SC 97; ed. and trans. G.M. de Durand; Paris: Cerf, 1964).

[6] For those who emphasise discontinuity in Cyril's writings, see John A. McGuckin, *St. Cyril of Alexandria and the Christological Controversy* (Crestwood, NY: St. Vladimir's Seminary Press, 2004), 207–10; Aloys Grillmeier, *Christ in Christian Tradition* (trans. John Bowden; 2nd rev. ed.; London: Mowbrays, 1975), 1:415–17. For continuity, see Eduard Weigl, *Die Heilslehre des heiligen Cyril von Alexandrien* (Mainz: Kirchenheim, 1905), 202; Henry Chadwick, 'Eucharist and Christology in the Nestorian Controversy', *JTS* 2 (1951): 145–64, at 150; Pius Angstenberger, *Der reiche und der arme Christus: Die Rezeptionsgeschichte von 2 Kor 8,9 zwischen dem 2. und 6. Jahrhundert* (Bonn: Borengässer, 1997), 189. Most discontinuity in his writing is primarily terminological and not substantial. This allows Donald Fairbairn (*Grace and Christology in the Early Church* [Oxford: Oxford University Press, 2003], 129–30) to write: 'when one considers the soteriological concerns that lie behind his Christology, it becomes apparent that the guiding principles of his thought remained constant throughout his career'.

[7] Lois M. Farag, *St. Cyril of Alexandria, A New Testament Exegete: His Commentary on the Gospel of John* (Gorgias Dissertations 29; Piscataway, NJ: Gorgias, 2007), 71.

we discussed earlier, all writers are historically situated, and they are responding to the questions of their day. Regarding his exegetical method, many have simply lumped him together with other Alexandrians in distinction to the Antiochenes. This distinction has been strongly challenged by most patrologists for years, but many biblical scholars, unfortunately, tend to repeat the neat taxonomy found in decades-old patristics textbooks.[8] For our purposes this exegetical distinction matters little anyway because the focus of debate centred on Old Testament and narrative texts. As non-narrative prose, the Pauline letters were accepted as authoritative and direct communication to be accepted and applied.

In our examination of how Cyril presents his theology of deification, we will first look at his theological framework and then more specifically at his presentation of deification. In section 2 I summarise Cyril's portrayal of the Trinity, humanity, and soteriology. Next, we move into a discussion of deification in Cyril, which includes an examination of passages where Cyril uses Ps 82.6 and 2 Pet 1.4 to explain the human-divine relationship (§3.1) and then an investigation of central themes that arise from those passages (§3.2).

2. The Trinity, Humanity, and Soteriology

Before understanding Cyril's theology of deification, we must understand his larger theological structure. With Cyril's concern about the Arian and Nestorian debates, we are not surprised to find developed accounts of the nature of divinity and humanity and the relationship between the two. Summarising these accounts, we will review Cyril's theological framework with a focus upon his views on the Trinity (§2.1), humanity (§2.2), and soteriology (§2.3).

2.1 The Trinity

Cyril's Trinitarian theology reflects a century of intense christological and Trinitarian debates.[9] In particular, Cyril's early works, which focus on Arian debates, argue for the equality of nature (ὁμοούσια) between the Father, Son and Spirit, such that the Son is uncreated and eternally exists together with the Father and the Spirit. Cyril reflects the positions agreed upon at Nicaea (AD 325) and Constantinople (AD 381), which strike a careful balance of unity in the midst of diversity within the Godhead (e.g., *In Jo.* 1.3, 1:53 [1:69]). Cyril's emphasis upon the consubstantial divinity

---

[8] Cf. Donald Fairbairn, 'Patristic Exegesis and Theology: The Cart and the Horse', *WTJ* 69 (2007): 1-19.

[9] For a recent treatment, see Ayres, *Nicaea and Its Legacy.*

of the Spirit, which reflects late fourth century explanations, significantly influences his soteriology and presents a clear development from Irenaeus.[10]

The councils of Nicaea and Constantinople helped clarify the relationship of the Son to the Father as being consubstantial; however, this affirmation provided the basis for debates about the relationship of the Logos to his humanity in which Cyril was involved.[11]　Specifically, the church debated how the impassible God is united to passible humanity in Christ.[12] The 'Nestorian' position emphasised the duality in the incarnation as a way of preserving the transcendence and impassibility of the divine essence.　Following those who responded to Apollinarius, Cyril maintained that the fully divine Word took on full humanity, with a rational soul and body (cf. *Quod*, 55 [316]).　He also understood God as impassible[13] but argued fervently for the unity in the incarnate person of Christ, such that Mary is rightfully called the *Theotokos* in distinction to Nestorius' appellation of *Christotokos*.　In particular, Cyril argues that the Nestorian position merely makes Christ a deified man alongside the Word.[14]　In other words, rather than God saving humanity, Christ would be merely the model of saved humanity.[15]

2.2 Humanity

While these debates about the nature of the incarnation drive Cyril's later work, his arguments against Arianism also reflect considerable thought about Christ's humanity.　Cyril's anthropology is best summarised in an explanation about the Word becoming flesh (John 1.14):[16]

Man then is a rational creature (λογικὸν ζῷον), being composite of soul and of this perishable and earthly flesh.　And when he was made by God and was brought into being,

---

[10] A significant development in Pneumatology occurred in the fourth century with the explicit ascription of consubstantial divinity to the Spirit. E.g., Athanasius, *ad Serapion* 1.24; Gregory of Nazianzus, *Oration* 31.4.

[11] See Janssens for the soteriological importance of this dual consubstantiality, particularly for Cyril's emphasis on exchange formulae: L. Janssens, 'Notre Filiation divine d'après Saint Cyrille d'Alexandrie', *ETL* 15 (1938): 233–78, at 237–43.

[12] John J. O'Keefe, 'Impassible Suffering? Divine Passion and Fifth-Century Christology', *TS* 58 (1997): 39–60.

[13] Cf. *Quod*, 54 and *In Jo.* 4.27, 1:354.

[14] Cf. *Quod*, 67–76.

[15] Fairbairn, *Grace*, 131–32.

[16] See also Cyril's Festal Letter of 418 (*Epistula Pascalis* 6) for a more detailed development of his anthropology: Cyril of Alexandria, *Lettres Festales, 1–6* (SC 372; ed. P. Évieux; trans. P. Évieux; Paris: Cerf, 1991). Cf. Susan Wessel, *Cyril of Alexandria and the Nestorian Controversy: The Making of a Saint and of a Heretic* (Oxford: Oxford University Press, 2004), 50–51.

not having of his own nature incorruption and indestructibility (for those things appertain essentially to God alone), he was sealed with the Spirit of life, by participation (σχέσις) in the divinity, gaining the good that is above nature. For, 'He breathed,' it says, 'into his nostrils the breath of life and the man became a living soul' [Gen 2.7]. But when he was being punished for the transgression, then rightly hearing 'You are dust and to dust you will return' [Gen 3.19], he was stripped of grace. The breath of life, that is the Spirit of him who says 'I am the life,' departed from the earthly flesh, and the creature falls into death, through the flesh alone – the soul being preserved (σῴζω) in immortality since it was said only to the flesh, 'You are dust and to dust you will return' [Gen 3.19]. Therefore it was necessary that the thing which was most of all endangered in us should be vigorously restored and should be recalled to immortality by intertwining again with Life by nature. It was necessary to find release from the suffering of evil. It was necessary that at length the sentence, 'You are dust and to dust you will return' [Gen 3.19], should be relaxed when the fallen body is united ineffably to the Word who gives life to all things. For it was necessary when his flesh came to partake of the immortality that is from him. (*In Jo.* 1.14, 1:108–9 [1:138–39])

We will thus address key aspects of Cyril's anthropology by using this passage as a window onto larger issues. Cyril speaks of humans as composite, being body and soul (§2.2.1); as derivative, participating in divine life (§2.2.2); and as under the problem of sin (§2.2.3). The narrative of salvation, or rather the *narrative of the Spirit*, which includes the giving, removal and restoration of the Spirit, will also be important for our discussions of his soteriology in §2.3.

2.2.1 Humans are Composite

From the passage above, we see a basic duality in his anthropology, in that humans are composed of a body and rational soul. Cyril notes that the body is perishable on its own and lives only by participation in life from God. The curse of death then is removal of that participation in the divine life, revealing the body for what it is – corruptible.[17] Accordingly, the body is primarily characterised as mortal and corruptible in Cyril's writings. On the other hand, the soul is also fundamentally corruptible by nature, yet it remains immortal since the curse is only applied to the body.[18] Thus, both soul and body are alive only by participation in the divine.

Interestingly, Cyril does not interpret the 'breath of life' from Gen 2.7 as referring to the giving of the soul, as did most, but rather the impartation of the Spirit. Marie-Odile Boulnois thus writes: 'L'insufflation, venant de Dieu, possède les caractéristiques divines. Par conséquent, elle ne peut s'identifier avec l'âme, puisque l'âme aurait alors été incorruptible, ce qui

---

[17] Cf. *In Jo.* 8.35, 1:631 [2:69–70]. This anthropology is similar to Irenaeus. Cf. Chap 2, §2.2.

[18] However, Cyril earlier makes clear that souls are not pre-existent and that being placed in the body is not punishment (*In Jo.* 1.9, 1:91 [1:117]).

n'est pas le cas, puisqu'Adam a péché'.[19] Though not addressed in this passage, it appears that he understands the human 'soul' and 'spirit' as being synonymous (e.g., *In Jo.* 3.5, 1:168 [1:219]).[20] With regard to the soul, he characterises the human as 'rational'; however, rational enlightenment is dimmed in the fall and is restored by Christ. Another aspect of the soul, which Cyril also develops elsewhere, is free will. When commenting on John 6.45 and the agency of God in revelation, Cyril highlights the necessity of the human will (*In Jo.* 6.45, 1:401 [1:507]). Drawing from this composite nature of humanity, Cyril views soteriology as addressing both aspects – body and soul.

2.2.2 Humans are Derivative

A correlate to the notion of humans being composite for Cyril is that they are also derived. That is, all that they have is from God through participation. Every good thing exists in God, but 'what is in the creature is compound, and nothing simple is in it' (*In Jo.* 1.9, 1:85 [1:109]). That which is simple (indivisible) is self-existing but something which is compound must derive from something else. By nature of their being created – moving from not being to being – humans are derived from true being, who is God. God is all wisdom, life, light, etc., and he communicates these to those that participate in him. Creatures are an amalgam of what they are by nature and what they partake in and receive from God.

One primary theme that Cyril develops is that of participation in divine life. As we see in the main passage above (*In Jo.* 1.14), the breath of life is the Spirit. In the first instance, this experience of the *Spiritual* life is described as 'participation in the divinity' and later 'partaking of immortality', which points back to the synonymity between immortality and divinity we discussed in Irenaeus.[21] In addition to life, Cyril also draws similar conclusions with the theme of light, which he draws from key passages in John (cf. John 1.4–5, 8–9). In the same way that life is restored through Christ and the Spirit, divine illumination is also restored to the rational creature.[22] In some ways, the dual categories of life and light correspond to the dual nature of humanity, body and soul, but this correlation is not exact.

---

[19] Marie-Odile Boulnois, 'Le souffle et l'Esprit: Exégèses patristiques de l'insufflation originelle de Gen. 2,7 en lien avec celle de *Jn* 20,22', *RechAug* 24 (1989): 3–37, 32.

[20] Cf. Walter J. Burghardt, *The Image of God in Man According to Cyril of Alexandria* (Washington: Catholic University of America Press, 1957), 20.

[21] See Chp 2, §3.1.2. Cf. *In Jo.* 1.4, 1:57–59 [1:74–76].

[22] Cf. *In Jo.* 1.5, 1:68 [1:88].

2.2.3 Problem of Sin

Since humans only experience life and light through participation in the divine, they must remain united to God to share these benefits. However, Adam's transgression presented a barrier to participation. Returning to our main passage discussed above (*In Jo.* 1.14), Adam's transgressions resulted in the curse of death upon the body (Gen 3.19), and God justly removes the grace of participation granted by the Spirit's presence. However, as a compound being, sin affects humans in both body and soul: 'man is, sirs, a compound animal upon the earth, that is, of soul and body. The slavery according to the flesh pertains to the flesh, but that of the soul, which takes place upon the soul, has for its mother the barbarian sin' (*In Jo.* 8.34, 1:627 [2:64]). Thus, the body that once participated in divine life is now mortal, and the soul that participated in divine light is now darkened, with only vestiges of each remaining.[23] Mortal and moral corruption reside in humanity which lives under the power of death, the devil, and sin (cf. *Quod*, 55–59 [316–28]).

2.3 Cyril's Soteriology

With the curse of corruption from the Spirit's departure as the central problem, Cyril portrays Christ as restoring incorruption through the Spirit. This curse is reversed through the union of believers with Christ and the restoration of the presence of the Spirit, who is the breath of life. We will briefly explore Cyril's depiction of salvation summarised in the account of Christ's baptism (§2.3.1) and then the accomplishment and realisation of salvation (§2.3.2).

2.3.1 Christ's Baptism

Cyril renders the work of Christ and the Spirit most clearly when he addresses the issue of why the Spirit came upon Christ at baptism since they already shared the one divine nature (*In Jo.* 1.32–33, 1:140–3 [1:181–85]).[24] Cyril repeats his *narrative of the Spirit* which centres upon the giving of the Spirit at creation, his departure due to Adam's sin, and his restoration to believers through Christ.[25] God formed Adam into the divine im-

---

[23] Quoting Rom 5.14, Cyril writes: 'corruption is extended against the whole nature of man, because of the transgression of Adam' (*In Jo.* 1.9, 1:96 [1:123]).

[24] See especially Daniel A. Keating, 'The Baptism of Jesus in Cyril of Alexandria: The Re-creation of the Human Race', *ProEccl* 8 (1999): 201–22. Cyril also discusses Christ's baptism in his homily on Luke 3.21–23. See §3.1.2.1 for further discussion of this passage. He repeats the emphasis upon our need for the Spirit, citing the benefits of sonship and re-creation (2 Cor 5.17).

[25] Throughout this chapter I use the phrases 'narrative of the Spirit' and 'narrative of salvation' whenever Cyril explicitly develops this gift-departure-restoration narrative.

age (Gen 1.27), which was impressed upon him through the Spirit as the breath of life (Gen 2.7). After sinning, God removed the presence of the Spirit and gave the curse of death (Gen 3.19), with the result that 'now the likeness to God was defaced through the inroad of sin, and the impress was no longer bright (λαμπρός), but fainter and darkened because of the transgression' (1:141 [1:183]). However, in his grace God relented and 'decreed to transform (μεταστοιχειόω) human nature anew to the ancient image through the Spirit, for it was not otherwise possible that the divine impress should shine forth in him again as it did formerly' (1:141 [1:183]). The Spirit however did not independently perform this renewal. Rather, it was the work of Christ, as the second Adam, that opened the door. The first Adam despised the grace of God, became mastered by 'corruption and death, [and] transmits the penalty to his whole race' (1:142 [1:184]). The second Adam came in obedience, and

he received the Spirit from the Father as one of us (not receiving anything for himself individually, for he was the giver of the Spirit); but in order that he who knew no sin might preserve (διασῴζω) him to our nature by receiving him as man and might again plant in us the grace which had left us. (*In Jo.* 1.32–33, 1:142 [1:184])[26]

Then, mentioning 2 Cor 8.9 for the third time in this passage, Cyril explains how by the death of Christ life through the Spirit was restored, 'sanctify[ing] our whole nature' (*In Jo.* 1.32–33, 1:143 [1:185]). Thus, the defaced image of God is restored through the Spirit as new life and sanctification.[27]

Continuing in his discussion on the baptism of Christ, Cyril argues for the close relation of Christ and the Spirit since they are of one essence (*In Jo.* 1.32–33, 1:145–6 [1:88–89]). Cyril is concerned to show passages that closely relate the work of Christ and the Spirit, such as Eph 3.16–17; Rom 8.9–10, 15; and 1 John 4.13.[28] One primary type of evidence is that of unified presence – if Christ is in you, so is the Spirit. Ultimately, the result of salvation then is a restoration to immortality and enlightenment that existed in the prelapsarian condition through the unified work of Christ and the Spirit. While the work of Christ and the Spirit is distinguishable for Cyril, they cannot be separated, especially after Christ's resurrection.

---

[26] It is in this context that Cyril describes the Spirit as growing accustomed to humans again, similar to Irenaeus in *AH* 3.17.1. See Keating, 'Baptism of Jesus', 207n.18.

[27] This argument is also repeated in *In Jo.* 8.39 (1:548–50 [2:76–78]), where Cyril presents his narrative of salvation in the context of the second Adam.

[28] When I list biblical verses throughout the chapter, these are texts that Cyril himself has directly quoted or alluded to.

2.3.2 Salvation Accomplished and Realised

With Cyril's emphasis upon the pre-existence of the Logos, the incarnation itself seems to take centre stage in the soteriological drama, particularly in the christological debates. For instance, the restoration of the Spirit begins at Christ's baptism. Also, the Pauline exchange formulae, especially 2 Cor 8.9; Phil 2.5–11; and Gal 4.6, serve an important role in Cyril's explanation of Christ's work.[29] These formulae with their descent-ascent structure give a general picture of the work of Christ without clarifying the specific aspects and can make the incarnation itself seem salvific. In addition, Cyril makes explicit in certain texts that the incarnation partially restores life and light back to all humanity.[30] Thus, the question of the relative importance of the incarnation vis-à-vis the death and resurrection in Cyril's soteriology arises. More specifically, one may ask what role each plays in Cyril's soteriology.

In distinction to Paul and his contemporaries, who present the death and resurrection of the Messiah as the surprising aspect of Christology, we might say that for Cyril and his contemporaries the incarnation itself was the most surprising (and debated), and thus it captures most of their attention. However, for Cyril the exchange formulae do not symbolise the incarnation alone but the whole work of Christ. As a result, when Cyril speaks of Christ coming in the 'flesh for our sakes ... to fashion [us] after His own likeness' as the second Adam (1 Cor 15.49), he explains this through one of his favourite exchange formulae, 2 Cor 8.9: 'He Who was rich shared our poverty, that He might raise man's nature to His riches: He tasted death upon the tree and the cross, that He might take away from the midst the offence incurred by reason of the tree (of knowledge), and abolish the guilt that was thereby, and strip death of his tyranny over us' (*In Luc.* 10.23–24, 1:308). Thus, for Cyril the exchange formulae include each aspect of Christ's work – incarnation, death, and resurrection.

Thus, the death and resurrection form the climax of Christ's soteriological work, rather than just the incarnation as some statements might imply.[31] Two particular aspects of his soteriology emphasise the necessity of

---

[29] E.g., Phil 2.5–11: *Quod*, 54, 58, 85, 121–22; 2 Cor 5.21: *Quod*, 56, 69, 115; 2 Cor 8.9: *Quod*, 59; Rom 8.3–4: *Quod*, 89; Gal 4.4–5: *Quod*, 60, 67–8. Koen notes that 'none of the eastern fathers before Cyril quotes Phil 2.5–11' as often as he. Lars Koen, *The Saving Passion: Incarnational and Soteriological Thought in Cyril of Alexandria's Commentary on the Gospel according to John* (Uppsala: Graphic Systems, 1991), 95.

[30] Regarding life, all humanity will be raised in the last day, for blessing or judgment. This resurrection before the judgment seat is the resurrection life all will experience (*In Jo.* 10.15, 2:84–5 [2:233–34]). Cf. *In Jo.* 3.36, 1:199–200; 5.25, 1:270–71; 8.51, 1:667–668. Regarding light, Christ has granted rational ability or enlightenment to all humanity (*In Jo.* 1.9, 1:86–87 [1:111]).

[31] Cf. Koen, *Saving Passion*, 106.

Christ's death and resurrection: 1) the problem of sin and death and 2) the giving of the Spirit. First, the transfiguration episode shows that the incarnation is not efficacious in itself. Cyril tells us that the consummation of resurrection life expressed by Phil 3.21 cannot be fulfilled until Christ has accomplished his work of suffering: 'For He redeemed all under heaven, by both undergoing death in the flesh and by abolishing it by the resurrection from the dead' (*In Luc.* 9.27–36, 1:228–29). Second, Cyril's narrative of the Spirit requires that sin be removed so that the Spirit can return. Based on John 7.39 and 20.22, Cyril repeatedly notes that the Spirit is not poured out on believers until after the death and resurrection of Christ.[32] Cyril affirms that Christ, though he is consubstantial with the Spirit, received the Spirit humanly for humanity as the second Adam; however, believers cannot experience the life of the Spirit until Christ had destroyed death and restored life to humanity through his own resurrection as the firstfruits of life. Noting the importance of the second Adam, new creation, and victory over death, Wilken proposes that Christ's resurrection is the centre of Cyril's soteriology: 'The central fact which supports and illuminates all these various senses of new creation is the resurrection of Christ .... New creation appears most regularly in connection with the typology of the second Adam'.[33] As a result, simplistic interpretations of his incarnation theology improperly neglect the role of Christ's death and resurrection.[34]

If we consider the question of atonement theories in relation to Christ's work, none seems to control centre stage. In some passages Cyril offers a large number of short summaries of Christ's work, which fit under the *Christus Victor* model. For example, Cyril regularly describes Christ as 'abolishing death'[35] or 'destroy[ing] and overcom[ing] the corruption set up against man's nature by the devil'.[36] His comments on John 16.33 provide an important summary of how Christ must have conquered death as a man and how the resurrection was integral to overcoming death.[37] How-

---

[32] See Robert L. Wilken, *Judaism and the Early Christian Mind: A Study of Cyril of Alexandria's Exegesis and Theology* (New Haven: Yale University Press, 1971), 136–37.

[33] Ibid., 176.

[34] Münch-Labacher helpfully explores Cyril's thoughts on Christ's suffering death, especially in light of Cyril's interest in Phil 2: Gudrun Münch-Labacher, *Naturhaftes und geschichtliches Denken bei Cyrill von Alexandrien: Die verschiedenen Betrachtungsweisen der Heilsverwirklichung in seinem Johannes-Kommentar* (Hereditas 10; Bonn: Borengässer, 1996), 132–58.

[35] *In Jo.* 1.9, 1:93 [1:119].

[36] *In Jo.* 5.16, 1:243 [1:313].

[37] *In Jo.* 16.33, 2:475–77 [2:655–57]. Cf. also, *In Luc.* 22.35–38, 678 and 22.39–42, 684–85.

ever, he does not often develop the depth of these declarations.[38] In addition, Cyril also uses sacrificial language regularly. For instance, when commenting on John 1.29 and John's appellation of Christ as the Lamb of God, Cyril expounds upon the sacrifice of Jesus.[39] Along with this sacrificial metaphor, Cyril uses a wide variety of other sacrificial images.[40] However, Cyril does not develop these metaphors much further than the plain biblical language. Along with *Christus Victor* and sacrificial imagery, Cyril uses a variety of other metaphors so we should not too quickly try to force Cyril into one particular model but recognise and respect the diversity he presents.

Moving from the objective aspects of Christ's work to the subjective experience of believers, we can look more directly at what Cyril presents as the results of Christ's work. The climax of the salvific event for humanity may be seen in the death and resurrection of Christ as second Adam; however, from Cyril's narrative of salvation the salvific event for individuals is not complete until they experience the restored Spirit, which is the goal of Christ's work.[41] Christ's work as the second Adam restores the capacity of humanity for salvation while the restoration of the Spirit to humanity serves as its realisation.[42] With repeated emphasis on the curse of death from Gen 3.19, he most often emphasises conquering the problem of death and thus restoring life.[43] For individuals to appropriate this divine

---

[38] McInerney notes this aspect in Cyril's writing and posits that it may be his sense of mystery that precludes him from trying to dig more deeply. J.L. McInerney, 'Soteriological Commonplaces in Cyril of Alexandria's Commentary on the Gospel of John' in *Disciplina Nostra,* ed. D.F. Winslow (Philadelphia: Patristic Foundation, 1979), 179–185.

[39] *In Jo.* 1.29, 1:131–2 [1:169–71]. Cf. *In Luc.* 22.7–16, 659–60 and *Quod,* 127–28. Koen (*Saving Passion,* 105) writes: 'It would be totally anachronistic to make Cyril into a proponent of the Anselmian doctrine of penal substitution, but he believes that the sacrifice and the death on the cross is a necessary consequence of the Incarnation'. In distinction to the *vertical* level of participation in the Spirit, O. Blanchette ('Saint Cyril of Alexandria's Idea of the Redemption', *ScEccl* 16 [1964]: 455–480) argues that Cyril intends these sacrificial metaphors as *horizontally* based and that they only refer to solidarity (or representation) rather than to substitution. However, her bifurcation of juridical and mystical along the lines of horizontal and vertical is not supported by the evidence and does not help explain how the two are related.

[40] Cf. Koen's discussion of the variety: Koen, *Saving Passion,* 105–27.

[41] Cf. Daniel A. Keating, *The Appropriation of Divine Life in Cyril of Alexandria* (Oxford: Oxford University Press, 2004), 103.

[42] Janssens ('Notre Filiation', 275, cf. 275–78) distinguishes between the incarnation as 'la cause formelle' and the individual experience of the Spirit through faith as 'l'effet formel'.

[43] In *In Jo.* 1.30 (1:132 [1:171]) Cyril also presents several other related concepts such as restoring the nature of man as second Adam, delivering from corruption, granting

life, baptism and the Eucharist are integral because they allow the believer to participate somatically (σωματικῶς) and spiritually (πνευματικῶς) in the divine.[44] As Christ received the Spirit for humanity at his baptism, so also believers receive the Spirit at theirs.[45] In addition, Cyril presents a direct continuity between the life-giving body of the person of Christ and the life-giving body distributed through the Eucharist, which is the means to incorruption.[46]

To complete our summary of Cyril's soteriology, we should also note a point of contrast with Irenaeus. The distinction lies in the way they present the prelapsarian state of Adam and how the future soteriological state relates to it. Irenaeus presented Adam as infantile, though morally pure, and emphasised the need for growth as inherent in the human condition even before the fall. As a result, the soteriological state was not presented as a return to but rather a culmination of creation, effected by the second Adam, Christ (e.g., *AH* 4.38.1–4). In contrast, Cyril presents the prelapsarian Adam as participating fully in the Spirit and, therefore, in the divine attributes, and salvation as a 'return'.[47] Fairbairn contrasts these two soteriological models as two-act (Irenaeus) and three-act (Cyril).[48] However, most note that Cyril does present some discontinuity between the salvific and Edenic states.[49] Accordingly, there are clear differences between Irenaeus and Cyril regarding the height that Adam attained but not necessarily the capacity to attain that height. Thus, the two-act/three-act dichotomy might imply differences that are not material.

---

eternal life, bringing reconciliation to God, being the source of godliness and righteousness, and serving as the way to the Kingdom of Heaven.

[44] See Keating, *Appropriation*, 54–104. He draws out the important σωματικῶς/ πνευματικῶς dialectic with regard to the sacraments. See also Ezra Gebremedhin, *Life-Giving Blessing: An Inquiry into the Eucharistic Doctrine of Cyril of Alexandria* (Uppsala: Borgströms, 1977).

[45] Cf. *In Luc.* 3.21–22 and 4.1–2.

[46] Cf. *In Jo.* 6.51, 1:410 [1:520].

[47] E.g., *In Jo.* 17.18–19, 1:410 [2:719–20].

[48] Fairbairn, *Grace*, 17–21, 65–69.

[49] M-O Boulnois ('Le Souffle et l'Esprit', 35) lists three aspects of how the second is greater than the first: 1) the presence of the Spirit is more stable, 2) the Creator-created union is more intimate because it is based upon the incarnation, and 3) humans experience the Spirit of adoption. See also Fairbairn, *Grace*, 66–67; G.M. de Durand, *Cyrille d'Alexandrie: Deux Dialogues Christologiques* (SC 97; Paris: Cerf, 1964), 90–91; Janssens, 'Notre Filiation', 262–69; Burghardt, *Image of God*, 114–118. Langevin distinguishes between the possibility of not dying (Eden) and the impossibility of death (Christian resurrection): G. Langevin, 'La Thème de l'Incorruptibilité dans le Commentaire de Saint Cyrille d'Alexandrie sur l'Evangile Selon Saint Jean', *ScEccl* 8 (1956): 295–316, at 297, 304–5.

As Cyril presents his soteriology, he regularly returns to his narrative of salvation with its emphasis on Adam and the Spirit in creation and also the second Adam and the return of the Spirit in redemption. As we now turn to discuss deification, we will see that his view of deification is just the expression of his soteriology discussed above. Or rather, his soteriology is deification.

3. Deification

After Irenaeus, various theologians began to use more specific deification terminology. In particular, the most popular was that of θεοποιέω and θεοποίησις, though a variety of other terms such as θεόω or later θέωσις were also used by intervening patristic writers. Russell notes how Cyril only uses θεοποιέω and θεοποίησις positively in two of his earliest works – the *Thesaurus* and *Dialogues on the Trinity*[50] – while using them negatively against Nestorius in his later works.[51] In contrast, Cyril prefers to use biblical language, and two central biblical passages serve as the foundation for his explicit expression of believers' deification: Ps 82.6 (81.6 LXX)[52] and 2 Pet 1.4.[53] This 2 Peter passage, which is used so widely in modern discussions, was barely used to describe deification until Cyril.[54] In our investigation of how Cyril presents deification, we will focus first on specific passages where Cyril uses these two verses (§3.1). After that, I will summarise central themes that arise out of that exploration (§3.2). We will find that as an act of grace deification fundamentally consists of the restoration of the image of Christ through participation in the Spirit, who grants life and sanctification. As with Irenaeus, the Pauline theme of divine adoption is the most consistently used metaphor to describe this process.

---

[50] This terminology is used with regard to Christ's humanity (*Thes.* 28 and *Dial. Trin.* 5) and of the transformation of the believer (*Thes.* 4; 15; and 33 and *Dial. Trin.* 7). Cf. Russell, *Deification*, 192–93.

[51] Cf. *Quod*, 86.

[52] 'ἐγὼ εἶπα θεοί ἐστε καὶ υἱοὶ ὑψίστου πάντες'.

[53] 'δι' ὧν τὰ τίμια καὶ μέγιστα ἡμῖν ἐπαγγέλματα δεδώρηται, ἵνα διὰ τούτων γένησθε θείας κοινωνοὶ φύσεως ἀποφυγόντες τῆς ἐν τῷ κόσμῳ ἐν ἐπιθυμίᾳ φθορᾶς'.

[54] Norman Russell, ''Partakers of the Divine Nature' (2 Peter 1:4) in the Byzantine Tradition' in *ΚΑΘΗΓΗΤΡΙΑ: Essays Presented to Joan Hussey for her 80th birthday,* ed. J. Chysostomides (Athens: Porphyrogenitus, 1988), 51–67, at 52.

3.1 Scriptural References

3.1.1 Believers as Gods and Ps 82.6

As with other patristic writers, Cyril continues to employ Ps 82.6, although the appellation of θεοί to believers is not limited to direct references to Psalm 82 in Cyril's writings. Because he routinely refers to believers as gods in his commentary on John, we have several texts from which to choose.[55] He gives a lengthy treatment in his discussion of John 1.12–14, so we will focus on this extended passage. In this section of John's gospel, John contrasts the rejection and reception of Christ, and those who receive Christ are children of God. Drawing upon the themes of rejection and reception, Cyril contrasts the Jews who rejected Christ with the Gentiles who received him, and he then recounts the benefits of Christ's work:

> For in none other way could the one who bore the image of the earthly escape corruption, unless the beauty of the image of the heavenly were impressed upon us, through our being called to adoption. For being partakers of him through the Spirit, we were sealed unto likeness with him and ascend to the archetypal character of the image, after which the divine scriptures say we were made .... Therefore, we ascend to dignity above our nature because of Christ, and we too shall be sons of God, not like him exactly, but by grace in imitation of him. (*In Jo.* 1.12, 1:104 [1:133])

With references to 1 Cor 15.49, Cyril develops the importance of Christ as the second Adam in redemption and links adoption through the Spirit with bearing the likeness of Christ. Then, based on Ps 82.6, he notes that believers are adopted and are gods by grace:[56]

> For since the Word by nature consists of something different from that which is by adoption, and that which is in truth from that which is by imitation, and we are called sons of God by adoption and imitation; he is therefore Son by nature and in truth, to whom we, who are made sons, are compared, gaining the good by grace instead of by natural endowments. (*In Jo.* 1.12, 1:105 [1:134])

Cyril again intertwines the concepts of image and imitation. Keating notes that imitation is one of the terms used in discourse about participation as a way to describe how the lesser reproduces the greater.[57] For Cyril, this imitation is characterised by reproducing divine attributes, which in the context he directly signifies as incorruption and love, which are somatic and moral in nature.

Continuing his discussion of being sons of god through adoption in terms of being begotten (John 1.13), Cyril again describes believers as

---

[55] E.g., *In Jo.* 1.3; 1.6–7; 1.9; 1.12–14; 3.33; 5.18; 6.27; 10.33–34; 15.9–10; 17.3; 17.4–5; 17.20; 17.26; 20.17.

[56] See also these passages using Psalm 82 that also highlight specifically the nature-grace distinction: *In Jo.* 1.3, 1:51; 1.9, 1:86; 10.34, 2:104; 17.26, 2:565.

[57] Keating, *Appropriation*, 146–47.

gods. As Cyril defends the uncreated deity of the Spirit, he notes the Spirit's ability to effect deification:

The Spirit [is] God and of God by nature. We too, being accounted worthy to partake of him through faith in Christ, are rendered partakers of the divine nature [2 Pet 1.4] and are said to be begotten from God. For this reason, we are called gods, not by grace alone winging our flight to the glory above us but also by having God already indwelling and lodging in us, according to what is said in the prophet, 'I will dwell in them and walk in them' [2 Cor 6.16/Lev 26.11–12]. (*In Jo.* 1.13, 1:107 [1:136–37])

Cyril repeats the deification-sonship connection, but he also emphasises the divine presence mediated through the Spirit and introduces the connection between gods language and participation language from 2 Pet 1.4. Cyril then uses Paul's association in 2 Cor 6.16 , and later 1 Cor 3.16, between the presence of God and human temples to describe the divine presence through the Spirit. Thus, the presence of the Spirit is central to Cyril's argument here, even in the midst of a discussion of Christ's incarnation.

Maintaining his focus upon the divine-human relationship, Cyril then discusses the nature of the incarnation (John 1.14) and its 'deep Mystery'. Importantly, as he discusses God becoming human, he explains how humans become gods:

For we were all in Christ, and the community of human nature ascends to his person; since on account of this he was named the last Adam, giving richly to the common nature all things that belong to joy and glory, even as the first Adam gave what pertained to corruption and dejection. The Word then dwelled in all through one in order that when the one is 'declared the Son of God in power according to the Spirit of holiness' [Rom 1.4], the dignity might come unto all the human nature. And thus the saying 'I have said you are gods and all of you are children of the Most High' [Ps 82.6] might come to us also because of one of us. Therefore in Christ the slave is truly made free, ascending to mystic union with him who bore the form of the slave, and it is in us according to imitation of the one because of the kinship according to the flesh. (*In Jo.* 1.14, 1:110 [1:141])

The work of the incarnate Christ thus forms the basis for the deification of believers, bestowing dignity to human nature as the last Adam.[58] This follows the line of thought given above when Cyril spoke of the earthly and heavenly image (*In Jo.* 1.12), and both concepts flow from 1 Corinthians 15. With the language of 'form of a slave' we see one of Cyril's many employments of Philippians 2, in which not only Christ's descent but also

---

[58] Robert L. Wilken ('Exegesis and the History of Theology: Reflections on the Adam-Christ Typology in Cyril of Alexandria', *CH* 25 [1966]: 139–56, at 150) writes: 'By the use of the Adam Christ typology Cyril found an image which could give expression to this conviction [that Christ is truly God and truly man]. For by calling Christ the second Adam he said that he is both man and God'.

his ascent is a model for believers.[59] By use of the exchange formula, Cyril argues that believers become gods because God in Christ became human. In this same passage Cyril then quotes 2 Cor 8.9 speaking of how we come to likeness of him and how we are 'made gods and children of God through faith' (*In Jo.* 1.14, 1:111 [1:141]). However, he does not end the discussion with Christ alone, but returns to the theme that the Son dwells in believers by the Spirit (Rom 8.15), using both adoption and temple language.

The Johannine text is based upon humans being children of God, and Cyril finds the language of Ps 82.6 useful for explaining this passage. In this passage key themes that arise in his exposition are image restoration, the distinction between nature and grace, participation, adoption, the presence of the Spirit, and Christ as second Adam. Through Christ's work as second Adam, the Spirit resides in believers by grace. In turn, they are gods and sons of God, imitating Christ through participation. Like Irenaeus, Cyril employs Pauline themes of adoption and exchange to develop this. One primary development over Irenaeus is the greater emphasis on the Spirit in this adoption context. At the same time, his inclusion of love with incorruption as the effects of this participation shows that Cyril sees the gods language as addressing the relational as well as the somatic aspects of adoption.

3.1.2 Participation in the Divine Nature and 2 Pet 1.4

In the discussions of becoming gods above, the idea of participation arose as a central theme. With these concepts playing an important role in Cyril's soteriology, the importance of 2 Pet 1.4 is not surprising. In fact, Russell notes that 'the text is quoted more frequently by him than by any other Greek ecclesiastical writer'.[60] With over 30 clear references to the verse in his commentaries on John and Luke, we will examine a representative sample for our study: *In Luc.* 3.21–23 and *In Jo.* 17.18–23.[61] In

---

[59] In Cyril's treatment of John 20.17, Cyril explicitly associates Philippians 2 and the appellation of gods to believers (*In Jo.* 20.17, 2:663 [3:122]). He underscores how Christ shares human mortality, and by implication of the resurrection human ascension is to his life. Cyril also draws out this connection between Philippians 2 and believers' exaltation to the status of gods more fully in his commentary on John 15.9–10 in the context of loving obedience. Cf. *In Jo.* 17.4–5 (2:496–97 [2:671–78]) where Cyril, again using Phil 2.5–11, speaks of the glory of Christ exalting humanity.

[60] Russell, 'Partakers', 57.

[61] While not capturing all the allusions and echoes of 2 Pet 1.4 this is a list of primary references to this verse in his commentaries: *In Jo.* 1.9; 1.13; 3.5; 6.35; 6.37; 7.24; 7.29; 10.14–15; 14.4; 14.6; 14.16–17; 14.20*; 14.23; 14.24; 15.1; 16.7; 16.12–13; 16.15; 17.18–19*; 17.20–21*; 17.22–23*; 20.22–23 and *In Luc.* 2.25–35; 3.16; 3.21–2; 4.1–2;

many cases, Cyril uses the phrase 'partakers of the divine nature' as short-hand for a group of concepts which form his theology of deification.

3.1.2.1 *In Luc.* 3.21–23

In this passage Cyril expounds the baptism of Jesus and describes how Jesus passed that grace onto all believers when he became a partaker of the Holy Spirit.[62] Using Phil 2.5–11 as his basis Cyril argues that since the Son is God, he did not need to be baptised or sanctified nor did he need to receive the Spirit since they share the same essence.[63] If Christ did not need this baptism, what role does it play? Cyril tells us that Christ shared our likeness and became 'the pattern and way of every good work' (*In Luc.* 3.21–23, 1:47). Thus, when a person confesses faith, they 'wash away all the filth of sin, and are enriched by the communication of the Holy Spirit, and made partakers of the divine nature, and gain the grace of adoption' (*In Luc.* 3.21–23, 1:47). In this passage, then, Cyril alludes to several aspects of salvation: life, cleansing from sins, and enablement to good works. The central point is that communication of the Spirit, participation in the divine nature and adoption are all used synonymously.

After exhorting his congregation to follow Christ's example in baptism, Cyril concludes by recounting the humiliation that Christ underwent in order that he might become the firstfruits, firstborn, and second Adam, who makes all things new as in 2 Cor 5.17 (*In Luc.* 3.21–23, 1:48).[64] Cyril alludes to the resurrection of Christ with Pauline language of firstfruits and the second Adam (1 Cor 15.20–23) and firstborn (Rom 8.29; Col 1.15, 18). Thus, Cyril probably has somatic resurrection in mind for believers, but he implies that Christ's resurrection has larger implications beyond the somatic.[65] Cyril does not explore the Adamic history or the narrative of the Spirit as in his discussions of Christ's baptism in the *Commentary on John*, but he does emphasise Christ's role as second Adam along with the Spirit

---

4.18; 5.24; 7.24–28; 22.7–16*. Those starred have multiple references or develop the topic beyond a mere statement.

[62] *In Luc.* 3.21–23, 1:43–48. See above §2.3.1 for a discussion of Cyril's treatment of Jesus' baptism in the *Commentary on John*. Cf. Keating, 'Baptism of Jesus', 208–11.

[63] Cf. Ibid. 210.

[64] Wilken, in particular, notes the numerous uses of 2 Cor 5.17 in Cyril and how Cyril associates it with the resurrection of Christ and the new covenant. Wilken, *Judaism*, 170–80, esp. 176. This confluence of new creation, second Adam, incorruption, the presence of the Spirit and participation in the divine nature also occurs *In Jo.* 7.39 (1:546–52 [1:690–8]), where the Spirit's indwelling forms the basis of renewed life, which is described as participating in the divine nature.

[65] Unlike Irenaeus who focused heavily upon incorruption, we see that Cyril speaks more generically about new life and new creation.

in raising believers to the heavenly realm. Thus, the fulfilment of the new creation work of Christ is the communication of the Spirit.

3.1.2.2 *In Jo.* 17.18–23

The most sustained discussion involving participation in the divine nature in his *Commentary on John* is that of *In Jo.* 17.18–23 (1:533–56 [2:717–3:4]), which includes at least seven direct references to 2 Pet 1.4. The biblical setting out of which this theme derives is Jesus' prayer just before he is arrested and crucified. In this section of the prayer Jesus mentions sanctification, sending, and divine indwelling. Based around this context Cyril presents a complex theology related to participation in the divine nature.

For Cyril sanctification and empowerment for mission are thoroughly situated in the context of divine indwelling, which is mediated by the Spirit in a Trinitarian fashion – through the Son and from the Father. Thus, from the consubstantial nature of the three, he argues for the unity in their interaction with humanity even when only one is the focus, as the Spirit is in this passage. Cyril draws upon his Spirit-centred narrative of salvation, and thus he mentions the giving of the Spirit (Gen 2.7) and his role in forming the divine image and likeness in humanity through sanctification and life as evidenced in Rom 8.29. The presence of the Spirit then is the presence of the Father and Son as well, and thus fulfils Christ's work of reconciliation (2 Cor 5.19) and peace (Eph 2.14), making us 'sharers (μέτοχοι) and partakers (κοινωνοί) in the divine nature' (*In Jo.* 17.18–19, 2:537 [2:722]). Cyril then highlights other aspects related to the Spirit's presence, such that believers are shown to be sons of God (Gal 4.6) and sanctified temples of God, as they partake of the Spirit and experience new life.

Through Rom 4.25 and Phil 2.6–7, Cyril then redirects the discussion back upon the work of Christ as the life-giving second Adam. To bring new life he destroyed the power of death by dying and bearing the sins of the world (Is 53.4, 12; Col 2.14). Thus, he is able to grant sanctification through participation in the Spirit. Christ's flesh was both sanctified and sanctifying: 'He is sanctified on our account in the Holy Spirit; no one else sanctifies him, but rather he works for himself for sanctification of his own flesh. For he takes upon himself his own Spirit, and receives in so far as he was man and gives this filling to himself as God' (*In Jo.* 17.18–19, 2:540 [2:724]). Though Adam was cursed to die (Gen 3.19), Christ returns life and incorruption to humanity through the Spirit, and restores believers to Adam's prelapsarian state.[66] We see here Cyril's twin pillars of salvation: incorruption and sanctification.

---

[66] Cf. Fairbairn, *Grace*, 65.

Turning to discuss John 17.20–21, Cyril continues to focus upon the work of Christ, particularly in his bringing peace. He begins by focusing upon Christ's work of restoration as the second Adam (1 Cor 15.47). Just as humanity bears the image of the earthly man, believers will experience the image of the heavenly man (1 Cor 15.49) since Christ has come from above and bestows the Spirit. Regarding the process of restoration to original glory, Cyril writes: 'And the Son is the exact image of the Father, and his Spirit is the natural likeness of the Son. For this reason, moulding anew, as it were, into himself the souls of men, he stamps them with the divine form and seals them with the image of the Most High' (*In Jo.* 17.20–21, 2:546 [2:731]). Thus, the formation of the believer is uniquely Trinitarian in character. With discussion of the soul, we see that the transformation described is moral and noetic in nature, in accord with the sanctification theme of the Johannine passage.

Concerning the unity Jesus prays for in the Johannine text, Cyril explores the unity of the Trinity, unity in the church, and divine-human unity and shows the correlation between them all. Regarding this divine-human unity, Christ in his incarnation has forged the way. Since he shares the divine nature as God and shares human nature as man, he enables humans to partake of the divine nature as they 'partake of the Holy Spirit and union with God' (*In Jo.* 17.20–21, 2:549 [2:735]). Believers are not only united to Christ through the Spirit but also through his Body, the Eucharist, as they partake of the one bread (1 Cor 10.17) and are joined in one body (Eph 4.14–16; 3.5–6). Cyril, using Eph 4.2–6, turns again to emphasise the Spirit's role in uniting believers. By taking on 'the transcendent formation (μόρφωσις) of the Holy Spirit', 'we are well-nigh transformed (μεθίστημι) into another nature, so to say, and we become no longer mere men, but also being called sons of God and heavenly men, because we have been proved partakers of the divine nature' (*In Jo.* 17.20–21, 2:551–2 [2:737]). This union is one of 'mental condition ..., and also in conformity to godliness, and in the fellowship of the holy body of Christ, and in the fellowship of the Holy Spirit' (*In Jo.* 17.20–21, 2:552 [2:737]). Thus, the presence of Christ and the Spirit brings moral transformation within the formation of the community.

As he moves on to John 17.22–23, Cyril repeats themes that have arisen before. He focuses mainly upon the incarnation as uniting humanity and God by highlighting the unity in Christ himself, and he draws out the difference between believers' 'somatic' (σωματικῶς) union with God and the 'spiritual' (πνευματικῶς) union. These generally represent the Eucharist and the Spirit, respectively, and result in our participation in the divine nature,[67] on account of which believers overcome corruption through somatic and spiritual union with God. Thus, God showers his love upon believers through Christ, which results in their resurrection and glory.

Through this extended discussion of John 17.18–23, several topics are regularly repeated. Cyril returns several times to the giving of the Spirit to Adam in Gen 2.7 and the subsequent loss of the Spirit through Adam's sin in Gen 3.19. Through union of the divine and human in Christ, he restores the Spirit to humanity. The Spirit communicates the presence of Christ and the Father and allows believers to partake in the divine nature and experience divine life, making them into sons of God. As the Spirit of Christ, one important aspect of the Spirit's work is to form believers into the image of Christ, the heavenly man, in his incorruption and sanctification. In addition to this spiritual indwelling, the Eucharist also bodily communicates Christ to those who partake of it. The concept of participation plays a central role in his exposition. He repeatedly speaks of participation in the Spirit and in the divine nature but also participation in the Eucharist as the body of Christ. Thus, Cyril presents a thoroughly Trinitarian presentation of the divine-human interaction, with a strong emphasis upon the work of Christ and the Spirit in deification.

With regard to participation in the divine nature and 2 Pet 1.4, Cyril uses this to describe both participation in the Trinity and participation in the attributes of the Trinity. He repeatedly writes that participation in the divine nature is a participation in the Spirit,[68] who allows participation in Christ and God.[69] Based on the consubstantial union of the three members of the Trinity, the presence of the Spirit mediates the presence of the other two members.[70] In addition, Cyril also speaks of participating in the attributes of the Trinity, in particular, incorruption, sanctification, and sonship.[71] This intimate relationship provided by the Spirit is transforming, in that the new creation work of the second Adam is fulfilled through grace. To sum up Cyril uses participation in the divine nature and the appellation of gods and sons of God to summarise the effect of this life-creating grace.

---

[67] Keating argues convincingly that the distinction between these two aspects, while important, has been overstated: Keating, *Appropriation*, 74–104.

[68] *In Jo.* 1.9; 3.4; 14.16; 16.7; 16.12–13; 17.18–19; 20.22–23; and *In Luc.* 3.16; 3.21–23; 4.1–2; 4.18; 5.24; 7.24; 20.7–16.

[69] In Christ: *In Jo.* 14.20; 14.24; *In Luc.* 22.7–16. In God: *In Jo.* 14.23; *In Luc.* 4.18.

[70] *In Jo.* 14.20; 14.23; 15.1; 17.18–19.

[71] Incorruption: *In Jo.* 6.35; 14.20. Sanctification: *In Jo.* 7.44; 14.4; 14.16; 14.24; 17.18–19; 17.20–23; *In Luc.* 4.1–2. Sonship: *In Jo.* 1.13; 3.4; 15.1; *In Luc.* 3.21–22; 4.1–2; 7.24–28.

3.2 Central Themes

Based on the passages employing Ps 82.6 and 2 Pet 1.4, several central themes are evident. Deification is based on a distinction between nature and grace (§3.2.1), is effected by participation in the divine (§3.2.1), results in a restoration of divine likeness (§3.2.3), and is most often characterised as adoption (§3.2.4).

3.2.1 Basis: Nature versus Grace

With Cyril's interest in refuting what he considers christological heresies, he regularly discusses issues related to nature – human and divine – with a clear distinction between each, and this metaphysical divide serves as the basis of all soteriological language.[72] Thus, when believers are called gods, Cyril often qualifies this appellation by stating that it is 'by grace' and not 'by nature'. For instance, he writes:

One will surely say that he is very God, the one in whom the dignity of lordship is inherent by nature, and it accrues not to any other rightly and truly, since 'to us there is one God and Father, and one Lord Jesus Christ' [1 Cor 8.6], as Paul said. Though there be many called gods by grace and lords in both heaven and earth, yet the Son is truly one with God the Father. (*In Jo.* 1.6–7, 1:70 [1:90])

Those things that can be identified with divine nature – being uncreated and the source of all things – cannot be identified with believers who become gods by grace.[73] Cyril maintains that divine qualities are only shared with humans through grace as participation. He thus makes clear the importance of human deification while affirming the unique deity of Christ.

3.2.2 Means: Participation in the Divine

With this nature-grace distinction that serves as the basis of the divine-human relationship, Cyril describes participation as the means for humans to experience salvation. Since both Christ and the Spirit consubstantially share in the divinity of the Father, as believers participate in them, they partake of the divine nature. Through participation God graciously allows believers to share in himself and to become like him. Thus, God is both the giver and the gift. Cyril uses a variety of terms when describing this process (e.g., κοινωνία, κοινωνός, μετοχή, μέτοχος, μετασχεῖν, μετάλημψις, μεταλαμβάνω, and μίμησις), and his emphasis on restored image and likeness (e.g., εἰκών and ὁμοιότης) fit within this larger category as

---

[72] Indeed, Cyril describes the 'interval between the Maker and the thing made [as] infinite' (*In Luc.* 10.22, 1:304).

[73] In another instance, Cyril explains that the imitation of Christ in 1 Cor 11.1 speaks of us imitating not his actions as Creator, but his virtue (*In Jo.* 1.10, 1:99–100 [1:127–28]).

well. From the passages discussed above, we saw that Cyril describes participation as being both in the Trinity and in Trinitarian attributes. A significant part of Cyril's soteriological narrative is the restored presence of the Spirit in believers as the basis for their participation in life.[74] For Cyril the presence of the risen Christ is mediated primarily through the Spirit of Christ (*In Jo.* 3.36, 1:198 [1:258]) but also through the Eucharist, though the former is predominant.[75]

In his commentary on John 1.3–10, Cyril regularly makes use of participation language while arguing for the consubstantial divinity of the Son. The Son is light and life by nature. He does not participate in them.[76] However, humans participate in these by grace. Keating summarises the basic principles that inform Cyril's discussion:

(1) That which participates is necessarily distinct (and distinct in kind) from that which is participated in; (2) that which participates possesses the quality it receives only in part and from without; that which is participated in necessarily possesses that quality fully and by nature; (3) that which participates can lose what is [*sic*] has by participation; that which has a quality by nature cannot lose it.[77]

Thus believers share the same divine appellations (e.g., θεοί and light[78]), which reflects the transformation resulting from sharing in divine attributes.

Cyril often uses imagery to help communicate his points, and his images regarding participation are helpful for understanding his theology. One image that he uses more than once is that of a boiling pot of water.[79] The water remains water by nature, but it takes on the qualities of heat from the fire (*In Jo.* 6.53, 1:419 [1:531]). In the same way, the Spirit transforms believers, sanctifying them and bringing them to incorruption. However, participation entails active agency of both God and humans: God shares (e.g., enlightening believers) and believers imitate.

The sacraments serve as important media for the divine presence. Through baptism, the Holy Spirit is granted to believers (*In Jo.* 20.22–23, 2:674 [3.134]) and sanctifies both body and soul (*In Jo.* 3.5, 1:168–69 [1:218–219]). Thus, this sacrament plays a fundamental role in Cyril's narrative of salvation and is the necessary requirement for taking the

---

[74] See §2.3.

[75] Most of Cyril's commentary on John 6 centres around the Eucharist (*In Jo.* 6.1–71, 1:312–457; see especially 6.35, 1:374).

[76] In the same way, the Spirit is God by nature and does not participate in divinity. Cf. *In Jo.* 16.15 (2:459).

[77] Keating, *Appropriation*, 162.

[78] See *In Jo.* 1.8 (1:74 [1:95]) where believers are called light.

[79] Also, compare his imagery of an iron in a fire, which conveys a similar idea (*Quod*, 130 and *In Luc.* 22.17–22, 664–65).

Eucharist.[80] Partaking of Christ through the Eucharist reinforces believers' participation in the divine nature and leads them to life and incorruption.[81] As discussed before, the sacraments allow the dual participation in the divine – somatically (σωματικῶς) and spiritually (πνευματικῶς).[82]

3.2.3 Result: Likeness to God

Understanding the *basis* of deification as by grace rather than nature and the *means* of deification as through participation in the divine presence, we now turn to the *result* of deification, which is likeness to God. We have previously touched briefly on issues of likeness as being lost in the fall (§2.2.3) and subsequently being restored through the work of Christ and the Spirit (§2.3). The concept of image fits hand in glove with participation because it maintains a *distinction* between nature and grace but also allows *similarity* with regard to attributes.

Central to Cyril's conception of image is the Adam/second Adam comparison, as evidenced by the almost ubiquitous references to 1 Cor 15.49 with the distinction between the image of the earthly man and the image of the heavenly man. According to Cyril's narrative of the Spirit, Adam received the Spirit and was formed in the image of God, but the image was lost after he sinned. Cyril notes specifically that humanity can lose or fall from the divine likeness, whereas the Son cannot because his is from nature (*In Jo.* 6.27, 1:352 [1:445–46]).[83] With regard to the effects of sin on the image of God, Burghardt writes: 'Those aspects of the image which are part and parcel of man's essential structure – basic rationality and psychological freedom – were not lost. Those facets of the image which owe their existence to the indwelling of the Spirit – holiness, incorruptibility, kinship with God – were lost'.[84] However, we noted the 'essential' feature of noetic enablement was dimmed through sin.[85]

If the image is dimmed, what constitutes its restoration? Christ is regularly characterised as the image, express image, and likeness of the Fa-

---

[80] Cf. *In Jo.* 20.17, 2:657–60 [3:120–24].

[81] Cf. *In Jo.* 6.35–37, 1:377–79 [1:476–78].

[82] Cf. *In Luc.* 22.7–16 (2:661–62) and 22.17–22 (2:664–65).

[83] The Son is the likeness of the Father in a way different from creatures. Creatures, by definition, are not uncreated and do not take on immutability (and other characteristics) by nature but only by reflecting the attribute as an image. These characteristics exist essentially (οὐσιωδῶς) in the Trinity but only by spiritual relationship (οἰκειότητος πνεθματικῆς) in the creature (*In Jo.* 6.27, 1:355 [1:449]).

[84] Burghardt, *Image of God*, 153.

[85] See §2.2.3

ther.[86] As the second Adam, Christ removes the sin barrier and receives the Spirit back to humanity, bringing new creation.[87] Thus, the Spirit is able to re-form the image of God, the image of Christ, in humanity.[88] In Cyril's larger discussion, the two central attributes in the context of image restoration are life and sanctification.[89]

3.2.3.1 Restored Life

One of the most repeated themes in Cyril is that Christ has gained victory over death and corruption, overcoming the mortality resulting from sin. As we saw in the extended passage quoted in §2.2, the main result of the work of Christ is restoration of immortality through a participation in the immortality of the Word (*In Jo.* 1.14, 1:108–9 [1:138–39]). In addition, Cyril routinely notes how the Son is life and that believers participate in his life (*In Jo.* 1.1–9), which is also reflected in Cyril's Eucharistic theology. At the same time, when believers participate in Spirit they experience incorruption (*In Jo.* 1.12, 1:105 [1:134]). Cyril presents the culmination of life as resurrection to eternal bliss as opposed to being raised to judgment.[90] Only those partaking of Christ and the Spirit experience the eternal blessing of true life.

3.2.3.2 Restored Sanctification

Along with life and incorruption, sanctification (or holiness) is central to Cyril's conception of the restored image of God in humanity.[91] Cyril himself states this plainly when he writes, 'Virtue restores us to the form of

---

[86] For example, Cyril writes: 'The Father then being considered as the source, the Word was in him, being his Wisdom and Power and express image and radiance and likeness' (*In Jo.* 1.1, 1:13 [1:18]). Cf. *In Luc.* 6.12 (1:95).

[87] Boulnois, 'Le Souffle et l'Esprit', 3–30.

[88] Cf. *In Jo.* 1.8; 5.2; 11.8; 11.10. A.M. Bermejo, *The Indwelling of the Holy Spirit according to Cyril of Alexandria* (Ona: Facultad de Teologia, 1963), 63–75; Keating, *Appropriation*, 136–37. Cyril does not make a distinction between image and likeness like Irenaeus in some passages. Cf. *Epistula ad Calosyrium* 5 (PG 76:1085b–1088c). Gross, *Divinization*, 221.

[89] This corresponds to our prior discussion of life and light; cf. Bermejo, *Holy Spirit*, 13–14. Janssens ('Notre Filiation', 252) also rightly associates the role of the sacraments and particularly the Eucharist with life and sanctification: 'Le corps du Christ est devenu vivifiant et sanctifiant en vertu de son union hypostatique avec le Verbe'.

[90] E.g., *In Jo.* 14.21, 324–25 [2:491–92].

[91] Cf. Burghardt, *Image of God*, 65–83. He writes: 'In a word, God is holy, and man images God if he is himself holy. In fact, this is divine resemblance at its loftiest level. Time and again Cyril identifies the image of God with the holiness of man' (*Image of God*, 65).

God, and imprints on our souls certain characters as it were of the supreme nature' (*In Luc.* 6.36, 1:113).[92]

In his *Commentary on John*, Cyril notes five different ways of being an image (*In Jo.* 5.23, 1:265–6 [1:139–40]).[93] According to Cyril, the five ways of being an image are: 1) a 'sameness of nature in properties exactly alike, as Abel of Adam;' 2) an artistic reproduction; 3) likeness of will as 'habits and manners, and conversation and inclination;' 4) a sharing in 'dignity and honour and glory and excellence' of another; or 5) something that reproduces 'any ... quality or quantity of a thing, and its outline and proportion' (*In Jo.* 5.23, 1:265–6 [1:339–40]). Of these five, he explicitly notes that humans and angels are only capable of a likeness of will as 'habits and manners, and conversation and inclination' (*In Jo.* 5.23, 1:265–6 [1:139]). As moral agents, humans are thus enabled to imitate the divine. This is not mere moral enablement, a gift. Rather, Cyril describes this as a benefit of participation in the divine presence, an experience of the Giver.

In particular, the *Holy* Spirit shares his power of *holiness* with believers as he shapes their will and desires.[94] Cyril uses a variety of Pauline metaphors such as new creation (2 Cor 5.17)[95] and circumcision of the Spirit (Rom 2.28–29) to expound this. In one passage he associates the latter with participating in the divine nature and in Christ through the Spirit (*In Jo.* 7.24, 1:507 [1:639]). Circumcision of the Spirit is a purification, a cutting away of lusts so one is 'persuaded only to love and do the will of God' (*In Jo.* 7.24, 1:501 [1:632]). As a refusal of the world's pleasures, circumcision of the Spirit signifies dying with Christ as noted in Col 3.3–4 and the resulting participation in his resurrection. Cyril notes how circumcision of the Spirit brings perfection in holiness and virtue and brings freedom from the devil and sin (*In Jo.* 7.24, 1:502, 508 [1:632, 641]). He thus associates the ethical formation of believers with participation in the Spirit, which results primarily in a mortification of passions and an ability to walk in holiness.[96]

---

[92] Cf. *In Luc.* 16.10–13, 514–15.

[93] Regarding the distinction between (1) and (3), Keating (*Appropriation*, 181–82) calls (1) 'ontological' in contrast to (3) as 'dynamic'.

[94] Cf. Bermejo, *Holy Spirit*, 48–63.

[95] Concerning new creation as described by 2 Cor 5.17, Cyril argues that based on the presence of Christ through the Spirit all things are made new 'in him and by him, both covenant and law, and mode of life,' with the result that believers can even love their enemies (*In Luc.* 6.27, 1:110).

[96] For more on mortification of passions see *In Luc.* 5.30 (1:88); 6.37 (1:113); and 6.46–49 (1:124–26).

3.2.4 Adoption as Children of God

We have noted that the anthropological result of salvation is a restoration of the divine image and likeness through the Spirit, which consists primarily of new life and sanctification. Following Irenaeus and other theologians, Cyril continues to associate this experience with adoption. In fact, no other metaphor or concept is as consistently associated with deification in Cyril as that of adoption.[97] Cyril almost always speaks of gods as sons of God in relation to Christ as the Son.[98] At the same time, his controlling emphasis on the Spirit's presence when speaking of participating in the divine presence readily drew him to the Pauline adoption passages that incorporate the Spirit and adoption: Rom 8.15 and Gal 4.6.

The metaphor of adoption is particularly suited to encapsulate the basis-means-result aspects of deification in Cyril. It captures the *basis* of deification, as the distinction between *nature and grace*: believers are not children by nature but are adopted by grace. In *In Jo.* 1.18 Cyril argues that the Word has a nature separate from those who are by adoption sons and gods (1:123 [1:156]). As a relational model, adoption also points towards a restored *participation* in the divine, as the *means* of deification. This is not surprising considering the repeated emphasis Cyril places on Pauline language of adoption related to the presence of Christ and the Spirit from Rom 8.15 and Gal 4.6.[99] For instance, Cyril writes: As 'sons by adoption, we are conformed to the Son, through whom we are called by grace to the dignity of adoption' (*In Jo.* 1.34, 1:147 [1:190]). Later, he writes more explicitly that 'we are adopted, ascending to the dignity above nature through the will of him that honoured us and gaining the title of gods and sons because of Christ who dwells in us through the Holy Spirit' (*In Jo.* 5.18, 1:245 [1:316]). Thus, Cyril directly associates the presence of Christ and the Spirit within us with adoption. Finally, adoption allows Cyril to discuss issues of *likeness*, as the *result* of deification.[100] In *Quod* Cyril

---

[97] de Durand (*Cyrille*, 93) writes: 'Quand Cyrille se risque à dire que nous sommes devenus dieux, ... c'est qu'il vient de mentionner que nous sommes fils'.

[98] Janssens ('Notre Filiation', 273) cautions that we should not look to human adoption as the source for our understanding of adoption but rather the sonship of Christ as the model. Marie-Odile Boulnois (*Le Paradoxe trinitaire chez Cyrille d'Alexandrie* [Paris: Institut d'Études Augustiniennes, 1994], 380) also writes 'La filiation du Monogène n'est pas seulement le modèle de toute filiation humaine, mais elle est la causalité formelle de l'adoption divine de l'homme par le Père'.

[99] See especially *Quod* (80) where Cyril associates divine presence (Eph 3.14–17) with Rom 8.15.

[100] Boulnois (*Le Paradoxe*, 380–83) discusses the distinction between creation in the image and adoption. She writes: 'Cyrille exprime ici un point important de sa doctrine de la filiation adoptive : l'homme n'est pas fils depuis le jour où il a été créé à l'image de

makes the distinct connection between the Son and the sonship of believers. He writes that 'whatever is by adoption or grace must always be in the likeness of that which is by nature and truth .... It is in relation to [the Son] that we too have been fashioned as sons by adoption and grace' (*Quod*, 81–82 [384]). In particular, Bermejo writes, 'The Spirit stamps on our soul the Son's image rendering thereby men sons of God [John 1.8; 1.9; 2.5]; we are chiselled into God's sons by the Indwelling Spirit'.[101] Also, believers are like the *Father* as they follow his will and live piously (*In Jo.* 8.37, 1:633 [2:72]).[102] Thus, this metaphor functions as a convenient expression for Cyril to encapsulate his views on deification.

4. Conclusion

4.1 Deification in Cyril

For Cyril, deification then is participation in the divine attributes such that believers become like God in life and virtue. This participation is based upon the distinction between humans becoming gods by grace and God who is divine by nature. In order to achieve deification, the presence of the Christ and the Spirit provides the means of participating in the divine both somatically and spiritually. In particular, the restoration of the Spirit to humans grants the grace of sharing in divine attributes, of which incorruption and sanctification are primary. In addition to new creation and second Adam themes, the metaphor that Cyril most often uses to describe this process is that of adoption.

This portrayal of deification cannot be separated from Cyril's larger soteriological framework because the two are identical. The narrative of the Spirit, who is given to Adam and is restored through the second Adam, is the narrative of deification. This fits directly with his discussion of believers as gods and in their participation in the divine nature. Thus, for Cyril the experience of salvation is deification.

4.2 Cyril and Paul

Although Cyril incorporates 2 Pet 1.4 into his language of deification, he employs many of the same Pauline themes and passages as Irenaeus to de-

---

Dieu, mais il devait un jour y être appelé' (*Le Paradoxe*, 382). Thus, she distinguishes between creation and re-creation and associates adoption primarily with the latter.

[101] Bermejo, *Holy Spirit*, 83. Cf. Janssens, 'Notre Filiation', 249–50.

[102] For instance, he writes: 'by thinking his thoughts and resolving to live piously because it is fitting and not secondary, we are called sons of God who is over all. Forming our own mind after his will so far as we can, we are his likeness (ὁμοιότης) and truly his family with reference to exact representation (ἐμφέρεια)' (In Jo. 8.37, 1:633 [2:72]).

scribe deification. With his explicit narrative of the Spirit leading from Adam to Christ, Cyril finds 1 Corinthians 15 with its Adam-Christ dialectic and the hope of immortality central. In particular, Christ is the heavenly man who draws believers into a deified state as they bear his Sprit-formed image, and Cyril thus utilises 1 Cor 15.49 ubiquitously. A difference from Irenaeus is his dependence upon the new creation language in 2 Cor 5.17 to capture this new state of being.

With this emphasis upon Christ as the divine and heavenly man, Cyril finds the Pauline exchange formulae very helpful. In particular, he regularly employs Phil 2.5–11; 2 Cor 8.9; and Gal 4.4–6 to describe both the descent by Christ and the ascent of believers to deification. By treating these passages as essentially identical, we can note that some of the particularities of the passages drop out, such as the discussion of the law in Galatians 4. He finds Philippians 2 especially helpful, using it more than any other writer to date, because not only Christ's descent but his ascent serves as a model for believers. Thus, while the divinity of Christ is most evident in his pre-existence and incarnation, Cyril balances this with his ascent as the heavenly man as model for believers' ascent in deification.

The Spirit's role in this process is crucial for Cyril because partaking of the Spirit is the primary way that partaking of the divine nature is characterised. Accordingly, when employing the Pauline passages speaking of adoption (Rom 8.15 and Gal 4.6), Cyril highlights the central role of Spirit in these passages to a depth not explored by Irenaeus. However, following Irenaeus Cyril makes this the primary way to describe humans as gods in that believers are adopted sons of God. Another Pauline theme associated with the Spirit that Cyril employs is the temple imagery of 1 Cor 3.16 and 2 Cor 6.16, where the Spirit's divine presence sanctifies humans. Thus, Cyril incorporates both the Spirit's life-giving and sanctifying personal presence.

These various Pauline texts and themes lie at the heart of Cyril's soteriological discourse. Wilken is thus correct in his analysis:

St. Paul provided Cyril with the key to the interpretation of the Bible. But his Paul was not the Paul of St. Augustine, the Paul of Romans 7 or Romans 9 (nor the Paul of justification by faith), it was the Paul of Romans 5, of 1 Corinthians 15 and of 2 Corinthians 5. From Paul Cyril learned to speak of the second Adam, the heavenly man, a new creation and, most of all, the centrality of the Resurrection in the biblical narrative.[103]

Even though we have discussed his commentaries on the gospels, this Pauline lens has been evident. Before developing questions for our study of Pauline texts we will draw together our readings of Irenaeus and Cyril in the next chapter.

---

[103] Robert L. Wilken, 'St Cyril of Alexandria: The Mystery of Christ in the Bible', *ProEccl* 4 (1995): 454–78, at 477–78.

4. Patristic Summary and Questions for Paul

In the previous two chapters we have explored how Irenaeus and Cyril of Alexandria described deification and how they used Pauline texts and themes in support of their theology. Before turning to the Pauline side of the conversation, a brief summary of the soteriology of our two patristic writers will help highlight the primary issues related to our discussion (§1). After this integrative summary, we will then explore several key areas of interest related to Pauline texts and delineate the questions that will guide our reading of Paul (§2).

1. Patristic Summary

Having examined the unique soteriological features in chapters 2 and 3, it will be helpful to summarise each writer's vision of salvation and its anthropological effects and then explore the larger theological structure that helps shape their soteriology.

Irenaeus' direct deification language relates specifically to his use of Psalm 82 where he identifies believers as 'gods' (θεοί) and adopted sons of God. However, this identification is integrated into his portrayal of the larger soteriological experience of believers. Particularly, Irenaeus presents the culmination of salvation as a restoration of the image and likeness of God. Christ, as the second Adam, became human so that believers could become what he is. Thus, believers become like God and are even called gods themselves. At times, Irenaeus distinguishes image and likeness, with image being associated with having a body and soul and likeness related to the restoration from the Spirit's presence. However, in other instances he speaks of the image and likeness as a hendiadys.

With regard to anthropological likeness to God, moral progression is prominent in Irenaeus' anthropology, but the ontological experience of immortality and incorruption is ubiquitous in his discussion. Since the spirit and soul remain immortal through the presence of the life of God, the primary locus of the soteriological change is that of the body, the flesh. As a result, much of Irenaeus' language focuses upon the future eschatological experience, rather than the current age. What does relate to the current age (and the next) is the growing relationship with God that allows believers to progress morally. He situates this salvific experience within a restored relationship with God, expressed through three primary models: adoption, vision, and union. As a result, salvation is always mediated relationally with Christ as the model and mediator and the Spirit as the agent.

Since Irenaeus does not use deification language widely, we should be cautious about overstating its position in his theology; however, we have seen that he integrates this language into key themes within his theological structure. Based upon this, many credit him with being one of the first to synthesize a Christian version of deification. Later proponents of deification certainly take up many of Irenaeus' emphases.

Like Irenaeus, Cyril uses Ps 82.6 to identify believers as gods and continues to associate this with being sons of God by adoption. However, he also incorporates this identification into his discourse about participation in the divine nature from 2 Pet 1.4. For Cyril, deification is participation in the divine attributes such that believers become like God in life and holiness, being restored to the image of God. Believers do not become what God is in his nature – being uncreated and the source of all things – rather they share in his attributes through participation and by grace. Thus, when believers are called gods, Cyril often qualifies this appellation by stating that it is 'by grace' and not 'by nature'.

Because of Adam's sin humans lost the presence of the Spirit, but through Christ, the second Adam, the presence of the Spirit has returned. Thus, believers do not participate in the divine in some abstract manner but through the personal presence of Christ and the Spirit. Since both Christ and the Spirit consubstantially share in the divinity of the Father, when believers participate in them, they partake of the divine nature. The presence of the risen Christ is mediated primarily through the Spirit of Christ but also through the Eucharist, such that Cyril describes this as spiritual and somatic, respectively. Importantly, the restored the presence of the Spirit to humanity restores the image and likeness of God as they participate in the divine attributes of incorruption and sanctification. In addition to new creation and second Adam themes, the metaphor that Cyril most often uses to describe this process is that of adoption. Those that are gods because they partake in these divine attributes of life and sanctification are thus called sons of God by adoption because they share in these attributes by grace and not by nature.

1.1 Problems and Solutions

Central to understanding the solution which their soteriologies represent, we must first understand the nature of the problem(s). Both Irenaeus and Cyril attribute corruption to the fall, and they have fairly developed accounts of Adam's pre- and postlapsarian states. Adam was created inno-

cent and in relationship with God. This relationship is particularly characterised by the presence of the Spirit, the means of life (Gen 2.7). Being
created in the image and likeness of God, Adam shared in the divine attributes of life and holiness. For Irenaeus, Adam was created in a position
of immaturity, and God designed him to mature in his intellectual and
moral capacity and grow into true immortality. In contrast, Cyril viewed
Adam as mature in his creation, fully understanding moral codes. When
Adam sinned, he lost the presence of God through the Spirit and thus experienced corruption as a consequence (cf. Gen 3.19). Thus, the problem
is fundamentally relational but results in noetic and physical mortality.
While condemnation and judgment are discussed, the resulting mortality
and corruption from the lost divine presence serves as the predominant
theme of their accounts. As a result, humans no longer reflect clearly the
image and likeness of God.[1]

The solutions offered by Irenaeus and Cyril cohere in that they both focus on a renewed relationship between humans and God that results in immortality and moral progression, or sanctification. Through his identification with humanity, Christ as the second Adam restored humanity to a relationship with God so that the presence of the Spirit may return.[2] The Spirit
in turn restores life and holiness to believers. Their emphasis on immortality and incorruption becomes one of the primary bases for ascribing the
name 'gods' to believers. For Irenaeus, the Spirit enables moral progression, and with Cyril, participation in sanctification also becomes a central
aspect of participating in the divine nature. Both physical and moral corruption is overcome by the life and incorruption of God.[3]

Both Irenaeus and Cyril understand soteriology to be fundamentally
about a restoration of the divine image and likeness in believers. The true
nature of the image is revealed through the Son who is the Image of God,
and as the Spirit returns to believers, they are restored to God's original

---

[1] One aspect repeatedly affirmed is that free will is not lost in this event.

[2] While Irenaeus and Cyril use exchange formulae that seem to emphasise the salvific
efficacy of the incarnation alone, we noted that both clarify that the incarnation entails
the saving death and resurrection of Christ as well.

[3] In distinction to those in the mystical tradition (see chapter 1) who emphasise the
purification and ascent of the soul, Irenaeus and Cyril also give a strong place to the body
along with the soul. For those in the mystical tradition, the goal of incorruption for the
already immortal soul is purification from corrupt passions as one moves towards *apa-
theia* and *gnosis* in ascent towards God. Irenaeus, in particular, focuses primarily upon
the physical expectation of resurrection of the flesh due to the polemical battle in which
he engaged. However, his sustained discussion regarding the vision of God and moral
progress shows that he does not neglect aspects identified more with the soul. With a
more balanced presentation than Irenaeus, Cyril incorporates both the soul and the body
and thus talks regularly of purifying the passions and of the physical expectation of resurrection, that is, of sanctification and of life.

intention. That is, they are restored to the image and likeness through the presence of the Spirit.[4] Accordingly, this unites creation and re-creation themes in their theology. This also explains why the Adam-Christ dialectic is so important since it also reinforces this connection between the beginning and the end.[5] While Irenaeus and Cyril present some distinctive aspects regarding image and likeness, they are in strict agreement that corruption and mortality represent a distortion of it. Thus, when incorruption and immortality are restored to believers, image and likeness are also restored. Cyril explores this further by also placing stress on holiness as another divine attribute associated with divine likeness.

While deification is not the sole designation of this salvific process, both theologians describe salvation with deification language. In particular, deification language stands at central points in their discussion, although we can see its greater importance for Cyril. Deification is a useful term for both theologians because the primary distinction between humans and the divine is immortality. By crossing that line and becoming immortal, humans become divine through sharing in divine life.

According to Russell's taxonomy of deification language in various patristic writers, both Irenaeus and Cyril would be classified as 'metaphorical', in distinction to 'nominal' or 'analogical'.[6] Russell segregates the metaphorical into two categories: ethical and realist, which focus on likeness (*homoiosis*) and participation (*methexis*), respectively. These are not mutually exclusive, but the distinction highlights the difference in emphasis. Those with a mystical theology who focus upon ascetic and philosophical endeavour are in the 'ethical' category are said to emphasise 'likeness/imitation', whereas those who focus upon the transformation offered by the incarnation and the sacraments are in the 'realist' category and are said to focus on 'participation'. Thus, while noting their significant interest in restoring likeness to God, Russell assigns Irenaeus to the realist/participation model, whereas he argues that Cyril brings together the ethical/likeness and realist/participation categories.[7] I agree with the gen-

---

[4] While likeness may be distinguishable from image in some passages (e.g., *AH* 5.6.1), Irenaeus most often uses them together as a hendiadys of the *telos* of humanity. Cyril does not present any distinction between image and likeness, treating the two as a hendiadys.

[5] Related to this is the distinction that Fairbairn (*Grace*, 17–21, 65–69) makes between two-stage and three-act soteriologies. He argues that Irenaeus presents both two-act and three-act models, while Cyril just presents a three-act model. While this raises important questions about the ways soteriology relates to protology, the helpfulness of this model is diminished because the differences are based on the depth of discussion about the prelapsarian state.

[6] Russell, *Deification*, 1–3.

[7] Ibid., 105, 191.

eral categorisation, but we must note that both maintain a twin emphasis on attaining *likeness* to God through *participation*.

Before exploring these twin emphases, I would like to propose a taxonomy that takes into account other versions of deification in order to situate patristic deification in light of other forms. As noted earlier, ancient notions of divinity (and therefore deification) centred around two poles: immortality and power.[8] The ascription of deity to humans, whether in the emperor cult or in Christian perspectives, incorporates these two poles though with emphasis on one or the other to a greater or lesser degree. In particular, in Christian forms of deification, immortality appears to be more central than the exercise of power. Based on this, I argue that there are two general ways of understanding deification in the ancient world: 1) culticly and 2) ontologically. These are not mutually exclusive, but they serve as helpful heuristic categories (see Figure 4.1).

Figure 4.1: Deification Models

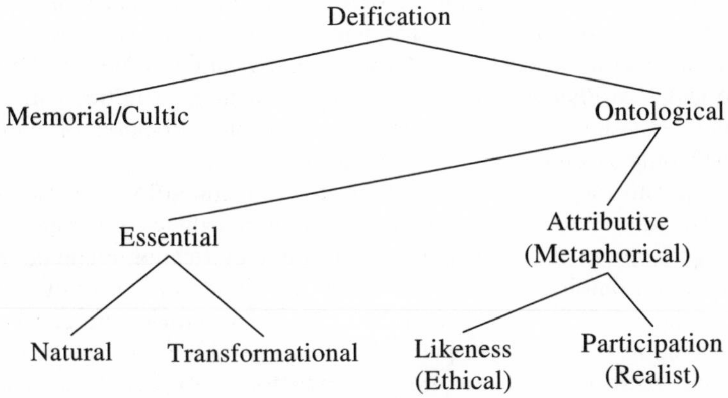

Deification

Memorial/Cultic   Ontological

Essential   Attributive
                   (Metaphorical)

Natural   Transformational   Likeness   Participation
                             (Ethical)   (Realist)

Note: Russell's terminology is shown in rounded brackets

Memorial/cultic deification commemorates the life of an honoured person and thus enables their name to live into perpetuity, which gives them immortality through remembrance.[9] Greco-Roman apotheosis of heroes and emperors is primarily situated in this category. Gradel strongly argues that the Emperor cult in particular had little to do with ontology, that is, assertions about the anthropological immortality of the emperors. Rather, di-

---

[8] See Chp 2, §3.1.2.

[9] Though not referring to deification, Wisdom represents a Jewish parallel, in that the righteous will be immortal because they are remembered by the community (Wis 3-4, esp. 4.1, 7-9, 18-19).

vinity was more about relative status and power.[10] As a result, cultic deification is a means to recognise that status differentiation. This does not mean that conceptions of ontology were not involved, but they were not necessary.

Ontological deification, on the other hand, entails some type of anthropological experience of immortality and power. This deification can be divided into two different aspects: an essential ontology or attributive ontology. With essential deification, the human shares ontologically in the essence of the divine, or rather they contain a divine element within themselves. This may occur naturally or transformationally, though this distinction may break down in some cases. Essential-natural deification is where a human being born with this divine element within themselves. Examples of this would be 'Gnostics' who share consubstantially in the divine essence, having a divine spark within themselves, and also some Platonic and (later) Neo-Platonic writers who taught a unity between the divine soul and human souls.[11] On the other hand those who are transformed or changed by taking on the divine element experience an essential-transformational deification. The tension between the two categories shines through with those who are deified by purification of the soul. With Platonic and Neo-Platonic writers the soul had natural affinities with the world-soul, but through purification by means of cultivation of virtue, one's soul could ascend higher, even to the gods.[12]

In contrast to these who are ontologically constituted by a divine element, those who merely participate in the divine attributes experience attributive deification. Those proposing attributive deification maintain that humans remain ontologically separate from the divine primarily due to a distinction between the Creator and the created, but humans are ontologically changed as they share in particular divine attributes such as immortality. One distinction between essential-transformational deification and attributive deification is the nature of *pneuma*. With essential-transformational deification, the pneuma is the divine material in which believers come to share and by which they are constituted. In contrast, attributive deification maintains the agency of the Spirit as one who mediates the divine presence and thus always remains distinct from believers, who nonetheless come to take on a pneumatic body through the relationship.[13]

---

[10] Gradel, *Emperor Worship and Roman Religion*, 25–32, 72, 305. Cf. S.R.F. Price, 'Gods and Emperors', 95.

[11] Cf. Louth, *Origins*, 73–75.

[12] Russell, *Deification*, 37–44.

[13] While not characterising their discussion as deification, the contrast between essential-transformative and attributive deification directly parallels the distinction of the role of pneuma in Troels Engberg-Pedersen, *Cosmology and Self in the Apostle Paul: The Material Spirit* (Oxford: Oxford University Press, 2010), and Volker Rabens, *The Holy*

Attributive deification corresponds to Russell's 'metaphorical' category. The choice of 'metaphor' is presumably used to guard against confusion with an essential deification.[14] Drawing from Russell's subcategorisation, this group could then be subdivided into the ethical/likeness and realist/participation categories. While these subcategories are heuristically helpful, and the titles 'ethical' and 'realist' are less so, whereas 'likeness' and 'participation' are a little more explanatory.[15] These subgroups are not mutually exlusive. In fact, likeness and participation terminology is drawn from Plato and thus rightfully has affinity to essentialist deification positions as well. As a result, I present this taxonomy for its heuristic value not because I expect that it properly captures all the diversity represented by ancient writers.

Returning to the discussion of Irenaeus and Cyril, we will briefly discuss the two primary pillars of attributive deification – likeness to God and participation in God – and then the Creator-created distinction which serves as a foundation for these.

1.2 Likeness to God

Both Irenaeus and Cyril focus heavily upon the divine image and likeness because they unite the protological and teleological aspects of their anthropology. The two writers present developed accounts of Adam and his creation in the image of God drawn from Genesis 1–2. At the same time, they both relate the protological event to the teleological restoration provided by Christ and the Spirit. Christ, as the perfect human, models true humanity, and the restoration of the Spirit to believers through Christ allows the image to be reformed within them. While rationality and free will are noted as aspects of this likeness to God, the central deifying dimension is primarily characterised as immortality and incorruption for both writers. Irenaeus notably associates this with moral growth into perfection, and Cyril regularly balances the experience of somatic incorruption with moral incorruption. Thus, while these two writers do not emphasise ascetic prac-

---

Spirit and Ethics in Paul: Transformation and Empowering for Religious-Ethical Life (WUNT 2/283; Tübingen: Mohr Siebeck, 2010).

[14] Later Greek theologians reinforced the distinction inherent to attributive deification by speaking of participation in the divine energies rather than the divine essesnce. Accordingly, 'energetic deification' could be another way of speaking about 'attributive deification', and both stand in distinction to 'essential deification', which was roundly refuted.

[15] To complicate matters further, Russell then subdivides the 'realist/participation' category into two further subgroups: ontological (changed by the incarnation) and dynamic (changed by the sacraments). This last subdivision is only marginally helpful in its emphasis, and creates more ambiguity than clarity through its terms, and so I have not employed it here.

tices in these works, they do encourage a moral rigour empowered by the presence of the Holy Spirit.

1.3 Relational Participation

An important correlate to image and likeness is that of participation because it simultaneously entails similarity and distinction. Both theologians describe image and likeness with participation language. Adam's original participation in the divine was lost because of his sin, and the restoration of the divine-human relationship restores this participation in the divine and therefore the divine likeness. Irenaeus described this participatory relationship in various ways: union with God, adoption, and vision of God. Cyril, on the other hand, preferred adoption as the primary model and always qualified it with language of participation. While Cyril's presentation of the relationship is more philosophically developed, we can easily describe the soteriological transformation of both as arising from relational participation. The work of Christ and the Spirit drive this relational participation. Christ unites God and humanity in himself and thus allows humanity to participate in God. The instantiation of this participation comes through the Spirit himself, who brings life and sanctification to believers. Neither Irenaeus nor Cyril seemed concerned with abstract qualities; rather, they emphasise the personal presence of God as the source of divine attributes within humanity.

1.4 Creation, Nature, and Grace

The often unqualified language regarding believers as gods can sound as if mere 'likeness' has been transcended so that the distinction between God and humanity is lost. That is, humans may seem to become divine as God is divine, or they become what he is in essence. However, Irenaeus and Cyril clearly affirm a fundamental distinction between the divine and human that cannot be crossed, and it is this firm distinction that allows them to make such unqualified statements about this human transformation. The human-divine separation is evidenced through their distinction between nature and grace and a theology of creation *ex nihilo*.

The distinction between nature and grace that is fundamental to Cyril's theology is implicit in Irenaeus' as well. For instance, Irenaeus describes adoption as 'by grace' and makes clear that believers do not become sons in the same way that Jesus is the Son. For Cyril this is not merely something he argues for but something he argues from in his defence of the divinity of Christ and the Spirit. With Cyril's interest in refuting what he considers christological heresies, he regularly discusses issues related to human and divine nature, with a clear distinction between each, and this metaphysical divide serves as the basis of all soteriological language.

Thus, when believers are called gods, Cyril often qualifies this appellation by stating that it is 'by grace' and not 'by nature'. Those things that can be identified with divine nature – being uncreated and the source of all things – cannot be identified with believers who become gods by grace. Rather than becoming divine, in the sense of being uncreated in nature, believers become like the divine, in the sense of participating in divine attributes by grace.[16] Importantly, they most often use the Pauline theme of adoption to describe this type of deifying relationship. It captures the new relationship of sonship but with separation between a natural and a created relationship. And, important for their larger deification claims, we saw how adoption was equated with the experience of incorruption, which holds close the connection between divine likeness and participation in the divine.

An implicit, and sometimes explicit, basis for this nature-grace distinction is the idea of creation *ex nihilo*. In distinction to some Platonic and (later) Neo-Platonic writers who taught a unity between the divine soul and human souls, most Greek patristic writers affirmed the idea of *creatio ex nihilo* that broke the strong Platonic and Stoic link between the soul and God.[17] Both Irenaeus and Cyril show evidence of influence from Greek philosophy (though not nearly to the extent of those with a 'mystical theology'), but they are both unambiguous about creation *ex nihilo*, as with most other patristic theologians. In particular, they describe the untraversable gulf, with regard to nature, between Creator and the created. For Irenaeus the idea of continual progression highlights the inexhaustible nature of God in contrast to the finitude of humanity (cf. *AH* 4.38–39).[18] Thus, the ultimate transcendence of God is maintained, and the 'dependence and contingency of creation' is maintained.[19]

---

[16] Some pre-Chalcedonians hint at this being based on a distinction between participation in the divine essence and participation in the divine energies; however, this idea is not systematically developed until Gregory Palamas.

[17] Cf. Louth, *Origins*, 73–75. Other Greek patristic theologians, particularly those influenced by Origen and Platonism, also emphasise the soul over the body. However, Louth (*Origins*, 110) distinguishes between those with a mystical *philosophy* (e.g., Origen and Evagrius), where the *nous* is central because God is knowable, and those with a mystical *theology* (e.g., Gregory of Nyssa and Denys), where *nous* is transcended because God is unknowable. According to our taxonomy, those with a mystical philosophy would come close to if not fall into the essential deification category, whereas those with a mystical theology would be situated in the attributive-likeness deification category.

[18] The transcendence of God is so emphatically maintained that theology is fundamentally apophatic. While this is most explicit in 'mystical' writers, we also saw the importance of progress, even eschatologically, with Irenaeus (cf. *AH* 4.38–39). This too reflects the distinction between the finite nature of humanity as opposed to the infinite nature of God.

[19] Frances Young, '"Creatio ex Nihilo": A Context for the Emergence of the Christian Doctrine of Creation', *SJT* 44 (1991): 139–51, at 147.

With this clear distinction between humanity and God in Irenaeus and Cyril, believers cannot experience an essential deification. In fact, believers explicitly become sons of God and gods, not by nature but by grace. They never connaturally share in the divine essence; rather, through the personal presence of the Spirit they share in the attributes of God embodied by Christ, namely life and sanctification. Consequently, attributive deification is the model of deification found in Irenaeus and Cyril.

Based on this categorisation, the modern concern about deification as absorption into God has no basis here.[20] Habets captures the general unease many feel: 'contemporary western scholars (particularly Protestant scholars) are regularly concerned with the problem of 'a pan(en)theistic concept of union in which the believer becomes dissolved into the essence of the divine nature so that he or she ceases to exist as a distinct entity'.[21] Absorption assumes an impersonal god whose essence is shared in some manner by disembodied souls, which is as far from the patristic conception as possible. Any of the following factors would refute this assumed problem of absorption, but the weight of them all excludes any hint of absorption: 1) the Creator-created distinction, 2) a Trinitarian God, 3) likeness through participation (which entails distinction; otherwise, it would identification), and 4) new creation as re-creation (namely, somatic immortality). With this understanding of how Irenaeus and Cyril situate their views of deification, we should now address the Pauline texts which they utilised to present their perspectives.

1.5 Pauline Texts and Themes

While Psalm 82 and later 2 Pet 1.4 are used as short-hand summaries of biblical notions of deification, Pauline texts and themes are the focal point for their explanations of what these verses mean. With the experience of immortality at the centre of notions of deification, Irenaeus and Cyril make repeated use of 1 Corinthians 15. Importantly, this passage contains explicit connections between Adam and Christ, and, therefore, Irenaeus and Cyril incorporate the restoration of humanity described in this passage to their larger theme of restoration of the image and likeness of God, especially through the language of bearing the Sprit-formed image of the heavenly man (1 Cor 15.49). Drawing upon creational themes, Cyril regularly employs the new creation language in 2 Cor 5.17 to capture this new state of being.

---

[20] David Cairns (*The Image of God in Man* [London: SCM, 1953], 41-43) offers but one example of someone who confuses deification with absorption. Perhaps it stems from a concern about eastern mysticism?

[21] Myk Habets, '"Reformed Theosis?": A Response to Gannon Murphy' *Theology Today* 65 (2009): 489-498, at 494.

Related closely to the emphasis upon Christ as the divine and heavenly man, Irenaeus and Cyril find the Pauline exchange formulae very helpful. While Irenaeus primarily employs Gal 4.4–6, Cyril also uses Phil 2.5–11 and 2 Cor 8.9 regularly to describe both the descent by Christ and the ascent of believers to deification. Cyril in particular finds Philippians 2 especially helpful because not only Christ's descent but his ascent serves as a model for believers. Thus, while the divinity of Christ is most clearly evident in his pre-existence and incarnation, Cyril balances this with Christ's ascent as the heavenly man, which becomes a model for believers' ascent in deification.

Drawing from the association of being gods and 'sons of the Most High' (Ps 82.6), the identification of deification and adoption as sons of God is ubiquitous in their accounts of deification. The central passages that they regularly return to are Gal 4.4–6 and Rom 8.14–16. Irenaeus even identified the adoption language from Galatians 4 with becoming immortal as described in 1 Cor 15.53–54. Cyril, to a much deeper level than Irenaeus, focuses especially upon the Spirit's role in this adoption process. Drawing off his close association with the Spirit, Cyril employs the temple imagery of 1 Cor 3.16 and 2 Cor 6.16, where the Spirit's divine presence sanctifies humans. Thus, Cyril incorporates both the Spirit's life-giving and sanctifying personal presence in the context of deification.

Although our two writers utilised a number of other Pauline texts and themes, these are primary. They integrate these texts into larger theological constructions, but we should remember that these constructions are strongly influenced by their readings of the Pauline texts.

1.6 Conclusion

We noted in the introduction that Irenaeus and Cyril broadly represent a similar tradition, and this characterisation has been reinforced in our study of the two writers. While Irenaeus' soteriology in totality may not be described as deification, deification themes intersect at key points with his description of God, Jesus and humanity and the relationship between them. Cyril on the other hand uses deification language regularly, such that we can rightly identify his soteriology with this term. Based on their similar vision, we can thus describe deification in Irenaeus and Cyril as the process of restoring the image and likeness of God, primarily experienced as incorruption and sanctification, through a participatory relationship with God mediated by Christ and the Spirit. Through the Son and the Spirit believers become adopted sons of God, even gods, by grace and not by nature, because they participate in divine attributes.

These writers discuss participation at the most intimate level as arising from Christ's work and the presence of the Spirit. However, they viewed humans as fundamentally different from the Godhead: there is a distinction between God and humanity – Creator and created – that can never be crossed. Even with this essential distinction, Irenaeus and Cyril did not hesitate to use language that seemed to blur the lines between human and divine. If anything, this divine-human distinction allowed even more freedom in their language because it enabled them to focus on the similarities without forgetting the differences.

That these boundaries are not crossed in this soteriological system is shown through the anthropological effects arising from this relational participation. With mortality and corruption as the centre of the problem related to sin, we are not surprised to see immortality and incorruption at the centre of the human experience of salvation. With immortality as the key identifying feature of the divine in the ancient Greco-Roman world, the ascription of immortality to believers easily led to the use of deification to describe this experience. However, deification quickly came to include any attributes shared by the Christian God with his redeemed creation.

2. Paul and His Patristic Interpreters

In this preliminary stage in our quest to explore whether and to what extent theosis helpfully captures Paul's presentation of the anthropological dimension of soteriology, we have seen the clear importance of Pauline texts for the development and use of deification language in both Cyril and Irenaeus. In particular, Irenaeus depends almost solely on Pauline texts when he unpacks Ps 82.6 and gives believers the appellation of gods. Cyril also leans heavily upon Pauline texts but he also makes use of 2 Pet 1.4. However, the fact that the use of 2 Pet 1.4 is relatively late in the development of notions of deification gives us further reason to consider the importance of Pauline texts and themes.

2.1 Questions for Paul

Now that we have explored the different aspects of these two writers' views on deification and how they have used Pauline texts to support their ideas, we can begin to consider the other participant in the conversation – Paul himself. Since Pauline texts served as an important foundation for their explanation of deification, several key areas of interest have become evident. In what follows, I will summarise these key areas of interest. After that, we will narrow these down to a manageable set of questions that will then guide our reading of Paul.

2.1.1 Areas of Interest

Life and Incorruption. Life and incorruption are central to Irenaeus' and Cyril's soteriological accounts. The question arising from this sustained emphasis on life and immortality is whether these hold such a central place with Paul. Is there a central problem-solution pair that forms his soteriological foundation such as mortality-immortality or condemnation-justification? Or, does Paul present a variety of problem-solution combinations without one being primary? If so, what place does life and incorruption play in his soteriology?

Relational Models/Transforming Presence of God. Though Irenaeus describes his soteriology in several ways, he primarily uses three relational models – adoption, vision of God, and union with God. We saw that adoption encompasses the whole of what Cyril understands by deification. With adoption, the Pauline links are clear with repeated reference to Romans 8 and Galatians 4. What association does Paul make between sonship/adoption and transformation? Does Paul identify divine sonship with immortality like Irenaeus and Cyril? Cyril's whole ontological structure is based upon a nature-grace distinction and the necessity of participation. Does Paul hold to such a nature-grace distinction? If not, does this render their ontological systems incompatible?

Both Irenaeus and Cyril place a distinct emphasis on the agency of Christ and the Spirit as mediators of the divine presence. Christ restores the connection between the divine and human, and the Spirit's presence in the believer primarily mediates participation in the divine, such that the divine likeness is restored. How does Paul situate the personal presence of the divine in his theology? Do Christ and the Spirit play such a central role in the divine-human encounter in Paul's theology? Does Paul ever employ the concept of restored divine likeness with regard to the Spirit or Christ?

Exchange Formulae. Irenaeus and Cyril use a variety of exchange formulae to describe the descent of Christ and the ascent of believers. With their focus upon Christ's pre-existent divinity, these formulae might appear to focus solely upon his incarnation, but they more likely serve as a shorthand for the whole of Christ's work. The height from which the Word descended seems to influence significantly the height to which believers ascend: as God became a human, humans can become gods. From what height do the Pauline letters present Christ as descending, and how does this affect the height to which believers may attain? What aspects are emphasised in the individual passages that may have been lost when the patristic writers read them together?

New Creation and Image Restoration. With explicit and developed narratives of creation and the fall, Irenaeus and Cyril integrate soteriol-

ogy/eschatology with protology. The intention of God when creating
Adam determines the destiny of recreated humanity.[22] A central aspect of
salvation is the restoration of the image and likeness of God given at creation. In what ways does Paul integrate creation and fall themes into his
soteriology? In particular, how does Paul portray image restoration? Does
Paul view soteriology/eschatology as in continuity with creation or is new
creation in discontinuity with creation? And if there is continuity, what
sort of continuity is implied?

2.1.2 Proposed Questions

These specific areas of questioning are important, but we do not want them
overly to influence our reading of Paul. We must remember the discussion
in Gadamer, Jauss, and Skinner about how particular texts arise out of individual contexts and are meant to be an answer for questions at that time.
If we focused just upon these questions, they could divert our attention
from other important issues in the Pauline texts. We need a framework of
questions that enables us to capture all the dimensions of Pauline soteriology, not just those utilised by Irenaeus and Cyril so that we are not imposing a pre-set agenda on Paul. These questions above will play a role in our
analysis of Paul, but in order to give him his own voice they cannot be the
only questions we ask. As a result, we will address his letters with the following general questions which will allow us to situate our specific questions noted above:

   1) What is the anthropological shape of Paul's soteriology? What aspects of the human condition change due to the soteriological encounter
with God?

   2) When do these soteriological changes occur? Paul's soteriology is
frequently characterised as being 'already/not yet', but how can we clarify
further when specific aspects of this soteriological experience take place?

   3) How does the soteriological change of the human condition come
about? What divine and human activities lead to the soteriological
changes expected by Paul?

   In addition, we noted the importance of the Adam-Christ narratives in
Irenaeus and Cyril. Since Andrew Louth locates a fundamental distinction
between theological traditions that move from creation to deification and

---

[22] While the Adam-Christ correlation in patristic and Pauline theologies is central to
this area of discussion, we will for the most part have to leave it to the side because it is
outside our primary area of interest which is the anthropological dimension of soteriology. That is, this is more about Christology than anthropology.

those that move from fall to redemption, the following question needs to be addressed specifically:[23]

4) How does Paul relate this soteriological change to creation themes? Does Paul view soteriology/eschatology as in continuity or in discontinuity with creation? That is, does Paul's soteriology represent a fulfilment of creation, or does he present his soteriology as something that surpasses creation?

These broad and structural questions are not the only questions one could ask, but neither are they so specific that they lead to prefigured answers. It is the breadth of these questions that give us the freedom to read Paul with a certain interest but without pre-set conclusions. In that way we can foster an open conversation between these Patristic writers and Paul on the topic of deification.

Being guided by these questions, our analysis of the patristic writers will function as a heuristic device in our reading of Paul. That is, they will introduce ways of reading Paul but will not limit our readings. In particular, we will not focus upon the presence or absence of specific terms or motifs that arise from our patristic writers, but we will allow the Pauline passages to shape our understanding of his texts. As a result, we can allow for the possibility that there might be a greater or lesser correlation between the theological structures offered by the different writers.

2.2 Pauline Passages

Now that we have chosen questions for the Pauline texts, we must choose the texts that will be the basis of our study. Irenaeus and Cyril drew from a wide variety of Pauline texts, but we must limit the number of passages analysed to make the project manageable. At the same time, we must remember that our question relates to the topic of deification in the Pauline letters and not simply patristic interpretation of the Pauline letters. As a result, we should not ignore the passages highlighted by our patristic authors, but neither should we be limited by them. Just as we do not want the particular issues raised by our reading of Patristic interpreters to overpower the discussion, we also do not want their selection of texts to rob Paul of his voice in this discussion. Rather than treating a number of texts thematically in a shallow manner, our conclusions would be stronger and weightier if we focused on close readings of a limited number of texts.

Based on our investigation of Irenaeus and Cyril, we noted several prominent passages. With the repeated use of adoption as a relational

---

[23] Andrew Louth, 'The Place of *Theosis* in Orthodox Theology' in *Partakers of the Divine Nature: The History and Development of Deification in the Christian Traditions,* eds. Michael J. Christensen and Jeffery A. Wittung (Grand Rapids: Baker, 2008), 32–44, at 34–35.

model, Romans 8 and Galatians 4 were regularly utilised. With its Adam-Christ contrast and the resurrection emphasis, they certainly found 1 Corinthians 15 central. With regard to the exchange formulae, Philippians 2 was popular with Cyril. At the same time, the description of the restoration of humanity to the image and likeness of God raises the profile of those Pauline passages that address this issue: Romans 8; Romans 12; 2 Corinthians 3; Philippians 3. These various passages are ones important for patristic writers, but we must also consider other texts important in the Pauline corpus.

While Paul integrates his soteriology into numerous parts of his letters, some soteriological passages in the Pauline corpus are more focused and more clearly address the anthropological condition, including 1 Thessalonians 4–5; 2 Thessalonians 1–2; Galatians 2–4; 1 Corinthians 15; 2 Corinthians 3–5; Romans 3–8; Philippians 2–3; Colossians 2–3; Ephesians 1–2; 4–5.

Our primary criterion is that the texts analysed need to give a variety of data points. That is, they should integrate the present and future aspects of salvation and address different aspects of the anthropological condition to give us a better picture of the variety of Paul's theology. This excludes passages that focus primarily upon present (Galatians 2–4; Romans 3–7; Philippians 2–3; Ephesians 4–5) or future (2 Thessalonians 1–2; 1 Corinthians 15) soteriology. Also, the present aspect of 1 Thessalonians 4–5 is primarily parenetic and thus less helpful in capturing the basis of his soteriology.

This leaves us with 2 Corinthians 3–5; Romans 8; Colossians 2–3; and Ephesians 1–2. With the primary place of the Spirit and adoption in Romans 8, as well as its importance for the patristic writers, this is an obvious choice. While Irenaeus does make use of Eph 1.10, 2 Corinthians 3–5 serves as a better candidate than Ephesians 1–2, but it provides more data points with regard to key themes such as image, creation, and resurrection that play into patristic conceptions of deification. Importantly, Romans 8 and 2 Corinthians 3–5 are sufficiently rich and varied to give a good sample of Pauline soteriology. As a result, they will provide ample evidence to answer our four primary questions because they contain various contours of Pauline soteriology related to the different aspects of humans in different time frames. In addition, these two passages also include image language as well as language related to justification, which are important for Eastern and Western readings. In order to capture some of the contingent nature of Paul's message, I will also include brief excursus on Colossians 2 and Galatians 3–4 (with Romans 8) and 1 Corinthians 15 and Philippians 2–3 (with 2 Corinthians 3–5) to round out the picture. We will turn first to our discussion of Romans 8.

III. Pauline Soteriology

5. Romans 8

1. Introduction

As we turn to the Pauline letters, we remember that Irenaeus and Cyril commonly employed Romans 8 due to the adoption passage in 8.14–17; however, the whole chapter addresses themes central for both Paul and patristic theologians, such as life and glory. As we address whether and to what extent theosis helpfully captures Paul's presentation of the anthropological dimension of soteriology, several questions will guide our discussion of this passage: 1) What is the shape of Pauline soteriology? 2) When do these soteriological changes occur? 3) How do these soteriological changes of the human condition come about? 4) How does this transformation of the human condition relate to creation? After discussing how the chapter fits into the context of the letter, we will consider these questions through the major sections of Romans 8: powers and the divine presence in 8.1–13 (§2), adoption in 8.14–17 (§3) and conformation to Christ in 8.17–30 (§4).

1.1 Romans 8 in Context

In order to understand the role of Romans 8, we should first consider the argument of the letter as captured in its thesis statement in Rom 1.16–17, where Paul describes the saving power of God as the revelation of the righteousness of God.[1] As a basis of this declaration, he quotes Habakkuk 2.4 (LXX), which associates righteousness with the soteriological goal of life: ὁ δὲ δίκαιος ἐκ πίστεως ζήσεται. Stuhlmacher, thus, describes the theme of the letter: 'the gospel of divine righteousness in and through Christ, by virtue of which those who believe from among the Jews and

---

[1] Most agree that Rom 1.16–17 is the thesis. One dissenter is J.R. Daniel Kirk (*Unlocking Romans: Resurrection and the Justification of God* [Grand Rapids: Eerdmans, 2008], 39–49), who argues that 1.1–7, with a focus upon Jesus resurrection in 1.4, better serves as the thesis of the letter. While I disagree, my reading is very much in sympathy with his, as will become clear, particularly with the central place that resurrection and new life play in the letter.

Gentiles (according to the promise from Hab. 2:4) obtain *life*'.[2] In other words, those who believe in Christ obtain life on account of their experience of divine righteousness.[3] Byrne draws on this connection between righteousness and life and describes the following as the unexpressed premise of Rom 1.16–17: 'eternal life (the fullness of eschatological existence, participation in the world to come) is gained by righteousness, by being found holy and blameless by God at the judgment: the just inherit eternal life; the wicked face perdition'.[4] Therefore, he argues that Rom 1–8 is an exploration of δίκαιος ἐκ πίστεως and ζήσεται: 'In this scheme Rom 1:18–4:25 deals with the establishment of the principle of justification by faith on the basis of the righteousness of God, while Chh [*sic*] 5–8 treat the reality of the new life in Christ'.[5]

While other issues are involved, the distribution of key terms supports Byrne's assertion.[6] For instance, (α)δικ- terms occur 72 times in the letter and over half (37) are in chapters 1–4. Likewise, ζωή and its cognates occur 37 times in Romans, with the majority (24) in chapters 5–8 and the others variously throughout the letter, except for a concentration of 5 occurrences in 14.7–9. We find a similar distribution of 'death' terminology (νέκρος, θανατός, and cognates) with 45 total occurrences and 36 within chapters 5–8.[7] Thus, as we approach chapter 8, we will pay close attention to the hope of life in the context of righteousness.

---

[2] Peter Stuhlmacher, 'The Theme of Romans' in *The Romans Debate,* ed. Karl P. Donfried (Edinburgh: T&T Clark, 1991), 333–345, at 335, emphasis added.

[3] A variety of opinions exist concerning the identity of ὁ δίκαιος. Whether it is Christ as, for example, Richard B. Hays (*Echoes of Scripture in the Letters of Paul* [New Haven: Yale University Press, 1989], 39–41) argues or any believer as I lean towards, the important aspect of the verse for our purposes is that righteousness is associated with life.

[4] Brendan Byrne, *'Sons of God' – 'Seed of Abraham'* (AnBib 83; Rome: Biblical Institute Press, 1979), 89.

[5] Ibid., 88. Gorman ('Romans') does not argue for a particular division in the argument of Romans as here, but with his emphasis on *dikaiosunē* and *doxa* as the two foci around which Romans runs, he clearly agrees with the centrality of righeousness and life.

[6] For a range of views on the purpose and audience of Romans, see Karl P. Donfried, *The Romans Debate* (Peabody, MA: Hendrickson, 1991). Many arguments exist regarding the subdivision of the argument in Romans. A clear transition in the argument occurs after 8.39, so our primary question is how to divide Rom 1–8. Main transitions in the argument have been proposed as occurring after chapter 4, after chapter 5, or at 5.12. I will not rehearse the details here, but two primary points strengthen the division offered by Byrne. First, the language at 5.1 appears to mark a transition in argumentation with the causal participle (Δικαιωθέντες οὖν ἐκ πίστεως). Second, the discussion of afflictions and glory serve as an inclusio of the second division: 5.1–5 and 8.17–39.

[7] Regarding death, C. Clifton Black ('Pauline Perspectives on Death in Romans 5–8', *JBL* 103 [1984]: 413–433, at 420) writes: 'Especially when viewed in the context of his

What role then does chapter 8 play in among chapters 5–8? Gieniusz contends that 5.20–21 'represent[s] not only the concluding point of the preceding presentation [5.12–21] but also and primarily the thesis (*propositio*) which Paul is going to work out in the following *probatio*. He will first defend it against possible misunderstandings, (chapters 6–7), and then positively unfold it in chapter 8'.[8] Accordingly, we find the themes of law, sin, grace, death and eternal life in 6–8. In particular, with the numerous noted connections between chapter 5 and 8,[9] we should not be surprised that the climax of chapter 5 in 5.20–21 is further explored in chapter 8.

Many themes might be proposed as important in Romans 5–8, but Feuillet argues that the death-life antithesis is central: 'Il nous paraît certain que l'antithèse *mort-vie* constitue le thème capital des chapitres 5–8 de l'Épître aux Romains'.[10] Particularly significant for Paul's argument in chapters 5 to 8 is language about ruling (βασιλεύω) and slavery (δουλόω), with which Paul personifies the power of death (5.12–21), sin (6.1–23), and the law (7.1–25).[11] Within this pattern of bondage, Paul repeatedly affirms that death is the result of sin: 5.12, 17–18, 21; 6.16, 21, 23; 7.5, 9–13, 24.[12] Hence, death is a central problem which the Christ-event addresses. In the same way that sin brings death, Christ is the agent of new life: 5.17–18, 20–21; 6.4–5, 8, 11, 13, 22–23.[13] Central to both chapter 6 and 7 is the incorporative death and resurrection of Christ in this act of liberation from death. The Christ event is effective but also paradigmatic for believers as they follow his pattern of death and life. Chapter 8 continues the death-life

---

discussion of the Christian's new life in Christ (chapters 6 and 8), Paul's main interest in this section is not the origin of sin but the origin of death'.

[8] Andrzej Gieniusz, *Romans 8:18–30: "Suffering Does Not Thwart the Future Glory"* (Atlanta: Scholars Press, 1999), 41.

[9] Douglas J. Moo, *The Epistle to the Romans* (NICNT; Cambridge: Eerdmans, 1996), 292–94. E.g., glory (5.2–5; 8.17–18, 21, 30), hope (5.2–5; 8.24–25), affliction (5.3; 8.35), endurance (5.2–5; 8.25), love of God (5.5–8; 8.35, 39), and the Spirit (5.5; 8.14–17, 26–27). For a discussion of how death and life stand at the centre of Paul's argument in 5.12–21, see Robin Scroggs, *The Last Adam: A Study in Pauline Anthropology* (Oxford: Blackwell, 1966), 81–2.

[10] André Feuillet, 'Les attaches bibliques des antithèses pauliniennes dans la première partie de l'Épître aux Romains (1–8)' in *Mélanges Bibliques,* eds. Albert Descamps and André de Halleux (Gembloux: Duculot, 1970), 323–49, at 333.

[11] For a discussion of the emphasis on these categories in this larger division of the letter, see James D.G. Dunn, *Romans* (WBC 38A–B; 2 vols.; Dallas: Word, 1988), 301–3.

[12] While Emma Wasserman ('Paul among the Philosophers: The Case of Sin in Romans 6–8', *JSNT* 30 [2008]: 387–415) rightly notes the internal aspects of death, she incorrectly minimises the apocalyptic personification of death and ignores the physical corruption related to sin as we will see in Rom 8.10.

[13] Cf. Byrne, *'Sons'*, 86.

discussion but now includes the Spirit, whose agency in granting life is central.

In many ways, Rom 7.7–8.30 serves as an exposition of 7.1–6 where Paul discusses freedom from the law. This freedom is for bearing good fruit through dying with and being joined to the risen Christ (7.4), which entails serving God through the life of the Spirit rather than through the law (7.6). Addressing the relationship between flesh, law, and Spirit in the context of death and life, 7.4–6 serves as the basis of 7.7–8.30.[14] Rom 7.7–25 develops the claim in 7.5 that the law aroused sinful desires in the flesh, which produce fruit for death rather than God.[15] The central issue is the goodness but *inability* of the law, as it is unable to stop death's invasion through sin (7.9–13), and the cry of desperation at the end of the chapter summarises the problem: 'Who will rescue me from this body of death?' It is to this inability of the law and the problem of death that chapter 8 responds concerning the *ability* of Christ and the Spirit to bring life and thus develops the claim in 7.6.[16]

Based on the thesis of the letter we have seen a basic division within chapters 1–8: in chapters 1–4 the emphasis is upon righteousness and in chapters 5–8 the emphasis is life. Chapter 8 stands as the climax of this latter section, in which the antithesis of death and life runs through. Sin brings death, and this death has moral and somatic consequences. As a development of the issue of the law's inability to bring life, summarised in 7.4–6 and developed in 7.7–25, chapter 8 spells out the life-giving work of Christ and the Spirit.

1.2 Summary of Chapter 8

With this larger context in mind, we can now address Romans 8 more specifically. Paul's response in 8.1–2 to the embattled cries of the person in chapter 7 sets the tone, indeed gives the thesis, for the rest of the chapter: rather than condemnation and death, Christ and the Spirit bring liberation and life.[17] Nygren argues that this is a culmination of the life spoken of in 1.17: 'Here we see how, in chapter 8, Paul draws the ultimate conclusion of his theme, that the Christian, he who through faith is righteous, shall

---

[14] Ulrich Wilckens, *Der Brief an die Römer* (EKK; 3 vols.; Neukirchen-Vluyn: Neukirchener, 1978), 2:118. Cf. Gordon D. Fee, *God's Empowering Presence: The Holy Spirit in the Letters of Paul* (Peabody, MA: Hendrickson, 1994), 504.

[15] Though not decisive for my interpretation of Romans 8, Romans 7.7–25 appears to be speaking of one under the law ('outside' Christ) rather than one freed by Christ ('in' Christ). Cf. Jason Maston, *Divine and Human Agency in Second Temple Judaism and Paul* (WUNT 2/297; Tübingen: Mohr Siebeck, 2010), 133–140; Fee, *Empowering Presence*, 511–15.

[16] Ibid., 513.

[17] Cf. N.T. Wright, *Romans* (NIB 10; Nashville: Abingdon, 2002), 574.

live: he describes the Christian life not only as free from wrath, sin, and the law, but also as *"free from death"*.[18]

Paul advances this thesis through discussion of resurrection life and glory and through language of adoption and the enablement of the Spirit. While key transitions are seen at the beginning of 8.12, 14, 18, each development in the argument draws closely upon what has just gone before, with the result that significant turns in the line of reasoning are hard to distinguish. As Paul expounds the experience of liberation in the Spirit, he first addresses the issue of what animates believers and gives them life if the Torah does not (Rom 8.1–13). It is the Spirit, who grants life based on Christ's work, in contrast to the flesh, which works death. In Rom 8.14–17 he then uses the adoption metaphor to describe the state of believers as a part of this liberating Spirit relationship. With issues of law fading into the background, the second half of the chapter addresses the follow-up question: If the Spirit's life is so determinative now, what place does suffering as the marker of death have in believers' lives? Continuing with this theme of adoption, in Rom 8.18–30 Paul then addresses liberation and glory in the midst of suffering by using terminology of creation and re-creation. As a conclusion of not only this chapter but also of chapters 5–8, Paul gives assurance of God's love in the face of difficulties in Rom 8.31–39. Since 8.31–39 presents a discreet concluding unit for chapters 5–8, we will limit our discussion to 8.1–30.

2. Powers and Divine Presence: 8.1–13

As the embattled person of chapter 7 struggled with both the problem of overcoming the will of the flesh and the resulting death that came from sin, Paul presents the deliverance from Christ through the Spirit in 8.1–13 that both animates the believer presently in moral action and also will restore life in the future. He does not describe persons uninfluenced and acting upon their own volition. Rather, he further develops a picture of contrasting powers exerting influence upon people as in chapters 5–7. In particular, Paul intermixes a variety of phrases to describe a life determined by different agents – by Christ and the Spirit or by the Flesh and Sin. We will first address the law and the Spirit and how these form the context of the larger discussion (§2.1). Afterwards, we will look at the respective roles of Christ's incarnation, death, and resurrection since they are central to the experience of freedom and to later discussions of theosis (§2.2). Then we will discuss the flesh and the Spirit as two spheres of existence (§2.3).

---

[18] Anders Nygren, *Commentary on Romans* (trans. Carl C. Rasmussen; London: SCM Press, 1952), 306, emphasis original.

2.1 The Law and The Spirit (8.1–2, 4)

With ἄρα νῦν in 8.1 Paul transitions from his development of the problem to his discussion of the solution. He writes: 'Therefore, there is now no condemnation for those in Christ Jesus' (8.1). The reference to condemnation (κατάκριμα) hearkens the reader back to 5.16–18, which speaks of *death* as the result of sin.[19] At the same time, the experience of those who are ἐν Χριστῷ is *life* through relationship with Christ.[20] Paul then makes this implicit life-death contrast in 8.1 explicit by speaking of the freedom which the Spirit of life attains 'in Christ Jesus' from the law of sin and death (8.2).[21]

The law (ὁ νόμος) has played an important role in Paul's argumentation through the letter, with specific emphasis in chapters 2 and 7. The problem with understanding νόμος is that Paul uses it in multiple ways, primarily 'Torah' (e.g., 3.21)[22] or a 'principle' (e.g., 7.21, 23).[23] In our passage, the term νόμος is found four times in 8.2–4, with two particularly debated occurrences in 8.2. With regard to the contrast between (a) ὁ νόμος of the Spirit and (b) ὁ νόμος of sin and death, scholars see different variations:[24] both a and b refer to Torah,[25] b refers to Torah and a acts as a rhetorical

---

[19] In 5.16 and 18 Paul contrasts κατάκριμα with δικαίωμα and δικαίωσις ζωῆς, respectively, as the opposite results of sin and the work of God. In particular, 5.18 makes clear that this condemnation is equated with mortality and death: 1) Condemnation is contrasted with justification of *life*. 2) In 5.12 Paul describes death spreading εἰς πάντας ἀνθρώπους as the result of sin. This εἰς πάντας ἀνθρώπους language is then repeated in 5.18, showing that condemnation is the death previously mentioned.

[20] To this point in the letter, ἐν Χριστῷ has only been used three times: 3.24; 6.11; and 6.23. The two occurrences in chapter 6 both explicitly occur in contexts of new life from Christ. In addition, in 3.24 justification and redemption stand implicitly as the life-giving solution for the mortality described in 3.23 through the loss of glory. Cf. Ben C. Blackwell, 'Immortal Glory and the Problem of Death in Romans 3:23', *JSNT* 32 (2010): 285–308.

[21] Ron C. Fay ('Was Paul a Trinitarian? A Look at Romans 8' in *Paul and His Theology,* ed. Stanley E. Porter [Leiden: Brill, 2006], 327–345, at 335) argues that in Romans the 'in Christ' phrase always modifies what precedes not what follows.

[22] E.g., Dunn, *Romans,* 1:416–8.

[23] E.g., C.E.B. Cranfield, *Romans* (ICC; 2 vols.; Edinburgh: T&T Clark, 1975), 1:375–76.

[24] Michael Winger, *By What Law?: The Meaning of Nomos in the Letters of Paul* (SBLDS 128; Atlanta: Scholars, 1992), 194–95.

[25] Dunn, *Romans,* 1:416–19; Robert Jewett, *Romans: A Commentary* (Hermeneia; Minneapolis: Fortress, 2007), 480–81; Wilckens, *Römer,* 2:122; N.T. Wright, 'The Vindication of the Law: Narrative Analysis and Romans 8.1–11' in *Climax of the Covenant: Christ and the Law in Pauline Theology,* (Minneapolis: Fortress, 1992), 193–219.

foil,[26] or both a and b refer to a principle or power.[27] Each position has strengths and weaknesses, and detailing the exegetical arguments is outside the scope of this chapter.

This verse, however, does raise the topic of agency. Paul's contention in Rom 7 is that Torah does not enable people to fulfil it, and this is reaffirmed in 8.3 with the language of 'inability' (ἀδύνατος). Sin takes the opportunity offered by the law, such that people cannot do what they want, resulting in death. By use of genitive modifiers, Paul speaks of different agents animating νόμος: for the good (πνεύματος, 8.2 and θεοῦ, 7.22, 25; 8.7) or for the bad (ἁμαρτίας, 7.23; 8.2; θανάτου, 8.2). With considerations of agency in mind, the thrust of 8.2 is that the Spirit of life has freed believers from the competing agents of sin and death. Thus rather than the power of sin and death ruling as Paul has portrayed in 5.12–21 and 7.7–25, a new power has entered the discussion – the Spirit of life, who is an agent of liberty.

While addressing νόμος, we should also consider 8.4, where the role of νόμος as 'Torah' seems clear as Paul describes the fulfilment of the δικαίωμα τοῦ νόμου in those walking κατὰ πνεῦμα. What does δικαίωμα τοῦ νόμου refer to and what is its relationship with the Spirit? Some have noted new covenant allusions (e.g., Jer 31.31–34; Ezek 36.24–32).[28] This is not the first time these concepts have been associated in the letter. Both 2.26 and 8.4 speak of the δικαιωμα(τα) τοῦ νόμου being 'kept' (φυλάσσω) and 'fulfilled' (πληρόω), respectively, in the context of the Spirit.[29] In 2.26–29 the discussion of circumcision of the heart has distinct new covenant echoes, which Paul may intend his readers to consider in chapter 8. At the centre of the new covenant promise, along with restoration from exile, is the agency of God in enabling his people to walk according to his ways. Ezek 36.27 (LXX), in particular, speaks of the ability to follow God's decrees (δικαιώματα) because of his Spirit (πνεῦμα) in the people (ἐν ὑμῖν), which has clear overlaps with the language in Romans 8.

---

[26] Ernst Käsemann, *Commentary on Romans* (trans. Geoffrey William Bromiley; Grand Rapids: Eerdmans, 1980), 215–16.

[27] Cranfield, *Romans*, 1:375–76; Fee, *Empowering Presence*, 523–24; Moo, *Romans*, 475–76; Colin G. Kruse, 'Paul, the Law, and the Spirit' in *Paul and His Theology*, ed. Stanley E. Porter (Leiden: Brill, 2006), 109–130, 124.

[28] John W. Yates, *The Spirit and Creation in Paul* (WUNT 2/251; Tübingen: Mohr Siebeck, 2008), 143–47. Cf. Cranfield, *Romans*, 1:384; Moo, *Romans*, 486n.66.

[29] In each passage Paul discusses πνεῦμα, νόμος, and σάρξ within the context of agency, law fulfilment, and pleasing God. In both 2.29 and 7.6 Paul contrasts πνεῦμα and γράμμα in the context of serving God.

While Ziesler associates fulfilling the righteous decree with the tenth commandment as in 7.7,[30] fulfilling the Torah by the Spirit should more likely be considered as 'bearing fruit towards God' (7.4) or pleasing God (8.7–8). Many scholars also point to Rom 13.8–10 and Gal 5.13–18 as places where Paul abstracts the law into the love command since 3.21, 28 and 7.4–6 speak of righteousness being separate from the law.[31] Based on this model, Paul associates the work of the Spirit with the eschatological new covenant promise of moral empowerment for pleasing God.

Another option for the fulfilment of δικαίωμα τοῦ νόμου is that of the *decree of life* or *of death*, which also fits well with the overall context of the chapter. Wright, for instance, argues that 'the thing that "the law could not do" in 8.3 was not to produce mere ethical behaviour, but to give *life* – that is, the life of the new age, resurrection life'.[32] Based on the connection of righteousness and life in the letter (e.g., 5.17–21; 8.10),[33] Wright then goes on to argue that 'δικαίωμα can perfectly properly bear the meaning "the covenant decree", i.e. the decree according to which one who does these things shall live (e.g. Deut 30.6–20)'.[34] Wright does not see this as an emphasis on 'ethical behaviour' but on somatic life as in 8.10–11 because it is 'the verdict that the law announces rather than the behavior which it requires'.[35] He links the use here to the just decree of death in 1.32 and the implicit promise of life in 5.16, where Paul makes the contrast between κατάκριμα and δικαίωμα explicit. On the other hand, Kirk sees the association of δικαίωμα with the death sentence (or 'judgment') in Rom 1.32 as controlling. He proposes that the use of δικαίωμα is tied to Jesus' death: 'As in 5:18, the means by which the δικαίωμα is accomplished is the death of Jesus; this seems precisely calculated to meet humanity's need as articulated in 1:32 (and 6:23): death'.[36] However, κατάκριμα and δικαίωμα do not appear to be synonymous here in 8.4 and 5.18, but rather antithetical.[37] With δικαίωμα meaning 'decree' in 1.32; 5.18; and 8.4, it appears that the outcome of the decree is driven by the

---

[30] J. A. Ziesler, 'The Just Requirement of the Law (Romans 8:4)', *ABR* 35 (1987): 77–82, at 79.

[31] E.g., Kruse, 'Paul, the Law', 125–29. See Maston (*Divine and Human Agency*, 163–66) for a good defense of this position.

[32] Wright, 'Vindication', 202. Cf. Brendan Byrne, *Romans* (SP 6; Collegeville, MN: Liturgical Press, 1996), 94.

[33] Paul closely associates righteousness with new life in Romans: 1.17; 4.5, 13–22; 4.25; 5.17, 18, 21; 6.13; 6.19–23; 8.10.

[34] Wright, 'Vindication', 203.

[35] idem., *Romans*, 577.

[36] J.R. Daniel Kirk, 'Reconsidering *Dikaiōma* in Romans 5:16', *JBL* 126 (2007): 787–92, at 791.

[37] Cf. §2.1 above, note 19.

context. As a result, the contrast here with κατάκριμα argues for the decree of life, as Wright has argued.[38]

With the love command in the background, the new covenant hope of moral enablement by the Spirit instantiates this new life encapsulated in this expression. This decree of life fits well with the new covenant hope. Thus, the declaration of new life is fulfilled by those who walk in the Spirit. As we will see in chapter 6, the hope of resurrection is not easily dissociated from moral enablement because both are aspects of the new life given by the Spirit. The declaration of life encompasses the present and future work of the Spirit. However, this occurs not only through the Spirit but also through Christ as well, as the intervening verse, 8.3, shows.

2.2 God Condemns Sin: Incarnation, Death, and Resurrection (8.3–4)

After declaring liberation from the powers of Sin, Flesh, and Death through Christ and the Spirit (8.1–2), Paul then explains the basis (cf. γάρ in 8.3) for these claims about liberation in light of the law's inability: God has condemned sin by sending Christ (8.3–4). Our focus is upon the shape of Paul's soteriology at the anthropological level but Rom 8.3–4 opens the door to his insight on how this is achieved. With Christ's incarnation, death, and resurrection as central to discussion of deification in patristic writings, we have the opportunity to explore how Paul presents these three foci.

While Paul does not dwell on Christ's incarnation, this is the most explicit aspect of the three foci in 8.3.[39] With regard to being sent by God, Dunn is correct: This phrase does not necessitate Jesus' divine pre-existence,[40] but Dunn is too cautious in his attempt to exclude pre-existence as an option here.[41] Though there is much talk of God sending people as his agents in the Bible (e.g., Exod 3.10; Isa 6.8; Jer 1.7), two

---

[38] Since the law could easily condemn, Hooker notes this must mean a 'declaration of righteousness'. Morna D. Hooker, 'Interchange and Atonement' in *From Adam to Christ*, (Eugene, OR: Wipf & Stock, 2008), 26–41, at 32.

[39] Although the term 'incarnation' carries much theological baggage, I use it here because it best captures the nature of the debate regarding Jesus' humanity.

[40] James D.G. Dunn, *Christology in the Making* (2nd ed.; London: SCM, 1989), 38–45. Moule regards this passage as 'ambiguous'. C.F.D. Moule, 'Review of *Chistology in the Making*', *JTSns* 33 (1982): 258–63, at 259.

[41] Cf. C.E.B. Cranfield, 'Some Comments on Professor J.D.G. Dunn's *Christology in the Making*' in *The Glory of Christ in the New Testament: Studies in Christology*, eds. L.D. Hurst and N.T. Wright (Oxford: Clarendon, 1987), 267–80, at 270–72; Jean-Noël Aletti, 'Romans 8: The Incarnation and its Redemptive Impact' in *The Incarnation: An Interdisciplinary Symposium on the Incarnation of the Son of God*, eds. Stephen Davis, et al. (Oxford: Oxford University Press, 2002), 93–115, at 106–7.

aspects are unique to Christ: being sent 1) as 'Son' and 2) 'in the likeness of the flesh of sin'.

Campbell points out that the son language used in Romans 8 (8.3, 14, 19, 29, 32) only occurs sparsely in the letter both before (1.3–4, 9; 5.10) and after (9.9, 26–27) and that its emphasis is primarily on the obedience of the Son in relation to the Father (and the Spirit).[42] Paul discusses Christ as 'God's Son' in the context of incarnation and resurrection (1.3–4) and death (5.10).[43] Based on his analysis of sending language in various ancient traditions, Schweizer notes how Pauline texts (Gal 4.4–5; and Rom 8.3) are similar to the sending of Wisdom, but he ultimately argues for the uniqueness of these sending passages because of the *son* language. [44] Though pre-existence is not explicit in the sending passages, Schweizer argues that these statements assume 'that Jesus was living in a filial relation to God before being sent by him'.[45] No evidence is given as to the nature of Christ's pre-existence, so this pre-existent state would presumably be that of divinity of some sort.[46] Schweizer importantly notes the consistent association in the NT with sending, sonship, and Christ's death. This becomes clear in discussion of the 'flesh of sin' language.

---

[42] Douglas A. Campbell, 'The Story of Jesus in Romans and Galatians' in *Narrative Dynamics in Paul: A Critical Assessment,* ed. Bruce W. Longenecker (London: Westminster John Knox, 2002), 97–124, 104, 107. According to Campbell ('Story of Jesus', 113–18), the basis of Paul's son language is two passages – Genesis 22 and Psalm 89. The Genesis passage which has a direct allusion in 8.32 (Gen 22.12 'οὐκ ἐφείσω τοῦ υἱοῦ σου') accounts for the sending work of the Father and the obedient death of the son, both of which show sacrificial divine love for humanity. At the same time, royal messianic theology in Psalm 89 and other related texts (2 Sam 7.14–16; Ps 2.7–8; and Psalm 110) foresee an elevated status of the messianic figure and use sonship language to communicate this.

[43] Other passages also mention suffering/death and resurrection (e.g., 5.5–8; 6.9–10; 8.34; 14.9) as central to Christ's work without explicitly noting his status as Son, though some of these are in son contexts (5.5–10 and 8.34).

[44] Eduard Schweizer, 'What Do We Really Mean When We Say "God sent his son..."?' in *Faith and History: Essays in Honor of Paul W. Meyer,* eds. John T. Carroll, et al. (Atlanta: Scholars Press, 1990), 298–312.

[45] Ibid., 306. Ultimately, the son language distinguishes these sending formulae from other Jewish and Greek writings, such that 'this excludes both a mere commission of human being (a prophet) and a sending of a being that is no "partner" of God (either a subordinate being, such as an angel, or the spirit, word, and wisdom of God, which are not really distinguishable from him)'. Schweizer, 'What Do We Really Mean', 311.

[46] Brendan Byrne ('Christ's Pre-Existence in Pauline Soteriology', *TS* 58 [1997]: 308–30, at 321) writes: 'In the light of the pre-existence implied in Phil 2:6–8 and 2 Cor 8:9, it makes good sense to see them, notably the sending statements in Rom 8:3–4 and Gal 4:4–5 (see John 3:16–17; 1 John 4:9), as also presenting the phenomenon of Christ as an invasion of divine grace and generosity into the human sphere from outside'.

Building upon his earlier discussion about Christ coming in the flesh (1.3), Paul now describes Christ's existence as 'in the likeness of the flesh of sin'.[47] Focusing on the nature of the 'likeness' (ὁμοίωμα) of the flesh of sin, a common interpretation is that this verse allows a dual focus: Christ had a real body which experienced physical corruption but was not under the power of sin in the flesh as a sinner.[48] Alternatively, Jewett argues against this bifurcated reading of ὁμοίωμα because it is based upon an unfounded dual emphasis: the concrete reality of Christ's humanity (of flesh) and only a similarity to the sinful flesh (flesh of sin).[49] Thus, while the discussion often focuses on the question of ὁμοίωμα,[50] ἁμαρτία is really the word that influences the meaning most. Accordingly, based on the context of the law and the power of sin, Paulsen argues 'daß in der Formulierung ἐν ὁμοιώματι σαρκὸς ἁμαρτίας in Verbindung mit σάρξ das ἁμαρτίας den Ton der paulinischen Argumentation trägt'.[51]

With the modifier ἁμαρτίας, one might expect that Paul is employing σάρξ pejoratively, functioning in an attributive sense: 'sinful flesh' or flesh that is characterised by sinfulness.[52] Like 7.5 and 7.25 where Paul also associates σάρξ and ἁμαρτία, we see that the flesh, similar to the law, is animated by other controlling influences. Wilckens appropriately offers this consideration: 'Doch der Gedanke der Sündlosigkeit Jesu liegt dem Text fern. σάρξ ἁμαρτίας ("Sündenfleisch") bezeichnet den *Wirklichkeitsbereich* der Sünde, in den hinein Gott seinen Sohn so gesandt hat, daß Christus *darin* den Menschen als Sündern gleichgeworden ist'.[53] Christ not only takes on flesh, the source of weakness of the law, but he comes in the 'flesh of sin'. This means 'identification with the human condition, not mere similarity. Had the Son been only "like" flesh, he could not have condemned the sin "in the flesh," precisely where Paul had located the problem'.[54] God sent Christ in the manner of the greatest weakness of humanity – in the flesh, which made the law weak and people unable to fulfil

---

[47] For Gnostic readings see Elaine Pagels, *The Gnostic Paul: Gnostic Exegesis of the Pauline Letters* (Philadelphia: Fortress, 1975), 33.

[48] Käsemann, *Romans*, 217. Cf. Moo, *Romans*, 478–80.

[49] Robert Jewett, *Paul's Anthropological Terms: A Study of Their Use in Conflict Settings* (Leiden: Brill, 1971), 151–52.

[50] E.g., Vincent Branick, 'The Sinful Flesh of the Son of God (Rom 8:3): A Key Image of Pauline Theology', *CBQ* 47 (1985): 246–62, at 248–50.

[51] Henning Paulsen, *Uberlieferung und Auslegung in Römer 8* (Neukirchen-Vluyn: Neukirchener Verlag, 1974), 59.

[52] Cf. τὰ παθήματα τῶν ἁμαρτιῶν (7.5).

[53] Wilckens, *Römer*, 2:125–26, emphasis original.

[54] Leander E. Keck, 'The Law And 'The Law of Sin and Death' (Romans 8:1–4): Reflections on the Spirit and Ethics in Paul' in *The Divine Helmsman: Studies on God's Control of Human Events, Presented to Lou H. Silberman*, eds. J.L. Crenshaw and S. Sandmel (New York: KTAV, 1980), 41–57, at 49–50.

God's requirements. However, this is not just flesh as in a physical body, but flesh characterised by mortality and corruption resulting from sin. In that way, God was able to condemn sin 'ἐν τῇ σαρκί', which points directly to Christ's death.[55]

By sharing in humanity's mortal condition and condemning sin through his death, Christ liberates believers from death and corruption stemming from the flesh (8.1–2).[56] God had to condemn sin in the flesh because the flesh rendered humans incapable of fulfilling the law, as 7.7–25 explores.[57] Thus, instead of the flesh being the cause of weakness of the law and the avenue for sin, God uses it to overcome sin, to condemn it.

Paul describes Christ's action as being sent περὶ ἁμαρτίας; this could mean generically 'for sins' or more specifically 'as a sin offering'. While I am drawn towards the 'sin offering' reading,[58] the nature of the cultic sacrifice here is outside our scope. However, the important point for our consideration is that his sacrificial death is the primary emphasis of the Son's sending.[59] No separation is made here between representation (believers die with Christ) and substitution (Christ dies for believers).

With Christ's incarnation and death evident in 8.3–4, does his resurrection have a soteriological role in the context? It does, but only in an implied manner. First, the closely related passage 7.1–6 explicitly marks Christ's death and resurrection as liberating events: believers die to the law through the death of Christ's body and are subsequently joined to the risen Christ (7.4).[60] Thus, freedom entails association with his resurrection and

---

[55] James D.G. Dunn ('Paul's Understanding of the Death of Jesus' in *Sacrifice and Redemption: Durham Essays in Theology,* ed. S.W. Sykes [Cambridge: Cambridge University Press, 1991], 35–56, 37, emphasis original) writes: 'Flesh is not evil, it is simply weak and corruptible. It signifies man in his weakness and corruptibility, his belonging to the world .... *Sarx hamartias* does not signify *guilty* man, but man in his *fallenness* – man subject to temptation, to human appetites and desires, to corruption and death'.

[56] Condemnation is associated with death in this letter (see §1.2 above) and other Jewish literature (e.g., Mark 10.33; 14.64; Daniel 4.37a [LXX]; Susanna 1.41, 53).

[57] Christ's death reconciles to God (e.g., 3.24–25; 5.6–10) and as a formative pattern for believers – they die with Christ to sin (6.6, 10–11) and the law (7.4) and are thus freed from their dominion. Clearly, Christ's death is foundational for the liberation of humanity from Sin and Death, which use the law and the Flesh as their minions.

[58] Περὶ ἁμαρτίας is used some 60+ times in relation to the sin offering in the LXX tradition, e.g., Leviticus 4, 5, 16. Earlier in Romans Paul describes Christ's death as a ἱλαστήριον, which also replicates cultic language.

[59] Wright ('Vindication', 223–25) demonstrates from chapter 7 that Paul compares Christ's death to that of the animal sacrificed for atonement in the context of unwilling sins. This along with the OT lexical association lends weight to the 'sin offering' reading.

[60] Cf. also 8.32 where Paul explicitly includes the resurrection.

the ability to serve by the Spirit. Second, we discussed in §2.1 how the declaration of *life* is fulfilled in those who 'walk (περιπατέω) according to the Spirit' (8.4). The only other use of περιπατέω in Romans to this point is 6.4, where Paul speaks of those who presently walk in new life based upon Christ's own resurrection. Later, we see Christ's resurrection as the model for believers in 8.11, showing that if God was powerful enough to raise Christ through the Spirit who now indwells believers, they will also experience that same resurrection. However, it is important to note that the focus is the efficatious act of Jesus' death in enabling believers to fulfil the law not the resurrection as it is in other passages. In fact, it is through the cross that the δικαίωμα is fulfilled 'in us' (ἐν ἡμῖν) not merely for us (8.4).

In contrast to Sin, Death, and the Flesh as powers dominating humans, Paul presents the liberating power of Christ's incarnation and death. The focus is not the incarnation itself; rather, the incarnation serves as one step in the larger process of defeating sin. Christ had to experience physically corrupted flesh in order to become the locus of God's condemnation of sin in the flesh. Those who begin to experience new life from the Spirit, which will be consummated fully in the future, experience the benefits of this atoning death.[61] Thus, no arbitrary separation should be made between these three foci.

2.3 Spheres of Existence: Flesh and Spirit (8.4–13)

With the purpose clause in 8.4, Paul turns to his development of the flesh-Spirit dualism in 8.4–13. In chapter 7 the law was shown to be ineffective due to the problem of sin and the flesh. Here in chapter 8 Paul now addresses the core problem of the flesh in contrast to the Spirit. In 8.5–6 he establishes the dualism between the two ways of life, or rather spheres of existence. Then he provides a more developed exploration of each aspect – flesh (8.7–8) and Spirit (8.9–11) – and concludes with an implied exhortation to live according to the Spirit rather than the flesh (8.12–13) as an inference of his discussion in 8.1–11.

Those that take 7.7–25 as speaking about a Christian tend to emphasise the flesh-Spirit dialectic as a present struggle within the believer.[62] Paul does not speak of moving between the realms of flesh to Spirit or upon an internal battle of the will. Rather, he presents the flesh and Spirit as mutually exclusive, alternative spheres of existence, which are ultimately characterised by death and life. Bertone captures this well: 'Paul uses σάρξ over against πνεῦμα not as a description of anthropological dualism (i.e., the internal struggle of the sinful nature with the Spirit) but as a descrip-

---

[61] If the reading of δικαίωμα as the decree of life holds in 8.4, the purpose clause in 8.4 offers a connection between Christ's death and resurrection.

[62] E.g., Cranfield, *Romans*, 1:385.

tion of one's orientation with respect to God in salvation-history'.[63] Thus, the picture Paul paints in 8.1–11 is black and white. He later presents a more nuanced picture with shades of grey in 8.12–13, where the power of the flesh intrudes on those who are ἐν πνεύματι.

Paul's anthropology shines through in this section, in that the outer-inner duality of humans is clear.[64] Importantly, this does not simply correspond to the flesh-Spirit dualism with which Paul works. The mind can be under the sway of the flesh or the Spirit (8.5–8). At the same time, the body is dead due to the effects of sin, whereas the body under the power of the Spirit will be raised to life, just as Christ was (8.9–11). Thus, the body-mind duality which is central for this section is intimately influenced by Paul's present-future duality.

2.3.1 The Problem of the Flesh

Christ and the law move to the background, and the Spirit and the flesh move to the foreground. This is interesting because the Spirit has played such a minor role in the letter to this point. Previous passages briefly, but significantly, mention the Spirit: Christ's Davidic sonship κατὰ σάρκα vis-à-vis divine sonship κατὰ πνεῦμα (Rom 1.3–4) and the love of God through the Spirit poured into hearts (Rom 5.5). A more engaged discussion occurs in Romans 2 where Paul explores obedience to the law and circumcision and then claims that the only true circumcision is of the heart by the Spirit (2.28–29). The same cluster of terminology from 2.28–29 – νόμος, σάρξ, πνεῦμα, and γράμμα – finds itself repeated in Rom 7.1–6. In addition, the theme of each passage centres on obedience and bearing fruit. Thus, we are not surprised that when Paul finally engages pneumatology extensively in chapter 8 as an exposition of 7.6, it centres around pleasing God through renewed obedience.

When discussing Christ's incarnation and death, I argued that corrupted physical nature is the meaning of flesh in that context, but the characterisation of flesh here seems to be taking on a greater scope. In Galatians Barclay finds three problems associated with the flesh – libertinism, social

---

[63] John A. Bertone, *"The Law of the Spirit": Experience of the Spirit and Displacement of the Law in Romans 8:1–16* (Studies in Biblical Literature 86; Berlin: Peter Lang, 2005), 184.

[64] Following Aune and others, I use 'duality' to denote a distinction and/or tension and 'dualism' to denote a conflict and/or opposition: David E. Aune, 'Anthropological Duality in the Eschatology of 2 Cor 4:16–5:10', in *Paul Beyond the Judaism/Hellenism Divide*, Troels Engberg-Pedersen, ed., (Louisville: Westminster John Knox Press, 2001), 215–239, at 220.

disunity, and law-observance – is this how we should summarise the problems associated with the flesh in Romans?[65]

Particularly important for Paul in Romans 6 and 7 is the negative influence the flesh (σάρξ) plays in conjunction with law. Σάρξ has been used in the letter several times previously, focusing on physicality without a necessarily pejorative meaning (1.3; 2.28; 3.20; 4.1), although its association with circumcision in 2.28 could make it a cipher here for law observance. However, in 6.19 Paul associates 'weakness' with the flesh and develops this further as he relates flesh to 'sinful desires' (7.5), 'nothing good' (7.18), and slavery to the law of sin (7.25, cf. 7.23). In fact, the flesh actively works against the mind and serves as the area in the individual where the law of sin has free reign (7.22–25).

Building on this negative characterisation in chapter 7, σάρξ becomes a focus of attention in the first half of chapter 8. Central to his portrayal of the flesh is its ability to weaken and subvert the law through the work of sin (8.3). It is associated with being an 'enemy of God' (8.7) and not being able to submit to him (8.7). The flesh is hostile to God (8.7) and ultimately leads to death (8.6). By associating it with death, Paul links it with the powers of Sin and Death. Also, this juxtaposition with the life-giving Spirit furthers Paul's death-life antithesis. The flesh is thus associated with law-observance, sinful desires, and individual disunity.

There are two general ways of reading this language: 1) as a description of a person's anthropology, or 2) a description of a personified agent working against the individual. These aspects – law-observance, sinful desires, and individual disunity – seem anthropologically focused and thus perhaps solely focused on the individual instead of as a personified agent. For instance, Engberg-Pedersen offers an individualistically-focused reading: 'The flesh will stand for any feature than an individual may single out as being specific to him- or herself as that particular individual – over and against any features that he or she will share with others'.[66]

In constrast, Barclay's discussion of the flesh-Spirit antithesis in Galatians presents an alternative perspective that would apply here as well. Following Käsemann's apocalyptic reading over the individualising ten-

---

[65] John M.G. Barclay, *Obeying the Truth: Paul's Ethics in Galatians* (Edinburgh: T&T Clark, 1988), 211–12.

[66] Troels Engberg-Pedersen, *Paul and the Stoics* (Edinburgh: T&T Clark, 2000), 153. Engberg-Pedersen more recently offered a more 'apocalyptic' reading of Paul, which attempts to integrate Paul's apocalypticism with his ethics: idem., 'The Material Spirit: Cosmology and Ethics in Paul', *NTS* 55 (2009): 179–97; and now his *Cosmology and Self*. The minimisation of the Spirit's agency is a central weakness to Engberg-Pedersen's construction. The Spirit in Paul's theology is not merely the material of the eschatological world, but the agent of God's eschatological renewal. Cf. Volker Rabens, *The Holy Spirit and Ethics in Paul*; Fee, *Empowering Presence*.

dencies of Bultmann, Barclay describes Paul's language of σάρξ in Galatians as 'what is merely human', as an apocalyptic category such that 'in the light of the glory of God's activity in the new age, all human achievements and traditions are put into the shade'.[67] In light of the overlap of the ages, Martyn notes that the flesh-Spirit war forms the antinomy of the new age surpassing the old antinomies, such as Jew-Gentile, slave-free, and male-female.[68] These are larger struggles beyond just that of the individual.

Paul's emphasis on φρόνημα in conjunction with both flesh and Spirit shows that the realm of the flesh is not just a power; rather, it infiltrates to the innermost region of the individual. Knox captures this interplay well with his discussion of σάρξ: 'the "fallen" world of which he is part is also a part of him – present within his own personality. Sin, which he thinks of as an external, demonic, almost personal power, has taken residence, so to speak, within the boundaries of his own personal existence'.[69] Accordingly, the problem of the flesh is both inter- and intrapersonal. The person who stands in the sphere of flesh cannot please God because s/he stands in opposition to God, as his enemy. However, the effections are not just relational. Ultimately, life in the flesh is characterised by corruption and death, affecting both the moral, noetic, and somatic aspects of an individual (7.4–5; 8.6, 13).

2.3.2 The Life of the Spirit

In contrast to the life in the flesh which places one in opposition to God and brings death, the Spirit of life unites believers to God and gives them life. In the early part of the passage the focus of this life is moral and noetic. Through Christ and the Spirit the inability to please God because of the flesh is overcome (8.3–8), and this new life is expressed as bearing fruit for God (7.4–6). The law cannot enable believers to please God because of the flesh, and those in the flesh are enemies of God (8.7–8). On the other hand, those who 'walk (περιπατέω) according to the Spirit' (8.4) implicitly please God. As noted above, this 'walk' reflects walking in new life in 6.4.[70] Cranfield thus writes: 'This newness of life is the moral as-

---

[67] Ibid., 208.

[68] J. Louis Martyn, *Theological Issues in the Letters of Paul* (Nashville, TN: Abingdon, 1997), 118.

[69] John Knox, *Life in Christ Jesus: Reflections on Romans 5–8* (New York: Seabury, 1961), 84.

[70] Paul regularly uses περιπατέω in moral contexts (cf. Rom 6.4; 13.13; 1 Cor 3.3; 7.17; 2 Cor 4.2; 10.2; Gal 5.16).

pect of that life which is really life which is promised in the scriptural quotation in 1.17'.[71]

A significant aspect of this present life is that of the mind. The φρόνημα, which is central to Paul's presentation of one's sphere of existence, is determined by flesh or Spirit and leads respectively to death or life and peace (8.6). Those in the Spirit stand in contrast to those whose thinking became depraved (1.18–32), and the noetic focused parenesis in 12.1–2 fits well Paul's subsequent encouragement not to live according to the flesh in 8.12–13.[72]

In the current overlap of ages, one's sphere of existence does not compel action in one way or another. Though believers exist in the sphere of Christ and the Spirit, they still have the opportunity to live according to the flesh, which produces death (8.12–13). However, those who 'by the Spirit put to death the practices of the body will live' (8.13). The fact that believers are no longer obligated to live according to the flesh shows that they have been liberated from its controlling power over them, but they still must battle against its influence in their lives through mortification. Just as in Deut 30.11–20 where the Israelites were given the option of choosing life or death by following the law or ignoring it, Paul presents the same life and death choice but now determined by the flesh or the Spirit.

The life in Christ and the Spirit is not limited to the mind and moral enablement in the present age. Paul correlates the present life of obedience with the future somatic experience of resurrection in 8.4–13 as in Rom 6.4–14.[73] Although the body is presently mortal because of the effects of sin (8.10),[74] Christ's resurrection is the model for believers in 8.11, showing that if God was powerful enough to raise Christ through the Spirit who now indwells believers, they will also experience that same resurrection.

In 8.10 this life through the Spirit is neatly juxtaposed to δικαιοσύνη.[75] This verse directly follows the same pattern we noted in 1.16–17, where

---

[71] Cranfield, *Romans*, 1:305. Cf. Gorman, *Inhabiting*, 66–68. *Pace* Käsemann (*Romans*, 166–67), who overemphasises Paul's eschatological caution here.

[72] The 'morphic' language later in the chapter in 8.29 and in 12.2 also shows the connections between these two chapters.

[73] This current new life is clarified in 6.11–13 where Paul encourages believers to obey God rather than allowing sin to reign as 'living to God' (6.11) or 'living from the dead' (6.13). Accordingly, as believers walk in the Spirit (of life) they experience the new life exhibited in Christ's resurrection. This present moral enablement serves as a sign for the future physical resurrection (6.5, 8).

[74] The reference to the body's death here does not, I think, correspond to the baptism event of dying to sin as Käsemann argues. Käsemann, *Romans*, 224. See Bertone, *Law of the Spirit*, 188–89.

[75] Rudolf Bultmann, *Theology of the New Testament* (trans. Kendrick Grobel; 2 vols.; London: SCM, 1952), 1:270–71. This association is clear in 4.25; 5.17, 18, 21; 6.13; 10.9–10. We will also see this association in 8.30.

righteousness leads to new life. The unique aspect here is the Spirit's agency. Paul does not develop it here, but several points may be made: 1) This justification is not merely an affirmation of status; rather it is established by the Spirit's presence. 2) Resurrection constitutes believers' vindication (justification). 3) Since resurrection life (8.10–11) is correlated to moral life (7.4–6; 8.4–10) through the Spirit, there does not need to be a bifurcation between acquittal and the later life of the believer. It is all the work of God through the Spirit on account of Christ. Thus, the presence of the Spirit and Christ will bring holistic renewal to believers as they experience moral, noetic, and somatic life.

In contrast to flesh as the agent of death, God enables believers to participate in him in order that they can experience life. Paul uses a variety of images, primarily through prepositional phrases, to present the idea of participation. Paul defines believers in 8.1 as οἱ ἐν Χριστῷ Ἰησοῦ, as those within the sphere of Christ's control and power (a local use of the preposition), whereas in 8.2 the act of liberation is described as ἐν Χριστῷ Ἰησοῦ, as through the work of Christ (an instrumental use of the preposition), which is further explored in 8.3–4[76]

At the same time, Paul describes human relationships with flesh/Spirit using prepositional phrases. He introduces the contrast as walking κατὰ σάρκα/πνεῦμα (8.4). As a clarification, Paul explains that οἱ ὄντες κατὰ σάρκα/πνεῦμα follow the ways of flesh/Spirit, as a party member to a way of thought (8.5).[77] Later, Paul describes them as οἱ ὄντες ἐν σαρκί/ πνεύματι (8.8–9).

In 8.9–14 Paul describes the believer-Christ/Spirit relationship with even more variety. Believers are ἐν πνεύματι if the Spirit οἰκεῖ ἐν ὑμῖν (8.9). Then, 'if someone does not have the Spirit of Christ, that one is not of him (αὐτοῦ)' (8.9). Also, just as Christ is ἐν ὑμῖν (8.10), the Spirit of the one who raised Jesus (ἐν)οἰκεῖ ἐν ὑμῖν (8.11, twice). Finally, Paul twice describes *living* κατὰ σάρκα in opposition to an implied κατὰ πνεῦμα (8.12–13).

The variety and the reciprocal nature of the phrases show that the relationships are deeper and more complex than any one phrase can describe. Being ἐν Χριστῷ seems to be equivalent to being ἐν πνεύματι and living κατὰ πνεῦμα. At the same time, Christ ἐν ὑμῖν is equivalent to the Spirit

---

[76] See §2.2 above for further discussion. The husband-wife metaphor in 7.1–6 also sheds light on the Christ-believer relationship. There, the widowed wife is free to remarry (γενομένην ἀνδρὶ ἑτέρῳ; 7.3). As Paul applies this metaphor to believers he describes them as being freed from the law through the death of Christ to be joined to another (εἰς τὸ γενέσθαι ὑμᾶς ἑτέρῳ), the risen Christ (7.4).

[77] Φρονέω here does not simply mean 'to think about' but reflects a choice to follow a particular faction or party: '*take someone's side, espouse someone's cause*' (BDAG, 1066).

ἐν ὑμῖν. Not only do believers now exist in the sphere of Christ and the Spirit, Christ and the Spirit reside personally within each believer.[78] The result of this self-communication to believers is that they experience their attributes – particularly, that of life.

2.4 Conclusion

Moving from the enslaved person in chapter 7, Paul presents a stark contrast of liberation secured through Christ and the Spirit. With the problem of the flesh, the law cannot enable those who attempt to follow it. In contrast, Christ and the Spirit serve as agents liberating those in Christ from sin and death. Through Christ's incarnation he shared in the heart of human weakness – the flesh of sin – and through death broke the power of sin. Instead of bearing the fruit of death associated with the flesh (cf. 7.5), believers enjoy the benefits of new life as they serve God through the Spirit (cf. 7.6). This new life is not just moral enablement and noetic life, but it also culminates in the resurrection of the body, also by means of the Spirit. This present-future experience of life and death reveals Paul's already/not yet eschatology. As the means to enjoying the benefits of Christ and the Spirit, Paul uses a variety of overlapping phrases to describe the participatory relationship.

2.5 Excursus: Colossians 2.6–3.4

One of the tensions in Rom 8.1–13 is the use of seemingly absolute language in 8.1-11, with being in the Spirit or in the flesh as mutually exclusive categories. Then Paul gives encouragement for those in the Spirit not to make provision for the flesh, as if the categories are more complex. Another central passage in the Pauline corpus that situates the believer between the past experience of dying and rising with Christ and the present (and future) life in light of that is Colossians 2–3. This passage was not used by either of our writers to support and express their conceptions of deification, but it has some of the most theotic language in the Pauline corpus. As a result, since it has similar thematic parallels to Romans 8 (and Romans 6), I have included our discussion of Colossians 2–3 here.[79]

While we are drawn to Colossians 2–3 out of interest in a broad sample of Paul's soteriological passages, we cannot help but focus on Col 2.9–10 because of its central role in the larger section but also its theotic emphasis. In 2.8 Paul says that the Colossians are being taken captive by phi-

---

[78] While the Spirit and Christ are closely related – God sending Christ to condemn sin explains the Spirit-given liberation – the distinction between the two is not lost.

[79] However, it should be noted that this passage has less direct affinities with Romans 8 than the other excursus do with their respective passages.

losophy and by empty deceit and this is 'according to human tradition, according to the στοιχεῖα τοῦ κόσμου and not according to Christ'. He then gives the basic response in 2.9–10 that serves as the basis of his warning through 2.23 and also his exhortations in chapter 3. He writes: this philosophy is not according to Christ 'because in him all the fullness of deity dwells bodily, and in him you are filled' (ὅτι ἐν αὐτῷ κατοικεῖ πᾶν τὸ πλήρωμα τῆς θεότητος σωματικῶς, καὶ ἐστὲ ἐν αὐτῷ πεπληρωμένοι; Col 2.9–10).

Questions often arise about the nature of this bodily dwelling of 'all the fullness of deity' (πᾶν τὸ πλήρωμα τῆς θεότητος) in Christ, but with the parallel use of filling language (πληρόω) in 2.10, it appears that believers are filled with this deity through Christ. This exegetical option is often quickly denied by most interpreters. For instance, O'Brien says that being filled with deity is 'asserting too much',[80] and Dunn calls it 'rhetorical and hyperbolic' language.[81] On the other hand, Wedderburn in his discussion of the theology of Colossians notes that the parallel nature of the language in 2.9–10 means that believers are 'also presumably [filled] with deity'.[82] Thus, with this debate before us, we will explore what it means to be 'filled in him' in 2.10 and how this relates to the question of deification. Before we can understand believers' filling, we must first attend to the nature of Christ's own filling in 2.9.

2.5.1 Colossians 2.9: 'All the fullness of deity dwells in him bodily'

Col 2.9 begins with an emphatic ἐν αὐτῷ. This reflects the Christo-centrism of this passage and the letter as a whole.[83] Since the deceptive philosophy is not in accordance with Christ, Paul provides a string of statements that are based around Christ throughout this chapter. And after the Christ hymn in chapter 1 this affirmation in 2.9, which echoes 1.19, is one of the explicit descriptions of who Christ is.

Although the focus on Christ is clear, the meaning of 'all the fullness of deity' is debated.[84] In particular, interpreters debate whether this 'dwelling

---

[80] Peter T. O'Brien, *Colossians-Philemon* (WBC 44; Waco: Word Books, 1982), 113.

[81] James D.G. Dunn, *The Epistles to the Colossians and to Philemon* (NIGTC; Grand Rapids: Eerdmans, 1996), 152.

[82] A.J.M. Wedderburn, 'Theology of Colossians' in *The Theology of the Later Pauline Letters*, Andrew T. Lincoln and A.J.M Wedderburn, eds., (Cambridge: CUP, 1993), 1–71, at 31.

[83] This Christo-centrism is evident from the repeated use of Christ with different prepositions: ἐν 1.14, 16, 17, 19, 28; 2.3, 6, 7, 9, 10, 11, 12, [15?]; also διά 1.16, 20 and εἰς 1.16, 20.

[84] Fullness does not seem to be drawn from the Colossian opponents because it is drawn from the Christ hymn. Cf. Petr Pokorný, *Colossians: A Commentary* (Peabody: Hendrickson, 1991), 121n71.

is' primarily ontological or functional. The former position appears to garner the majority of support. Pointing to literary Greek, Dunn, for instance, argues θεότης 'was sufficiently familiar in literary Greek to denote the nature or essence of deity, that which constitutes deity'.[85] Most taking this route point back to Lightfoot who quotes Plutarch on the distinction between θεότης (divine essence or nature) and θειότης (divine attributes), a distinction between deity and divinity. While this may be the case, investing heavily in this distinction in this *hapax* for Paul seems unwarranted.[86]

An alternative reading for this phrase focuses on the functional aspect of Christ's embodiment of deity. That is, Christ's identity is established along functional rather than ontological terms. Thus, as Christ fulfils the divine mission in the world, God's will is revealed and accomplished. O'Brien, in particular, takes issue with this reading of this passage: The filling in verse 10 is 'meaningful only if [Christ] is the one in whom the plenitude of deity is embodied. If the fullness of deity does not reside in him then the Colossians' fullness would not amount to much at all'.[87] Others, while not addressing this passage directly, have challenged this distinction between ontology and function, such as Barth, Gunton, and Watson as they argue that being is displayed through act.[88] We can affirm that Christ embodies divine activity, but there is little evidence here to separate this from ontology. While Hay works from a distinction in function and ontology, he still captures the sentiment of this verse:

Christology does not replace theology, but interprets it .... Hence, in fundamental ways Christ can be understood only when his relationship to God is grasped; on the other hand, God is known through Christ and, evidently, adequately know only through Christ. The distinction between Christ and God is developed in functional rather than ontological terms.[89]

Consequently, the ontological reading seems best, but it should not be separated from the functional expression of it.

---

[85] Dunn, *Colossians and Philemon*, 151.

[86] I have not seen any interaction with H.S. Nash ('θειότης – θεότης, Rom. i.20; Col. ii.9', *JBL* 18 [1899], 1–34), who argues strongly against seeing a firm distinction between these two terms here.

[87] O'Brien, *Colossians-Philemon*, 112.

[88] See the discussion in Gorman, *Inhabiting*, 32–34. Cf. Bruce McCormack, 'Participation in God, Yes, Deification, No: Two Modern Protestant Responses to an Ancient Question' in *Denkwürdiges Geheimnis: Beiträge zur Gotteslehre. Festschrift für Eberhard Jüngel zum 70. Geburtstag,* eds. Ingolf U. Dalferth, et al. (Tübingen: Mohr Siebeck, 2004), 347–74.

[89] David M. Hay, 'All the Fullness of God: Concepts of Deity in Colossians and Ephesians' in *The Forgotten God: Perspectives in Biblical Theology,* A. Andrew Das and Frank J. Matera, eds., (Louisville: WJK, 2002), 163–79, at 169–70.

Paul qualifies this dwelling with the term σωματικῶς. While most understand this σωματικῶς indwelling as referring to Christ's own bodily experience, the other primary options for interpreting σωματικῶς stem from other ways that Paul uses the term σῶμα in Colossians. In 1.18 and 1.24 (cf. 2.19; 3.15) Paul appositionally describes Christ's σῶμα as 'the church', but in 2.17 Paul also contrasts σῶμα with σκιά, which draws out the contrast between that which is temporal and substantial. Thus, it can be read literally as Christ's body, metaphorically as the church, or as that which is substantial (i.e., 'in reality').

Since the meaning of 'reality' in 2.17 is highly influenced by the co-occurrence of σκιά, that referent seems less likely here. Besides the affirmation of the σῶμα as the church in 1.18 and 1.24, the present tense of κατοικέω also stands as evidence for the ecclesial reading.[90] This reading is plausible (cf. Eph 1.23; 3.19) but not likely because the ecclesial reading makes the statement in 2.10 a tautology, and it presents difficulties for reading 1.19.[91] Thus, I follow the majority in reading σωματικῶς as a referent to Jesus' bodily existence.

With 2.9 Paul attempts to reorient the Colossians' theology around Christ rather than a merely human philosophy driven by the στοιχεῖα τοῦ κόσμου. He thus affirms God's divine indwelling in Christ bodily. The distinct implication is that God's work is not antithetical to somatic existence, nor is the body necessarily ruled by the στοιχεῖα τοῦ κόσμου, as the later discussion in chapter 2 shows. Also, Christ's bodily experience redefines what we understand as God's work. That is, for Paul we can no longer talk about what God does without first and foremost looking to the experience of Christ.

2.5.2 Colossians 2.10: 'You are filled in him'

If 2.9 argues that Christ is the only proper *basis for* soteriology because of the divine indwelling, 2.10 argues that the only true *experience of* soteriology is through him. Just as all the fullness (πλήρωμα) of deity dwells in Christ, believers 'have been filled (πληρόω) in him'. Since the Colossians were being drawn away by this empty philosophy, they were looking into various spiritual exercises for fulfilment. Paul's response is that these are

---

[90] M. Bogdasavich, 'The Idea of Pleroma in the Epistles to the Colossians and Ephesians', *The Downside Review* 83 (1965), 118–30, at 127–28; Bradley J. Matthews, 'A Theology of Christian Maturity with Special Reference to Ephesians and Colossians' (Ph.D. Thesis, University of Durham, 2008), 153–55. Primary proponents for a functional reading of the Christology also seriously entertain or argue for an ecclesial reading of σωματικῶς: Hay, 'All the Fullness of God' and Suzanne Watts Henderson, 'God's Fullness in Bodily Form: Christ and Church in Colossians' 118 *ET* (2007): 169-73.

[91] Pokorný (*Colossians*, 122) points out that Christ is the head not the body.

all inadequate avenues to the most fulfilling experience. Deity is to be found in Christ and your experience of completeness and fullness is through being filled in him.[92]

While Paul represents the fullness of deity dwelling in Christ with a present tense verb (κατοικέω), he describes the filling of believers with a periphrastic construction with a present form of εἰμί with a perfect participle, which, according to standard grammar, points to a filling that began in the past with continuing effects in the present.[93] Believers are thus already filled and will continue to experience its effects. The purpose of Paul's assertion seems clearer than the content of his assertion. Commentators are almost unanimous on this account, but they differ on the nature of the filling if they discuss it at all. So what is the nature of this fullness or this filling? There are three primary options which have been proposed.

2.5.2.1 Presence of Salvation

The majority position is that Paul is pointing out that the fullness of the presence of salvation is found in Christ. This is therefore a comprehensive statement about how all things pertaining to salvation are experienced through Christ, and some summarise this with the language of 'fullness of life'.[94] Agreeing with this, O'Brien points to the variety of 'fillings' that Paul uses to describe 'godly qualities or graces', such as, 'joy and peace' (Rom 15.13), 'fruit of righteousness' (Phil 1.11), 'every need' (Phil 4.19), 'knowledge of his will' (Col 1.9).[95] Others like Barclay associate this with Paul's concern for maturity in the letter.[96] To be sure this filling is comprehensive, and this reading makes sense of the purpose of the statement, but I would argue that the immediate context leads us to be more specific.

2.5.2.2 Noetic Enlightenment

The next proposal is that of noetic enlightenment, a theme prominent in the letter. Another key text in Colossians with the terminology of πληρόω or

---

[92] This statement about filling seems to counter Paul's eschatological reserve in other letters; however, O'Brien argues that Paul is not concerned about Corinthian over-realised eschatology. The Colossians misunderstanding 'was the opposite temptation of thinking that "fullness" was beyond their grasp unless they took sufficient account of the spiritual powers and followed a strict discipline of ritual and ascetic observance' (*Colossians-Philemon*, 114).

[93] Daniel B. Wallace, *Greek Grammar Beyond the Basics: An Exegetical Syntax of the New Testament* (Grand Rapids: Zondervan, 1996), 647–48.

[94] Dunn, *Colossians and Philemon*, 153.

[95] O'Brien, *Colossians-Philemon*, 113.

[96] John M.G. Barclay, *Colossians and Philemon* (London: T&T Clark, 2004), 88. Cf. C.F.D. Moule, '"Fullness" and "Fill" in the New Testament', *SJT* 4 (1951), 78–86, at 85–86.

πλήρωμα is that of Col 1.9, where Paul speaks of being 'filled with the knowledge of God's will in all spiritual wisdom and understanding'. In two other texts Paul uses πληροφορία: Col 2.2, which speaks of 'all the riches of complete understanding', knowing the mystery of God which is Christ, and Col 4.12, 'stand mature and fully assured in God's will'. These three texts have a noetic focus with their discussion of knowledge, assurance of God's will and complete understanding of the mystery of God. Thus, the nature of the fullness would be a full understanding of God's work in Christ. This also would make sense of the the noetic emphasis of 3.1ff. While I do not think that this line of interpretation is wrong, I do not think it captures the breadth of the fullness. For instance, the context here does not seem to emphasise a singularly noetic fullness. Importantly, with the parallelism between 2.9 and 2.10, the fullness of deity dwelling in Christ *bodily* does not easily point to a *noetic* filling.

2.5.2.3 Functional Mission

Those who emphasise both the bodily language and the functional nature of the divine indwelling point towards a functional filling and rightly note Christ's authority over powers in 2.10. David Hay, for example, writes: 'Believers in verse 10 experience the divine fullness evidently because they share in Christ's sovereignty over all powers, but also because the energy of God is at work within them to give them new life in Christ'.[97] I agree that this filling entails a functional aspect, and Hay importantly brings in the issue of the powers and authorities, but he also works from a distinction between ontology and function that I have already argued against.

Each of the three readings of the filling highlight different aspects that need to be considered. How do we correlate this fullness of life with an embodiment of its truth and also this close placement of the discussion of the powers and authorities? Also, what importance does the fullness of deity play in this soteriological filling? My own reading draws these together.

2.5.3 Filled with Christ: The Embodiment of Christ's Death and Life

Rather than drawing from lexical parallels in other passages in Colossians, my proposed reading draws meaning from the immediate literary context of this passage. As a positive statement of Paul's core theology, Col 2.9–10 serves not only as a summary of the response to the empty philosophy

---

[97] David M. Hay, *Colossians* (ANTC; Nashville: Abingdon, 2000), 90. Cf. Hay, 'All the Fullness of God', 169–70; Watts Henderson, 'God's Fullness in Bodily Form', 172–73.

in 2.11–23 but also as the basis of his exhortations in chapter 3. Thus, my thesis is that being filled with Christ entails the narrative embodiment of Christ's death and life, as explicated in chapters 2 and 3. I will focus on 2.11–15 but we will note the repetition of key themes in later verses. Paul is not just discussing death and life as abstract soteriological experiences. Rather, he is using these fundamental categories to respond to the Colossian error, and specifically their relationship with the authorities and rulers, the στοιχεῖα τοῦ κόσμου, as we will see.

Col 2.12 aptly summarises Paul's emphasis of embodying Christ's death and life as the key to this passage: 'having been buried with him in baptism, you have also been raised with him through faith in the power of God'. In 2.11–13 Paul first discusses dying with Christ not only in terms of baptism but also of circumcision.[98] He then clarifies the problem: the Colossians were previously dead in their transgressions and in their uncircumcision of the flesh (2.13). Through this metaphorical circumcision by Christ and baptism with him, the source of death is removed from the believers.

But this is only one half of the coin. In 2.12, Paul writes: 'having been buried with him in baptism, ... you were also raised with him'. And also in 2.13: 'When you were dead in your transgressions and in the uncircumcision of your flesh, he made you alive with Christ'. Thus, death with Christ makes sense only when it is simultaneously associated with the life which God brings.[99] Importantly, Paul does not separate this past experience with Christ from their present ethical action and future somatic resurrection. For instance in 3.1 Paul repeats the terminology of συνεγείρω and συζωοποιέω from 2.12–13.[100] Space does not permit an exploration of these ideas here, but this moral and somatic life also correlates with the experience of glory (1.27, 3.4) and the conformation to Christ's image (1.15, 3.10).[101]

We cannot simply note the fullness of life because interpreters have also rightly noted the role the powers and authorities play in our text. Just as

---

[98] Believers' circumcision not made by human hands removes the flesh. The referent here is not fully clear because this is the first metaphorical use of σάρξ in the letter. The four previous occurrences refer to a physical body (1.22, 24; 2.1, 5).

[99] Thus the forensic and liberative aspects of soteriology are brought together in the new life given by God as believers are both forgiven and released from the powers over them.

[100] Cf. Barclay (*Colossians and Philemon*, 84) who writes: 'In 3.1–4 and in 2.11–13 the emphasis rests on the inclusion of the believer in the death-resurrection event, with notable statements that Christians have been raised with Christ (contrast Rom. 6.1–8)'.

[101] Thus Hay ('All the Fullness of God', 177) writes: 'The future "glory" or "inheritance" of believers seems conceived largely as a revelation or amplification of benefits already essentially experienced'.

Christ's own death disarmed the powers and authorities (2.15), when believers died with Christ, they are released from the powers and authorities (2.20). As a result, the embodiment of Christ's death and life explains both the fullness of the presence of salvation and the functional release from power of the στοιχεῖα τοῦ κόσμου.

Just as Christ's ontology is not separated from his narrative acts of death and life. This embodiment of Christ's death and life is not merely a metaphorical filling. Rather, their narrative embodiment of death and life is shown to be transformational. In particular, this death sets believers free from the powers. Also, this life is shown to be expressed morally and ontologically in 3.1–4 as believers think and experience eschatological life. Accordingly, there is not a simple division between act and being.

2.5.4 Conclusion: Christoformity is Theoformity

As the Christ hymn shows and then 2.9 reinforces, believers' understanding of God, that is, of deity, is now only understood in light of Christ. Christ, in fact, embodies deity, and Christ's divine ontology is revealed through his functional narrative of death and life. And believers are filled with Christ and thus embody a narrative of death and life in the past, present and future, which allows them to participate in deity through him.

Does this mean the believers are divine as Christ is divine? These compact verses of 2.9–10 do not give an absolute response, but we can see a key distinction in the terminology. All fullness of deity dwells in Christ, whereas believers are filled in him. That is, Christ is full; believers are filled. He has an unmediated experience whereas believers' experience is mediated. Thus, while act and being are not easily separated, we see that Christ and believers remain separate agents. As believers embody Christ's death and life, they are made christo-form, and even dei-form since deity dwells in him.

Other Pauline passages do not set Christ's relationship to God as explicitly as this passage, but the participatory relationship with Christ that determines the believers experience is directly equivalent to other Pauline passages that we will explore. While the death-life dialectic and the christo-form nature of salvation is central to this passage like that of Romans 8, what sets this passage apart from our Romans 8 context and our patristic interpreters is the lack of the Spirit's activity in mediating this experience. Thus, while this passage appears as one of the most theotic passages in the Pauline letters, perhaps it is the lack of the discussion of the Spirit that contributed to its neglect. Another central metaphor for deification in the patristic interpreters is that of adoption, and it draws directly from the next passages in our discussion of Romans 8.

3. Adoption: 8.14–17

Flowing from Paul's discussion of the work of the Spirit, he turns to adoption and sonship to explain further believers' experience of life and liberation. Serving as a transition, this passage maintains Spirit themes from earlier verses but introduces the dialectic of suffering and glory which is foundational for the next section. Yates rightly notes that 'from this point on his interest shifts to focus not on the contrast between the present life and former life, but on the tension between present life and future, glorified life'.[102] In our discussion of adoption, we will address how it shapes the people of God (§3.1), how it expands upon the liberation theme of the chapter (§3.2) and then how it is more than just a relational metaphor but presents a new ontological reality (§3.3). After exploring Romans 8, I then present an excursus on the sonship language in Galatians 4 because of its relevance to the topic (§3.4). As before, we will continue to see the role of new life as a present/future dialectic.

3.1 Adoption and the People of God

Central to the modern interpretation of the passage is the debate about whether Jewish or Greco-Roman conceptions of adoption and sonship lie behind Paul's discussion.[103] Rather than focusing on the socio-cultural

---

[102] Yates, *Spirit and Creation*, 152.

[103] This debate smacks of an unnecessary either/or. Although there is no specific mention of adoption in Jewish writings because of the Levirate system that provided a means to maintain property within a family, several Jewish backgrounds have been proposed.   James C. Hester, *Paul's Concept of Inheritance: A Contribution to the Understanding of Heilsgeschichte* (Edinburgh: Oliver & Boyd, 1968), 10–12. With passages like 2 Sam 7:14 and Psalm 89, some draw a correlation between adoption of the Messiah and of believers. James M. Scott, *Adoption as Sons of God: An Exegetical Investigation into the Background of ΥΙΟΘΕΣΙΑ in the Pauline Corpus* (WUNT 2/48; Tübingen: Mohr Siebeck, 1992), 221–58; Campbell, 'Story of Jesus', 116. Others argue that adoption refers to a second Exodus, based on the slavery-freedom antithesis. Sylvia Keesmaat, *Paul and His Story: (Re)Interpreting the Exodus Tradition* (JSNTSup 181; Sheffield: Sheffield Academic, 1999), 54–96. The concept of sonship as signifying God's eternal redemption appears regularly in intertestamental literature. Cf. Byrne, 'Sons', 216–21. On the other hand, adoption is expressly attested in Greek and Roman society, even with legal instructions regulating its practice. Cf. Trevor Burke, *Adopted into God's Family: Exploring a Pauline Metaphor* (NSBT 22; Downers Grove: Intervarsity, 2006); James C. Walters, 'Paul, Adoption, and Inheritance' in *Paul in the Greco-Roman World,* ed. J. Paul Sampley (Harrisburg: Trinity Press, 2003), 42–76, at 42–55; Francis Lyall, 'Roman Law in the Writings of Paul: Adoption', *JBL* 88 (1969): 458–66; Hester, *Inheritance*. However, the majority of documented Greek and Roman adoptions occur only at the highest levels of society, particularly in the imperial household (e.g., Hadrian by Trajan) to maintain family political control.

context, we will focus on the literary context. In the letter to the Romans, Paul's presentation of Christology, election, and the formation of the people of God intersect in the collection of themes involving sonship and inheritance. As discussed above (see §2.2), Paul presents Christ as God's Son (1.4, 9; 5.10; 8.3, 29, and 32) and as David's descendant (ἐκ σπέρματος Δαυίδ, 1.3). Now, Paul introduces believers as adopted sons (υἱοί), children (τέκνα), and heirs (κληρονόμοι) of God in this passage. Standing in the background of this passage is Romans 4, where these sonship terms are first used of believers, both Jews and Gentiles, as children of Abraham. The focus in Rom 4.13–16 is upon Abraham's descendants (σπέρμα) and his faith in God's promise for them. Abraham and his descendants received the promise that they would be heirs of the world (4.13),[104] and his heirs are those who share his faith rather than ethnic descent or legal observance (4.16).

In addition to chapters 4 and 8, Paul continues his use of sonship language into chapter 9. He begins by noting adoption as one of the benefits of being Jewish (9.4) and also resumes the connection to Abraham's descendants, where the children of the promise are the true seed (9.7–9). In this context, Paul associates the τέκνα τοῦ θεοῦ with the children of the promise as opposed to the children of the flesh (9.8). The promise for those who are 'not my people' is that they will be called 'sons of the living God' (9.24–26), and a remnant will be saved from the numerous 'sons of Israel' (9.27).[105]

Rom 8.14–17 thus fits within this theme developed in the letter. Thus, Eastman rightly emphasises adoption language as formative for the people of God.[106] As we turn to discuss Rom 8.14–17, we will see hints of this formation of a new people in relationship to God, but the focus will be primarily upon the new ontological reality related to the resurrection ex-

---

[104] In the intertestamental literature Hester (*Inheritance*, 32) argues that 'the whole earth becomes the inheritance of the children of Israel (Jubilees 17.3, 22.14, 32.19; Enoch 5.7)'. Noting other Second Temple writings, Edward Adams (*Constructing the World: A Study in Paul's Cosmological Language* [Studies in the New Testament and Its World; Edinburgh: T&T Clark, 2000], 168–69) writes: 'Almost certainly, then, the construction τὸ κληρονόμον αὐτὸν εἶναι κόσμου relates to the reinterpreted promise to Abraham in which the promised inheritance is no longer just the land of Palestine but the whole world...,which is the eschatological inheritance of God's elect, that is to say, the new or restored creation'.

[105] Paul draws from Hosea 2.25; 2.1; and 1.10.

[106] Susan Eastman, 'Whose Apocalypse? The Identity of the Sons of God in Romans 8.19', *JBL* 121 (2002): 263–77. However, I disagree with the corporate reading of 'body' in 8.23, since there is no indication that it is not referring to the believers' physical bodies.

perience. That is, those who are children of God become like him, inheriting his life.

3.2 Adoption as Liberation

With liberation as the theme of the chapter (8.1–2), adoption provides Paul with a metaphor that enables him to develop the theme of deliverance within the contexts of enslavement and of the Spirit. With the γάρ introducing this passage in 8.14, Paul presents an explanation of the ζήσεσθε in 8.13. Those who put to death the actions of the body by the Spirit (8.13) are those who are led by the Spirit and are thus sons of God (8.14). Whereas those in the flesh were enemies of God because they did and could not obey God, believers obey God, being led by the Spirit, and are thus not only friends but also children. Thus, an implicit obligation to obey is combined with an explicit enabling freedom through the Spirit.[107] This Spirit-based sonship serves as the foundation of 8.15–17.

In 8.15 Paul then explains (γάρ) what being sons of God means by another set of statements: he contrasts adoption with slavery in the context of the Spirit.[108] Like in Rom 8.2 with its two 'laws', Paul refers to two spirits – of slavery and of adoption.[109] Slavery is here presented as negative, leading to fear. With the strong and repeated association with sin in 6.6, 16–22, we should most likely see slavery to sin as the referent. Δουλεία is also associated with corruption in 8.21. As such, in light of the contrast in 8.2 Gieniusz is correct to see both sin and death as the referent of the enslaving powers.[110]

In contrast to fear-inducing slavery, Paul presents adoption and the hope of inheritance arising from it. The contrast with slavery shows that Paul associates adoption with freedom and liberation, which continues the theme from Rom 8.1–2. This slavery-freedom contrast is later confirmed with Paul's double emphasis on freedom with regard to sonship in 8.21. In light of the whole passage, the inheritance includes present and future aspects, but at this point there is no indication that the status of being sons is not fully present. The present tense verbs (εἰσιν, 8.14 and ἐσμέν, 8.16) with sonship terms argue strongly that the state of adoption is a present reality. In addition, the aorist use of λαμβάνω also points in this direc-

---

[107] Hester, *Inheritance*, 92–94.

[108] Cf. Galatians 4 and John 8 where slavery and sonship are also contrasted.

[109] The two spirits could be a reflection of ideas like those in 1QS 3.16–4.26 but this is unlikely since Paul rarely uses πνεῦμα to refer to anything but the divine πνεῦμα and that of humans (except in 1 Cor 2.12: πνεῦμα of the world). Thus, the first is probably just a rhetorical device.

[110] Gieniusz, *Romans 8:18–30*, 48. However, based on the parallel in Galatians 3 with slavery being associated with the law, the implicit reference in 7.6 may be relevant.

tion.[111] Later, however, Paul speaks of adoption as a future experience, associated with the redemption of bodies (8.23).

Regarding the present, Paul offers two statements about the Spirit and believers: 1) the Spirit enables believers to call to God as 'Abba, Father', and 2) the Spirit communicates to believers' spirits that they are children of God. Thus, the Spirit facilitates both ascending and descending communication between believers and God.[112] Believers are free not only to serve God but to communicate and relate to him. Like in 8.1–13, the relational aspect cannot be segregated from the moral and ontological. The benefit of this adoptive relationship becomes clear in verse 17 where Paul reintroduces inheritance.[113] Walters argues that, for Paul, inheritance language is primary and that we can only understand adoption language in light of inheritance.[114] Scott points to the only other occurrences of inheritance language in the letter, which speak of Abraham being 'heir of the world' (κληρονόμος κόσμου). He thus argues strongly for 'heirs *of the Abrahamic promise*', reigning over the world.[115] Scott summarises:

The messianic Son of God is heir to the Abrahamic promise of universal sovereignty, because, just as in Gal. 3–4, the 'seed' of David (cf. Rom. 1:3) fulfills the Abrahamic promise (Gen. 15:18) and the Davidic (2 Sam. 7:12–14). Hence, those who are in Christ (Rom. 8:1) participate in the divine sonship and Abrahamic heirship of the Messiah (Rom. 8:17, 29).[116]

Paul closely associates the inheritance of believers with Christ since they are not just heirs of God but also co-heirs with Christ. Thus, the 'inheritance' that believers receive is the same as that of Christ, which Paul describes as suffering (συμπάσχω) and being glorified (συνδοξάζω) with him (8.17). Horn notes that Paul presents 'das Heilsgut christologisch' rather than in terms of βασιλεία as in other contexts (1 Cor 6.9–11; 15.50; Gal

---

[111] Bertone (*Law of the Spirit*, 197) notes: 'The presence of λαμβάνειν in association with πνεῦμα by this point in time for believers had become a *technicus terminus* for their initial reception of the Spirit': e.g., 2 Cor 11.4; Gal 3.2, 14.

[112] Thus, in distinction to normal convention, Paul presents the benefits of this relationship from the perspective of the adoptee rather than that of the adopter. Walters ('Adoption', 50) writes: 'Because the ultimate reason for adoption was to preserve the *oikos*, inheritance and adoption were always intricately interrelated in Athenian law.... Concern for the welfare of a child was not the primary motive for most Greek adopters'. Cf. Walters' ('Adoption', 58) similar assessment regarding Gal 4.

[113] The metaphor breaks down since God is eternal and cannot die for his children to receive an inheritance. However, regarding Gal 3.15, E. Bammel ('Gottes ΔΙΑΘΗΚΗ (Gal. III.15–17) und das jüdische Rechtsdenken', *NTS* 6 [1959–60]: 313–19) argues for an *inter vivos* will effective during one's lifetime, which could also apply here.

[114] Walters, 'Adoption', 55.

[115] Scott, *Adoption*, 251, emphasis added, cf. 248–56.

[116] Ibid., 254–55.

5.21; cf. Luke 10.25; 18.18).[117] We will explore the nature of suffering
and glorification more fully in §4, but we will first investigate the reality
of adoption as eschatological reality in light of this shared experience with
Christ.

3.3 Adoption as Eschatological Reality

We have already noted the community formation aspects of adoption lan-
guge, and many others take the adoption metaphor as explaining a renewed
and intimate relationship between God and believers.[118] The relational
aspects of the passage are clear and important, particularly with the renewed communication between believers and God by the Spirit. Also,
within the context the connection to love in 5.1–8 and 8.31–39 is important. However, Paul advances the metaphor far beyond this plain 'relational' level and moves it into the 'ontological' sphere, by associating it
with resurrection. In particular, divine sonship has somatic consequences
for those whom the Spirit indwells, which in turn relate to inheriting the
world.

Continuing from prior discussions of resurrection in 8.9–13, Paul now
associates the experience of bodily resurrection with divine adoption. The
association between Christ's resurrection and sonship was briefly discussed above (§2.2) with regard to Rom 1.4; 4.16–22 and 9.22–29. The
link within this passage stands at the transition from 8.13 to 8.14. In explanation of 'you will live', Paul introduces their sonship of God.[119] Byrne
describes it in this manner: 'Sonship of God is not introduced simply as a
further privilege of Christians of which in Paul's opinion mention may appropriately be made at this point. It is introduced precisely as a status that
points towards eschatological life'.[120] In other words, 'you are sons of
God' explains and qualifies 'you will live'. As both heirs of God and co-
heirs with Christ, believers presently suffer and are glorified in the future
with Christ as part of this inheritance (8.17).

---

[117] Friedrich Wilhelm Horn, *Das Angeld des Geistes: Studien zur paulinischen
Pneumatologie* (Göttingen: Vandenhoeck & Ruprecht, 1992), 398.

[118] E.g., Dunn (*Romans*, 1:460) writes: 'The contrast is clearly between the status of
slavery and that of sonship, and all that meant in terms of personal freedom and social
relationships.... Sonship as such, including adoptive sonship, by contrast speaks of freedom and intimate mutual trust, where filial concern can be assumed to provide the motivation and direction for living, and conduct be guided by spontaneous love rather than
law'.

[119] Gieniusz (*Romans 8:18–30*, 48n.150) writes: 'The essential aspect of divine sonship is life which results not only from the reflection on the nature of fatherhood in general, but is clearly indicated in the passage itself. Its immediate aim is to support
ζήσεσθε of v. 13'.

[120] Byrne, *'Sons'*, 98.

In this passage, the hope of glory (5.2; 8.24–25) is particularly emphasised as the expectation for the sons and children of God. Creation awaits
the 'revelation of the *sons* of God' (8.19), which is coterminous with the
'revelation of glory in us' (8.18). Again, Paul speaks of the hope that creation will be freed according to the 'freedom of the glory of the *children* of
God' (8.21). In the same way, believers eagerly expect their *'adoption*, the
redemption of their bodies' (8.23),[121] which is the only explicit definition
Paul gives of adoption. Finally, Paul describes believers as being conformed to the image of God's *Son*, with the result that Christ is the *'firstborn* among many *brothers and sisters'* (8.29). In each of these verses,
Paul talks about the nature of eschatological hope and the experience of
liberation life within the context of family metaphors: sonship, adoption,
inheritance, and brotherhood with Christ. Thus, as believers are a part of
God's family, they share in the ontological gift of life – the redemption of
the body – because of that relationship.

Based on 8.10–11, the bodily experience of resurrection life is wholly
future since the 'body is [currently] dead because of sin' even if 'the Spirit
is life' (8.10). While the direct statement about sonship in 8.14 and the use
of the aorist in 8.15 leads the reader initially to understand adoption as a
present reality, Byrne rightly points to Paul's qualification which makes
adoption a future experience as well:

> In v.15 Paul does not speak of the receiving of υἱοθεσία *simpliciter* but of a *Spirit* of
> υἱοθεσία – just as in v.23 he refers to the Spirit as 'first-fruits', as a preliminary gift or
> 'earnest' (2 Cor 1:22; 5:5; cf. Eph 1:13f.) of something more to come. Similarly, the
> intervening passage (vv.19–21) has spoken of sonship as something to be 'revealed',
> implying the hidden character of its present possession ....[122]

As such, while adoption may be a present relational *reality*, the phenome-
nological *experience* of adoption as bodily resurrection is future.[123] Is this
present/future dialectic the same for the other main adoption text in Paul?

3.4 Excursus: Galatians 3.23–4.11

Besides Romans 8–9, adoption language also appears in Gal 4.5 and Eph
1.5. Importantly, Patristic authors read these adoption texts in tandem, so
this excursus provides us with the means to see the distinct contours in

---

[121] 𝔓46 D F G 614 it[d, g] Ambst, which include some weighty sources, omit υἱοθεσία.
However, with its seeming contradiction to 8.15, the inclusion of υἱοθεσία is the more
difficult, and thus the preferred, reading.

[122] Byrne, *'Sons'*, 109.

[123] Horn (*Angeld*, 398) puts it in this manner: 'Es ist deutlich, daß mit dem Begriff
‚Angeld des Geistes' und den juridischen Termini υἱοθεσία und κληρονομία in den pl
Spätbreifen eine terminologische Verdichtung einhergeht, welche die gegenwärtige
Heilsgabe in ihrer Ausrichtung auf die Zukunft begreift'.

Paul's thought. Galatians 4, with its significant parallels with Romans 8, contains a substantial discussion of the abrogated status of the law in contrast with the promise made to Abraham and the new work of Christ. In this context, the same key terms from Romans arise: υἱός, σπέρμα, τέκνον, κληρονόμος, and υἱοθεσία. After considering the context in which Gal 3.23–4.11 stands, we will then explore key themes that arise out of the passage.

The themes of Gal 3.23–4.11 develop directly from Paul's discussion in 3.1–22 where Paul correlates the presence of the Spirit with justification and the coming of Christ with the abrogation of the law.[124] By believing like Abraham, the community has the opportunity to experience the promise given to him as his sons, a promise which is none other than the Spirit (3.14). The law did not bring life, which is God's ultimate soteriological intention, but rather guarded everyone until the blessing and promise came through Christ (Gal 3.19–22). In this discussion about what constitutes the people of God, Paul rebuts the idea that law observance serves this function.[125] The law had a role, but the people of God have always been established on faith, which has been fulfilled in Christ and the Spirit. Thus, the people of God are founded on them, not the law. In Gal 3.23–4.11 Paul builds upon this role of the law as 'imprisoning/guarding' and contrasts it with the freedom that sons and heirs enjoy through Christ and the Spirit. He gives two accounts (3.23–29 and 4.1–7), which contain the same themes.[126] In both accounts, Paul uses illustrations of children under the control of others being freed at their age of majority. The law serves as this enslaving power from whom believers as children of Abraham and of God are freed through the liberation of Christ and the Spirit.

---

[124] See Sam K. Williams, 'Justification and the Spirit in Galatians', *JSNT* 29 (1987): 91–100.

[125] While the repeated use of repeated use of ὑπό (3.23, 25; 4.2, 3, 4, 5) and the terminology of φρουρέω, συγκλείω, παιδαγωγός, ἐπίτροπος and οἰκονόμος do not necessarily connote negative meanings of authority, the discussion of the enslaving στοιχεῖα τοῦ κόσμου in 4.3 unambiguously presents a negative picture. Cf. Martyn, *Theological Issues*, 370–72.

[126] Why the recapitulation in 4.1–7? Walters ('Adoption', 65) argues that the difference in the restatement between 3.23–29 and 4.1–7 is that 'Galatians 4:1–7 is the bridge for this transition [from "who are descendants of Abraham" to "who is free"] and adoption supports the span connecting the heir's status directly to God via God's cosmic invasion through Christ'. While partially correct, the role of the Spirit in the recapitulation should not be ignored. This return to the Spirit in 4.1–7 brings Paul's larger argument full-circle from 3.1: the experience of the Spirit as the promise of God shows the law to be unnecessary. If sonship comes through Christ, the law is unnecessary for receiving the promise of God, which is the Spirit. The conclusion then is that believers are not slaves but sons, and if sons, then heirs. Thus, the purpose of the restatement appears to be the desire to include the Spirit within the context of freedom from the law.

The participatory union with Christ in 3.26–29 serves as a fundamental piece of his argument: it is not through law observance but Christ that one participates in the inheritance of Abraham as his children.[127] In 3.26–29 Paul uses a range of metaphors and prepositions to express similar, yet nuanced conceptions of the believer. This passage focuses on identity more than transformation per se, but the fact of believers being wrapped up in Christ and his destiny, making them heirs to the promise, is clear. While in other passages these different metaphor fields are used separately, in this context Paul weaves together several different phrases to speak of believers and Christ. This new divine-human relationship also fundamentally changes human-human relationships.[128]

Paul previously made use of Christ as Son of God (1.16; 2.20) and as σπέρμα of Abraham (3.16–19) and he now calls believers 'sons of God' (3.26) and 'σπέρμα of Abraham and heirs according to the promise' (3.29). In Gal 4.4–5 Paul then associates Christ's relationship as Son with that of believers through sending language like that of Rom 8.3. Many note the chiasm formed with the following ἵνα clauses:

A   God sent his son, born from a woman

     B   Born under law

     B'   ἵνα he might redeem those under law

A'   ἵνα we might receive adoption.[129]

Christ's sonship then is thematically paired with believers' receipt of adoption (υἱοθεσία). Based on the parallel nature of the Christ's work and the benefit of believers, this has been categorised as one of the interchange statements by Hooker.[130] Not to be forgotten though are the B and B' statements that include the issue of the law. Paul's argument is not just about sonship, but sonship shows the freedom from the law.[131] Accordingly, Christ's experience as a Jewish human ὑπὸ νόμον serves the basis of his securing freedom for humans ὑπὸ νόμον. Rather than writing about the result of Christ's incarnation – in the flesh of sin (Rom 8.3) – Paul presents the means of his incarnation – born of a woman – as a basis for his interac-

---

[127] Frank J. Matera, *Galatians* (SP 9; Collegeville, MN: Liturgical, 1992), 147.

[128] Martyn (*Theological Issues*, 120) terms the social, racial, and gender distinctions as antinomies of the old age that are abolished by the coming of Christ, leading the way to the flesh-Spirit antinomy during the overlap of the ages.

[129] Richard Longenecker, *Galatians* (WBC 41; Waco: Word, 1990), 166.

[130] Hooker, *From Adam*, 13–69.

[131] Irenaeus provides a reading of this passage that focuses only on the sonship language: 'the Word of God was made man, and He who was the Son of God became the Son of man, that man, having been taken into the Word, and receiving the adoption, might become the son of God' (*AH* 3.19.1). See further comments on this difference in chapter 8.

tion with humanity. The use of ἐξαγοράζω as the description of Christ's work reminds the reader of Gal 3.13, which also stands in the form of an interchange text, where Christ's death is characterised as redeeming and not just his incarnation. Interestingly, both Gal 3.13–14 and 4.4–6 present a move from interchange to the promise of the Spirit.

While Paul speaks presently about the status of believers as sons and heirs (3.26, 29; 4.6–7), the association of κληρονόμος points to a future fulfilment. For instance, we note the future expectation of *inheriting* the kingdom of God in 5.21, which may be associated with reaping eternal life (6.8). Thüsing describes sonship as 'ein schon gegenwärtiges Heilsgut', but notes that the use of the term κληρονόμος points to 'der eschatologischen Erfüllung der Verheißungen Gottes'.[132] At the same time, the turn of the ages has already come, as the evidence of the Spirit shows (3.1–5), the fulfilment of the promise to Abraham (3.14). Though Paul may have the kingdom of God and life in mind, the promise of inheritance seems primarily associated with the Spirit.

In the new age beginning with Christ, believers are liberated from the law and find adoption as the people of God. They have the hope of inheritance, which is the promise of the Spirit.[133] Thus, Paul shows that the people of God are constituted around the liberation offered by Christ and the Spirit and not the law. He explicitly renews this theme of liberation in 4.21–31 and in 5.1, which serves as the transition into his parenetic discourse.

Romans 8 and Galatians 4 overlap significantly, and not merely due to the repetition of the term 'adoption'. In both settings Paul describes the people of God as those liberated by Christ and the Spirit, who stand as the basis of the people of God. While Paul has been concerned with the place of law in the Romans passage, this adoption language serves to draw together Paul's discussion of present empowerment by the Spirit and his discussion of future resurrection like Christ's. In contrast, the law stands at the centre of the discussion in Galatians 4, and adoption through Christ and the Spirit shows that legal observance does not constitute the people of God. In Romans the inheritance is an immortal, glorified body like Christ, whereas the inheritance in Galatians is the Spirit himself.

---

[132] Wilhelm Thüsing, *Per Christum in Deum: Gott und Christus in der paulinischen Soteriologie* (Münster: Aschendorff, 1986), 118.

[133] Walters ('Adoption', 55) overstates the importance of inheritance by making it the central uniting concept of 3.1–4.7, but he rightly recognises the association of the Spirit with inheritance, the blessing of Abraham and the promise.

3.5 Conclusion

In Romans 4 Paul argues that Abraham is the father of all who believe and that they would inherit the world as his heirs (4.11–13). Echoing this previous discussion, Paul later speaks of believers as sons and heirs of God in 8.14–17. The close association of sonship and inheritance in Galatians 3–4 supports our reading of Rom 8.14–17 in light of Rom 4.11–22. In Galatians 3 Paul intermixes sonship of God and descent from Abraham, showing that he probably does not see much distinction between them. Interestingly, there Paul interprets the promise as that of the Spirit, rather than inheritance of the world. He uses the presence of the Spirit in both passages to demarcate those who are God's children as the people of God. The confluence of life, glory, image, and resurrection in association with adoption language shows that Paul stands within larger Jewish discussions about sonship.[134] Accordingly, Paul infuses a Graeco-Roman metaphor with Jewish meaning, which allows him to emphasise the common feature among all systems of inheritance: the 'continuity of family property within the family unit', which for Paul is the inheritance of life through the Spirit.[135]

As with Galatians 3–4, Paul uses sonship to emphasise freedom in opposition to slavery. In Galatians 4 that freedom is from the law and the *stoicheia*, whereas he is probably referring to freedom from sin and death in Rom 8.15. This association with sin and death shows the relevance of adoption and sonship to Paul's larger theme of new life that is running through the chapter. Like the earlier section of Romans 8, we have the twin themes of moral enablement along with eschatological life in this passage as well. The sons of God are presently led by his Spirit, putting to death the actions of the body. However, the discussion of the expected freedom of the glory of the children of God (8.21) and adoption as redemption of the body (8.23) point towards a yet future experience. Adoption thus continues the pattern of the eschatological present/future dialectic in Paul associated with moral enablement and somatic resurrection.

4. Conformation to Christ: 8.17–30

As with several passages in this letter, the conclusion of his initial discussion of adoption, sonship, and inheritance serves as the foundation for his next development in the argument (e.g., Rom 5.20–21). Thus, 8.18–30 more likely serves as a discreet unit, but with the introduction of the con-

---

[134] Byrne, *'Sons'*.
[135] Hester, *Inheritance*, 19.

cepts of suffering and glory in 8.17, we will consider 8.17–30 together.[136] By incorporating the problem of corruption in creation, Paul places the anthropological problem of death and corruption in a larger, cosmological context.[137] With this cosmological context in mind, our focus will primarily remain on the human experience. Three συν-compound words carry the meaning of the section from 8.17–30: συμπάσχω (8.17), συνδοξάζω (8.17), and σύμμορφος (8.29). As a result, we will analyse the issues of suffering and glory (§4.1) and then sonship as conformation to Christ (§4.2). With its creation themes, this passage allows us to conclude with a discussion of Adam, creation and re-creation (§4.3).

4.1 Suffering and Glory

Suffering and glory serve as the twin pillars upon which this passage stands. Paul introduces this pair in verse 17 as he explains the nature of inheritance as co-heirs with Christ: believers suffer with him in order that they may be glorified with him. In verse 18 he then gives his thesis statement for the remaining discussion through 8.30: these sufferings are not comparable to the glory to be revealed in/to believers. What then is the nature of this suffering and glory? To understand these themes, we must first understand how this passage fits in the larger argument and then we will address each aspect in turn.

---

[136] With regard to the structure of 8.17–30, Hahne details several ideas that have been offered: Harry Alan Hahne, *The Corruption and Redemption of Creation: Nature in Romans 8.19–22 and Jewish Apocalyptic Literature* (LNTS 336; London: T&T Clark, 2006), 173–76. The association and contrast between suffering and glory in both 8.17 and 8.18 with the repetition of these themes until 8.30 (and even 8.39) speaks highly for Hahne's proposed structure of the passage:

- 0. Transition: believers share in the present suffering of Christ and will share in the future glory of Christ (v. 17).
- 1. Thesis: the present suffering is insignificant compared with the future glory of believers (v.18)
- 2. Hope of future glory amidst present suffering
  - a. All creation groans in suffering, yet looks forward with hope to future glory (vv. 19–22).
  - b. Believers groan as they await in hope the future redemption of their bodies (vv. 23–25).
  - c. The Spirit's groaning in intercession helps believers in this age of suffering (vv. 26–27).
- 3. Confident assurance of the coming glory (vv. 28–30).

Hahne, *Corruption and Redemption*, 175.

[137] Several note the soteriological importance of this chapter and make statements similar to Günter Kehnscherper ('Romans 8:19 – On Pauline Belief and Creation' in *Studia Biblica 1978*, ed. E. Livingstone [Sheffield: JSOT Press, 1978], 233–243, at 236), who writes: 'Rom. 8:19–23 is not a marginal note, but the climax of Pauline soteriology'.

As we consider Paul's discussion, we should briefly note the different approaches to this section. Many understand that 'Paul's purpose in 8:18–39 is to legitimate the sufferings of his readers ...'.[138] Osten-Sacken and Bindemann, in particular, see Paul's emphasis as the hope of glory to encourage those in the midst of suffering.[139] On the other hand, Käsemann argues that Paul is addressing enthusiasts like those in Corinth, so Paul emphasises suffering with Christ as the nature of present experience. Any glory is left until the eschaton. He writes: 'The theme of hope is obviously approached from the standpoint of struggle'.[140] He therefore argues for an 'unmistakable break between vv. 18 and 19' that shows this.[141]

Käsemann, along with Beker, appears to reduce the complexity of the passage.[142] Paul's discussion throughout the chapter is based on an overlap of the ages. He is balancing the new life of the Spirit with the presence of suffering, but he also presents the hope of future resurrection as well. As we approach this section we should be conscious of the already/not yet framework that runs throughout. The reality of suffering and the reality of hope are both here in the passage, and I will attempt to maintain a balance between the two while examining this passage.

---

[138] Adams, *Constructing*, 183. See also Otto Kuss, *Der Römerbrief* (3 vols.; Regensburg: F. Pustet, 1963–1978), 2:621; Nygren, *Romans*, 335–36; Peter Stuhlmacher, *Paul's Letter to the Romans: A Commentary* (Louisville: Westminster John Knox, 1994), 120. Gieniusz (*Romans 8:18–30*, 110) argues that the reason for Paul's writing is to counteract the ideology arising from Deuteronomy that suffering is a sign of God's wrath.

[139] E.g., Peter von der Osten-Sacken (*Römer 8 als Beispiel paulinischer Soteriologie* [FRLANT; Göttingen: Vandenhoeck & Ruprecht, 1975], 264) writes: 'Die durch die Wendung εφ' ελπιδι [*sic*] hergestellte eschatologische Finalität des Leidens stimmt deshalb in ihrer Struktur mit derjenigen des Gesetzes überein, wie sie z.B. in Gal 3,21ff. zum Ausdruck kommt'. Cf. Walther Bindemann, *Die Hoffnung der Schöpfung: Römer 8,18–27 und die Frage einer Theologie der Befreiung von Mensch und Natur* (Neukirchen-Vluyn: Neukirchener, 1983).

[140] Käsemann, *Romans*, 231.

[141] Ibid.

[142] With the issue of suffering standing at the centre of the second half of the chapter, J. Christiaan Beker ('Suffering and Triumph in Paul's Letter to the Romans', *HBT* 7 (1985): 105–119, at 110) argues that Paul gives two different pictures of the church's experience. The first is one of peace and liberty in separation from the world (8.1–17a) and the second shows the reality of suffering in union with the world (8.17b–30). In other words, he sees Paul as focused upon *present* deliverance in the first half and *future* deliverance in the second. However, we will later see how suffering and glory recapitulate the themes of death and life from 8.1–17. As such, they are further developments from the death-life contrast which runs through the whole chapter. As such, Beker overstates the already (8.1–17) versus not yet (8.18–30) divide within the chapter.

4.1.1 Suffering With Christ

As we consider Paul's presentation of suffering, Gieniusz cautions the interpreter not to 'yield too easily to the temptation to subordinate the theme of suffering, as if it were only a dark background against which the other themes shine more brightly'.[143] Rather, he argues that the discussion of suffering in the *exordium* (5.1–11) and the *peroratio* (8.31–39) show its importance for understanding Paul's argument for chapters 5–8. This section is particularly important because Paul presents it in its fullest measure here.

In verses 17 and 18, Paul does not explicitly develop what he means by suffering, but he gives a fuller picture when the immediate context is included. Based on the contrasts with glory, suffering relates to futility (ματαιότης; 8.20), slavery (δουλεία; 8.21), corruption (φθορά; 8.21), and possibly weakness (ἀσθένεια; 8.26), in addition to being the reason for groaning (8.20–23). Nothing among these characteristics are specifically associated with suffering related to the Christian faith. Adams, along with others, distinguishes between 'Christian' suffering as persecution in 8.17 with creational suffering in 8.18–22, and argues: 'Paul links believers' specific afflictions with the general suffering that characterizes creation as a whole and emphasizes believers' solidarity with the world and its suffering'.[144] While the text does not exclude this reading, it also gives no clear indication for it. The discussion of creation does broaden its scope but, it just shows that all suffering is interrelated. Importantly, Paul describes this suffering as not only solidarity with the world but solidarity *with Christ* (συμπάσχω; 8.17). With no clear indication that Paul has changed his emphasis, the move to distinguish the two goes against the surface reading of the text.

If we look at the wider context, Paul explains why believers boast in the 'hope of glory': they boast in afflictions (θλῖψις), which in turn lead to perseverance, character, and then hope (5.1–8). And this hope of future glory 'does not put to shame/disappoint because of the love of God poured out in [their] hearts through the Holy Spirit' (5.5), and this love is initially confirmed by God's action in Christ. Later, in 8.35–36 Paul again mentions afflictions (θλῖψις) in the context of the love of Christ, along with hardship, persecution, famine, nakedness, danger, and the sword (8.35).[145]

---

[143] Gieniusz, *Romans 8:18–30*, 53.

[144] Adams, *Constructing*, 183. Gieniusz (*Romans 8:18–30*, 71–76) argues that verse 17 is not the thesis of 18–30 (as Osten-Sacken), though it introduces the issues. In particular, it does not have the formal structure of a *propositio* and the argument from 18–30 only speaks of suffering rather than suffering with Christ. Cf. Beker, 'Suffering'.

[145] Beker ('Suffering') understands suffering presented in Romans 8 as distinct from that in Romans 1, as suffering from the power of death (natural evil) and suffering from

These things do not separate from the love of God and believers are 'more than conquerors' in all these things.

There is no evidence that the Roman Christians were facing suffering or persecution in the introduction (1.1–17) and concluding sections of the letter (15.14–16.23) like there are in other letters (e.g., 1 Thes 1.2–10; 2 Cor 1.3–11), although Rom 12.12–21 mentions struggles in a non-specific manner. Based on the general nature of the physical and emotional troubles described in 5.1–5; 8.18–30; and 8.31–39, Paul does not appear to be specifying any specific 'Christian' suffering as different from that of others. In fact, since he immediately introduces the groaning of creation as commensurate with that of believers, the implication is that believers suffer similar struggles. In this case, suffering with Christ would appear to be suffering common to all humanity, without excluding trials faced only by believers.

Since this suffering is 'with Christ' (συμπάσχω), something must set it apart from simply suffering like the world. Just as Christ's submission to suffering death subverted the power of death, so when believers put to death the activity of the sin through suffering, they subvert the power of death that still holds sway.[146] Suffering then does not subvert God's plan

---

human injustice (moral evil). He maintains this distinction in order to make sense of the problem of evil. The discussion in Romans 1 clearly has moral overtones with the direct mention of intentional human sin, whereas Paul's discussion of evil in Romans 8.17–22 just mentions suffering, corruption, and futility. However, when seen in light of Rom 5.1–11 and 8.31–39 we see that the suffering of Romans 8 includes what might be called natural evil related to the problems in the natural world (e.g., λιμός) but also evil at the hands of humans as well (e.g., διωγμός and μάχαιρα). This latter aspect may point to the possibility of Christian suffering in the midst of general suffering.

[146] We should then consider how Paul portrays Christ's suffering in the letter. The central theme that Paul associates with Christ is his death (1.4; 3.25; 4.24; 5.6–8; 6.3–4, 8–9; 7.4; 8.11, 34; 10.9; 14.9, 15). [I have included verses that mention Christ being raised from the dead as an indication of the fact that Christ died.] He is also noted as being obedient to God (5.19), being sent by God for sins (8.3), and becoming a servant and minister to Jews and Gentiles (15.3, 8, 16). Thus, suffering with Christ may be considered in terms of dying with Christ. Rom 6.1–14, where Paul speaks of being baptised into his death, addresses this theme. This is described as dying to sin (6.2), crucifying the old self, and doing away with the body of sin, which results in freedom from sin (6.6). Paul also presents believers as dying to the law through the body of Christ, through Christ's death (7.4). This death to sin and the law, while it is presented as complete (e.g., 6.2; 7.4), must be lived out in believers' lives. Accordingly, Paul encourages them to continue to put sin to death in the body (6.11–14) and to put to death the deeds of the body (8.13). Thus, suffering through physical and emotional affliction, when it is done 'with Christ' may be considered an experience of death to sin and the law. This is in distinction to L. Ann Jervis (*At the Heart of the Gospel: Suffering in the Earliest Christian Message* [Cambridge: Eerdmans, 2007], 103–4) who argues for a difference

for believers. Rather, it becomes one of the means chosen by God to facilitate the freedom from sin and the law, which he has explained through the chapter.[147] In other words, Rom 8.17 is just a restatement of Rom 8.13 in that new life (glory) follows on from death with Christ.

As evidence of corruption, suffering plays the role of death in the current age (ὁ νῦν καιρός; 8.18). Similarly, all creation has been groaning and straining ἄχρι τοῦ νῦν (8.22). Although the new age has begun (as noted in 8.1), the problem of corruption still plagues believers and creation. This corresponds to Paul's earlier affirmation that the body is dead even in the midst of the Spirit's current activity (8.10). However, Paul's message here is clear: suffering is limited to the current age and believers should hope for something better in the future. It is to this hope of glory that we now turn.

4.1.2 Being Glorified With Christ

Although Paul initially promotes suffering with Christ as the means to being glorified with him (συνδοξάζω, 8.17), Paul predominately characterises glory (δόξα) as liberation from suffering. Paul associates glory with freedom (ἐλευθερία, 8.21), revelation (ἀποκάλυψις, 8.18, 19),[148] adoption (υἱοθεσία, 8.23), and redemption of the body (ἀπολύτρωσις, 8.23). At the same time, he contrasts glory with corruption (φθορά, 8.21) and, by implication, futility (ματαιότης, 8.20). Within the letter as a whole, Paul synonymously associates glory with immortality, eternal life, and resurrection and contrasts it with corruption and mortality in 1.23; 2.7–10; 6.4, 11; 8.21–23; and 9.23. At the same time, Paul uses other honour discourse language, such as τιμή, in the same contexts: 2.7–10; 9.21–23. Based upon his use throughout the letter we can conclude that 'in these ontological contexts glory denotes the honourable status of incorruption'.[149] As such, being glorified is the experience of somatic resurrection in remedy to the problem of corruption. Glorification serves as the culmination of new life, and it therefore fits within the larger soteriological sphere of 'life'.

Several points of evidence show that the consummate experience of this life is in the future:[150] 1) Paul speaks of this in the future tense (8.18, 21).

---

between suffering 'with Christ' and 'in Christ' in Paul's thought. She therefore conceptually separates Rom 6.3–11 from Rom 8.17.

[147] Consider again the progression from affliction to perseverance, to character to hope in 5.1–5. Cf. Robert C. Tannehill, *Dying and Rising with Christ: A Study in Pauline Theology* (Eugene, OR: Wipf & Stock, 2006), 122.

[148] This liberation, in contrast to suffering, is that of glory that will be revealed εἰς ἡμᾶς. cf. Gal 1.16 for 'reveal' with ἐν ἐμοί.

[149] Blackwell, 'Immortal Glory', 297 .

[150] So, e.g., Moo, *Romans*, 512–22, 535–36; Preston Sprinkle, 'The Afterlife in Romans: Understanding Paul's Glory Motif in Light of the Apocalypse of Moses and 2

2) This glory-experience is something that is eagerly expected (ἀποκαρα-δοκία) and patiently waited for (ἀπεκδέχομαι) (8.19, 23–25). 3) Paul contrasts the experience of suffering in 'the present age' and creation's groaning 'until now' with this glory that will be revealed in the next age (8.18, 22). 4) Finally, Paul goes to some lengths to describe that this hope of glory (cf. 5.2–5) is something not yet seen but rather a matter of hope, of confident expectation (8.23–25). These arguments point strongly to a 'future only' experience of glory.

At the same time, aspects of Paul's glory language hint at a present experience.[151] In 8.28–30 Paul gives a sequence of aorist verbs related to God's activity in conforming believers to the image of his Son, including ἐδόξασεν. While an aorist verb does not always signify the past tense, that is often its function. For those who see the event as future only, the standard arguments are that it is a proleptic aorist or that the chain is merely described from God's viewpoint.[152] Justification, also appearing in the chain of aorists, is often considered a past experience (cf. 5.1, 9), but aspects of justification are not consummated until believers experience resurrection (e.g., 8.10).[153] Justification, then, is more than just right standing, it is rather new creation, so that we can say with Thüsing: 'Die Gewißheit der Verherrlichung ist darin begründet, daß in der Dikaiosyne schon das Angeld der Doxa gegeben ist'.[154] Though these terms appear in the aorist, they are not completed actions in the past. The aorist use of σῴζω in 8.24 also fits this pattern since Paul normally uses it in the future tense (e.g., 5.9, 10; 10.9). In this manner, life is already present in some fashion but just waiting to be revealed like that of the sonship of believers (8.18–

Baruch' in *Lebendige Hoffnung – ewiger Tod?!: Jenseitsvorstellungen im Hellenismus, Judentum, und Christentum,* eds. Michael Labahn and Manfred Lang (Leipzig: Evangelische Verlagsanstalt, 2007), 201–33, at 213–20.

[151] Commentators often use 2 Cor 3.18 as evidence for a present experience of glory. E.g., Gorman, 'Romans', 29; Cranfield, *Romans,* 1:433.

[152] See Moo, *Romans,* 572–73.

[153] Cf. Bultmann, *Theology,* 1:270–71, 278–79; William Wrede, *Paul* (Eugene, OR: Wipf & Stock, 2001), 135; James D.G. Dunn, 'Jesus the Judge: Further Thoughts on Paul's Christology and Soteriology' in *Convergence of Theology,* eds. Daniel Kendall and Stephen T. Davis, (New York: Paulist, 2001), 34–54.

[154] Thüsing, *Per Christum,* 130. Thüsing (*Per Christum,* 132) also writes: 'Nach Jervell ist Doxa das Gepräge des Rechtfertigungsstandes. Richtiger würde man sagen, daß Doxa zunächst das Gepräge des Vollendungsstandes ist; nur deshalb, weil der Vollendungsstand von Christus her das Moment des „Lebens für Gott" mit der leiblichen Herrlichkeit verbindet, kann auch der irdische Rechtfertigungsstand, sein Angeld, als Doxa bezeichnet werden'. Cf. Horst R. Balz, *Heilsvertrauen und Welterfahrung: Strukturen der paulinischen Eschatologie nach Römer 8,18–39* (München: Chr. Kaiser, 1971), 115.

19).[155] As a central aspect of life, glory too may be proleptically experienced.

What is this present aspect of glorification, if somatic resurrection is future? In other Pauline passages he speaks of a present experience of glory as noetic enlightenment and moral transformation (2 Cor 3.11–4.6). A similar association might be justified here. As discussed above, Paul associates Christ's resurrection experience with moral enablement of believers in Rom 6.4 (cf. 6.11, 13) and 7.4–6. Importantly, Paul associates 'walking in new life' in 6.4 with the 'glory of the Father'. Later he explains this moral life of bearing fruit for God as animated by the Spirit (8.1–13). In the same way that believers die to sin and live to God through the Spirit, they suffer with Christ and are glorified with him. Since 'moral corruption results in the physical corruption of the natural world',[156] the resulting somatic incorruption from redemption implies that a commensurate moral incorruption will accompany it. This life in God is only truly consummated when the body is freed from the corruption of this present age.

Thus, the focus of glory language is the experience of immortal life rather than luminous bodies. Glory is presently experienced by believers as an experience of the firstfruits of immortal life through the Spirit (8.23, cf. 8.10), and this glory-life will be consummated in the future as the resurrection of the body.[157] From this, three points are important to note:

First, this glorification, however, is not just the mere possession of life but a participation in God's life mediated through Christ as believers are glorified with him (συνδοξάζω).[158] Drawing from glory as the instantiation of God's presence in the OT,[159] believers are now drawn up into God's mode of existence through participation. Several times in the letter, Paul describes δόξα as τοῦ θεοῦ (1.23; 3.23; 5.2, cf. 8.21 τῶν τέκνων τοῦ θεου) or τοῦ πατρός (6.4). At the same time, God is the agent of glorification

---

[155] Cranfield, *Romans*, 1:433; Gorman, 'Romans', 27–29.

[156] Hahne, *Corruption and Redemption*, 222.

[157] Jervell writes: 'Am nächsten kommt man der Bedeutung, wenn man sagt, daß Doxa, auf Gott bezogen, seine gerechtmachende χάρις bedeutet, was sowohl seine Wesens- als seine Wirkungsart bezeichnet; von Gläubigen verwendet, heißt Doxa ihre Dikaiosyne, ihre Gottebenbildlichkeit ...'. Jacob Jervell, *Imago Dei: Gen. 1.26f. im Spätjudentum, in der Gnosis und in den paulinischen Briefen* (Göttingen: Vandenhoeck & Ruprecht, 1960), 183.

[158] Byrne states: ' Glory" (δόξα) here particularly connotes the sense of immortality: to bear the glory of God, to be "like God" in this sense, means sharing God's own immortal being'. Byrne, *Romans*, 261. See especially Adolf von Schlatter, *Romans: The Righteousness of God* (trans. Siegfried S. Schatzmann; Peabody, MA: Hendrickson, 1995), 186–87.

[159] Cf. Carey C. Newman, *Paul's Glory-Christology: Tradition and Rhetoric* (NovTSup 69; Leiden: Brill, 1992), 17–78.

(8.17, 30) and the Spirit mediates this to believers.[160] Accordingly, glory is from God, and only shared with believers, particularly as they worship God properly (cf. 1.18–32; 4.20; 15.5–13).[161]

Second, this experience of new life – moral enablement and resurrection – fits squarely within Paul's eschatological present/future schema like adoption and salvation.[162] In the same way that the Spirit brings resurrection life in the future, the present enablement of the Spirit determines believers' existence. The present transformation is located primarily in the sphere of mind (8.5–8; cf. 12.1–2) and expressed in moral action,[163] whereas the future is more holistic as it also includes the body.

Third, we see a culmination of the righteousness-life focus that has driven the letter to this point. Those who are justified, are also glorified (8.30). In this 'golden chain', the following activity is the logical outcome of the prior one. Seifrid thus writes: 'The "glorification" which Paul attaches to this "justification" ... does not represent a subsequent act, but the vindication which accompanies the divine verdict. It consists in the resurrection from the dead, in which the children of God are glorified with Christ ...'.[164] As such, the granting of glory as resurrection is the logical outcome of the work of justification.[165] While our focus here is not to detail justification in the letter to the Romans, we noted earlier that justification is the response to condemnation, or we may say a reversal of a status of judgment by God; however, this status also entailed its outcome of death. Justification then stands as the response to this dual problem of condemnation and death. That is, the pronouncement of justification of entails both acquittal from this judgment *and* a restoration of life as experienced through participation in divine glory, a resurrection of the body,

---

[160] God is often the explicit or implicit agent of Christ's resurrection, as he raises Christ (ἐγείρειν [ἐκ νεκρῶν], 4.24, 25; 6.4, 5; 7.4; 8.11; 8.34) to resurrection (ἀνάστασις, 1.4; 6.5).

[161] Jervis (*Heart of the Gospel*, 105–6) even boldly contends that participation in glory is a participation in 'God's being'.

[162] Key verses that would support this are Rom 5.1–5; 6.4; 8.18, 23, and 29–30.

[163] The transformation discussion in 12.1–2 also draws on the theme of ethics and having a mind focused on God's will, which relates to the discussion of the mind set on the Spirit in chapter 8.

[164] Mark A. Seifrid, *Christ Our Righteousness: Paul's Theology of Justification* (Downers Grove: InterVarsity Press, 2000).

[165] Balz (*Heilsvertrauen*, 115) writes: 'Gottes Gerechtigkeit schafft Heil, indem sie den Glaubenden den Weg in ein Sein eröffnet, das von Christus her bestimmt ist und damit letztlich Gottes Doxa-Wirklichkeit unter den Bedingungen dieser Existenz repräsentiert. Rechtfertigung und Verherrlichung sind lediglich zwei verschiedene Aspekte des Heils der Glaubenden, denn das neue Urteil Gottes und die damit gesetzte Neuwerdung (ἐδικαίωσεν) bedeuten nichts anderes als die Verwirklichung des neuen Seins der Gotteskinder in dieser Welt (ἐδόξασεν)'.

through Christ and the Spirit. Beyond just a mere pronouncement, justification is God's act of new creation, which points to a participationist view of justification.[166] Much more could be explored here, but for the sake of our discussion we must not miss the climax in Paul's argument that he began in chapter one: the righteous one by faith will live. That is, those he justified, he also glorified.

4.2 Sonship as Conformation

Having addressed the first two of the three συν-prefixed words (συμπάσχω and συνδοξάζω), we now turn to consider the third – σύμμορφος, which captures the meaning of the first two. In the midst of a five-step salvation-historical progression of God's action towards believers (the 'golden chain'), Paul presents God's intention (πρόθεσις) that believers become 'conformed (σύμμορφος) to the image (εἰκών) of his son, so that he may be the firstborn among many brothers and sisters' (8.29).[167]   Van Kooten notes the importance of Paul's morphic theology because it links his Christology, anthropology, and soteriology.[168]   God's intention for believers is that they are to be christoform in their experience. While other passages contain a combination of morphic (σύμμορφος), image (εἰκών), and glory (δοξάζω) terminology (2 Cor 3.18; 1 Cor 15.40–49; Phil 3.21), the unique aspect of this passage is its motif of sonship.[169] We may ask then what the relationship is between these three: being conformed to Christ's image, sonship, and glorification.[170]

With the inclusion of τοῦ υἱοῦ αὐτοῦ modifying εἰκών, the motif of Christ the Son serving as the model for believers as sons returns from

---

[166] Gorman ('Romans', 27) writes: '*Paul does not conceive of sanctification as a stage of salvation between justification and glorification.* Rather, righteousification [*sic*] and glorification, new life [in the present] and eternal life [in the future], *dikaiosunē* and *doxa*, are two inseparable dimensions of God's overall salvation project'.

[167] The overlap between 9.23 and 8.29–30 is important. In 8.29–30 the πρόθεσις climaxes in glorification. In the same way, in 9.23 God has prepared beforehand (προετοιμάζω) believers for glory as their ultimate destiny.

[168] George van Kooten, *Paul's Anthropology in Context: The Image of God, Assimilation to God, and Tripartite Man in Ancient Judaism, Ancient Philosophy and Early Christianity* (WUNT 232; Tübingen: Mohr Siebeck, 2008), 71. Paul uses the term σύμμορφος (and its cognates) here and in Phil 3.10 and 3.21, which both have strong death-life associations. He also uses other 'morphic' (μορφή) language at other key points: Rom 12.2; Gal 4.19; 2 Cor 3.18; and Phil 2.6–7. While van Kooten traces the Jewish background to image language, he primarily places Paul in a Greco-Roman context and thus deemphasises the importance of resurrection in Paul's soteriology.

[169] Reidar Aasgaard, *'My Beloved Brothers and Sisters!': Christian Siblingship in Paul* (JSNTSup 265; London: T&T Clark, 2004), 139–41.

[170] This association between image and glory raises associations with Adam that we will discuss below in §4.3.

8.14–17. Rather than emphasising the 'image of God' (Gen 1.26–27), this conformation is to the 'image of his son' (Rom 8.29). Accordingly, Thüsing writes: 'Der Gedanke setzt einen engen Zusammenhang zwischen dem Sohn-Gottes- und dem Eikon-Gottes-Begriff voraus. Christus ist Eikon Gottes als der Sohn Gottes'.[171] This reminds the reader of the connection Paul makes between Jesus' status as Son of God and his resurrection in Rom 1.3–4.[172] Paul confirms this association with Christ's sonship through the purpose clause (εἰς τὸ εἶναι): 'in order that Christ would be firstborn (πρωτότοκος) among many brothers and sisters' (8.29).[173] Aasgaard notes Jesus as firstborn places him in the role of a model for the other siblings and culminates in their 'participation in an eschatological state of being'.[174] As believers are conformed to Christ's resurrection glory, they are fulfilling their status as sons of God.

While the Spirit is not overtly mentioned in these concluding verses, his role is implicit in the process. With the association of sonship and new life as glorification, Horn interestingly associates the Spirit's activity in glorification based on seeing the 'golden chain' as part of a baptismal rite.[175] Similarly, Campbell writes:

Implicit throughout this argument – whether in its ethical emphasis or its concern with assurance – is the notion that the Spirit is creating Christians at the behest of the Father but using the template (literally "image") of the Son (see 8:29). What the Son has done, and where he has been, is what Christians are currently being "mapped onto" by the activity of the Spirit.[176]

This, then, corresponds to my previous assertion that glorification is both present and future through the work of the Spirit.

With the density of familial language in 8.29 (son, firstborn, and brothers and sisters), Paul returns to themes that we saw in 8.14–17 and 8.23. As we saw earlier, Christ's obedience is closely related to his status as Son. Believers' role as co-heirs with Christ in 8.17 implies a fraternal relationship, which is explained as one of sharing his suffering (συμπάσχω) and glory (συνδοξάζω). Rowe writes: 'To suffer and die in the present with the hope of resurrection is in a precise sense to be in the εἰκὼν τοῦ

---

[171] Thüsing, *Per Christum*, 125. Cf. Byrne, *'Sons'*, 119. The Son-image connection also might form the basis of an exchange: the Son became like (ὁμοίωμα) humanity in their weakness (8.3) and now believers are conformed (σύμμορφος) to the εἰκών of the Son (8.29) in his glory.

[172] Cf. Scott, *Adoption*, 244–45.

[173] See Col 1.15–18 for πρωτότοκος and εἰκών in the same context. Also, cf. Ps 89.28 as a messianic background for the notion of the firstborn. Ibid., 252–55.

[174] Aasgaard, *Brothers and Sisters*, 144–45, 149. Cf. Gieniusz, *Romans 8:18–30*, 274–75.

[175] Horn, *Angeld*, 422–24.

[176] Campbell, 'Story of Jesus', 106.

υἱοῦ or to share the form (σύμμορφος) of his image: the pattern that is the life, death and resurrection of Jesus Christ'.[177]   As believers are conformed to the Son, this conformation is not only ontological in the resurrection but also moral, as they more fully obey the Father as Christ did. This fits within our previous discussion of adoption as not merely an intimate relationship but also an ontological reality culminating in resurrection life. In this confluence of glory, sonship, and conformation language, Paul is again arguing that sonship culminates in the experience of resurrection life as an inheritance but is also embodied presently. Thus, as Paul associates conformation to Christ with familial language in 8.28–30, he draws together the primary themes of 8.14–30 so that σύμμορφος becomes the umbrella under which υἱοθεσία as συμπάσχω and συνδοξάζω stands.

4.3 Adam, Creation, and Re-creation

Though we have focused on believers' anthropological experience in this passage, creational themes are clear.   With diverging opinions within apocalyptic and salvation historical interpretations of Paul, a particularly important question is the role of continuity and discontinuity with regard to creation and eschatology.   Those focusing on apocalyptic tend to emphasise discontinuity due to God's eschatological in-breaking, whereas those focusing on God's salvation-historical activity tend to emphasise continuity in his work.   Early patristic writers, and Irenaeus in particular, often focus on the continuity between creation and re-creation, but he also noted the necessity of progression between the two stages.   Patristic authors may be open to the charge of minimising Paul's apocalyptic language with regard to re-creation.   That Paul is drawing from Genesis 1–3 in the context of eschatological fulfilment seems clear since he uses the term κτίσις four times in 8.18–22 and notes its subjection to futility and bondage to corruption (8.19–21).[178]   Stanley points out that Paul is uncommon in his regular use of creation themes from Genesis, and so we should not ignore its purpose in his writing.[179]   As a result, we have the opportunity to consider

---

[177] C. Kavin Rowe, 'New Testament Iconography? Situating Paul in the Absence of Material Evidence' in *Picturing the New Testament,* eds. Annette Weissenrieder, et al. (Tübingen: Mohr Siebeck, 2005), 289–312, at 303.

[178] Edward Adams, 'Paul's Story of God and Creation: The Story of How God Fulfils His Purposes in Creation' in *Narrative Dynamics in Paul: A Critical Assessment,* ed. Bruce W. Longenecker (London: Westminster John Knox, 2002), 19–43, at 28–29.

[179] David M. Stanley, 'Paul's Interest in the Early Chapters of Genesis' in *Studiorum Paulinorum,* (Rome: Pontifico Instituto Biblico, 1963), 241–252, at 241–43, 251.   With Paul's earlier presentation of an Adam-Christ dialectic (Rom 5.12–21), Adam's presence becomes even more clear since Christ is presented as the eschatological telos of humanity, resolving the problem of corruption from Adam.   Adams (*Constructing,* 37) writes: 'The concentration of Adam motifs in the opening and closing sections of the argument,

how he presents soteriological continuity and discontinuity. We will first consider the problems faced by creation and then address how Adam fits within Paul's narrative.[180]

In this passage, Paul presents creation's problem and solution as intimately tied to that of humanity.[181] Adams reminds us that since sin entered εἰς τὸν κόσμον in 5.12, the implication is that 'the κόσμος is not inherently sinful or mortal'.[182] Thus, creation is not something against God but rather the disputed territory of cosmic powers. In like manner, κτίσις has been made subject to futility (ματαιότης; 8.20), which is most likely a reference to God's curse after the fall as in Gen 3.17–19.[183] In this manner, Paul follows traditions within other Jewish apocalyptic writings that highlight humanity's role in introducing corruption into creation in distinction to those that lay blame at the feet of external agents.[184] However, rather than just being a neutral battleground, Cranfield describes the implicit positive role of creation in light of the fact that this futility is a 'frustration of not being able properly to fulfil the purpose of its existence'.[185] Under this curse, creation groans (συνωδίνω) in anticipation of restoration.[186] Adams then notes the continuity between αὐτὴ ἡ κτίσις (8.21) and re-creation: In distinction to 1 Corinthians Paul here emphasises the 'continuity between this creation and the transformed creation', such that 'the linguistic role of κόσμος in 1 Corinthians as the main negative theological term of the epistle has been taken over in Romans by the triad ἁμαρτία, θάνατος, and σάρξ'.[187] This experience of non-human creation (as most interpreters[188]) is not separate from humanity, since in solidarity both groan together and have the same expectations (8.19–23).

1:18–32 and 8:18–30, suggests that the story frames the overall presentation of Romans 1–8,' especially with the explicit discussion in the centre 5.12–21.

[180] While our focus is primarily on the anthropological aspects of this passage, John Bolt ('The Relation Between Creation and Redemption in Romans 8:18–27', *CTJ* 30 [1995]: 34–51) challenges interpreters also to see the place of creation itself.

[181] Cf. John G. Gibbs, *Creation and Redemption: A Study in Pauline Theology* (NovTSup 26; Leiden: Brill, 1971), 40–41.

[182] Adams, *Constructing*, 173.

[183] Again, noting the neutral aspect of creation, Adams states: 'Paul makes clear that ματαιότης was not inherent in or original to the creation'. Ibid., 178.

[184] Hahne, *Corruption and Redemption*, 186–93, 210–13. However, we should also note the personified powers that hold sway over the current age: Sin, Death, and the Flesh.

[185] Cranfield, *Romans*, 1:413.

[186] This is also a possible Genesis association related to pain in childbearing (Gen 3.16).

[187] Adams, *Constructing*, 190–91.

[188] E.g., Cranfield, *Romans*, 1:411–12; Adams, *Constructing*, 176–78.

If Paul appears to point to continuity between creation and re-creation, how does that influence specifically human concerns? Is glorification a return to the prelapsarian state or something much greater by comparison? To address this question, we will consider the apparent Adamic allusions within this text. These allusions include the discussion of κτίσις, problems from the fall, the glory/corruption contrast, and image language. Adams thus describes Rom 8.19–22 and 8.28–30 as having clear 'Adam' motifs, along with 3.23 and 7.7–13.[189]

While Christ serves as the telos of humanity (the image to which they are conformed) in this passage, Paul does not present a developed protology here. That is, Paul does not explicitly state what Adam's prelapsarian state is. Paul only explores Adam's role as the one who introduces sin and death into humanity's story (5.12, cf. 3.23). Other Jewish writings interact more fully with Adam traditions, incorporating ideas regarding his protological and eschatological glory.[190] While Paul is probably drawing from these traditions, he makes clear that humanity lost participation in God's immortal glory (1.23; 3.23). In the same manner, the restoration to glory is not a return to Adam's glory, as characterised by the three texts preserved in Qumran (1QS 4:22–23; CD 3:19–20; 1QH^a 4:14–15 [17:14–15]) which speak of אדם כבוד כול ('all the glory of Adam') to describe the eschatological state, but rather a participation in the glory of Christ. In fact, this glorification is predetermined before creation (8:29), and so it predates creation and Adam's loss of glory. Thus, as a model of the in-

---

[189] Adams, 'Paul's Story', 26. Interestingly, A.J.M. Wedderburn ('Adam in Paul's Letter to the Romans' in *Studia Biblica 1978,* ed. E. Livingstone (Sheffield: JSOT Press, 1978), 413–30) does not mention Romans 8 in his discussion of Adam in Romans. In summary of his view of Adam in Paul, he ('Adam', 423) writes:

Certainly, Adam is not for Paul just one individual human being among others, any more than Christ is; like Christ, he is by virtue of his position in God's plan, representative of other men and he blazes a trail for them to follow. But, unlike Christ, he is still, for Paul, chronologically the first man, and this is also significant for Paul; he is not just some timeless exemplar of a certain existential experience of man with his God. By insisting on the guilt of this man Paul, along with his fellow Jews, insists on the universality of sin: all men are in its clutches; from the first it has dominated human history. The history of sin is co-terminous with the history of mankind.

[190] Cf. Blackwell, 'Immortal Glory', 287–91. Adam's fall from glory is represented by several Jewish texts – *Apoc. Mos.* 20–21; 38.1–2; *Gen. Rab.* 12.6; and *3 Bar.* 4.16 (Greek). At the same time, several texts present the eschatological goal for the righteous as an experience of glory like Adam's: 1QS 4.6–8, 22–23; CD 3.19–20; 1QH 17.15; *T. Abr.* 11:8–9. Byrne (*'Sons'*, 66, cf. 68–70) points to the restoration of humanity to be like 'man at the beginning'. However, John R. Levison (*Portraits of Adam in Early Judaism: From Sirach to 2 Baruch* [JSPSup 1; Sheffield: JSOT Press, 1988], 160) notes that this is not universal because 4 Ezra and 2 Baruch do not associate Adam with the *Endzeit.*

stantiation of glory, Christ is the better place to focus.[191] We may draw
from the Adam-Christ comparison in Rom 5, where Christ's obedience is
all the greater than Adam's disobedience. By analogy, Christ's glory is all
the greater than Adam's glory.[192] Accordingly, the eschatological state is
most likely not just a return to the protological state but rather something
greater by comparison.[193]

We may now consider the intersection of re-creation and the restoration
of humanity. Death and corruption are intrusions into God's order that
need to be conquered and undone. Thus, Christ is fulfilling the goal of
God's original intention. Adams describes this as 'a *creation history*
rather than a salvation history'.[194] Hahne labels it a 'transformation' rather
than a singularly new creation, a simple reversal of sin's effect, or a return
to pre-fall conditions.[195] The connection with creation highlights the holistic aspect of Christian redemption. Black writes:

> Redemption is not confined to our soma but is operative with respect to the whole of the
> Creator's work. The lordship of Christ, sealed by his resurrection from the dead, func-
> tions as nothing less than the universal reclamation of God's sovereignty over everything
> that has been created.[196]

Paul carefully associates new creation with old creation such that continuity is maintained. However, with the christocentric nature of soteriology, believers do not merely return to Adam's former glory. Rather, they
are now moulded into Christ's glory. Just as the incarnation is not the em-

---

[191] Even with Dunn's emphasis on Adam Christology, he notes that in distinction to
other Jewish writings Christ becomes central even though Adam themes are throughout:
'In Paul's theology Adam is pushed aside at this point, and Christ alone fills the stage'.
Dunn, *Christology*, 106.

[192] Cf. Jervell, *Imago Dei*, 284–92.

[193] The focus of this essay is on the anthropological experience of glory, which leads
to an emphasis on the role of Adam. However, were we to focus on the related issue of
glory as the mediation of God's presence, OT themes related to the Temple and Moses'
reception of the law would need to be explored. The correlation between worship and the
experience of God's presence is clear (e.g., 1:23; 5:2). Accordingly, we cannot simply
disaggregate Adam and Temple themes in the letter, and particularly in 1:23. Cf.
Newman, *Glory-Christology*, 17–78; Wright, *Romans*, 556.

[194] Adams, *Constructing*, 38, emphasis original.

[195] Hahne, *Corruption and Redemption*, 227. Beker ('Suffering', 118) writes: 'Paul
posits the coming triumph of God as a reality which embraces and glorifies the created
world rather than annuls or destroys it'.

[196] Black, 'Death', 428. Humanity then serves as a microcosm and mediator of creation. As microcosm, humanity reflects the problems faced by all of God's creation. As
mediator, humanity is shown to be the cause of trouble but also the source of its restoration (8.21). See Maximus the Confessor for a development of this. Cf. Lars Thunberg,
Microcosm and Mediator: The Theological Anthropology of Maximus the Confessor
(Lund: Gleerup, 1965).

phasis of Christ's work in 8.1–4 but stands as a necessary and important prerequisite for his death and resurrection, creation stands in the background of the soteriological emphasis of being conformed to Christ in his suffering and glory.

4.4 Conclusion

Based on our discussion of 8.17–30 centred around συμπάσχω (8.17), συνδοξάζω (8.17), and σύμμορφος (8.29), we have seen that Christ's experience is determinative for those who follow him. His suffering and glory are both the means and model of life for believers as they reproduce his image. Being glorified, or experiencing the resurrection life of Christ through the agency of the Spirit, is the pinnacle of being conformed to Christ's image. With the confluence of conformation, familial, and glorification language within the passage, we see that they are all three different ways of discussing the same eschatological result of sharing Christ's immortal life.

5. Summary and Conclusion

In Romans 8, Paul recounts divine liberation as new life and associates this liberation with various overlapping images, concepts, and themes. This new life fits directly in the larger of the scope of the letter (and particularly, chapters 1-8), where Paul is drawing out the implications that the righteous one by faith will live. We saw a primary emphasis here on the the basis and experience of that new life, and Paul also reiterated the direct connection between righteousness and new life (8.10, 30).

To begin the chapter Paul presents an intimate relationship between believers and God through Christ and the Spirit (8.1–13). Through this divine-human relationship, God has liberated believers from the grip of death, imparting somatic and ethical life. Paul then explains the divine-human relationship in terms of adoption and the parent-child bond (8.14–30). In addition to describing the new people of God as closely united to him as children, Paul furthers his discussion of liberation, developing it as an ontological reality of somatic resurrection life arising from this relationship. Transitioning to a discussion of suffering and glory (8.17–30), Paul continues to develop the theme of new life and liberation. While he notes sharing in both aspects – suffering and glory – with suffering being imperative for glory, Paul later portrays the experience of glory as liberation from present suffering. This process of sharing in Christ's suffering and glory culminates in being conformed 'to the image of [God's] son' (8.29), with the result that sonship and conformation are different ways to speak of the same process. Accordingly, we may say that being conformed to Christ's image is nothing other than the eschatological process of adoption and glorification. This same pattern of embodying Christ's death and life was evident in our discussion of Colossians 2–3, whereas in Galatians 3–4 adoption through identification with Christ and the Spirit was central. Through these chapters Paul has developed several key soteriological issues which addressed our central questions: the shape of soteriology, the timing, the means, and the relation of eschatological soteriology and creation, which we will address in turn.

5.1 Primary Questions

5.1.1 The Shape of Soteriology: Death and Life

Our primary question concerns the shape of Pauline soteriology in this chapter as it relates to the human. The fundamental thesis of Romans 8 is that Christ and the Spirit liberate believers from sin and death by granting them new life. This contrast of death and life permeates the whole chapter (and also Colossians 2–3). Focusing on the tension between the present and past, Paul discusses moral enablement and somatic resurrection in the first half (8.1–13). He then addresses the tension between the present and future as he focuses on suffering and glory as instantiations of death and life in the second half (8.14–30).

At the basis of Paul's discussion is the interplay of inter-personal and intra-personal problems and solutions. Regarding the inter-personal issues, Paul presents the fundamental human plight as a breakdown in their relationship with God. Those under the flesh are 'hostile to God' and 'unable to please him' (Rom 8.6). Earlier in Romans the foundation of this problem originates from humans' faithlessness and refusal to worship God alone, turning to other gods (Rom 1.18–32). This leads to wrath and judgment from God, and in our passages this is reflected in condemnation language (Rom 8.1). Humans have also broken relationships with one another and with creation (Rom 8.19–23), but their relationship with God is most central to our texts. Personalized agents of Sin, Death, and the Flesh facilitate this breakdown. In addition, the law plays an ambiguous role because believers are freed from it (Rom 7.1–6; Gal 3.21–4.7), but they also fulfil it (8.4). In Galatians 4 the domination of the law is also correlated with the enslaving στοιχεῖα τοῦ κόσμου (Gal 4.3, 11), which is not unlike the situation in Col 2.8, 20.

This inter-personal struggle with these 'external' agents cannot be separated from the intra-personal struggle that instantiates the fruit of their work. Drawing from chapter 7, Paul begins with the weakness of the flesh, in that it subverts the ability of the law to enable moral action, and the result of this life in the flesh is death (7.4–5; 8.5–8, 12–13). The intra-personal problem of death is literal in that it refers to physical corruption (8.10) but also metaphorical as it refers to ethical inability (7.4), noetic death (8.6) and the problem of suffering (8.17–23). As a result, inter- and intra-personal problems are deeply intertwined.

In response to these problems, God through Christ and the Spirit restores inter- and intra-personal harmony. The soteriological models that Paul employs throughout this chapter capture the relational and personal restoration. For instance, as Christ and the Spirit liberate believers from sin and death (8.1–2), this is both a release from 'external' domination and an internal empowerment to live for God. In the same way, adoption is a means of a reinstated relationship with God (8.14–16), but it also serves as a description of the resurrection of the body (8.23). While Paul does not develop justification language here, it too points to a relationship set right (3.21–26), but it also is tied closely to new life (8.10, 30; Gal 3.21). In the same way, believers had their record of debt cancelled before God through death with Christ and were therefore made alive with him (Col 2.9–15). In Romans, we also noted how glorification denotes both relational honour and ontological incorruption. With all these models, the ultimate outcome is life. Just as death pervaded the whole person, so does life. This new life actuated by the Spirit entails moral (7.6), noetic (8.6), and somatic (8.10–11, *passim*) effects. As a result, the climax of the soteriological event is sharing in divine glory and immortality modelled by Christ and effected by the Spirit.

5.1.2 The Timing: Present/Future

As we turn to the question of the timing of the experience of life, we see that Paul's death-life dialectic stands firmly in the midst of his eschatological present/future framework. The passage begins with the emphatic 'Οὐδὲν ἄρα νῦν κατάκριμα' (8.1). God's work of liberation is a present experience, wrought through the decisive work of Christ and the Spirit (8.2–3). This turn of the ages is very evident in Galatians 3–4, which is also marked by the advent of Christ and the Spirit. While present tense verbs do not always denominate time, their consistent use throughout the discussion of 8.4–17 with regard to the Spirit and the flesh indicates these two spheres of existence are present realities. Thus, the moral enablement granted by the Spirit is a current experience for believers. At the same time, the somatic experience of resurrection life is presented consistently as future – ζῳοποιήσει and ζήσεσθε (8.11, 13), as the present experience of dead/mortal bodies confirms (8.10, 11). The Spirit's activity then brings both current life (8.2, 6) and future life (8.11, 13). While Christ's and the Spirit's work over sin and death is decisive, the consummation of victory over mortality has not yet been actualised.

To be sure, the language in Colossians 2.12-13 is ambiguous about the the timing due to its 'raised' language in the aorist. However, by stating that 'you' have been raised, this can (and probably should) be read metaphorically in a way consistent with Romans 8 (and 6). This is clear from Col 3.4, which speaks of Christ appearing (somatically) in the future and the believers' experience of (somatic) glory. Although the language appears more 'realised' in Colossians, this points strongly to the consistency between the two letters in which they have been made alive in Christ presently but will experience somatic glory in the future.

With regard to adoption, this present/future paradigm is also clear. Those led by the Spirit are (εἰσιν) sons of God, for they have (already) received the Spirit of adoption (8.14–15). In the same way, they are children, heirs and co-heirs (8.16–17). All these statements affirm believers' current status as the people of God and would give little indication that this is anything but a completed event. In fact, the language in Galatians 4 focuses primarily on the current status of the people of God. However, the heir language in both passages points to a future experience, and this future experience becomes explicit in Romans when Paul writes that believers are eagerly awaiting their adoption, the redemption of their bodies (8.23). This discussion of redemption of bodies correlates with the hope of future resurrection noted in 8.11.

Paul continues to present a mixed picture of the soteriological benefits when discussing suffering and glory. The current experience is described as one of suffering, which is associated with ὁ νῦν καιρός (8.18). At the same time, all creation has been groaning and straining ἄχρι τοῦ νῦν (8.22). However, in the midst of these current difficulties, Paul notes the hope for future glory displayed in eager expectation, and this hope is confirmed by the ἀπαρχή of the Spirit (8.23–25). Interestingly, Paul notes that believers have been saved (ἐσώθημεν) in this hope. This is the only aorist use of σῴζω in the undisputed letters, but it is based on hope for a future work, as yet unseen.[197] Future glory, experienced as immortal life, is held out as the consummation of salvation (8.18–30). However, ambiguity enters the picture with Paul's use of the aorist with δοξάζω in 8.30 (Cf. Col 3.4). Vollenweider writes: 'Endlich setzt Paulus in Röm 8 gerade die der Eleutheria korrespondierenden Begriffe der *Sohnschaft* und der *Verherrlichung* sowohl in den Modus der Gegenwart wie der Zukunft'.[198] Accordingly, believers' lives are presently characterised by suffering and the Spirit's enabling power of life. The future will be characterised by the life

---

[197] Cf. Eph 2.5, 8; Tit 3.5.

[198] Samuel Vollenweider, *Freiheit als neue Schöpfung: Eine Untersuchung zur Eleutheria bei Paulus und in seiner Umwelt* (Göttingen: Vandenhoeck & Ruprecht, 1989), 386.

of the Spirit transforming bodies into the immortal archetype, which is Christ.

5.1.3 The Means: Participation in the Divine

With regard to the means of experiencing this eschatological life, participation in Christ and the Spirit is the centre of Paul's description. Christ shared in the depths of human mortality and died on the cross as a sin offering. God raised him from the dead and promises that same life to those who follow in his pattern of suffering and glorify by means of the Spirit working in them. Some (e.g., Schweitzer[199] and Wrede[200] and more recently Campbell[201]) draw a stark distinction between a forensic-only justification, which addresses the problem of condemnation and an apocalyptic participation which addresses the problem of death, and promote the latter. However, Romans 8, Galatians 3–4, and Colossians 2 subvert this proposed division.

Paul presents sin as producing condemnation and mortality, and the solution for sin as rectifying one's status before God and creating new life. From the beginning of the chapter, Paul presents the problem by mixing the forensic with apocalyptic terminology: There is no (forensic) condemnation because the (apocalyptic) Spirit has freed those who participate in Christ from sin and death (8.1–2). He then describes how those who walk κατὰ πνεῦμα (8.4) fulfil the righteous decree of the law. The height of the forensic-participation intersection is found in 8.10: 'If Christ is in you, the body is dead on account of sin but the Spirit is life on account of righteousness'. The connection between justification and the giving of the Spirit is central for Galatians 3 where the promise of the Spirit is intimately intertwined with the discussion of justification by faith. Thus, the life-giving work of the Spirit is the means of life-giving righteousness. This association between righteousness and life culminates in 8.30, where Paul draws the conclusion that those who are justified are glorified. Through the work of Christ who condemned sin and its effects and the Spirit who actualises the resurrection life in believers, God carries out his justifying work of new creation.

Paul describes participation in this chapter primarily through his use of prepositions and oblique cases. In the Rom 8.1–11, Gal 3.26–29, and Col 2.6–15, he uses ἐν and κατά repeatedly with both Christ and the Spirit: in Christ, into Christ, of Christ, Christ in you, (living/walking) according to the Spirit, in the Spirit, having the Spirit, the Spirit dwelling in you.

---

[199] Schweitzer, *Mysticism*, 224–26.

[200] Wrede, *Paul*, 127–37.

[201] Douglas A. Campbell, *The Deliverance of God: An Apocalyptic Rereading of Justification in Paul* (Grand Rapids: Eerdmans, 2009).

These are used reciprocally, overlapping in various ways. He then transitions to adoption and sonship language to describe the divine-human relationship in 8.14–30; however, he quickly returns to his use of prepositions as well. This time συν- prefixed words are the emphasis, used in conjunction with the familial metaphors and image language. As we consider participation, Paul's discussion of unity in Christ in Gal 3.26–29 (cf. Col 3.11) also reflects the variety of prepositional phrases and images, which centres around baptismal language. The repetition and variety in both passages points to the importance of participation for Paul, but it also shows the limitation of any one idea or phrase as centre. Rather, Paul compounds the imagery like overlapping circles that reveal participation as the centre without any one image fully describing the experience (See Figure 5.1).

Figure 5.1: Overlapping Images of Participation

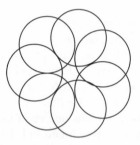

The fruit of participation in Christ and the Spirit is that believers become like Christ, particularly like his somatic resurrection, as the culmination of salvation. Just as he exists in a divine state of glory, this will be the state of believers as well.[202] And, thus, Morna Hooker's use of the language of 'interchange' helps capture the mutuality between Christ's experience and that of believers.[203]

5.1.4 Eschatology and Protology

Our final question centres around the level of continuity and discontinuity between eschatological soteriology and original creation. Paul does not present a developed account of creation from which one might make a full analysis. However, at certain points in the letter Paul notes the entrance of

---

[202] C.F. Evans (*Resurrection and the New Testament* [London: SCM, 1970], 160) writes: '... the present possession of spirit, which is all there is, is a foretaste and promise of something further, which is the full life of "glory", an eschatological term which comes nearest to denoting the divine life itself'.

[203] Hooker, *From Adam*, 13–69.

corruption into the created order (e.g., 5.12; 8.20). Based on this, we can infer that Paul understood original creation as free from the corrupting influences of sin. In addition, Paul presents creation as seeking the fulfilment of God's plan since creation will benefit from the eschatological restoration (8.19–22). Rather than needing to be destroyed, creation is renewed, or 'transformed', in Paul's presentation.

When we consider the protological anthropology in this passage, we see only allusions to Adam in Romans 8. Through Christ the true image is restored to humanity such that they share in his glory. Therefore, the original intention of God in creation is fulfilled in humanity, but this is not just a return to Eden. Rather, we see hints that the work of Christ in sharing the glory of God with humanity surpasses the original state of glory, which was not permanent.

5.2 Conclusion

Through their relationship with divine agents believers are formed in such a way that they take on divine characteristics, of which life and glory are primary. The Son of God and the Spirit of God mediate the life and glory of God to believers. 'The Spirit of life' (8.2), also 'the Spirit [who] is life' (8.10), grants that life to believers somatically (8.11, *passim*) but also noetically (8.6) and ethically (8.12–13). When considering the readings of this chapter offered by Cyril and Irenaeus, we see a striking overlap with their theologies of deification. In particular, they emphasised that 1) life and death are central soteriological poles, 2) adoption is not just a relationship but an ontological reality, 3) the telos of believers is to be conformed to the image of Christ, 4) the Spirit is central in the experience of new life, and 5) this experience of new life is fundamentally a liberation from sin, death, and the flesh. At the same time, the question of the law is central to Paul's exposition, does not play the same function due to their different contexts. With the issue of law being so central to Paul's discussion, we must ask what is lost by not including it. Can you reach the same ends (immortal life) by ignoring aspects of the means (freedom from law) to get there? We will return to these observations and questions in chapter 8.

6. 2 Corinthians 3–5

1. Introduction

Our next text for discussion is 2 Corinthians 3–5, where Paul explores key soteriological themes in the midst of a justification of his ministry. Like Romans, Paul addresses righteousness, resurrection, glory, and life in the context of the law, suffering, and death. As with our discussion of Romans 8, several questions will guide our analysis: 1) What is the anthropological shape of Pauline soteriology? 2) When do the changes occur? 3) How does this come about? 4) How does this relate to creation? After considering how the chapter fits into the context of the letter, we will consider these questions through the major sections of 2 Corinthians 3–5: 3.1–4.6 (§2), 4.7–5.10 (§3), and 5.11–6.2 (§4). In addition to 2 Corinthians 3–5, we will also have short excursus on Philippians 2–3 (§3.2) and 1 Corinthians 15 (§3.4) since they address related issues.

In order to understand the role of 2 Corinthians 3–5, we should first consider the larger argument of 2.14–7.4.[1] In the introduction to chapters 1–9, Paul describes two distinct soteriological emphases, comfort (παράκλησις, 1.3–7) and deliverance (ῥύομαι, 1.8–11), in the context of mutuality. God provides present comfort in the midst of difficult circumstances faced by both Paul and the Corinthians, and God also delivers Paul from temporal troubles.[2] In his justification of his travel decisions (1.12–2.13) the contentious nature of Paul's relationship with (some of) the Corinthians, which sets the stage for our passage, comes to the fore.

---

[1] Due to disjunctive turns in the argument within the canonical form of 2 Corinthians, scholars have proposed that it is a combination of two or more letters written by Paul. The major sections include chapters 1–8; 9; and 10–13. In addition, many see 2.14–7.4 (excluding 6.14–7.1) as a distinct section. Since chapters 3–5 fit wholly within this section, theories regarding the division of the canonical text will not influence the argument. However, for any issues that arise I treat 1–9 and 10–13 as distinct units, based upon Watson's argument: Francis Watson, '2 Cor. 10–13 and Paul's Painful Letter to the Corinthians', *JTSns* 35 (1984): 324–46. See particularly Margaret E. Thrall, *2 Corinthians* (ICC; 2 vols.; London: T&T Clark, 1994), 1:3–49.

[2] Cf. David Briones, 'Mutual Brokers of Grace: A Study in 2 Corinthians 1.3–11', *NTS* 56 (2010): 536–56.

In the remainder of chapter 2 through chapter 6, Paul sets out a defence of his ministry. In an introductory passage (2.14–17), Paul argues that although God is working through him in his frank and sincere proclamation, his ministry may not appear externally successful. This seeming failure stems from two primary reasons: 1) true ministers participate as much in Christ's death as in Christ's life, and 2) others do not properly perceive the message and thus do not accept it. These themes will also run throughout his following argument. Paul's difficult experiences (1.8–11; 4.7–12; 6.3–10; cf. 11.23–29; 12.10–11) do not reveal God's disapproval but rather divine approval of his ministry, in that the difficulties are the experience of the death and life of Jesus.[3] Even though 'evidence' appears to the contrary – regular troubles and a perceived lack of understanding and response – God is working through his ministry. Paul is calling the Corinthians to a proper understanding of God's agency within the ministry of the gospel, which is evidenced by the Spirit in the midst of death and life. Martyn describes it in this way: 'Paul defends his apostleship by various arguments, all of which refer to the turn of the ages,' such that there is 'an inextricable connexion between eschatology and epistemology'.[4] Thus, the evidence from Paul's ministry, which reflects the Christ event, demands the Corinthians adopt a new epistemology.

That Paul defends his ministry by explaining the soteriological content of his message makes these chapters appropriate for our study. For example, we see from the beginning the clear use of soteriological language: ζωή, θάνατος, σῴζω, and ἀπόλλυμι (2.15). Thus, by weaving together an apology for his ministry with his soteriology, Paul supports them both. While the defence is central, as we walk through key passages within this section, the soteriology that undergirds it will be our focus.

2. The Spirit, Life, and Transformation: 3.1–4.6

After setting out the key themes in 2.14–17, Paul unpacks different aspects of his defence through the next several chapters. He contrasts the old and new covenants, centred around the issues of glory, veiling, and transformation to support his argument about the Spirit's work. Following Martyn's contention that the issue of epistemology permeates the whole section (2.14–6.10), Duff rightly notes: 'Paul's attention to accurate and faulty

---

[3] The opponents argued otherwise. Accordingly, Jerry L. Sumney (*Identifying Paul's Opponents: The Question of Method in 2 Corinthians* [JSNTSup 40; Sheffield: JSOT Press, 1990], 147, emphasis original) writes: '*The entire debate between Paul and his opponents centers on the proper manifestation of divine power in apostles' lives*'.

[4] Martyn, *Theological Issues*, 92.

perception throughout 2 Cor 2:14–4:6 – and particularly his claim that the clarity of one's perception is tied to one's status vis-à-vis salvation – recommends that this entire section is concerned with the distinction between appearance and reality'.[5] Paul uses the reality of the new covenant experience as support for his style of ministry. That is, the Spirit-driven nature of the new covenant stands as the legitimation of Paul's ministry as divinely inspired and open.

2.1 Spirit of the New Covenant (3.1–6)

Using the theme of letters of commendation, Paul quickly builds his argument around a distinction between the old and new covenants. Calling into question the need for these letters, he claims that the Corinthian believers are themselves the letters based upon the Spirit's action (3.1–3). The competence (ἱκανότης) that ministers of a new covenant have comes explicitly from God (cf. 4.4–6). This is clear from the contrast of the life-giving Spirit and the death-dealing letter. As we explore this passage, the Spirit's new covenant work will be our focus.

Paul weaves together several intertextual references within 3.2–3 by associating letters of recommendation with the old and new covenants. As he contrasts the old and new covenants, Paul builds his case from OT textual echoes and allusions. For the new covenant he uses language from Jeremiah and Ezekiel: 'written on our hearts (ἐγγεγραμμένη ἐν ταῖς καρδίαις ἡμῶν)' (3.2; Jer 38.33 LXX [31.33 MT]) and 'fleshy hearts (πλὰξ καρδία σαρκίνα)' (3.3; Ezek 36.26). Regarding the old covenant, Paul's primary focus is Exodus 31–34, as he alludes to Moses' two Sinai experiences and the giving of the law on 'stone tablets (πλάκες λίθιναι)' (3.3; Exod 31.18; 32.15–16; 34.1, 4, 28–29). In 3.3 he implicitly identifies the stone tablets of the Mosaic covenant with hearts of stone (and with letters of commendation). In 3.6 Paul makes this contrast explicit by directly associating his ministry with the 'new covenant' (διαθήκη καινή) from Jer 38.31 (LXX, 31.31 MT) in contrast to the 'old covenant' (παλαιὰ διαθήκη) in 3.14.

This explicit interaction with the new covenant promises demands closer attention. Paul's quotations come from two of the primary new covenant promises in the prophets: Jer 38.31–33 (LXX) and Ezek 36.26–27 (cf. the parallel passage in Ezek 11.19–20). These read:

Jer 38.31–33 (LXX): 'Behold, days are coming, says the Lord, and I will make a new covenant (διαθήκη καινή) with the house of Israel and the house of Judah. It will not be like the covenant I made with their fathers in the day when I took them by the hand to bring them out of the land of Egypt, because they did not abide by my covenant, and I

---

[5] Paul B. Duff, 'Transformed 'from Glory to Glory': Paul's Appeal to the Experience of His Readers in 2 Corinthians 3:18', *JBL* 127 (2008): 759–780, 775.

was unconcerned for them, says the Lord .... Giving I will give my laws in their mind, and I will write them on their hearts (ἐπὶ καρδίας αὐτῶν γράψω αὐτούς), and I will become God to them, and they will become a people to me' (NETS).

Ezek 36.26–27 (LXX): 'And I will give you a new heart, and a new spirit I will put in you, and I will remove the stone heart (τὴν καρδίαν τὴν λιθίνην) from your flesh and give you a heart of flesh (καρδίαν σαρκίνην). And I will put my spirit in you and will act so that you walk in my statutes and keep my judgments and perform them' (NETS).

Ezek 11.19–20 (LXX): 'And I will give them another heart, and I will put a new spirit in them, and I will draw forth the heart of stone (τὴν καρδίαν τὴν λιθίνην) from their flesh and I will give them a heart of flesh (καρδίαν σαρκίνην) so that they might walk in my ordinances and keep my statutes and perform them, and they will become a people to me, and I will become God to them' (NETS).

Reading these texts together as Paul did, we see that the new covenant expectation consists primarily of God 1) granting the πνεῦμα, 2) putting his law in their minds and writing it on their hearts that they might obey it, 3) reforming his people, and 4) returning this people to the land.[6] All three texts specifically refer to a change of heart, and Ezekiel closely associates that new heart with a new spirit (πνεῦμα). In contrast to the law as external under the current system, the new heart and new spirit is the basis of the law as internal under the promised system, which provides the means to fulfilling the law. As exilic restoration promises, these passages are found within the context of restoration to the land and an expectation of a re-established relationship between God and his people.

In addition to intellectual illumination, divine empowerment, people formation, and restoration to the land, the πνεῦμα is also the basis of resurrection imagery in Ezek 37.1–14, which complements the Ezekiel 36 passage. The πνεῦμα returns to their dry bones, and the passage ends with this promise: '"I will put my spirit in you, and you shall live, and I will place you on your own soil; then you will know that I, the Lord, have spoken and will act", says the Lord' (Ezek 37.1–14 LXX, NETS). As with the earlier Ezekiel texts, the presence of the Spirit is central to this future promise of somatic life. The hope of restoration to the land is thus closely related to this promise of new life.[7]

---

[6] Cf. Scott J. Hafemann, *Paul, Moses, and the History of Israel: The Letter/Spirit Contrast and the Argument from Scripture in 2 Corinthians 3* (Peabody, MA: Hendrickson, 1996), 126–56.

[7] Andrew Chester explores the individual and corporate aspects of this verse. Andrew Chester, 'Resurrection and Transformation' in *Auferstehung – Resurrection: The Fourth Durham-Tübingen Research Symposium: Resurrection, Transfiguration and Exaltation in Old Testament, Ancient Judaism and Early Christianity,* eds. Friedrich Avemarie and Hermann Lichtenberger (Tübingen: Mohr Siebeck, 2001), 47–77, at 48–54. Chester also notes the associations between creation themes in Genesis 1–2 and Ezekiel 36–37.

With his direct quotation from these passages, we can be sure that Paul identifies these promises with the covenant inaugurated through Christ (cf. 1 Cor 11.25). However, what aspects of these promises is Paul drawing into his present context? His main emphasis here is on the Spirit's work of writing on their hearts.[8] As a result, the intellectual illumination and moral empowerment promised in these texts appear to be Paul's referent. Paul thus draws upon the soteriological vision of a renewed ability to obey God based upon God's personal, pneumatic presence permanently established within his people. This heart change and empowerment by the Spirit is a key aspect of Paul's soteriology that serves as the basis of his argument throughout the chapter.

In 3.6 Paul moves the analogy from hearts of stone and flesh (letters of ink and Spirit), to the contrast between letter (γράμμα) and Spirit (πνεῦμα), noting that the one kills (ἀποκτείνω) and the other gives life (ζῳοποιέω), respectively. Concerning the nature of this death-dealing letter, Hays writes: 'The problem with this old covenant is precisely that it is (only) written, lacking the power to effect the obedience that it demands. Since it has no power to transform the readers, it can only stand as a witness to the condemnation'.[9] However, is the old covenant just a witness to condemnation? Watson rightly argues that Paul's interaction with Exodus includes chapters 31–34, not just chapter 34. That is, it includes the giving of the first set of tablets and not only the second. He writes:

> The reference can only be to the story of Moses' first descent from the mountain: for Moses' first advent with the first pair of stone tablets issues in the death of three thousand of the people of Israel, who had earlier flouted the divine prohibition of idolatry when they 'sat to eat and drink and rose to play' (Ex. 32.6; 1 Cor. 10.7).[10]

Thus, the death-dealing letter is not just a reference to an aphoristic truth but also to a narrative reality associated with the Mosaic law.

In contrast to this, Paul emphasises the role of the Spirit as life-giving, which he sees as confirmation of the new covenant promises in Christ. In 3.6 Paul does not explain directly in what manner the Spirit gives life. Rather, this verse stands as the thesis for the following passage (3.7–18), where Paul explores this idea more fully. However, based on the employment of new covenant themes, we can initially contend that the content of this life is Spirit-wrought understanding and moral obedience. However, two pieces of evidence point towards eschatological life experienced as

---

[8] The eschatological outpouring of the Spirit repeatedly serves as the foundation of the current experience of the early Christian community (cf. Galatians 3; 1 Corinthians 12–14; Romans 8).

[9] Hays, *Echoes*, 131.

[10] Francis Watson, *Paul and the Hermeneutics of Faith* (London: T&T Clark, 2004), 288.

resurrection as also included here. First, if the old covenant brings physical death (Exodus 32), as pointed out by Watson, then we might expect a requisite physical life as its opposite. Second, the resurrection imagery in Ezekiel 37 associates πνεῦμα with a renewed and embodied life. As we will explore below, the association between glory and resurrection in chapters 4 and 5, which builds upon chapter 3, supports this reading.[11] We will see that this Spirit-given life is both noetic – including inward enlightenment and moral enablement – and somatic. Since the Corinthians currently serve as Paul's letter of recommendation, we can safely assert that the inward aspects of this life are a present work of the Spirit within the community.

2.2 Transformation into Unveiled Glory (3.7–18)

Continuing with his discussion of the new covenant in juxtaposition to the old, in 3.7–18 Paul focuses more specifically on Moses' experience narrated in Exodus 32–34, with emphasis on Exod 34.25–29. Rather than a rebuttal of the opponents' use of the Moses story[12] or an interpolation,[13] 2 Cor 3.7–18 primarily serves to further the discussion about letters of recommendation and specifically illustrates his concluding claim of 3.6: 'the letter kills, but the Spirit gives life'.[14] Paul, thus, explains the Spirit's new covenant work (3.8, 17, 18) through an exposition of Exodus 34. The centre of the comparison between the old and new is the presence of glory (3.7–11) and the use of a veil (3.12–18). While this discussion serves as a validation of his ministry,[15] the basis of the argument is about the nature of the new covenant itself and the Spirit's work of life, and thus the discussion goes well beyond just his ministry. Since the new covenant is about life and righteousness from the Spirit in contrast to the old covenant which is about death and condemnation, Paul can act with openness and freedom.

---

[11] As with Romans 8, moral enablement and physical resurrection are not easily separated.

[12] E.g., Dieter Georgi, *The Opponents of Paul in Second Corinthians* (Philadelphia: Fortress, 1986), 6. Paul may be re-appropriating this passage about Moses' glory from his opponents, especially when considered in light of 5.12. However, Sumney is correct that mirror reading opponents in the text can lead to too much speculation. Sumney, *Identifying*.

[13] Hans Windisch, *Der zweite Korintherbrief* (KEK; Göttingen: Vandenhoeck & Ruprecht, 1924), 112.

[14] cf. N.T. Wright, 'Reflected Glory: 2 Corinthians 3:18' in *Climax of the Covenant*, (Minneapolis: Fortress, 1992), 175–92, at 184; Morna D. Hooker, 'Beyond Things That Are Written? St Paul's Use of Scripture' in *From Adam to Christ*, (Eugene, OR: Wipf & Stock, 2008), 139–154, at 149–50.

[15] For the importance of διακονία language, see James D.G. Dunn, '2 Corinthians 3.17 – "The Lord is the Spirit"', *JTSns* 21 (1970): 309–20, at 310.

2.2.1 Moses' Glory (3.7-11)

When we consider the nature of the δόξα (glory) of Moses (3.7–11), the emphasis is primarily upon the visible splendour shining from his face (πρόσωπον), which arises from his direct interaction with God as detailed in Exodus 34 (cf. Exod 34.29). As a noun δόξα appears 15 times in Exodus (LXX), and 11 times the term is modified by a genitive noun or pronoun (δόξα κυρίου) referring to Yahweh (Exod 15.7; 16.7, 10; 24.16–17; 29.43; 33.18–19, 22; 40.34–35). Thus, the 'glory of the Lord' signifies the divine presence in Exodus and other OT texts.[16] God's glory rested on the mountain and by virtue of the fact of his presence with God, Moses face was glorified (δεδοξασμένη) because he spent 40 days with the Lord (Exod 34.28). In fact, during this 40 days Moses asks to see the glory of the Lord, and the Lord partially complies with the request (Exod 33.18–34.9). In distinction to this personal presence from Exodus, the glory in 2 Cor 3.7–11 stands almost as an abstract quality, but it cannot be separated from the personal encounter that stands as its basis.[17] In fact, Renwick argues that within the diverse employment of glory language, 'the one abiding element in each use of δόξα concerns the presence of God'.[18]

The glory of the new covenant comes in distinction to this glory. Based on Moses' physical transformation, Paul argues *a fortiori*: If Moses – although he represents the covenant of death (3.7), letters on stone (3.7), and condemnation (3.9) – experienced glory, how much more will those associated with the Spirit (3.8) and righteousness (3.9) experience glory. Paul thus situates the new covenant glory within the context of life and righteousness rather than radiance. While there is no explicit redefinition of glory in this passage, the shift in emphasis from external to internal is evident.[19] Paul still speaks of glory in contexts of visibility (cf. 3.18 with use of the mirror and 4.4–6 with shining), but it becomes metaphoric, signifying primarily noetic illumination. The result is that the surpassing glory of the new covenant nullifies that of the old because the new covenant glory is permanent (τὸ μένον) as opposed to that which does not last.[20] Accord-

---

[16] Newman (*Glory-Christology*, 190) concludes that in the OT, '... glory is a technical term to refer to God's visible, mobile divine presence'.

[17] It is interesting to note that Paul prefers the nominal form (δόξα) here to the verbal form (δοξάζω), which is found in Exod 34 (34.29, 30, 35).

[18] David A. Renwick, *Paul, the Temple, and the Presence of God* (Atlanta: Scholars Press, 1991), 103.

[19] Hooker ('Beyond', 143) also notes this transition from a discussion of old covenant glory to new covenant glory and mentions how it goes unnoticed by most commentators. Also, see the further discussion of glory in §3.3.

[20] Scholars debate the nature of the passive form of καταργέω applied to Moses' glory (3.7, 11, 13). Instead of the traditional interpretation of Moses' glory as 'fading', Hays (*Echoes*, 133–35) argues that it is 'nullified' because it has been eclipsed by Christ's

ingly, this glory is commensurate with the permanence of the new covenant (Jer 38.32, 40 LXX).

2.2.2 *Moses' Veil (3.12–18)*

After contrasting the old and new covenants based on glory (3.7–11), Paul
then focuses on Moses' veil (τὸ κάλυμμα) and its contemporary application (3.12–18). As with 3.7–11, Exod 34 continues to stand at the centre
of Paul's argument.[21] Rather than simply a foil for Paul's *a fortiori* argument (3.7–11), Moses serves as both a positive (an unveiled, direct interaction with God) and negative (one who veils himself before others) example. Hays accordingly describes Paul's use of Moses as dissimile.[22]
Moses' ambiguous role makes interpreting this passage difficult. Indeed,
much has been written to discuss the nature of the old covenant and the
veil upon those who currently read the text, but we will pass over this for
the sake of our study. We will focus primarily upon 3.17–18 as the crux of
this section.

Continuing the theme of perception, the veil serves to limit one's understanding of God's work. With the interchangeable use of mind/thoughts
(νόημα, 3.14) and hearts (καρδία, 3.15) in this section, we see that the inward, new covenant work of the Spirit described earlier in 3.3–6 is still
central to Paul's discussion. Along with the Spirit, Paul also reaffirms
Christ as integral to new perception and to reversing Israel's hardness of
heart (3.14–15). Paul further clarifies this in 3.16 where he generalises
Moses' action of removing the veil to speak with God (Exod 34.34) and
thus draws a universal application from this narrative event: Anyone who

---

greater glory (3.10). He writes: 'Paul's *katargoumenēn* is not a narrative description but
a retrospective theological judgment' (*Echoes*, 134). Watson, however, makes a strong
case for Paul being able to infer from the context of the Exodus account that the glory
was fading. He writes: 'This [Moses' veiling after speaking to them] makes it possible
for the people of Israel to suppose that the glory must be his own permanent possession,
and not the temporary after-effect of specific occasions of communion with the deity... .
They believe that what is concealed is a permanent state of transfiguration; but what is
actually concealed is the fading of the glory' (*Hermeneutics*, 293). Accordingly, Moses'
limited disclosure characterises his giving of the law, and Paul exploits this (intentional)
hiddenness for his argument.

[21] Linda L. Belleville (*Reflections of Glory: Paul's Polemical Use of the Moses-Doxa
Tradition in 2 Corinthians 3.1–18* [JSNTSup 52; Sheffield: JSOT Press, 1991], 175–91)
helpfully notes the text-interpretation pattern of these verses: Paul cites a passage from
Exodus 34 and then interprets it. This pattern occurs twice: 3.13 (text, Exod 34.33) –
3.14–15 (interpretation) and 3.16 (text, Exod 34.34) – 3.17 (interpretation). Belleville
also argues that 3.18 also follows this pattern of noting the text of Exod 34.35, with a
following comment, but the evidence of a quotation is not clear. Rather, 3.18 serves as a
conclusion of 3.7–17, and thus 3.1–17, by explaining in what manner the Spirit gives life.

[22] Hays, *Echoes*, 140–43.

turns to the Lord, as Moses did, gains a correct perception because the veil of limited perception is removed. Paul then interprets the text he has just quoted by clarifying that 'the Lord is the Spirit' (3.17) and draws the reader's mind to his larger task of showing how the new covenant is based upon the life-giving Spirit. As a result, Lambrecht writes: 'The reason why Paul in v. 17 and v. 18 explicitly brings in the Spirit is his characterization of the new covenant as a covenant of the Spirit (see vv. 3, 6 and 8) over against the old, that of the letter (v. 6)'.[23] The crux of Paul's argument, thus, depends on the present experience of the Spirit.[24]

Paul explains the benefit of the presence of the Spirit as freedom (ἐλευθερία). Van Unnik argues against Windisch's interpretation of this freedom as 'freedom in the relation towards God' because 'it ignores the fact that in this context Paul deals with his relation not towards God, but towards men'.[25] van Unnik, with many others, rightly sees this freedom as associated with the παρρησία in 3.12.[26] Thus, the Spirit enables Paul to

---

[23] Jan Lambrecht, *Second Corinthians* (SP 8; Collegeville, MN: Liturgical, 1999), 54.

[24] While meant to clarify, this is one of the most debated parts of the passage. Is 'the Lord' (κύριος) in 3.16, 17a, 17b, 18 Christ? E.g., Windisch, *Der zweite Korintherbief*, 125; C.K. Barrett, *The Second Epistle to the Corinthians* (BNTC; London: A & C Black, 1973), 123; Mehrdad Fatehi, *The Spirit's Relation to the Risen Lord in Paul* (WUNT 2/128; Tübingen: Mohr Siebeck, 2000), 289–94. Alternatively, does it refer to God/Yahweh? E.g., Dunn, '2 Corinthians 3.17'; Fee, *Empowering Presence*, 311–20; J.-F. Collange, *Énigmes de la deuxième épître de Paul aux Corinthiens: Etude exégétique de 2 Cor. 2:14–7:4* (SNTSMS 18; Cambridge: Cambridge University Press, 1972), 111. Neither reading is without its problems. In support of reading Christ, 'Lord' is Paul's typical designation of Christ (e.g., 1 Thes 1.3; 1 Cor 1.3; Rom 1.4). The parallelism of v. 14 (the veil is abolished in Christ) and v. 16 (the veil is removed for those who turn to the Lord) speaks in favour of reading Christ here. In addition, Paul clearly identifies Christ with κύριος in 4.5. However, the question of how Christ is identified with the Spirit in 3.17, 18 is difficult to answer (Cf. Rom 1.3–4; 1 Cor 15.45.). An alternative reading is that the anarthrous κύριος in 3.16, 18 serves as evidence that Paul is speaking of Yahweh from the Exodus passage (e.g., Exod 34.34), and thus the use in 3.17b would be anaphoric. Since 3.7–18 is an exposition of how the Spirit gives life, I find the weight towards reading Yahweh in each of these uses of κύριος. Accordingly, Dunn ('2 Corinthians 3.17', 318) writes: 'The fact is, however, that the central antithesis in this passage is between the law and the Spirit, not between the law and Christ'. This reading of people turning to the Spirit is unique within Paul's letters, and thus the mediating role of Christ must not be forgotten. C.F.D. Moule ('2 Cor 3.18b, καθάπερ ἀπὸ κυρίου πνεύματος' in *Neues Testament und Geschichte,* eds. Heinrich Baltensweiler and Bo Reicke [Tübingen: Mohr Siebeck, 1972], 231–237, at 236) captures this sentiment: 'the point he is making is that the Yahweh of the Exodus story is no longer remote on the mountain top ... but is permanently present (through Jesus Christ) as Spirit'. This seems to be the probable reading but with the ambiguity in the passage not the certain one.

[25] W.C. van Unnik, '"With Unveiled Face', An Exegesis of 2 Corinthians 3.12–18', *NTS* 6 (1963): 153–69, at 159–60. Cf. Windisch, *Der zweite Korintherbief*, 126.

[26] Cf. Wright, 'Reflected Glory', 179–81.

speak the gospel freely. However, in his attempt to highlight the importance of Paul's ministry to the argument, van Unnik presents a false dichotomy. For Paul believers' openness with God corresponds to the minister's openness with others. By making the appeal general with 'whoever turns to the Lord' (3.17), Paul speaks of the experience of all believers. He too turned to the Lord with an unveiled face, and this openness with God is then the basis of his openness with others. Noting the soteriological aspect of this, Hafemann argues strongly for seeing this not primarily as a freedom *from* something (particularly, the veiled heart) but rather a freedom *for* obedience to God, which corresponds directly to the new covenant promise of moral enablement.[27]

2.2.3 Glory and Transformation (3.18)

This brings us to 3.18, where glory (3.7–11) and unveiled faces (3.12–17) come together as the climax of the Spirit's life-giving work (3.6).[28] The text reads: ἡμεῖς δὲ πάντες ἀνακεκαλυμμένῳ προσώπῳ τὴν δόξαν κυρίου κατοπτριζόμενοι τὴν αὐτὴν εἰκόνα μεταμορφούμεθα ἀπὸ δόξης εἰς δόξαν καθάπερ ἀπὸ κυρίου πνεύματος (3.18). With each phrase being debated, this verse has several ambiguous aspects that obscure its meaning. The major exegetical problems are the following: 1) who is the 'we', 2) what does it mean to have unveiled faces, 3) does the 'we' see or reflect the glory, 4) who is the Lord, 5) what is the 'same image', 6) what is the nature of the transformation, and 7) what does 'from glory to glory' signify? We will address these questions in turn. With all the exegetical problems in this verse, the lack of any consensus is not surprising.[29]

Who is the 'we'? By comparing Moses' Sinai experience to Paul's Damascus road experience, Kim argues that the 'we' of this passage can only refer to Paul himself.[30] However, this neglects the context of the argument. While Paul's own experience may stand in the background here as a confirmation of the reality of his calling, he expects all believers to be able to interact with the glory of the Lord. That is, all believers encounter God through the Spirit's presence – the Lord who is the Spirit (3.17). With the 'we all' Paul widens the import beyond just Moses, new covenant minis-

---

[27] Hafemann, *Paul, Moses*, 401–7.

[28] Dunn, '2 Corinthians 3.17', 314.

[29] We may liken it to a child's 'choose your own adventure story', where the reader makes a decision at each page and this determines the final outcome so that everyone comes out with a different ending. Or, in the same way, it is similar to the game where children have a picture of a person but are able to spin the head, torso, and legs independently of one another. As with these books and games, interpreters here create their own 'image' of what the verse means from their decisions about the various pieces.

[30] Seyoon Kim, *The Origin of Paul's Gospel* (Grand Rapids: Eerdmans, 1982), 235.

ters, or even only himself, and includes all believers. The emphatic πάντες and the general 'whoever' from 3.16 both point to the universal availability of this experience. Importantly, this transformation is the basis of Paul's argument in 3.1–3 regarding the Spirit's work in the Corinthians. This shows that the nature of new covenant soteriology is at the centre of Paul's discussion. Not wanting to err on the other side of van Unnik's false dichotomy between ministry and soteriology,[31] we can affirm with Wright this statement: 'Difference in style of ministry is occasioned by difference in the spiritual condition of the hearers ...'.[32]

What does it mean to have unveiled faces? By speaking of unveiled faces, some argue that Paul is either comparing believers with Moses[33] or with the Israelites.[34] This presents a false dichotomy because both can serve as models.[35] As we noted before, Moses serves as a dissimile.[36] He is a positive model in that he interacts directly with God with an uncovered face (3.16), but, in contrast, he later covers his face when not with the Lord (3.13). As such, Paul uses his positive example of 'turning to the Lord' as a model for believers in 3.16. The Israelites with their hardened hearts appear to serve only as foils because of their hardened hearts (cf. 3.14–15). See Figure 6.1, where the arrows represent the process of seeing or reading. In Figure 6.1A. (3.13), Moses sees God in the tent, but the people cannot see the glory on Moses' face because of the veil. In Figure 6.1B. (3.14–15), the people read 'Moses', but they cannot understand ('see') Moses because their hearts are veiled. They needed the heart change offered by the Spirit of the new covenant, and until they turn to the Lord as Christian believers, in the manner of Moses, their hearts are hardened, not being able to see. When believers encounter God 'with unveiled faces', they are able to understand the reality of the new covenant through the

---

[31] By ignoring the association of glory in 3.18 with its following context of 4.16–5.10, Frances Back (*Verwandlung durch Offenbarung bei Paulus: Eine religionsgeschichtlich-exegetische Untersuchung zu 2 Kor 2,14–4,6* [WUNT 2/153; Tübingen: Mohr Siebeck, 2002], 198) declares that this passage only relates to the mark of ministry in '*dieser Welt*' as opposed to a soteriological statement about '*der himmlischen Welt*'. This clearly overstates the soteriology-ministry distinction.

[32] Wright, 'Reflected Glory', 180. However, Wright emphasises ministry over soteriology, and I think the evidence points to soteriology as the basis of ministry.

[33] E.g., Belleville, *Reflections*, 284.

[34] E.g., Victor Paul Furnish, *II Corinthians* (AB 32A; New York: Doubleday, 1984), 213–14; Fee, *Empowering Presence*, 314–16.

[35] Jacques Dupont, 'Le Chrétien, Miroir de la Gloire divine d'après II Cor. III,18', *RB* 56 (1949): 392–411, at 398–402.

[36] Moses is not only ambiguous as a character in Paul's narrative, Hays also notes the ambiguity of his status with regard to the law. 'A coherent reading of 2 Cor. 3.12–18', writes Hays (*Echoes*, 144, emphasis original), 'is possible only if we recognize that in these verses a metaphorical fusion occurs in which Moses *becomes* the Torah'.

Spirit. While this may seem like the human agent's action, the discussion
of veiling and shining in 4.3–6 show that external agents are central to this
action of unveiling.

Figure 6.1: Veils in 2 Cor 3.13–15

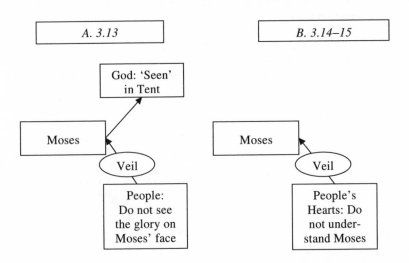

The next question – Do believers 'see' or 'reflect' the glory of the Lord? –
cannot be separated from these related questions: Who is the Lord, what is
the 'same image', and what is the nature of the transformation? Central to
these problems is the meaning of the mirror metaphor from κατοπτριζόμενοι: Does it refer to seeing or reflecting?[37] In the active voice the verb
focuses on the reflecting (to produce a reflection), and the passive voice
focuses on the image reflected (to be mirrored), whereas the middle (as
here) captures aspects of seeing and reflecting (usually, seeing one's reflection in a mirror).[38] Regarding the mirror idea, the literary use of
κατοπτρίζω was not common enough at the time for the metaphor of 'mirror' to become a dead metaphor.[39] As a result, the mirror aspect must not
be lost. According to the nature of a mirror, something is reflected and

---

[37] Dupont gives the classic defence for 'reflect as in a mirror': Dupont, 'Miroir'. See
also, Belleville, *Reflections*, 278–81. Hugedé gives the best argument for 'behold as in a
mirror': Norbert Hugedé, *La métaphore du miroir dans les Epítres de saint Paul aux
Corinthiens* (Neuchatel: Delachaux et Niestlé, 1957). See also, Thrall, *2 Corinthians*,
1:290–95.

[38] LSJ, 929; BDAG, 535.

[39] Cf. Jan Lambrecht, 'Transformation in 2 Cor 3:18', *Bib* 64 (1983): 243–254, at 248.

that reflected image is seen, and so we may not need to make hard distinctions between seeing and reflecting. [40]

When explaining this phrase, interpreters first determine whose experience (Paul or believers generally) is captured by the metaphor and then how the metaphor works. See Table 6.1 for a summary of primary positions. Figure 6.2 represents the three main positions noted in Table 6.1 that relate to believers.

Table 6.1: The Mirror Metaphor in 2 Cor 3.18

Figure 6.2	Whose Experience	Mirror	Object Seen	Proponents
—	Paul	Christ	Christ as God's Glory	Thrall, Barrett, Harris, Barnett, Hafemann[41]
A	Believers	Gospel	Christ as God's Glory	Lambrecht, Barrett, Harris, Barnett[42]
B	Believers	Believers	Believers	Wright, Belleville[43]
C	Believers	Believers	Christ Embodied	Duff, Blackwell[44]

If interpreters discuss Paul's experience, most point to Christ as the mirror who reveals God's glory to Paul. However, this reading of the mirror metaphor breaks down because the 'image' seen, Christ (4.4), is at the same time the mirror. When these interpreters turn to describe the general experience of believers ('we all'), they primarily assign the gospel as the mirror that reflects the glory of God in Christ (cf. 4.4, 6) (see Figure 6.2A). However, the weakness in the argument is that no indication is given that

---

[40] Frances Young and David F. Ford, *Meaning and Truth in 2 Corinthians* (SPCK: London, 1987), 91–92; Hooker, 'Beyond', 147n.12.

[41] Thrall, *2 Corinthians*, 1:284–85; Barrett, *Second Corinthians*, 125–26; Murray J. Harris, *The Second Episitle of Paul to the Corinthians* (NIGTC; Grand Rapids: Eerdmans, 2005), 315; Paul Barnett, *The Second Episitle to the Corinthians* (NICNT; Grand Rapids: Eerdmans, 1997), 205–206; Hafemann, *Paul, Moses*, 411n.239.

[42] Lambrecht, 'Transformation', 245–46. With Hafemann's (*Paul, Moses*, 412n.241) discussion of Paul (in comparison to Moses) as the mediator, it becomes unclear whether Paul (or Paul's gospel) implicitly becomes the mirror in Hafemann's account or not.

[43] Wright, 'Reflected Glory', 185–89; Belleville, *Reflections*, 290–96.

[44] Duff, 'Transformed', 773–74. While I agree with Duff regarding this primary structure, he emphasises the seeing aspect of κατοπτριζόμενοι. Thrall (*2 Corinthians*, 284–85) also points to my position that believers (though she only mentions Paul) reveal Christ in their dying and rising (cf. 4.10–11).

the *gospel* reveals God through Christ *indirectly*, as they argue. These interpretations that emphasise *seeing* 'as in a mirror', thus, find it difficult to give the mirror imagery a proper place.

Figure 6.2: The Mirror Metaphor in 2 Cor 3.18

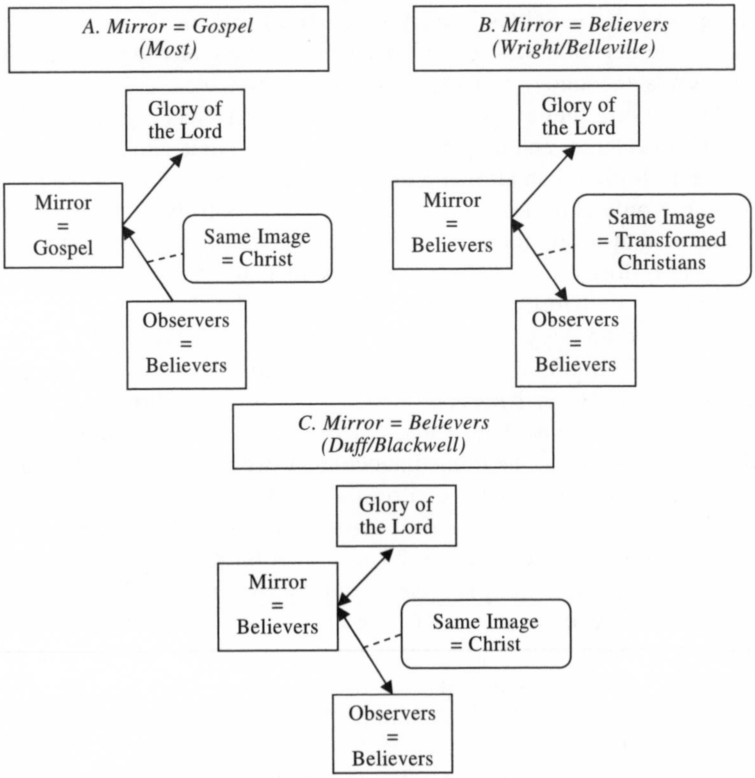

A. Mirror = Gospel
(Most)

Glory of the Lord

Mirror = Gospel

Same Image = Christ

Observers = Believers

B. Mirror = Believers
(Wright/Belleville)

Glory of the Lord

Mirror = Believers

Same Image = Transformed Christians

Observers = Believers

C. Mirror = Believers
(Duff/Blackwell)

Glory of the Lord

Mirror = Believers

Same Image = Christ

Observers = Believers

In contrast, Wright and Belleville interpret the believing community as the mirror (see Figure 6.2B). Accordingly, the community reflects 'the same image' back to one another. This reading maintains the importance of the metaphor and makes more sense of Paul's overall argument that transformed believers serve as his letters of commendation (3.1–6). However, the primary weakness of their construction is evident from the multiple roles that transformed believers play in their interpretation. Since believers are both the mirror and the image seen, the metaphor breaks down.

My reading is similar to Wright and Belleville, but I, along with Duff, understand 'the same image' to be a reference to Christ (see Figure

6.2C).[45] As believers encounter God with unveiled faces, directly like
Moses, they serve as the mirrors that reflect the glory of the Lord. In distinction to Moses' illuminated face, Paul's emphasis is now upon changed
hearts and lives that embody Christ. The nature of the embodiment is
characterised in 2 Corinthians 4. When compared to Figure 6.1, we see
how my reading represented by Figure 6.2C best corresponds to the models
of Moses and the Israelites already employed by Paul. Like Moses, believers encounter God with unveiled faces, but they also do not hide the
effects of this encounter, with the result that all may see.

In this reading, believers are the mirror, they reflect the glory of the
Lord which is Christ, and they are transformed into that same image which
they reflect. Rather than allowing this to be a mere reflection of the Lord's
glory, going only skin deep, Paul clarifies that it is truly a transformation
of the heart that takes place.[46] The mirror becomes like the object it reflects, as did Moses' face. Thus, the centre of Paul's argument is that 'we
all ... are being transformed into the same image'.[47]

With the terminology of 'the same image' (ἡ αὐτὴ εἰκών), Paul points
back to the reflection in the mirror just mentioned. We noted the weakness
of reading this image as believers, and so most point to Christ as the referent of the εἰκών because Paul calls him the εἰκὼν τοῦ θεοῦ in 4.4.[48] Besides the evidence from the immediate context, we also saw a similar association of morphic language – conform – and the christological image in
Rom 8.29–30. In addition, the most consistent use of εἰκών in Paul's letters is christological: 1 Cor 15.49; 2 Cor 4.4; Rom 8.29; Col 1.15 (cf. Col
3.10). Thus, the 'same image' – the image that was reflected in the mirror
– is the image of Christ. It is not Christ himself but a person experiencing
the life-giving new covenant work of the Spirit. Christ serves as a concrete image of what this looks like.

Being associated with Christ, the importance of cruciformity emerges in
a manner that it might not otherwise. Thus, as we shall argue below, the
passage of 4.1–18 with its discussion of death, life, and glory stands to
clarify and expound what Paul has stated generally to this point. Accordingly, Collange writes: 'Cette transformation n'a donc pas qu'un aspect
intérieur de renouvellement, mais aussi un aspect extérieur de conformation aux souffrances du Christ (cf. 4:7ss)'.[49] Savage also writes:

---

[45] See below for evidence for the reading of 'the same image' as Christ,

[46] The only other use of μεταμορφόω in Paul's letters is in Rom 12.2, where the transformation relates to a renewal of the mind, which is not unlike our context here.

[47] On the use of the accusative direct object with a passive verb, see BDF §159.4 (and
§155), where they explain that the object remains in the accusative for a verb which normally takes a double accusative.

[48] E.g., Lambrecht, 'Transformation', 245–46; Litwa, '2 Corinthians 3:18'.

[49] Collange, *Énigmes*, 120.

By using the word εἰκών instead of δόξα Paul seems to be drawing attention to the visible character, the salient image, of Jesus Christ. He is underscoring the fact that Christ, in his resolve to live for God's glory and not his own and in his act of consummate self-sacrifice on the cross, demonstrates not only what God is like but also, dramatically, what humans ought to be like.[50]

Therefore, this image that believers are transformed into is not merely some abstract replication but one of the dying and rising Christ, as evidenced by the suffering and life described in 4.7–18.

As the climax of the argument that the Spirit gives life, this transformation ultimately includes not only noetic illumination and moral enablement, but also the resurrection of the body. Paul directly discusses in 4.1–6 noetic enlightenment and in 4.7–18 the inner and outer experience of transformation, which culminates with resurrection glory in 4.17–18.[51]

What does 'from glory to glory' signify? Reiterating that glory is at the centre of this transformation, Paul writes that it is ἀπὸ δόξης εἰς δόξαν. This is most often interpreted as a description of the progressive nature of glory (cf. 2 Bar 51.3, 7, 10),[52] while Duff has recently argued for a transition from old covenant glory to new covenant glory.[53] Collange, on the other hand, argues that this shows source and goal ('la source et le but').[54] He contends that ἐκ with εἰς denotes progression, whereas ἀπό with εἰς denotes source and goal. However, examples where ἀπό and εἰς are parallel – Rom 6.22; 8.21; 15.31; 1 Cor 14.36; 2 Cor 1.16; Gal 1.16 – and where ἐκ and εἰς are parallel – Rom 1.17; 11.36; 1 Cor 8.6; 2 Cor 1.10; 2.16; Gal 6.8; Col 1.13 – do not bear out this distinction. The two prepositions are important, but the *crux interpretum* lies in determining the referents of the first and second δόξαι. With the reading of progression, both of the δόξαι refer to believers' experience of glory. Duff's distinction between old and

---

[50] Timothy B. Savage, *Power Through Weakness: Paul's Understanding of Christian Ministry in 2 Corinthians* (SNTSMS 86; Cambridge: Cambridge University Press, 1996), 151–52.

[51] Several of those who have focused on the transformation of 3.18 commendably note that the discussion of 4.7–18 gives a description of the nature of that transformation; however, each spends the majority of their time on 3.18 and gives little, if any, explanation of how this transformation works out. For example, Lambrecht (*Second Corinthians*, 81) writes: 'The renewal in 2 Cor 4:16 is the equivalent of the transformation mentioned in 3:18'. See also, Wright, 'Reflected Glory', 190; Duff, 'Transformed', 779. Accordingly, we will specifically address the connection.

[52] E.g., Harris, *Second Corinthians*, 316–17; Ralph P. Martin, *2 Corinthians* (WBC 40; Waco: Word, 1986), 72.

[53] Duff, 'Transformed', 771–74.

[54] Collange, *Énigmes*, 122–23. See also Carey C. Newman, 'Resurrection as Glory: Divine Presence and Christian Origins' in *The Resurrection – An Interdisciplinary Symposium on the Resurrection of Jesus,* eds. Stephen T. Davis, et al. (Oxford: Oxford University Press, 1998), 59–89, at 86; Hafemann, *Paul, Moses*, 408n.229.

new covenant glory, separates the two glories, but it does not fit well with the mirror metaphor and it implies a Jewish only audience. Collange's reading, however, fits better with the mirror metaphor earlier in the verse: from the glory (of the Lord) to (believers') glory.

At the same time, this reading of source and goal also fits with his reading of the final phrase: καθάπερ ἀπὸ κυρίου πνεύματος. The use of καθάπερ is an awkward construction to most, with a debate whether it is comparative ('just as') or causative ('from').[55] If comparative, interpreters question what Paul is trying to compare. Hays provides a potentially helpful answer by describing this as 'contrapuntal', so that the Lord is contrasted with Moses (οὐ καθάπερ Μωϋσῆς, 3.13) and competency from ourselves (οὐχ ὅτι ἀφ᾽ ἑαυτῶν, 3.5).[56] However, the statement here lacks a clear parallel with the previous verses, with no ἀπό in 3.13 and no comparative in 3.5. With the preferred source-goal reading of the previous phrase, we can also read the καθάπερ as comparative: The ἀπὸ δόξης is clarified as ἀπὸ κυρίου, the source. As with my reading of 3.17, I see no dominant reason to posit Christ as the referent of κύριος. Rather, Paul here just reiterates his point in 3.17 that the Spirit is the divine agent behind this transformation, as he has been arguing from 3.1–6.

Now that we have discussed the individual pieces of 3.18, it would be helpful to reassemble them into a whole again: 'we all with unveiled faces, reflecting the glory of the Lord, are transformed into the same image from glory to glory, just as from the Lord who is the Spirit'. As all believers encounter God directly (with unveiled faces) through the Spirit's presence (the glory of the Lord) they reflect this glory as mirrors. Being transformed by this experience, the image reflected is that of the dying and rising Christ, who is the image of God. This is from the Spirit and experienced by believers, who reflect the glory of the Lord and are themselves glorified in the process (from glory to glory). To clarify, this is from the Spirit who is the Lord. This transformative process thus confirms the Spirit's life-giving work in Paul's gospel and ministry.

With the discussion of letters of recommendation, Paul defends himself by arguing that the Corinthians themselves serve as his letters because of the Spirit's work in their hearts. The primary nature of the Spirit's work is that of giving life (3.6), which Paul then explains through an exposition of Exodus 34 in 3.7–18. Accordingly, the transformation described in 3.18 functions as the climax of the life-giving work of the Spirit.[57] Based upon the new covenant hope in chapter 3 and Paul's discussion in chapter 4, this

---

[55] See Furnish, *II Corinthians*, 216.

[56] Hays, *Echoes*, 144.

[57] Hays writes: 'The veiled telos is ... the glory of God in Jesus Christ that makes itself visible in fleshy communities conformed to Christ's image' (*Echoes*, 146).

noetic, moral, and somatic embodiment consists of inward renewal in the midst of present sufferings and outward renewal in glorified, resurrected bodies in the future. The return to the agency of the Spirit at the end of the chapter drives home the new covenant hope of renewal through the Spirit. However, with the use of glory and image to clarify the shape of this transformation, we see that it transcends just a mere inward transformation to include a full christoformity that involves both suffering and death but also future glorious resurrection, which is directly in line with the new covenant hope Paul has explored throughout chapter 3. As such, the full shape of this soteriological vision will become clearer as we discuss chapters 4 and 5.

2.3 Transformation and Deification (3.18)

Probably more than any other verse in the Pauline corpus, the transformation in 2 Cor 3.18 has attracted comments about deification in modern literature.[58] Hence, Finlan calls this passage 'the most frankly theotic passage in Paul'.[59] This is not to say that the majority of scholars address the issue of deification, but when they do address it, they tend to consider this verse.

Some some past interpreters spoke in terms of mysticism and apotheosis when discussing this verse. For instance, drawing from a history of religions methodology, Boussett writes: 'This verse [3.18] is saturated with mystical piety. Out of the mysterious words we hear the great theme sound forth quite clearly: deification through the vision of God'.[60] His assessment helped set the parameters for much of the later discussion, and the majority of interpreters dismiss deification because they associate it with these older claims of mysticism from the mystery religions. For example, Lambrecht writes: 'Even if the term [μεταμορφόω] is a borrowed one, its content has little or nothing to do with a Hellenistic-eastern magic ritual; it is not a privileged mystic deification by vision'.[61]

At the same time, as interpreters attempted to come to grips with the transformation described, they affirm something significant is going on, but they lack the categories to describe it. For instance, Barrett writes: 'If the result of the transformation is not apotheosis (Bousset, *Kyrios Christos* (1913), p. 203) it is not far away from it. Kümmel (*Theologie*, p. 199), however, rightly insists that the thought is not properly mystical; the be-

---

[58] Interestingly, Irenaeus makes no use of the verse in his extant writings, and Cyril only uses it sparingly.

[59] Finlan, '*Theosis* in Paul?', 75.

[60] Wilhelm Bousset, *Kyrios Christos* (trans. John E. Seely; Nashville: Abingdon, 1970), 227n.68.

[61] Lambrecht, 'Transformation', 251–52.

liever remains distinct from God'.[62] However, Barrett further writes, '... and seeing Jesus the image of God they are, not deified but, *transformed into the same image*, the glory they share with him ever increasing'.[63] Collange, as well, affirms an 'événement immanent et mystique', but this must be balanced by 'la conception paulinienne de la transcendance divine et sa perspective eschatologique'.[64] Where then can we situate this transformation?

As noted in chapter 1, Finlan, Litwa, and Gorman all affirm that 3.18 describes an aspect of theosis. Finlan emphasises the transformation into glory, which he holds to be both an inward quality of spiritual knowledge and an outward radiance.[65]

In his exploration of 3.18 and 4.4, Litwa makes two primary arguments. First, 'the same image' in 3.18 refers to Christ as the divine image of God in 4.4. Thus, when believers are transformed into that image, they share in Christ's theological (divine) and anthropological (human) reality.[66] Second, this participation in the humanly divine and divinely human image 'is not an ontological state – let alone a mystical one – but consists (at least in this life) in a mode of being that is manifested in concrete ethical acts'.[67] At this point in his article, Litwa leans heavily upon the parallel use of μεταμορφόω in Rom 12.2 and then discusses the problem of deification in context of the struggle with sin. Unfortunately, the concept of 'image' that was so important to the first argument plays little role in the second, and so the connection between the two feels strained. This disjunction is due in part by the fact that he determined that the lexical parallels in 1 Corinthians 11 and 15 for εἰκών and Romans 12 for μεταμορφόω were more informative for his argument. Thus, he intentionally left behind the epistolary context of 2 Corinthians.[68]

Despite this weakness, the fundamental issue that he has raised is important because he specifically notes the common, but disjunctive interpretation of 'image' between 3.18 and 4.4: many interpreters often claim that 4.4 points to Christ's divine identity (the theological image), but they then argue that when believers are transformed into that 'same image', it refers to Christ in his humanity (the anthropological image).[69] While I do not think that Litwa sufficiently incorporated the importance of the human as-

---

[62] Barrett, *Second Corinthians*, 125.

[63] Ibid., 125, emphasis original.

[64] Collange, *Énigmes*, 119.

[65] Finlan, '*Theosis* in Paul?', 75.

[66] Litwa, '2 Corinthians 3:18', 118–28.

[67] Ibid. 129.

[68] Ibid. 117n.1.

[69] E.g., Hafemann, *Paul, Moses*, 416–17.

pect arising from the allusion to Genesis 1–2 in 2 Cor 4.4-6, the conundrum about the theological and anthropological aspects remains.

This passage is not central to Gorman's work on theosis, but, citing Litwa, he does note its importance. In distinction to Finlan and Litwa, Gorman makes the important point that it is not the abstract divine Christ-image that believers gaze upon. Rather, since the 'exalted Christ ... remains forever the crucified one, their ongoing metamorphosis into the image of God, or the image of the Son (2 Cor 3:18), is a participation in his cruciform narrative identity and the transformation into his cruciform image'.[70] Allowing the literary context to inform his reading, Gorman brings the content of chapter 3 and 4 together. With the importance of the literary context for understanding the passage, we therefore need to address chapter 4 before making final assessments about 3.18.

2.4 The Glory of Christ (4.1–6)

Building upon this implicit support of his ministry in 3.7–18, Paul now explicitly affirms that his ministry is true to the new covenant with its gift of freedom because he speaks openly and without deception. However, in spite of his direct speech, the veil remains for those who are perishing and not everyone responds to his message. Paul earlier mentioned that those who are perishing viewed the gospel as the smell of death (2.15–16), and they are like the Israelites who still have a veil over their hearts (3.15). He now introduces the agency of the 'god of this age' as the basis of this (4.4), and this god stands in distinction to the God who shines out the light of the *knowledge* of the gospel of Christ.[71] This blinding activity stands in direct contrast to the noetic illumination offered in the new covenant by the Spirit (3.3, 16–18) and God's illumination to believers through Christ (4.4, 6).

The context is filled with the imagery of light and seeing: blinding, seeing, light, and glory (4.4) and light, shine, darkness, and glory (4.6). This is a metaphorical use of vision imagery, which points to a proper perception, a proper epistemology, of God's work through Christ.[72] God's activity of creating light out of darkness is similar to his bringing the light of the gospel to those who have been blinded (4.6). This metaphorical use of glory and light that refers to knowledge and noetic illumination corresponds to that of 3.18.

Whereas the Spirit played a primary role in chapter 3, Christ's position in chapter 4 becomes central. The identification of Christ as the 'image of

---

[70] Gorman, *Inhabiting*, 92.

[71] Timothy B. Savage, *Power Through Weakness: Paul's Understanding of Christian Ministry in 2 Corinthians* (SNTSMS 86; Cambridge: Cambridge University Press, 1996), 127.

[72] Cf. Martyn, *Theological Issues*, 104n.47.

God' (εἰκὼν τοῦ θεοῦ) in 4.4 complements the discussion of 'the same image' (ἡ αὐτὴ εἰκών) in 3.18. Just as image is repeated from 3.18, so is the term glory (δόξα), and this glory is both 'of Christ' (4.4) and 'of God' (4.6). Accordingly, Hafemann writes: 'Christ is not merely reflecting the glory of God as Moses did, he *is* the glory of God'.[73] It is the light of this glory that the god of this age hinders and that God shines out.

In contrast to the focus upon noetic illumination, Kim and Newman both argue for Paul's conversion experience as the foundation of this language.[74] As a result, they emphasise Paul's literal vision of Christ in his glorious, resurrected body. Whether the background of Paul's conversion is in view here or not, the somatic experience does play a role in 4.17-5.5, as we will see. Newman thus draws the important conclusion about Jesus' glory and his divine identity: 'Notably, then, Jesus as a bearer of eschatological divine presence is tied to believers' faith and hope. It is not just that God raised Jesus (as crucial for Christian theology as that is!), but that, in his resurrection, the divine character of Jesus, his Glory, becomes an essential confessional element'.[75] As believers are transformed into Christ's divine glory, they are participating in the divine presence. 'Therefore', Nguyen writes, 'as with δόξα and εἰκών in 3.18 and 4.4, Paul's use of πρόσωπον and εἰκών in 4.4, 6 should be regarded as synonymous, which indicates that the πρόσωπον of Christ is also depicting Christ as the visible image and representation of God'.[76] Thus, this implies that the transformation into this glory is not only noetic but also embodied because it is a visible manifestation, an idea we will explore further.

Several texts have been proposed as the basis of Paul's allusions. Savage has proposed Isa 9.1,[77] but there appear to be more connections to Wis 7.25-26 and Genesis 1-2. With regard to Wisdom 7, an important aspect is its inclusion of image language along with glory and light (δόξα, ἀπαύγασμα, φῶς). In the context of a praise of wisdom, Wis 7.25-26 reads: 'For she is a breath of the power of God, and a pure emanation of the glory of the Almighty (τῆς τοῦ παντοκράτορος δόξης); therefore nothing defiled gains entrance into her. For she is a reflection of eternal light, a spotless mirror of the working of God, and an image of his goodness'.[78]

While this Wisdom reference has much to commend it, the association with God's creation of light in conjunction with image language appears to

---

[73] Hafemann, *Paul, Moses*, 416, emphasis original.

[74] Kim, *Origin*, 229–30; Newman, *Glory-Christology*, 220–21, 229–35.

[75] Newman, 'Resurrection as Glory', 80.

[76] V. Henry T. Nguyen, *Identity in Corinth: A Comparative Study of 2 Corinthians, Epictetus and Valerius Maximus* (WUNT 2/243; Tübingen: Mohr Siebeck, 2008), 180.

[77] Savage, *Power*, 112.

[78] Cf. Wis 2.23, which also has a striking reference to εἰκών. See the discussion in Thrall, *2 Corinthians*, 1:310.

be a more likely allusion to Genesis 1–2.[79] After recurring several times in the beginning chapters of Genesis (Gen 1.26, 27; 5.1, 3; 9.6), image language plays a minimal role in the rest of the OT and occurs variously (outside of idol contexts) in Jewish texts until Wisdom and Philo.[80] With such a limited register from which to draw, the explicit reference to Christ as εἰκὼν τοῦ θεοῦ (4.4) takes us directly back to Gen 1.27 LXX where Adam was made according to the εἰκὼν θεοῦ. This particular textual link with Genesis gives evidence that Christ reveals God not as wisdom but as a human, in a manner similar to Adam at the beginning.[81] This assessment is supported by Lorenzen's recent study on Paul's understanding of εἰκών, where she argues strongly that for Paul εἰκών is fundamentally somatic.[82] Speaking of the theomorphism of εἰκών, Scroggs writes: 'Christ is the true revelation of God *precisely because* he is true man. The reverse is equally true'.[83] Noting the importance of this association of image and revelation, Jervell rightly argues for the *Offenbarungsqualität* of the image concept.[84] Thus, as God's divine agent Christ reveals God as the 'image of God' only as he lives a human life, which the association with the creation language from Genesis 1–2 makes evident.

That Christ reveals God in a human context is important, but for Paul Christ's specific experience of death and resurrection is central. It is through this dying and rising that Christ most clearly reveals God and restores humanity.[85] This narrative of Christ's death and life as the model of human existence comes to the fore in Paul's discussion in 4.7–18. In particular, this aspect of revealing the work of God through Christ becomes evident when we consider 4.4 alongside 4.10–11. The same conceptual language of revelation, *Offenbarung*, is made explicit by Paul in 4.10–11 when he speaks of the life of Jesus being manifest (φανερόω) in their bod-

---

[79] Wolfgang Schrage ('Schöpfung und Neuschöpfung in Kontinuität und Diskontinuität bei Paulus', *EvT* 65 [2005]: 245–259, at 248) writes: 'Ἐκ σκότους steht zwar nur beim Schöpferhandeln Gottes am Anfang und ist vermutlich in Analogie zum *nihil* in Röm 4,17 zu verstehen ...'.

[80] See van Kooten, *Paul's Anthropology*, 1–69.

[81] Savage, *Power*, 148–51.

[82] Stefanie Lorenzen, *Das paulinische Eikon-Konzept: Semantische Analysen zur Sapientia Salomonis, zu Philo und den Paulusbriefen* (WUNT 2/250; Tübingen: Mohr Siebeck, 2008), 139–256. She also writes: 'Das Wissen um diese somatische Gemeinschaft im Eschaton bewirkt bereits eine Verwandlung der Gegenwart des Menschen, weil er seinen leidende und schwachen Körper in der Nachfolge des Gegreuzigten nicht mehr als Ausdruck der Schwäche interpretiert, sondern darin ein Zeichen der zukünftigen Auferstehung sieht' (261).

[83] Scroggs, *Last Adam*, 98, emphasis original.

[84] Jervell, *Imago Dei*, 218.

[85] Cf. Gorman's similar conclusion with regard to Philippians 2: Gorman, *Inhabiting*, 16–29.

ies through the process of suffering (see §3.1 below). Concerning this suffering Güttgemanns writes: 'Die Leiden des Apostels haben ... *Offenbarungscharakter.* Sie sind ein Epiphaniegeschehen, und zwar ... ein christologisches Epiphaniegeschehen'.[86] We see then a direct parallel between Christ's embodied death-life narrative that reveals God and the believers' re-enactment of this death-life narrative that also reveals the life of Jesus. Thus, being transformed into 'the same image' and reflecting divine glory in 3.18 is nothing other than the embodiment of the dying and rising of Christ, and that, in turn, is an epiphanic event.[87] Capturing this narrative movement, Rowe writes:

> God's image is a human image, and thus a living image. Paul's iconism is not about a static image but a life-story, first of a particular human and then of a community that embodies the pattern which is the story of that human life: in Jesus Christ and the community of the ἐκκλησία God stands on the side of humanity and is known humanly. In this way the image of God is in fact God's humanity.[88]

Accordingly, as believers are transformed into this same image they are transformed into this christoform narrative of death and life.

If being transformed into Christ's image is the embodied revelation of God, are believers the same as Christ? Believers encounter the glory of God through the Spirit (3.17–18) and through Christ (4.4–6). Although they are transformed by this experience, their transformation derives from a *reflection* of that glory. Thus, the transformation is from God's glory to their glory, that is, from God to believers. Since their experience of God is reflected 'from' God, this shows a distinction between humanity and God. Besides the mediation of glory from God to believers, other aspects support this distinction in this section. The emphasis upon sufficiency coming only from God and not from themselves (2.16–17; 3.5; cf. 4.7), as well as the distinction between the Spirit (3.17) and Christ (4.5) as Lord and Paul's ministry team as slaves (4.5) also reflects this. That is, believers' experience of elevated status, power or sufficiency is mediated from God through Christ and the Spirit. Paul avoids a confusion of the created with the Creator, while still describing human participation in divine attributes of glory and power.

2.5 Conclusion

Regarding the shape of Paul's soteriology of 3.1–4.6, we have seen hints of future resurrection with the language of life, the presence of the Spirit,

---

[86] Erhardt Güttgemanns, *Der leidende Apostel und sein Herr* (FRLANT 90; Göttingen: Vandenhoeck & Ruprecht, 1966), 107.

[87] See especially Lorenzen for sustained argument for somatic embodiment as central for εἰκών in this context: Lorenzen, *Das paulinische Eikon-Konzept*, 214–56.

[88] Rowe, 'New Testament Iconography?', 311.

and the experience of glory, but the emphasis has been on present noetic enlightenment and moral enablement. The life-giving Spirit, who is the centre of the new covenant promise of inward renewal, is the one who brings glory and transforms believers. As believers encounter the Spirit through Christ, the veil that hindered their understanding and action has been removed so that they can know and experience the gospel of the glory of Christ. Since this noetic illumination and moral enablement begins when one turns to the Lord, this is a present experience. In fact, Paul's argument that the Corinthians are his letter of commendation depends on the fact that they have seen the work of the Spirit in their midst. With the emphasis on glory and image along with creation of light language, Paul makes use of Genesis 1–2 imagery. Just as the first humans served as the image of God, so now Christ as a human has fulfilled that role. That image now serves as the basis for the transformation of believers so that they can reveal God to the world by embodying a christoform narrative of death and life.

3. Death and Life in Christ: 4.7–5.10

In the previous section, Paul discusses the Spirit's work of transforming believers into the image of Christ. I have argued that this transformation cannot be separated from this passage that follows, where Paul plumbs the depths of Christ's experience as embodied by believers. Lest he give the idea that all believers are simply transformed into Christ's image of glory, Paul qualifies the nature of current existence by emphasising participation in Christ's death as well as his new life. Accordingly, we will see how Christ's narrative of death and resurrection form the basis not just for Paul's life but for all those who follow Christ. Whereas present, inward renewal was the focus of the previous section, Paul now explicitly balances this with the hope of an embodied resurrection in the future.

3.1 Embodying Christ's Death and Life (4.7–15)

Paul begins this section with a contrast between 'this treasure' (θησαυρὸς οὗτος) and 'clay jars' (ὀστράκινα σκεύη).[89] This contrast highlights a distinction that will run throughout chapter 4 and is reflected in 5.11 – the distinction between the inner and the outer. With the use of οὗτος, Paul

---

[89] Although Paul distinguishes gospel ministers, 'we' (*passim*), from the Corinthian congregation, 'you' (4.12), in 4.7–12, Paul ultimately presents his suffering and hope as common to all in 4.14 (cf. 4.16–18). Accordingly, I treat Paul's experience as a paradigm for all believers because Christ's suffering is not only a paradigm for Paul but for all those who follow Christ.

indicates that the treasure relates to what he has previously discussed. While this may refer back to Paul's ministry (4.1),[90] the referent is most likely 'the knowledge of the glory of God' (4.6, cf. 4.4) because of its proximity.[91] As the outward aspect, the clay jars signify believers' embodied existence. Thus, this inward-outward duality Paul presents has its basis in a mind-body distinction, though we will see later how he emphasises different aspects of anthropology without separating them.[92]

Returning to the primacy of God's agency (cf. 1.8–9; 3.5–6), Paul associates the treasure and the clay jars with that which is 'of God' and 'from us', respectively (4.7). This duality is not one that devalues the body – that which is 'from us' – because it serves as the context in which God's treasure is situated. On the other hand, the transforming knowledge comes from the creative work of God as he makes the light of knowledge shine in the darkness. In particular, Paul describes this knowledge from God as a 'surpassing power' (ὑπερβολὴ τῆς δυνάμεως), which emphasises its potent efficacy in contrast to the clay jars which connote weakness and instability.[93]

Paul then gives the first of several peristasis catalogues that occur in 2 Corinthians (4.8–9; 6.4–10; 11.23–27 cf. 1.8–10). This catalogue exemplifies the weakness connoted by the clay jar imagery. However, each mark of weakness is paired with a qualification: the weakness is not carried out fully, as God's implicit deliverance carries them through (cf. 1.8–11). Most of the terms have a physical and social connotation – θλίβω, διώκω, and καταβάλλω, but one seems primarily mental and emotional – ἀπορέω.[94] Thus, this inner-outer duality is not absolute. However, Paul summarises this catalogue by stating that they are 'always carrying around the death of Jesus in the *body* (σῶμα)' (4.10). That the term 'clay jars' signifies the embodied aspect of believers is now confirmed with the use of σῶμα. Although the nature of this suffering is not limited to physical

---

[90] E.g., Lambrecht, *Second Corinthians*, 71; Rudolf Bultmann, *The Second Letter to the Corinthians* (trans. Roy A. Harrisville; Minneapolis: Augsburg, 1985), 112. However, Bultmann interestingly says that τοῦτον points to 4.6 rather than 4.1, which speaks against his conclusion.

[91] See Hans Dieter Betz, 'The Concept of the 'Inner Human Being' (ὁ ἔσω ἄνθρωπος) in the Anthropology of Paul', *NTS* 46 (2000): 315–41, at 332.

[92] Following Aune ('Anthropological Duality', 220) and others, I use 'duality' to denote a distinction and/or tension and 'dualism' to denote a conflict and/or opposition.

[93] Fitzgerald rightly notes the role of God's divine empowerment that runs throughout the whole passage: John T. Fitzgerald, *Cracks in an Earthen Vessel: An Examination of the Catalogues of Hardships in the Corinthian Correspondence* (SBLDS; Atlanta: Scholars, 1988), 170–72.

[94] Harvey provides a helpful summary of the economic, social, and emotional consequences that suffering caused in the ancient world: A.E. Harvey, *Renewal Through Suffering: A Study of 2 Corinthians* (Edinburgh: T&T Clark, 1996), 20–23.

problems, the context for the suffering is the present, embodied state. With the repetition of the adverbs of time (πάντοτε and ἀεί), Paul shows that this is the consistent state of humanity, and ministers in particular.[95]

Paul metaphorically identifies these afflictions with the *death* (νέκρω-σις) of Jesus (4.10). Similar to the construction in Rom 8.17, the leaders 'carry around the death of Christ in the body in order that (ἵνα) the life of Jesus may be manifested in [their] body' (4.10).[96] In 4.11, Paul again reiterates that this 'life of Jesus' is manifested in the body, but this time he describes this body as 'mortal flesh' (θνητὴ σάρξ).[97] The paradox becomes more enigmatic: Those who are living die in order to experience life in dead bodies. Since we have noted the importance of the body for Paul's discussion, we should briefly note the scholarly discussion about Paul's anthropology.

3.1.1 Excursus: The Body

I have argued that the basis of Paul's anthropology is an inner-outer duality, and that the body represents this outer aspect. As we analyse the various interpretations of the body here, our discussion will also prefigure the debated concepts of the inner and outer person in 4.16. While a variety of interpretations of Paul's thought has been offered, we shall look at three representative positions: Bultmann, van Kooten, and Käsemann.

Bultmann views the body as representative of the human as a whole.[98] For instance, he writes: 'It is clear that the *soma* is not something that outwardly clings to a man's real *self* (to his soul, for instance), but belongs to its very essence, so that we can say man does not *have* a *soma*; he *is*

---

[95] Accordingly, Wolfgang Schrage ('Leid, Kreuz und Eschaton. Die Peristasenkataloge als Merkmale paulinischer *theologia crucis* und Eschatologie', *EvT* 34 [1974]: 141–75, at 158) writes: 'Der leidende Herr, der leidende Apostel und die leidende Christenschar gehören zusammen'.

[96] While arguing that tribulation lists were much more widespread than previously appreciated, Robert Hodgson ('Paul the Apostle and First Century Tribulation Lists', *ZNW* 74 [1983]: 59–80, at 79) provocatively places Paul's peristasis catalogues alongside those of Heracles, among others. However, the Heracles stories are provocative in that they often portray 'tribulation as the path to deification'. Though Hodgson does not pursue the parallel, he concludes that 'the mythological labours of Heracles, as they were understood in the first century by Plutarch and Arrian, is a history of religions background which illumines Paul's trial list[s] as effectively as Stoic and apocalyptic parallels, and perhaps even more' (61).

[97] Cf. Robert H. Gundry, *Sōma in Biblical Theology: With Emphasis on Pauline Theology* (Cambridge: Cambridge University Press, 1976), 31–32.

[98] Robinson and Best generally follow Bultmann's reading but are both concerned with communal aspects as well: John A.T. Robinson, *The Body* (London: SCM, 1952); Ernest Best, *One Body in Christ* (London: SPCK, 1955), 215–25.

soma'.[99] With regard to our current passage, Bultmann notes that the language in 2 Cor 4–5 sounds dualistic, but contends that this does not overrule his primary conclusions.[100] Unfortunately, Bultmann argues from the premise that any duality must be equivalent to a dualism of the Gnostics, such that the body must be depreciated.[101] However, this does not allow for the complexity of thought that existed in the ancient world.

As a more recent interpreter, Betz follows Bultmann and describes human identity as σῶμα, and the inner person as an aspect of the identity of the ἄνθρωπος. Concerning the inner-outer distinction Paul uses in 4.16, he writes: 'Abandoning the inferior part to save the superior ἔσω ἄνθρωπος is not what Paul has in mind. Rather, the entire ἄνθρωπος must be saved, and that is the σῶμα'.[102] Betz argues that Paul uses Platonic language but does not use it in a Platonic manner with a sharp dualism. Rather, Paul speaks about different aspects of the human.[103] The recognition of the importance of the body is right, but does σῶμα really encapsulate the totality of the Paul's anthropology?

In distinction to Betz and Bultmann, van Kooten argues that Paul's language shares the philosophical emphasis from which the terminology arises.[104] Therefore, Paul's language represents a strict material-immaterial dualism, expressed in a trichotomous anthropology.[105] In his understanding, the immaterial aspect is the centre of Paul's anthropology, and in contrast to the sophists who emphasise the body, Paul minimises the body, similar to what we see in Philo.[106] Interestingly, van Kooten appears to use the same structural premises as Bultmann: there are two options, unity or dualism, and a dualism entails a de-emphasis on the physical. In contrast to Bultmann, van Kooten argues that Paul falls on the side of dualism and thus devalues the body. While van Kooten rightly notes Paul's noetic emphasis in passages like 2 Corinthians 3–4, he excludes Paul's eschatological hope for the body (cf. 2 Cor 4.16–5.10; Romans 8; Phil 3.20–21) that provides for more balance and unity in his anthropology. Also, the

---

[99] Bultmann, *Theology*, 1:194, emphasis original.

[100] Ibid., 1:199–202.

[101] E.g., Ibid., 1:202.

[102] Betz, 'Inner Human Being', 338.

[103] Betz ('Inner Human Being', 334) writes: 'the apostle interprets the concepts in ways characteristically different from the Platonic tradition, from which they have come. Evidently, he does not identify the ἔσω ἄνθρωπος with ψυχή, νοῦς or πνεῦμα. In principle the ἔσω ἄνθρωπος does not have a higher status than the ἔξω ἄνθρωπος, but both are the two aspects of the same ἄνθρωπος'.

[104] van Kooten, *Paul's Anthropology*, 363–64.

[105] Ibid., 298–308.

[106] For instance, van Kooten (*Paul's Anthropology*, 388–92, cf. 310) argues that the renewal of the mind in Rom 12.2 is the 'climax of Paul's anthropology'.

similarity of Paul's language to philosophical schools should not override Paul's use of that language to rebut traditions that minimise the body.

A mediating position would be that of Käsemann, who views the body as a central aspect of anthropology, but not an overarching category like that of Bultmann. Käsemann writes: 'The coherence of Pauline soteriology is destroyed once we modify in the slightest degree the fact that for Paul all God's ways with his creation begin and end in corporeality'.[107] He later clarifies: 'corporeality is the nature of man in his need to participate in creatureliness and in his capacity for communication in the widest sense, that is to say, in his relationship to a world with which he is confronted on each several occasion'.[108] The body allows humans to interact with the physical world, but this does not necessitate a separation from other aspects of the individual. This reading affirms a body-mind duality, but this is not reduced into a dualism.[109]

Bultmann's rejection of an absolute dualism in Paul's anthropology appears correct, but the use of σῶμα to incorporate the unified person stretches the meaning of the term beyond its referent. The mediating position advocated by Käsemann emphasises anthropological unity while taking the dualistic language seriously. We will see that this corresponds well with our later conclusion that although the inner-outer duality frames the discussion, Paul is not denigrating the somatic aspect of humans. On the contrary, this embodied state specifically serves as the context for Christ's death and life to be formed in believers.

Returning to 2 Corinthians, we see this inner-outer duality at work. That physical and emotional suffering is the metaphorical experience of death seems clear, but the experience of the 'life of Jesus' is not as clear (4.10–11). Since Paul describes the outward, bodily experience as one of corruption (4.16), the nature of the life 'in the body' or 'in the mortal flesh' should not be taken as a description of a present vivification of physical bodies. The 'mortal flesh' is not presently vivified, but rather this *life* is experienced while believers live in the mortal flesh, that is, presently. Thus, the body and the mortal flesh describe the present context in which this life is experienced.

Since this life is not present resurrection, we see from the context that it consists of deliverance from specific trials and inward strengthening. If the suffering of trials is expressed as a metaphorical death, then the implicit divine act of deliverance from the troubles listed in 4.8–9 is likely a

---

[107] Ernst Käsemann, 'On Paul's Anthropology' in *Perspectives on Paul*, (London: SCM, 1971), 1–31, at 18.

[108] Ibid., 21.

[109] More recent support of Käsemann's general position is represented by Robert Gundry, *Sōma*, 31–32 and Aune, 'Anthropological Duality', 220–222.

part of the way the life of Jesus is manifest through this deliverance.[110] In that way, verses 10–11 give a 'theological interpretation' of the concrete examples in 4.8–9.[111] However, the life in the body appears to be larger than just deliverance from specific trials. God also offers inward comfort and enablement in the midst of present somatic struggles. Tannehill rightly notes: 'The power of the old dominion has been transformed into a power which serves the new dominion in its present form'.[112] Based on the knowledge of the gospel as a treasure within believers' weak bodies (4.7), as believers face outward struggles in their embodied state, God reveals his comfort and transforming knowledge through these circumstances.

Support for this reading comes from the way 4.7–12 reflects primary aspects of 1.3–11 where Paul speaks of suffering troubles and God's requisite inward comfort and deliverance. In the earlier passage, Paul experienced troubles (θλῖψις) and the sufferings (πάθημα) of Christ, and he was granted comfort (παράκλησις) and deliverance (ῥύομαι) from God through Christ. However, in the midst of this discussion Paul states that if he is troubled, it is for the Corinthians' comfort, and even their salvation (σωτηρία; 1.6), which parallels Paul's death leading to the Corinthians' life (4.12).

The correspondence between 1.3–6 and 4.7–12 helps us understand the nature of this life experienced paradoxically in the midst of death. We see a clear correspondence between the two passages, both conceptually and terminologically, with troubles (θλῖψις, 1.4, 6, 8; 4.8), suffering (πάθημα, 1.5, 6, 7) and death (θάνατος, 1.9, 10; 4.9–12). In chapter 1 God provided comfort (παράκλησις, 1.3–6), salvation (σωτηρία, 1.6) and deliverance (ῥύομαι, 1.10), whereas the result in chapter 4 is the 'life of Jesus' (4.10–13). As a result, we can postulate that 'life' signifies mental and emotional support (παράκλησις) in the midst of distress and, at times, deliverance (ῥῦσις) from the events causing the distress so that believers do not experience its culmination with bodily death. Wright correctly notes the expectation of a fuller experience of life: 'The present life, caught between the present age and the age to come, held in tension between the past resurrection of Jesus and the future resurrection promised to all his people, is thus itself appropriately spoken of with the *metaphor* of resurrection, as in 4.10–12'.[113] This limited experience of life will give way to a fuller expression in the future, as we will see in the coming section.

---

[110] Cf. Fitzgerald, *Cracks*, 171.

[111] Also see Harris, *Second Corinthians*, 345.

[112] Tannehill, *Dying and Rising*, 85. Cf. Savage, *Power*, 176.

[113] N.T. Wright, *The Resurrection of the Son of God* (London: SPCK, 2003), 371, emphasis original.

Interestingly, Paul does not just say that believers merely have the life of Jesus, but that this death comes in order that the life of Jesus may be manifested, or become visible (4.11). In case the point was missed, Paul repeats it in 4.12. Earlier, we briefly noted the importance of this manifestation language for Paul's discussion.[114] Just as the image language relates to revelation and manifestation, Paul clarifies that the suffering believer is the place where the revelation of God's life occurs. This is important for Paul's apologia in that it serves to support his claim for divine approbation of his ministry.[115] This experience of the life of Jesus comes through trials which are embodied as the death of Jesus, and interestingly this life is also mediated through leaders who experience these trials on behalf of others, so 1.6 and 4.12. We remember that in 3.18–4.6 believers serve as a mirror reflecting the image of Christ for others to see, that is, for the benefit of others. In the same way here, Paul reveals the context of how this transformation and mediation occur – suffering and trials. As they face these trials, believers experience the life of Jesus – comfort and deliverance. At the same time, their experience of these trials is the basis of this life within others (cf. 5.14–15). We might say that these trials act as a mirror polish that allows the image of Christ to be reflected more clearly in their lives.

An important aspect of this exchange is that both the death and the life are τοῦ Ἰησοῦ.[116] That is, believers embody Christ's cruciform narrative in the present which reveals his life.[117] This process of death (suffering) and life (comfort, deliverance, and illumination) clarifies the nature of the transformation proposed by Paul in 3.18. The OT promise of new covenant, Spirit-given life (3.6) primarily entails inward renewal and moral enablement,[118] and the transformation described in 3.18 summarises this life-giving work of the Spirit. The nature of that renewal becomes clearer now as Paul fleshes out the context in which it occurs. Believers experience this life in the somatic context of suffering so that Christ's image, characterised by death and resurrection, is formed in them. This implicitly entails the enablement of the Spirit in order that they maintain their faithfulness in the midst of trials.

---

[114] See §2.4.

[115] Fitzgerald, *Cracks,* 160–201.

[116] Jan Lambrecht ('The Nekrōsis of Jesus: Ministry and Suffering in 2 Cor 4,7–15' in *L'Apôtre Paul,* ed. A. Vanhoye [Leuven: Leuven University, 1986], 120–143, at 124) notes that Paul refers to Christ as 'Jesus' six times in verses 10, 11, and 14, which points towards Jesus' earthly experience.

[117] Michael J. Gorman, *Cruciformity: Paul's Narrative Spirituality of the Cross* (Grand Rapids: Eerdmans, 2001), 30–35.

[118] See §2.1 above.

In 4.13–15, Paul clarifies the basis of this bold declaration about life in the midst of death. This is a matter of faith because it is unseen – its manifestation is not presently materialised. To help make his point Paul uses Ps 116 (114–115 LXX), which is a prayer of praise highlighting God's work of deliverance for the one who faced troubles. Using this phrase 'I believed therefore I spoke' (Ps 115.1 LXX), Paul draws on the hope of unseen deliverance in the midst of present affliction that fills the Psalm. The content of his faith is the fact that 'the one who raised the Lord Jesus will also raise us with Jesus and present us with you' (4.14).[119] Turning from the problem of death Paul presents the hope of an embodied resurrection in the future.[120] Regarding σὺν Ἰησοῦ, Bultmann writes: 'It indicates that though the acts of raising are temporally distinct (cf. 1 Cor. 15:23), in face of the essential unity ... the temporal distinction disappears – Christ's raising and that of believers is an eschatological event'.[121] Thus, Jesus' resurrection cannot be disassociated from that of believers any more than the future restoration of believers' bodies cannot be disassociated from their present experience of death as suffering. Therefore, they can have a confident expectation that God will carry them through.[122]

3.2 Excursus: Philippians 2–3

The hope of resurrection in the midst of present suffering at the centre of 2 Corinthians 4 is also reflected in the soteriological themes of Philippians 2–3. In this passage, Paul also juxtaposes the death and life in Christ's narrative and that of believers. We remember that Cyril of Alexandria found the Christ hymn (2.5–11) fruitful for his soteriological exposition, but we explore Philippians 2 and 3 since important themes connect the two chapters.[123]

---

[119] Earlier Paul declared that his firm hope in God's deliverance was based on his ability to raise the dead (1.9–10). He now reasserts his trust that God's raising Jesus serves as the basis for his willingness and ability to save now.

[120] With the use of ἐγείρω, Paul points to the hope of believers' resurrection and does not refer back to the manifestation of the life of Jesus presently. See Lambrecht, 'Nekrōsis', 134. *Pace* Jerome Murphy-O'Connor ('Faith and Resurrection in 2 Cor 4:13–14', *RB* 95 [1988]: 543–550), who argues that this points to present, 'existential' life.

[121] Bultmann, *Second Corinthians*, 122.

[122] In 4.14, presenting (παρίστημι), in the context of a future event, probably relates to a judgment scene and holiness (Rom 14.10; Col 1.22; cf. Eph 5.27).

[123] Some have posited that the canonical text of Philippians is a combination of a number of letters. However, the weight of evidence is against this perspective as Watson and Reed show: D.F. Watson, 'A Rhetorical Analysis of Philippians and its Implications for the Unity Question', *NovT* 30 (1988): 57–88; J.T. Reed, *A Discourse Analysis of Philippians: Method and Rhetoric in the Debate over Literary Integrity* (JSNTSup 136; Sheffield: Sheffield Academic, 1997).

In the preliminary section Phil 2.1–18, Paul primarily urges 'the Philippians to *adopt* a new disposition towards one another'.[124] In the context of suffering (1.27–30), Paul emphasises the mental and emotional support offered by Christ and the Spirit as a basis for their proper relations with each other (2.1–4). He then uses the Christ hymn both as a model for their thinking and acting and as confirmation of his lordship which demands obedience (2.5–11).[125] In his descent, Christ moves from the form of God through incarnation to death, and his ascent is one of exaltation to a position of authority over all.[126] As a model for Christians, most attention is placed upon Christ's descent because the subject shifts to God's work of exaltation in the second half of the hymn. However, the implication is that since God vindicated Christ in his suffering, he will vindicate believers also.[127] This vindication of believers is later confirmed in chapter 3.

In Michael Gorman's chapter on the Christ hymn, his primary argument is that Christ reveals the divine identity and that his activity of death and resurrection is that of God himself.[128] As the basis of this argument Gorman focuses particularly on the language of Phil 2.6 with its 'although [x], not [y], but [z]' formula.[129] Based upon his analysis, Gorman contends that inherent in the 'although' is a 'because', and, thus, Christ acts in a kenotic and cruciform manner *because* he is divine. Consequently, when believers are drawn up into the pattern of death and resurrection through participation and conformation, they are living in a divine way. He concludes: 'To be truly human is to be Christlike, which is to be Godlike, which is to be kenotic and cruciform'.[130] Gorman's proposal has much to commend it because he shows how Paul connects Christ's divine identity with his cruciform character and then applies that to believers. Gorman's

---

[124] Markus Bockmuehl, *The Epistle to the Philippians* (BNTC; London: A & C Black, 1997), 122, emphasis original.

[125] Cf. Gerald F. Hawthorne and Ralph P. Martin, *Philippians* (WBC 43; Nashville: Thomas Nelson, 2004), lxxiii–lxxvii. An association between Christ and Adam is not explicit, but Dunn and others have argued strongly for seeing it in the background of Paul's argument in 2.5–11: James D.G. Dunn, 'Christ, Adam, and Preexistence' in *Where Christology Began: Essays on Philippians 2,* eds. Ralph P. Martin and B.J. Dodd (Louisville: Westminster John Knox, 1998), 74–83. Cf. Hawthorne and Martin, *Philippians*, 105; Peter T. O'Brien, *The Epistle to the Philippians* (NIGTC; Carlisle, UK: Paternoster, 1991), 263–68. While this hypothesis has interesting implications, it falls outside the scope of this excursus.

[126] Whether Paul presents Christ as pre-existent here is debated, but the weight of evidence does seem to support the idea. Cf. N.T. Wright, 'Jesus Christ is Lord: Philippians 2.5–11' in *The Climax of the Covenant,* (Minneapolis: Fortress, 1991), 56–98.

[127] Bockmuehl, *Philippians*, 140.

[128] Gorman, *Inhabiting*, 9–39.

[129] Ibid., 16–25.

[130] Ibid., 39.

focus is on what might be termed 'moral deification', with its emphasis on moral action, in distinction to 'ontological deification', which focuses on embodied resurrection. From the parenetic focus of 2.1–18 the moral emphasis is clear, but the hope of resurrection cannot be separated from this passage because of the numerous thematic connections in Phil 3.20–21 that Paul establishes, as we will see below.

Paul continues his parenesis in the paragraph following the Christ hymn as he encourages ethical obedience (2.12–18). Interestingly, Paul describes this as 'work[ing] out your own salvation (σωτηρία) with fear and trembling' (Phil 2.12). Salvation, then, is not merely a past or future event but a process lived out by the agency of God who enables both the willing and activity (Phil 2.13). Within this discussion of ethical obedience, Paul identifies believers as 'children of God' (2.15). In Romans 8 the children of God appellation was associated with embodied incorruption, whereas here it is associated with moral incorruption (cf. Deut 32.5). The shining here, rather than an embodied radiance, is one related to moral character as 'they shine as stars' in the world (2.15).[131] Paul then summarises the hope of the Christian gospel as the 'word of life', which seems to have both moral and somatic implications due to the mention of the 'day of Christ' (2.16). Paul then uses Timothy and Epaphroditus as examples of those who follow the Christ model (2.19–29).

In Phil 3.1–11 Paul distinguishes between useful and unuseful objects of confidence and boasting. In distinction to the aspects of his former way of life, knowing Christ is now of primary importance in such a way that all other things have no relative value. This passage is indicative of the other Pauline texts that associate righteousness, law, faith, and the flesh, in that Paul argues that the Spirit and Christ have superseded the law and any ethnic nationalism as a means to righteousness. Paul describes a fundamentally relational knowledge of Christ as 'gaining Christ' and 'being found in him' (3.8–9), and this serves as the basis of his righteousness (3.9). However, this relationship transforms Paul's own experience according to Christ's own death and life. He has lost all things (3.8) and 'shares in his sufferings by being conformed (συμμορφίζω) to his death' (3.10). At the same time, he has the hope of knowing 'the power of his resurrection' (3.10). Like 2 Cor 4.10–11 and Rom 8.17, Paul genetically links suffering with resurrection when he writes about 'sharing in his sufferings by being conformed to his death if somehow (εἴ πως) I may attain the resurrection from the dead' (3.10–11). Paul again uses morphic language (συμμορφίζω) to describe the christoform nature of believers' experience, but this

---

[131] Fee notes the importance of the Daniel 12.1–4 allusion, where Paul uses resurrection imagery for present moral behaviour: Gordon D. Fee, *Paul's Letter to the Philippians* (NICNT; Grand Rapids: Eerdmans, 1995), 246–48.

passage is unique in that the morphic language focuses primarily on the aspect of suffering. Although the resurrection is something to be attained in the future, knowing the power of the resurrection appears to be a present and future phenomenon similar to that of Rom 6.4, 11 and 2 Cor 4.10–11 where the life of God is at work in believers' lives.[132]

Continuing on from the discussion of suffering with Christ and the hope of resurrection, Paul describes his present struggle towards the goal of maturity and resurrection in Phil 3.12–21. In 3.12–16 the progressive nature of Christian maturity is clearer than in any other in Paul's letters. As in 1 Corinthians 15 and 2 Corinthians 5, Paul works from an earthly-heavenly duality. On the one hand, he describes the enemies of the cross as those whose thoughts are on 'earthly things' (3.19). In contrast, he speaks of the 'upward (or heavenly)[133] call of God in Christ Jesus' (3.14) and the 'commonwealth in heaven, from which we are expecting a Saviour, the Lord Jesus Christ' (Phil 3.20).[134] Christ's 'body of glory' (3.21) most likely corresponds with his position of being 'from heaven'. The commonwealth presently exists in heaven, so this cannot merely be a temporal distinction between earthly existence now and heavenly in the future.[135] Rather, as believers' bodies are transformed into conformity with Christ's heavenly glory, they are drawn up into a heavenly mode of existence. However, there is no evidence that they will leave earth because the Saviour will come 'from there'.

In this final section, Paul draws together a thread that he has woven through Philippians 2–3. The humility-glory dialectic[136] in 3.20–21 corresponds to death-resurrection in 3.10–11 and kenosis-exaltation in 2.6–11. Thus, Lincoln writes: 'This christological pattern of humble suffering as the path to glory in chapter 2 is now applied to believers in chapter 3'.[137] See Table 6.2 for the similarities between 2.6–11 and 3.20–21, in particular.

---

[132] Joseph A. Fitzmyer, '"To Know Him and the Power of His Resurrection" (Phil 3.10)' in *Mélanges Bibliques*, eds. Albert Descamps and André de Halleux (Gembloux: Ducolot, 1970), 411–25.

[133] Cf. Andrew T. Lincoln, *Paradise Now and Not Yet: Studies in the Role of the Heavenly Dimension in Paul's Thought with Special Reference to His Eschatology* (SNTSMS 43; Cambridge: Cambridge University Press, 1991), 93.

[134] Lincoln argues for 'commonwealth' as the translation of πολίτευμα: Ibid., 97–100.

[135] O'Brien, *Philippians*, 461.

[136] Like in Rom 9.22–23 Paul contrasts destruction (ἀπώλεια) and shame (Rom: ἀτιμία; Phil: αἰσχύνη) and glory (δόξα) as ultimate destinies. This reflects the social and ontological aspects of glory. Cf. Blackwell, 'Immortal Glory', 292–99.

[137] Lincoln, *Paradise Now*, 107.

Table 6.2: Similarities between Phil 2.6–11 and 3.20–21[138]

Phil 2.6–11	Phil 3.20–21
μορφή (6, 7)	σύμμορφος (21)
ὑπάρχω (6)	ὑπάρχω (20)
σχῆμα (7)	μετασχηματίζω (21)
ταπεινόω (8)	ταπείνωσις (21)
ἐπουράνιος (10)	ἐν οὐρανοῖς (20)
πᾶν γόνυ κάμψῃ ... καὶ πᾶσα γλῶσσα ἐξομολογήσηται (10–11)	κατὰ τὴν ἐνέργειαν τοῦ δύνασθαι αὐτὸν καὶ ὑποτάξαι αὐτῷ τὰ πάντα (21)
κύριος Ἰησοῦς Χριστός (11)	κύριος Ἰησοῦς Χριστός (20)
δόξα (11)	δόξα (21)

Christ's pattern of death and exaltation then is mapped onto the believers' experience of suffering and resurrection. Thus, we see how the moral and ontological aspects of Paul's soteriology cannot be separated. Again, Paul uses morphic language to capture this transformation, which he locates in the body. This time, Christ's body of glory, his new life, is the model to which believers are conformed (σύμμορφος; 3.21). Just as the heaven does not negate the earth, this bodily transformation is not separated from the creational order. Rather, it is 'by the power that also enables him to subject all things to himself' (3.20). By 'all things' Paul does not merely refer to creation, but he surely includes it. This implicitly points to a correspondence between human somatic transformation and creational restoration.

Three central themes from Philippians 2–3 are worth noting. First, Paul uses 'morphic' language in each of the three key sections (2.5–11; 3.10–11; and 3.20–21). Paul associates μορφή in the first instance with the visible aspect of God and humans (2.6–7), and later he describes believers as being conformed (συμμορφίζω; σύμμορφος) to Christ's death (3.10) and his resurrection (3.21). Thus, as believers suffer with Christ and experience his resurrection life as heavenly glory, they do not become the μορφή θεοῦ/κυρίου, but they do share in divine attributes of life and glory. The shape of this soteriology is decidedly christoform in nature, both in present suffering and in future resurrection.

Second, related to the morphic language, Paul introduces explicit language of participation in the divine with the use of κοινωνία (2.1; 3.10). This language is not new to Paul (e.g., 1 Cor 1.9; 10.16), but it does introduce explicit participation language into our discussion. Whereas we have previously noted Paul's use of overlapping prepositional phrases and oblique cases to describe the divine-human relationship, Paul here employs

---

[138] Ibid., 88.

explicit participation language regarding the Spirit and Christ (through his sufferings). Its synonymous function in this latter case in 3.10 vis-à-vis the conformation language shows how the morphic language corresponds with his conception of participation.

Third, the earthly-heavenly duality recapitulates a theme we will soon address in both 2 Cor 5.1–5 and 1 Cor 15.35–49. Christ has been elevated over all in heaven and earth (2.10), showing his reign over all. He will then return from there and share heavenly glory with believers as they are resurrected. With the employment of pre-existence motifs in Phil 2.5–11, we may infer his pre-existent presence in heaven. However, when Paul describes the anthropological transformation of believers, he primarily relates it to Christ's exaltation rather than to his pre-existent state.[139]

In our excursus on Philippians 2–3, we have seen similar themes to those in Romans 8 and 2 Corinthians 3–5. In particular, Paul reiterates the importance of Christ's death and life as the basis of the Christian life. While believers suffer presently, their bodies will be transformed into heavenly bodies of glory in the future. During the present time, they are to strive towards maturity by the agency of God as they 'work out their salvation'. Notably, Paul places this discussion in the context of law, flesh, the Spirit, and righteousness, as in other passages. While God and the Spirit play a role in this process of salvation, Christ stands at the centre because believers are conformed to his death and resurrection. As we return to 2 Corinthians 4, we will see how this death-life dialectic continues to play out in the argument.

3.3 Hope of Resurrection (4.16–5.10)

While 2 Corinthians 4–5 continues in an uninterrupted flow from 4.7 to 5.10, Paul takes a decisive turn in his argumentation in 4.16. The present state of weakness and trouble are central in 4.7–15, and Paul shifts to a focus upon the future resurrection in 4.16–5.10.[140] However, the present-future interaction is clear throughout both sub-sections. Although Lambrecht notes a shift in the discussion from the Corinthian addressees to all Christians,[141] this does not negate the universal significance of the prior discussion.

---

[139] Bockmuehl (*Philippians*, 145) notes that the language of exaltation points to the possibility that Christ was raised to a higher position than in his pre-existence.

[140] Cf. Furnish, *II Corinthians*, 288.

[141]Lambrecht, 'Nekrōsis', 123. Regarding Paul's rhetoric, Fredrik Lindgård (*Paul's Line of Thought in 2 Corinthians 4:16–5:10* [WUNT 2/189; Tübingen: Mohr Siebeck, 2005], 221) notes that in 4.7–15, 'the suffering of Paul is "relation-centered" and "functional" since it benefits the Corinthians. In 4:16 the emphasis moves to Paul's inner attitudes and emotions'. However, Lambrecht's assessment that the 'we' addresses all

3.3.1 2 Corinthians 4.16–18

In spite of the troubles facing Paul, his faith in the resurrection power of
God and in his promise to raise believers in the future means that he does
not lose heart (4.16; cf. 4.1). Summing up the death-life dialectic explored
since 4.7, Paul writes of outwardly wasting away and being inwardly renewed (4.16). The use of 'outer person' (ὁ ἔξω ἄνθρωπος) and 'inner person' (ὁ ἔσω [ἄνθρωπος]) has given rise to a debate about the nature of
Paul's anthropology. While some attempt to minimise the anthropological
duality in Paul's language by associating this language with the 'old/new
person' (cf. Col 3.10),[142] the distinction Paul makes here is consistent with
his anthropology throughout the previous passage.[143]

The 'outer person' refers back to the (mortal) body of 4.10–11 and the
clay jar of 4.7. This is the locus of the death of Jesus, and we are not surprised to hear Paul describe it in terms of corruption (διαφθείρω).[144] The
'inner person' refers to the other aspects noted previously by Paul, specifically, heart (καρδία, 3.3, 15; 4.6) and mind (νόημα, 3.14, 15; 4.4).[145] Jewett rightly notes that 'the fact that [Paul] does not explicitly identify [the
inner person] with the heart, the mind, the gospel or the indwelling Christ'
means that 'he seems to consider the term ἔσω ἄνθρωπος self-
explanatory'.[146] This inward renewal corresponds to the transformative
knowledge granted by God (3.18; 4.4, 6), which is strengthened daily. In
other words, this inward renewal is the experience of life (3.6; 4.10–12).[147]

Whereas in 4.10–11 death was the basis of the new life showing in their
lives, in 4.16 Paul contrasts corruption with renewal. This earlier causal
relationship returns in 4.17 where the corruption is characterised as a
'momentarily light trouble' (θλῖψις) that produces an 'eternally weighty

---

Christians better fits Paul's purpose of placing the problem of present suffering in the
context of eternal glory.

[142] E.g., Savage, *Power*, 182–83.

[143] Robert Gundry (*Sōma*, 135–37), in particular, argues strongly that the inner-outer
human duality cannot be simply mapped on the new-old human language in Paul.

[144] This use of corruption (διαφθείρω) to describe the problem in distinction to incorruption and glory reflects similar discussions in Rom 8.18–30 and 1 Cor 15.42–54. Cf.
Blackwell, 'Immortal Glory', 294–97.

[145] Aune ('Anthropological Duality', 220–222) supports a reading that sees the inward–outward here, but he is reticent to see specific terms associated with ὁ ἔσω
[ἄνθρωπος] in this specific context, though he agrees that these are the realities that Paul
is referring to. This inner-outer taxonomy is later repeated in 5.12 with the contrast between the face (πρόσωπον) and heart (καρδία). Cf. Rom 12.1–2.

[146] Jewett, *Anthropological Terms*, 397.

[147] Due to the prior associations of the Spirit with this activity of inward change (1.22;
3.3–6, 17–18), we have reason to expect that this daily renewal here occurs through the
Spirit, but this is not explicit here.

glory' (δόξα) beyond comparison.[148] The glory that was central to Paul's argument in chapter 3 returns to describe the eschatological hope of believers.[149] Unlike Romans, Paul has used a variety of terms related to *visible* glory. Most important is the discussion of Moses' luminous face (3.7–11), but he also spoke of 'reflecting in a mirror (κατοπτρίζω) the glory of the Lord' (3.18), 'the light (φωτισμός) of the glory of Christ' (4.4), and God shining (λάμπω) 'in our hearts the light (φωτισμός) of the knowledge of the glory of God' (4.6).[150] With this co-occurrence of glory with light language, even if metaphorical, it seems clear that glory connotes luminosity. However, the association with light is not repeated in this context; rather, somatic life comes to the fore.[151]

Several data indicate the association between glory and resurrection life in this context. First, in contrast to the present state of corruption (δια-φθείρω, 4.16) and trouble (θλῖψις, 4.17), Paul describes a new state of glory (δόξα, 4.17) that awaits believers. We encountered the same contrast in Rom 8.17–30 with similar language, where it was clear that Paul was discussing the somatic life of the believers. Second, the double ascription of the adjective 'eternal' (αἰώνιος) to this state of glory in 4.17–18 supports this reading. The importance of the term αἰώνιος becomes even clearer when Paul uses it in 5.1 to describe the eternal 'house' (οἰκία). Accordingly, αἰώνιος becomes the hinge-term that helps Paul connect the context of future glory to that of the future resurrection body (5.1–5). As such, textual and contextual evidence supports understanding this glory as denoting an embodied state of existence characterised by incorruption.

---

[148] This reminds us of Rom 8.17–23 where suffering is the basis of glory but also something from which believers are to be freed.

[149] Pate argues that the background to this discussion is Adam's lost glory: C. Marvin Pate, *Adam Christology as the Exegetical and Theological Substructure of 2 Corinthians 4.7–5.21* (Lanham, MD: University Press of America, 1991). While there is evidence that Paul employs traditions related to Adam and glory in Rom 3.23, the evidence that Pate supplies here is forced. See Blackwell, 'Immortal Glory', 301–2. James D.G. Dunn ('Adam in Paul' in *The Pseudepigrapha and Christian Origins,* eds. Gerbern S. Oegema and James H. Charlesworth [London: T&T Clark, 2008], 120–135) is quite sanguine about the role of Adam in Paul's theology, but he does not mention 2 Cor 4–5 in the passages where Adam themes play a role. Paul does not mention Adam in this context, but rather Moses. Also, the glory here is modelled after Christ and not Adam. Pate, however, takes what might be implicit and tries to make it the key to the whole passage, thus overstepping the usefulness of the speculation.

[150] Paul's use of glory serves to trump the glory or honour being claimed or exhibited by other ministers. Rather than an external show of honour, this glory is one of incorruption and honour before God.

[151] In fact, this glorious state of existence is described as 'unseen' because it is eternal (4.18). This is probably a statement about temporality rather than ontology. That is, the glory cannot be seen *now* but will be in the future.

With this use of glory, Paul develops his statement in 3.10–11 that Moses' glory has been set aside. Paul describes Moses' glory as τὸ καταργούμενον as opposed to τὸ μένον. This glory in 4.17f is also outward and somatic like that of Moses, but it is associated primarily with incorruption and permenance. The move from mental enlightenment to embodied resurrection represents the temporal progress within the Christian life. The continuity is evident because the Spirit is the agent of the enlightenment (3.18) and of resurrection (5.5). At the same time, believers are conformed to Christ in each stage. Paul has previously associated the 'glory of the Lord' with the presence of the Spirit (3.17–18), and he has described this glory as being of God (4.4) and of Christ (4.6). As they reflect this glory, being transformed into the image of Christ, they share in a divine mode of existence as modelled by Christ.

With this discussion of resurrection life, Paul brings together several dialectical threads explored through this whole passage: clay jars and treasure (4.7), death and life (4.10–12), the outer and the inner (4.16), momentary affliction and eternal glory (4.17), and the visible and invisible (4.18). The centre of the discussion appears to be death and life and what these mean in believers' lives. This death-life experience drawn out by Paul depends heavily upon a body-mind duality. While the mind and body experience temporal troubles, the mind is the locus of present renewal. Thus, Bultmann's overemphasis on anthropological unity does not capture the duality in the passage. However, with the culmination of life being centred on the body, we also see that van Kooten's overemphasis on the the mind in the context of an anthropological dualism does not hold up.[152] Van Kooten rightly sees the present emphasis on the renewal of the mind in the midst of physical corruption, but he ignores the hope of future resurrection and thus the importance of the body in Paul's anthropology. While an anthropological duality is central for Paul's theology, his temporal duality is more formative.[153] The current age with its already/not yet characteristic means that death and life both pervade believers, such that their inner and outer aspects experience this differently. However, in the eschaton believers will experience life fully, and, thus, when this temporal duality is overcome, believers will experience greater intra-personal unity, as the next section makes clear.

3.3.2 2 Corinthians 5.1–10

In 5.1–10 Paul continues his discussion of the resurrection and as well as other aspects of eschatological life. He talks about the 'eternal house',

---

[152] See the Excursus on the body in §3.1 above.

[153] Lincoln, *Paradise Now*, 70.

being away from/with the Lord, and judgment. Because of Paul's use of the tent/house distinction and his contrast of being in the body and being with the Lord, this passage has attracted a great deal of discussion. However, many of the questions that interest others fall outside the scope of this study. As a result, we will leave behind questions about the intermediate state or whether Paul has changed his mind about certain aspects of eschatology because they do not directly concern our consideration of the shape of his soteriology.

Paul began his discussion of the resurrection in 4.16–18, and he continues that discourse in 5.1–5 where he now draws on two metaphors, that of buildings and clothing, in order to describe the bodily existence of believers. He first describes two states of existence, using the term 'building' (οἰκία) to characterise both. In particular, a 'tent' (σκῆνος), which is temporary and earthly (ἐπίγειος), is contrasted with a 'house' (οἰκοδομή), which is eternal (αἰώνιος), not made by hands (ἀχειροποίητος), and is in the heavens (οὐρανός). In 5.2 Paul mixes metaphors as he introduces the aspects of being clothed and naked while still using building terminology. The tent-house contrast continues similar themes based on the outer-inner and temporal-eternal contrasts developed by Paul in the previous section. The temporal and ephemeral character corresponds to the outer person wasting away in contrast to the incorruption of eternal glory awaiting the outer person, as in 4.16–18. As such, the house presents the future and 'unseen' aspect of the Christian hope for the body that is in distinction to the current state of bodily corruption (4.16).[154]

A debated aspect of these verses relates to the timing of the reception of the glorified body.[155] In 5.1 Paul uses a present tense form of ἔχω to describe the possession of the building 'not made with human hands in the

---

[154] In contrast to reading this section as referring to the physical body, Ellis posits that this building is not physical but ecclesial and that being unclothed corresponds with being condemned at the judgment rather than speaking about a disembodied state: E. Earle Ellis, '2 Corinthians 5:1–10 in Pauline Eschatology', *NTS* 6 (1960): 211–224, at 216–21. Several points of evidence indicate that Paul is discussing the physical body. See especially Gundry, *Sōma*, 148–54. The primary piece of evidence is that the death-life language throughout chapter 4 continues into chapter 5. Accordingly, Manuel Vogel (*Commentatio mortis: 2Kor 5,1–10 auf dem Hintergrund antiker ars moriendi* [FRLANT 214; Göttingen: Vandenhoeck & Ruprecht, 2006], 371, cf. 226–38) writes: '2Kor 5,1–10 liegt auf derselben gedanken Linie wie der voranstehende Kontext seit 4,7, wo es um die Niedrigkeits- und Leidensgestalt des irdischen Leibes geht'. If the building here is the church, then the language of chapter 4 would have to be interpreted ecclesially as well. Second, the outer-inner dialectic serves as the basis for this discussion about the hope of restoration of the outer person, not of a corporate body. Third, in 5.6–10, the discussion of the body (σῶμα) would make little sense if taken corporately. Together, these speak against Ellis' interesting but unsupportable thesis.

[155] E.g., Harris, *Second Corinthians*, 374–80.

heavens'. The primary question is whether the glorified body is a present possession or acquired in the future. It is difficult to affirm this 'heavenly building' as a present state.[156] As we have argued above, 5.1 is a continuation of the description of the hope of resurrection described in earnest from 4.13 onward. This is a future resurrection since it is set in distinction to the current experience of corruption. Thus, the present ἔχω should be understood as describing a *'probable future'* event.[157] This reading is strongly supported by the following context: the current groaning (5.2), the future putting on of the new body (5.3),[158] the Spirit as a deposit (ἀρραβών, 5.5), and the progression in 5.6–8.

If the reception of this body is in the future, is it received at death or the parousia? Will believers that die before the parousia experience some sort of disembodied, intermediate state, where they are 'naked'? What does it mean to be away from the body and at home with the Lord (5.6–8)? While these are interesting and highly debated questions, we can bypass them because questions related to an intermediate state are not central to our discussion of the shape of soteriology. Whatever is decided regarding these questions, the intermediate state is just that, intermediate. The expected telos is not one of a disembodied soul, but of mind and a resurrected body fully united together. As such, the hope of resurrection as a permanent (3.11) and everlasting (4.17) state of being, characterised as new life (5.4), is the telos of believers.

Paul's emphasis is on the fact of this transformation rather than its mode. However, an important aspect is the role God's agency plays. Paul makes clear that the eternal building is described as 'from God' (ἐκ θεοῦ) and 'not made with (human) hands' (ἀχειροποίητος) in 5.2. Since ἐκ θεοῦ (5.1) is used synonymously to ἐξ οὐρανοῦ (5.2), when believers are drawn up into this heavenly mode of existence, it is not without basis that we can say they are drawn up into a divine mode of existence. This is not an esoteric experience but rather an experience of immortal life. As he speaks of life swallowing up the mortal (5.4), Paul re-introduces the agency of the Spirit into the discussion. In 5.5, God is described as the one who makes this happen (ὁ κατεργασάμενος) and the one who gives believers the Spirit

---

[156] E.g., Richard Reitzenstein, *Hellenistic Mystery-Religions: Their Basic Ideas and Significance* (trans. John E. Steely; Eugene, OR: Pickwick, 1978), 451–52.

[157] Wallace, *Greek Grammar Beyond the Basics*, 696–97, emphasis original. As a third class condition, this could refer to a present or future event.

[158] With the external support of 𝔓46, ℵ, B, C, D², Ψ, 0243, 33, 1739, 1881, 𝔐, lat, sy, and co, the reading should be ἐνδυσάμενοι (put on) and not as ἐκδυσάμενοι (take off) in NA²⁷, following Bruce M. Metzger rather than the committee: *A Textual Commentary on the Greek New Testament* (2nd ed.; Stuttgart: Deutsche Bibelgesellschaft, 1994), 511. Surely, this nearly tautological reading is the more difficult. Cf. Harris, *Second Corinthians*, 368.

as a deposit (ἀρραβών). This is the first unambiguous mention of Spirit since 3.3–18, where the Spirit's role in giving life was central.[159] However, by reintroducing the Spirit here Paul clarifies that the Spirit is the agent of all life – both inward renewal and somatic resurrection. Whereas the adjective πνευματικός in 1 Cor 15.44–45 stands at the centre of discontinuity with the current existence for most interpreters, Belleville helpfully notes the Spirit's role in continuity between the 'present and future modes of existence' here in 2 Corinthians 3–5.[160]

Like the question of the intermediate state, the question of the nature of the judgment described in 5.9–10 takes us beyond our topic of interest. However, we can draw conclusions about the anthropology expressed by this discussion. If, as Paul has argued, the mortal body is a tent to be exchanged in the future, some might argue that what happens in the body does not really matter. Paul reminds his audience that while the present body is temporary, the activities done 'in the body' (5.10) will have future consequences as believers stand before the judgment seat. Just as God's work of life in the body was manifest (4.10–11), believers' work in the body will be made manifest (5.10). Thus, Paul again guards against entirely negative views of the body.

Our primary focus has been on the shape and timing of Paul's soteriology, but we must consider Pate's monograph on this passage since it relates to our question about the relationship of creation and soteriology.[161] Building on his argument about Adam's loss of glory and the suffering righteous in 4.7–18, Pate continues to see the Adam tradition behind Paul's discussion in 5.1–10. While there was only a little room for seeing Adam in 4.7–18, Pate's arguments find little ground in this passage as well.

According to Pate, the nakedness language echoes the Adam tradition related to his loss of glory.[162] Pate, in particular, cites 2 *En* 22.8; 30.12; and *Gen Rab* 20.12 as key examples of this association between Adam's loss of glory and nakedness.[163] Of these, 2 *En* 22.8 speaks of Enoch and not Adam, and 2 En 30.12 speaks of Adam being created 'glorious' but clothing is not mentioned. In *Gen Rab* 20.12 a brief association is made between garments of skin (עור) and garments of light (אור), which gives more basis for an argument. While this association between garments of

---

[159] One could possibly read the 'spirit of faith' (πνεῦμα τῆς πίστεως) in 4.13 as referring to the divine Spirit, but there is little in the context to commend this reading. *Pace* Fee, *Empowering Presence*, 323–24.

[160] Linda L. Belleville, 'Paul's Polemic and Theology of the Spirit in Second Corinthians', *CBQ* 58 (1996): 281–304, at 288.

[161] Pate, *Adam Christology*.

[162] Ibid., 115–116.

[163] For a recent assessment of Jewish traditions related to Adam's glory, see my 'Immortal Glory'.

light and nakedness may reflect larger traditions, building the case upon these tenuous pieces of evidence is speculative at best. Thus, Pate is right to see the hope of eschatological vindication for God's suffering people, but the associations with Adam are weak and difficult to substantiate.

If cannot substantiate dependence upon Adam traditions, what, if any, relationship with creation can we see? Importantly, the heaven-earth dialectic appears here (5.1–2), as with 1 Corinthians 15 and Philippians 3. In distinction to Christ who comes from heaven to glorify believers' bodies (Phil 3.20), this new building is from God, in the heavens.[164] In this passage future experience seems to be in heaven and not on earth, and thus the duality between earth and heaven appears strong in this passage. The earthly, as part of creation, appears to be destroyed (καταλύω; 5.1), while the heavenly is eternal. However, the 'put on over' (5.2, 4) and 'swallow up' (καταπίνω) language might point towards some type of continuity. Also, both states are described as buildings (οἰκία), so that some type of continuity is seen between the two. In this passage, however, the discontinuity is stronger here than continuity. Accordingly, Schrage writes: 'Gottes schöpferischer Neubeginn bewirkt einen radikalen Bruch mit dem bisher Gültigen und das Ende des alten Wesens und Wandels'.[165]

3.4 Excursus: 1 Corinthians 15

The discussion of the resurrection body and the association with Adam and creation calls for a brief discussion of 1 Corinthians 15 where similar themes also arise. Significantly, this passage is one of the most important for Irenaeus and Cyril in their soteriological explorations. Central to this rich passage on the resurrection is the correlation between Christ's resurrection and that of believers who belong to him. Paul begins the passage by mentioning that the Corinthians 'are saved' through the gospel (1 Cor 15.2). Most take this as a 'futuristic present' in light of the discussion in the rest of the chapter and Paul's other uses of σῴζω (e.g., Rom 5.9).[166] Although Paul relates the argument to present parenesis (1 Cor 15.30–34, 58),[167] our concentration is on the future bodily resurrection.

The Adam-Christ dialectic plays a significant role in Paul's argumentation. Although Christ is a man (ἄνθρωπος) like Adam, he is also distinct

---

[164] Lincoln notes that this use of ἐν τοῖς οὐρανοῖς has more of a qualitative sense ('heavenly') than merely a locative sense ('in the heavens'). Lincoln, *Paradise Now*, 61, 63.

[165] Schrage, 'Schöpfung und Neuschöpfung', 247.

[166] C.K. Barrett, *The First Epistle to the Corinthians* (2nd ed.; BNTC; London: A & C Black, 1971), 336.

[167] Richard B. Hays, *First Corinthians* (Interpretation; Louisville: John Knox, 1997), 253–54.

from him (1 Cor 15.21–22, 47–49). Working from these two representative figures, Paul describes human existence as 'bearing the image' (φορέσωμεν τὴν εἰκόνα) of the earthly Adam and the heavenly Christ (1 Cor 15.49).[168] This introduction of 'heavenly' language is important because it is used to characterise Christ's present elevated status and the future elevation of believers, not unlike Phil 3.20–21.

The nature of the continuity and discontinuity between the earthly and heavenly aspects of the resurrected body reflects this balance between the continuity and discontinuity between Adam and Christ. Focusing on the discontinuity, Bousset writes, 'The relation between the first and the second Adam is that of blunt opposition. The first man and the second actually have nothing in common but the name'.[169] In distinction, Scroggs, while still noting the contrast between Adam and Christ, notes how Paul uses the term ἄνθρωπος to signify the continuity between the two (15.21, 47).[170] When we consider the different characterisations of the two somatic states of existence based upon Adam and Christ, Paul is focusing on the contrast (see Table 6.3). While much debate typically focuses on the nature of the σῶμα πνευματικόν,[171] Paul's emphasis is on new life experienced as incorruption and immortality through Christ in distinction to the corruption associated with Adam.

Table 6.3: Somatic States of Existence in 1 Corinthians 15

Verse	Adam	Christ
15.21	θάνατος	ἀνάστασις νεκρῶν
15.42	φθορά	ἀφθαρσία
15.43	ἀτιμία	δόξα
15.43	ἀσθένεια	δύναμις
15.44–45	ψυχικός	πνευματικός
15.47	ἐκ γῆς	ἐξ οὐρανοῦ
15.48–49	χοϊκός	ἐπουράνιος
15.53–54	φθαρτός	ἀφθαρσία
15.53–54	θνητός	ἀθανασία

---

[168] Against NA[27] I read the text here as φορέσωμεν rather than φορέσομεν. The weight of the exegetical argument should not outweigh the very strong external evidence (e.g. 𝔓46 ℵ A C D F G Ψ 𝔐 etc.).

[169] Bousset, Kyrios Christos, 178.

[170] Scroggs, Last Adam, 88, 93.

[171] For instance, Wright (Resurrection, 348–52) argues that the distinction between ψυχικός and πνευματικός has nothing to do with material-immaterial dialectic, but rather describes the animating agent. In response to Wright, Finlan, ('Theosis in Paul?', 71) argues that the future state is embodied but not physical. Wright's reading appears more amenable to the passage, but there is not enough evidence to rule out Finlan's reading.

What role does the heaven language play, then? Wright points out that Paul does not characterise this as a movement towards heaven by believers but 'from heaven' by Christ.[172] Thus, believers participate in a heavenly, πνευματικός manner of existence but are not taken away from the earth in that process. This implies that the earthly context remains but believers will have a changed manner of existence primarily characterised by incorruption. The focus then is not upon a return to the state of Adam but upon an elevation to the condition of Christ, that is, to a heavenly manner of existence. Thus, Lincoln writes: 'The terminology of "heaven" in connection with that of "image" provides one way for Paul of expressing the fact that conformity to Christ's image is not simply a restoration of something lost by the first Adam but involves a distinctly new element, a new quality of existence'.[173] However, as Adam and Christ are both ἄνθρωποι, this manner of existence will be human.

With its emphasis on the resurrection and the resurrection body, 1 Corinthians 15 obviously resonates with 2 Cor 4.16–5.10. The primary similarity between the two passages is the stark contrast between the earthly and heavenly/glorified states of existence. In 1 Corinthians 15 this is based around the Adam-Christ dialectic, but in 2 Cor 5.1–5 no mention is made of Christ at all. Rather, the Spirit is the uniting factor between the two passages. In 2 Corinthians 5 the Spirit serves as a means of continuity between God's current work and the future resurrection, whereas in 1 Corinthians 15 the σῶμα πνευματικόν stands at the heart of the discontinuity. In either case, Paul presents the hope of inward renewal. Separation from the body at death is not the ultimate hope of believers; rather, their ultimate hope is the somatic experience of incorrupt glory so that the heavenly life that infuses the inner person will also infuse the outer person as well.

3.5 Conclusion

In the midst of the defence of his ministry, Paul gives an intensely theological discussion of soteriology in 2 Cor 4.7–5.10. He does not make explicit conclusions about his ministry, but by exploring various contrasts – death and life, outer and inner, present and future – Paul makes clear what expectations of a present ministry should be. These three antitheses are brought together as Paul shapes his soteriology in three forms: 1) inward, noetic transformation, 2) personal deliverance from trying circumstances, and 3) somatic resurrection. The first two occur in the present age, and the last is reserved for the future.

---

[172] Wright, *Resurrection*, 355.
[173] Lincoln, *Paradise Now*, 51–2.

In the present age believers struggle with troubles and corruption in the context of their bodily existence, which Paul metaphorically termed bearing the death of Jesus. However, alongside this death is the experience of the life of Jesus, which consists of inward comfort and renewal and even deliverance from out of particular struggles. Presently a disjunction stands between the outward and inward, but Paul presents the hope of reuniting the inner and outer as the body also experiences incorruption as eternal glory consistent with the inward illumination of glory. Consequently, the life of Jesus will consume the totality of believers in that future state, and death will be overcome.

4. Salvation Explored: 5.11–6.2

In the prior section, the implications of Paul's soteriology for a proper understanding of ministry became more implicit than explicit in his discussion. As he turns to a new section, Paul again makes the soteriology-ministry connection explicit. Moving from a discussion of commendation, Paul explores ideas of new creation, reconciliation and righteousness. With regard to the transition, Bultmann writes: 'If 4:7–5:10 had shown that ζωή is hidden beneath θάνατος, but proves itself to be operative precisely in θάνατος, then 5:11–6:10 explains that ζωή is manifest in proclamation'.[174] The soteriological themes remain, but Paul employs them more directly for a defence of his ministry.

4.1 Death and Life in Christ (5.11–15)

As we have seen throughout chapters 3–5 Paul continues to intertwine the theological basis of his ministry with the explicit implications arising from it. Thus, after describing his ministry (5.11–13), Paul then explores the message of Christ's work that undergirds and propels it (5.14–15). In the midst of this renewed attention to his ministry, Paul addresses the problem of those who boast in the outward appearance (πρόσωπον) rather than the heart (καρδία).[175] In this way, he draws together the importance of the evidence he provided in 4.7–5.10. The outward πρόσωπον will not be renewed until the eschaton, and the current outward experience is characterised by weakness, corruption, and fragility, otherwise known as death. Nguyen writes: 'Paul, then, is not simply criticising the outer person and emphasising the inner person, but he is criticising the outward appearance

---

[174] Bultmann, *Second Corinthians*, 145.

[175] Surely, this reflects 1 Sam 16.7 LXX where the account of Samuel choosing David as the next king is recorded: Assessing others based on their appearance (πρόσωπον) is what humans do, but the Lord looks at the heart (καρδία).

that reflects superficial values and commending, instead, outward appearance that is based on and reflects the spiritual transformation taking place in the inner person'.[176] As a result, believers should expect to boast not in the outward appearance, but rather the heart where inward transformation and enlightenment occurs. The καρδία is where the Spirit dwells in believers (1.22), where the Spirit confirms evidence of his work (3.3) and where the light of the glory of God shines (4.6).[177] The locus of God's present work is this inner aspect, and no mention is made here of future transformation of the outward.

Paul then discusses the love 'of Christ' (5.13–15), that is, Christ's love for others.[178] Christ's dying for all shows his love, and this has ramifications for all: 'one died for all; therefore all died' (5.14). This use of 'all' is notoriously difficult: in what sense did 'all' die because (ὅτι) he died?[179] Looking to the death-life contrast in 5.15, we can see that they died to themselves (ἑαυτοῖς), in order that they may live for Christ, who died for them and was raised.[180] Christ's death and resurrection were literal, but Paul applies these metaphorically to believers.[181] In distinction to 4.7–12 where the death of Jesus describes the ongoing problems in life, Paul here appears to point to a one-time event, as the repetition of the aorist of ἀποθνήσκω indicates.

Twice Paul characterises Jesus' death as being 'for all' (ὑπὲρ πάντων). The nature of the ὑπέρ's meaning has been debated – is it more like ἀντί ('instead of') or ἕνεκα/διά ('for the sake of')? While either reading would make sense here, the context points more towards the latter reading. Against 'instead of', Christ does not die so that humans do not have to die. Rather Christ's death is inclusive: 'he died for them, therefore (ἄρα) they all die' (5.14). Substitution is not excluded because, as we will see in 5.21, Christ dies to sin in a way that believers will not. However, the emphasis here is upon believers' embodiment of the path of Christ. That is,

---

[176] Nguyen, *Identity in Corinth*, 174.

[177] See also 3.14, 15; 4.4 for the related use of νόημα to describe the inward faculty.

[178] The description of Christ's self-sacrifice supports reading this genitive construction as a subjective genitive, that is, Christ's loving, rather than an objective genitive pointing to Paul's love of Christ.

[179] Cf. Rom 5.18 for another instance of a difficult use of 'all' to describe Christ's work.

[180] Cf. Rom 6.1–11 that bears many similarities to this passage. C.F.D. Moule ('Death "to Sin", "to Law", and "to the World": A Note on Certain Datives' in *Mélanges Bibliques,* eds. Albert Descamps and André de Halleux [Gembloux: Ducolot, 1970], 367–75) argues that these should be characterised as 'datives of relationship' and not 'datives of obligation' (374–75).

[181] Jack P. Lewis, 'Exegesis of 2 Corinthians 5:14–21' in *Interpreting 2 Corinthians 5:14–21: An Exercise in Hermeneutics,* ed. Jack P. Lewis (Lampeter: Edwin Mellen, 1989), 129–41, at 133.

they must experience this death in themselves; otherwise, it will remain external to them. Therefore, the objective accomplishment of salvation in Christ's death meets the subjective experience of believers as they follow him in death.

Just as believers die like Christ, they also live: those who died now live for (ὑπέρ) the one who died and was raised (5.15; cf. Rom 6.4). This use of ὑπέρ must be 'for the sake of' and thus coheres with our interpretation of 5.14. Christ's motivation for action was not his own benefit but that of others, and this same love compels Paul, and even all believers, to live for Christ on behalf of others (cf. 4.13). This 'living' corresponds to proper conduct on behalf of Christ. Thus, with this accent on moral living, the focus here is on the present experience of believers.

4.2 New Creation, Reconciliation, and Righteousness (5.16–6.2)

Returning to the distinction between judging others based on their appearance as opposed to their heart (5.12), Paul states: 'we now regard no one according to the flesh' (5.16). If the model and motivation for living is the death and resurrection of Christ, then measuring people's ministry by any other standard is regarding them 'from a human point of view'. Noting the use of epistemological terms throughout this whole section of 2 Corinthians, Martyn convincingly shows how the epistemology of the ages culminates in these verses here.[182] Taking κατὰ σάρκα adverbially to describe the manner of thinking rather than adjectivally to describe Christ's manner of existence, Martyn distinguishes between the old way of thinking and the way appropriate to the new age inaugurated in Christ. The old way of thinking looked at the outward appearance and only considered Christ as cursed and crucified. According to this, he was a failure, in the same way that Paul's own suffering indicates his failure. However, by challenging this view of Christ, Paul also forces the Corinthians to recognise the correct view about his own situation. Paul describes the basis for this new mindset with his discussion of new creation in 5.17.

4.2.1 New Creation: 2 Corinthians 5.17

In a rather direct manner, Paul explains why the old way of thinking associated with the flesh is inappropriate: Christ brings 'new creation' (καινὴ κτίσις) to any who are in him: 'the old has passed away; see, the new has come' (5.17).[183] With such a general exclamation, this verse, along with

---

[182] Martyn, *Theological Issues*, 89–110.

[183] Irenaeus makes no use of this text in his extant writings, which makes sense in light of his polemical context where he is arguing for continuity in the creative work of God rather than discontinuity. Cyril, on the other hand, finds this text quite useful because it sums up the work of Christ as the new Adam.

its parallel in Gal 6.15, has engendered much debate about whether this statement is focused upon individual conversion or a cosmic transition of the ages. We will address these two positions and then explore some of the OT texts that seem to be the basis of Paul's discussion before drawing conclusions about the verse.

Several features encourage an individualist reading. The context contains several soteriological themes: the language of Christ's death and resurrection (5.14–15), the close discussion of reconciliation (5.18–20) and justification (5.21), and a challenge to accept God's salvation today (6.1–2). Within the verse itself, the strongest evidence is the use of the singular τις. This 'new creature' that God creates is thus able to put away the improper ways of thinking and acting drawn from the immediate context: 'boasting in appearances (5.12), living for self (5.14–15), and judging others κατὰ σάρκα (5.16)'.[184] However, those following this individual-focused reading typically allow this verse to speak to the whole soteriological experience and not just those aspects in the immediate context. For instance, Hubbard gives this summary of the idea: 'New creation refers to the new inner dynamic of the Spirit which has begun the process of restoring the *imago dei* marred by Adam's sin, and which enables those who rely on its power to fulfill the (true) requirement of the law'.[185] With such a synthetic description, Hubbard captures much of Paul's discussion from 3.1 following.

This willingness to incorporate a larger perspective within the concept is also captured by those who see Paul discussing eschatological and cosmological realities not limited to individuals.[186] Martyn, in particular, calls this 'the turn of the ages, the apocalyptic event of Christ's death/ resurrection'.[187] In distinction to other passages that maintain an already/not yet balance, Paul strikingly affirms that the old has passed away and the new has come, not unlike his flesh-Spirit distinction in Rom 8.5–11.

While Paul's focus is on the individual (τις), this change can only happen in correspondence with God's overarching new creation act. Capturing this thought, Adams writes:

---

[184] Moyer V. Hubbard, *New Creation in Paul's Letters and Thought* (SNTSMS 119; Cambridge: Cambridge University Press, 2002), 183. Cf. Harris, *Second Corinthians*, 432–34.

[185] Hubbard, *New Creation*, 235.

[186] Peter Stuhlmacher, 'Erwägungen zum ontologische Character der καινὴ κτίσις bei Paulus', *EvT* 27 (1967): 1–35, at 4–7; Ulrich Mell, *Neue Schöpfung* (Berlin: Walter de Gruyter, 1989), 364–72. Cf. Martyn, *Theological Issues*, 89–110; ibid., *Galatians: A New Translation with Introduction and Commentary* (AB 33A; New York: Doubleday, 1997), 565, 570–74.

[187] Martyn, *Theological Issues*, 95.

Paul's meaning is that the individual believer (τις) as part of the believing community (ἐν Χριστῷ), in advance of the coming physical destruction of the universe, already participates in the life of the new eschatological world. Though the final eschatological event lies in the future, for Christians, in some partial and non-material way, the old things have passed away, and new things have already come (τὰ ἀρχαῖα ... καινά). Again, the underlying thought is that Christ's death and resurrection has in some way set in motion the change of the ages.[188]

While the use of 'anyone' (τις) focuses the meaning on the anthropological level, Hubbard inappropriately limits this to believers. By use of the term new creation, Paul speaks in the broadest of terms, which allows him to address anthropological issues in light of the larger eschatological transition.

Within this larger scope, we can determine the shape of this new creation by looking at related language in the letter and from OT texts that Paul draws from. The closest passage in 2 Corinthians that contains καινός language is 4.16, where Paul speaks of the inner person being renewed (ἀνακαινόω) daily.[189] The only other use of καινός in the letter is that of 3.6 where Paul speaks of the *new* covenant (καινή διαθήκη). While the new covenant is probably a primary instantiation of what new creation entails, the old that has passed away is not merely limited to the old covenant (παλαιὰ διαθήκη).[190] These connections are tentative, but the new covenant change does correspond to the turn of the ages.[191]

In addition to echoes of the new covenant through the καινός language, many also see echoes of another OT promise of future restoration from Isa 43.18–19 and 65.1–25. Danker, in particular, notes that we should be aware of the larger context in the Isaiah passage, and that Isa 42.1–44.5 as a whole is relevant to this new creation context.[192] In Isa 43.18–19, the writer speaks of not remembering the old because of new things characterised by making 'a way in the wilderness and rivers in the dry land' (NETS).[193] Regarding the rivers, several verses later the writer clarifies

---

[188] Adams, *Constructing*, 235.

[189] Cf. Hubbard, *New Creation*, 185.

[190] Note the difference in language between the old (τὰ ἀρχαῖα) that has passed away in 5.17 and the old covenant (παλαιὰ διαθήκη) in 3.14.

[191] The new covenant themes from Ezekiel 36–37 possibly draw from creation motifs (e.g., πνοὴ ζωῆς in Gen 2.7 LXX) and thus may support this reading. Cf. Chester, 'Resurrection and Transformation', 48–54; Yates, *Spirit and Creation*, 118–19.

[192] Frederick W. Danker, 'Exegesis of 2 Corinthians 5:14–21' in *Interpreting 2 Corinthians 5:14–21,* ed. Jack P. Lewis (Lampeter: Edwin Mellen, 1989), 105–126, at 116–17.

[193] E.g., Mark Gignilliat, 'A Servant Follower of the Servant: Paul's Eschatological Reading of Isaiah 40–66 in 2 Corinthians 5:14–6:10', *HBT* 26 (2004): 98–124, at 121–22; Hubbard, *New Creation*, 182; Windisch, *Der zweite Korintherbrief*, 189–90. For scepticism about the Isaiah background, see Harris, *Second Corinthians*, 432–33.

what God's promise of pouring out streams of water entails: 'I will pour out my Spirit on your descendants' (Isa 44.3). We cannot be definitive but with the verbal echoes of the *new* covenant language and the Isa 43–44 promise of renewal associated with the Spirit, we can posit that Paul drew the Spirit into his conception of new creation. A more speculative suggestion is that an implied κατὰ πνεῦμα of the new age would correspond to the κατὰ σάρκα of the old.[194] In any case, while the Spirit's activity in new creation is implicit, the numerous points of contact give reason for seeing his work here.

Later in Isaiah another promise of new things, the promise of the new heaven and new earth (ὁ οὐρανὸς καινὸς καὶ ἡ γῆ καινή) looms large (Isa 65.17 LXX). This promise is a response to the former troubles (θλῖψις), which they will not remember (Isa 65.16–17 LXX). The intertextual allusion may be a call to view suffering differently. If the new age has dawned, one should not view suffering in the same way. At the same time, the hope in Isaiah 65 is that of long life, a restored community, and fruitful labour (Isa 65.20–23). Thus, it pertains most fully to the time of resurrection.

The creation terminology is relevant to our question of continuity and discontinuity between creation and redemption. While the contrast is not as stark as that between the heavenly and earthly (5.1–2), the emphasis on the old passing away seems to follow a similar pattern. However, the restoration imagery being drawn from Isaiah 65 shows that there is a balance between continuity and discontinuity. Though he emphasises discontinuity, Käsemann catches that balance when he writes: 'In the new creation, there is a reference back to creation *ex nihilo* and a reference forward to the resurrection of the dead'.[195] Something new happens but there is identity with the past. Adams also notes how κόσμος and καινὴ κτίσις stand juxtaposed: 'In Gal 6:14–15, the cross of Christ announces the birth of the new creation and the *death* of the κόσμος. In 2 Cor 5:17–19, the death of Christ announces the birth of the new creation and the *reconciliation* of the κόσμος'.[196] Therefore, we can conclude that although the emphasis is on the newness of God's activity of those 'in Christ', Paul also makes use of OT texts that speak in terms of renewal.

If we are right to find the new covenant hope recapitulated in new creation, we can see that Paul primarily refers to new life through the presence

---

[194] In favour of this position, see Harris, *Second Corinthians*, 434; Collange, *Énigmes*, 259. In opposition, see especially Hubbard, *New Creation*, 183–84; Martyn, *Theological Issues*, 107–8.

[195] Ernst Käsemann, 'The "Righteousness of God" in Paul' in *New Testament Questions of Today*; trans. W. J. Montague (Philadelphia: Fortress, 1979), 168–82, at 180.

[196] Adams, *Constructing*, 236.

of the Spirit, based on the death and resurrection of Christ. This turn of the ages not merely draws in humans but looks forward to the restoration of all creation (cf. Isaiah 65). Nevertheless, as individuals are drawn up into this restoration, they are empowered to leave behind old ways of thinking and acting. That is, through participation in the one who died and was raised they too may be drawn up into his new life.

4.2.2 Reconciliation: 2 Corinthians 5.18–20

In 5.18–20 we again find the pattern of Paul first explaining God's sote-riological activity and drawing ministerial implications from it. God is the one who reconciles humanity to himself through Christ, and, accordingly, Paul and his companions have become ministers and ambassadors of this message, calling others to reconciliation.[197] Mead aptly notes: 'So far as we know, no one at Corinth was disputing God's reconciling activity in Christ, but there were mutterings against the "ministry of reconciliation" (as Paul called himself and his colleagues); and that governed the aims of the latter'.[198] That being said, our interest is in the soteriological aspects, so we will leave aside the discussions of Paul's ministry.

Using the terminology of reconciliation (καταλλαγή), Paul points to the problem of a ruptured relationship between humanity and God, which finds its source in human trespasses (παράπτωμα, 5.19). Since God does not count these trespasses against them, believers are reconciled to God (5.19b). This act of reconciliation is twice described with God as the principal and Christ as the agent: 'God ... reconciled us to himself through Christ' (διὰ Χριστοῦ, 5.18), and 'God was reconciling the world to himself in Christ (ἐν Χριστῷ), not counting their trespasses against them' (5.19).[199] Even though humans are the ones who have broken the relationship, God through Christ is the one who restores it.[200] Paul does not explore the logic that explains the connection between Christ's work and this reconciliation through forgiveness, but in 5.21 he continues to explore Christ's work with regard to the problem of sin.

---

[197] Regarding the implications for Paul's ministry, see especially Anthony Bash, *Ambassadors for Christ* (WUNT 2/92; Tübingen: Mohr Siebeck, 1997).

[198] Richard T. Mead, 'Exegesis of 2 Corinthians 5:14–21' in *Interpreting 2 Corinthians 5:14–21*, ed. Jack P. Lewis (Lampeter: Edwin Mellen, 1989), 143–62, at 154.

[199] Some take the latter dative phrase as primarily locative ('God was in Christ'). E.g., Harris, *Second Corinthians*, 440–43. However, due to the parallel nature of the statements of God's work in reconciliation, an instrumental reading better fits the context.

[200] Mead ('2 Corinthians 5:14–21', 154) notes a transition at 5.18 due to the shift in primary agents. In 5.14–17, Paul or 'we' is primary, whereas in 5.18–6.2 God's agency is primary. He has a point, but this overstates the lack of divine agency in 5.14–17.

4.2.3 Sin and Righteousness: 2 Corinthians 5.21

Like 3.18, virtually every aspect within verse 21 is debated. The complexity is increased because it is asyndetic, and so more disputes arise regarding its relationship to Paul's larger argument.[201] Regarding its place in the argument Bieringer concludes: 'Die wichtigste Frage besteht für die Forscher darin, ob 5,21 zu den Aussagen über das vergangene Heilsereignis (5,14cd; 5,18b; 5,19ab) oder zur gegenwärtigen Versöhnungsbitte (5,20d) zu rechnen ist'.[202] We must ask whether this is a plain statement about soteriology or if Paul is explicitly using this to describe an aspect of his ministry. As a description of God's soteriological activity through Christ, it serves as the basis for ministry implications, without forcing an unnecessary dichotomy between the two. Following the contours of the verse, we will explore Christ being made sin and then what it means for believers to become the righteousness of God. Since the emphasis of our study is on the anthropological shape of Paul's soteriology, the latter aspect will naturally receive more attention.

As with Rom 8.3, the association between Christ and sin is integral for the argument here. Paul qualifies Christ's association with sin by asserting that the one who was made sin *did not know sin.* Since Jesus' sinlessness is probably in view here,[203] we must ask: in what sense was Christ made sin? Bieringer details six different ways of interpreting this phrase: Sünden*fleish* (Menschwerdung), Sünd*opfer* (Kreuzestod), Realität der Sünde (Substitution or Repräsentation), Sünden*macht* (Herrschaftswechsel), and Sünder (Abschreckungseffekt).[204]

We may dismiss some of these without much discussion. Regarding becoming human (Sündenfleish/Menschwerdung), the association with sin appears to relate to Christ's death rather than his incarnation *per se*, though ideas of incarnation may be implicit.[205] Regarding the sin offering (Sündopfer), the use of ποιέω in conjunction with ἁμαρτία possibly hints at OT sacrificial ideas regarding a 'sin offering', but the evidence is weak. A

---

[201] Reimund Bieringer ('Sünde und Gerechtigkeit in 2 Korinther 5,21' in *Studies on 2 Corinthians,* eds. Reimund Bieringer and Jan Lambrecht [Leuven: Leuven University Press, 1994], 461–514, at 462–63) lists three views on the function of the passage in its context: 1) it is independent from the context and simply represents traditional material thrown in, 2) it represents a development of the salvation language of 5.14–15 and 5.18–19, thus describing the basis of reconciliation with God, or 3) it is part of the challenge to reconciliation with God from 5.20.

[202] Ibid., 464.

[203] E.g., Bultmann, *Second Corinthians,* 164–66.

[204] Bieringer, 'Sünde und Gerechtigkeit', 473–94, esp. 495, emphasis original.

[205] Pace Morna D. Hooker, 'Interchange in Christ' in *From Adam to Christ,* (Eugene, OR: Wipf & Stock, 2008), 13–25, 17. She partially bases her conclusion on parallel verses.

rough parallel to Paul's statement here is in Exod 29.36 LXX and Lev 4.20 LXX, where there is a discussion of making a calf a 'sin offering'.[206] However, the fact that in those cases ἁμαρτία is a genitive modifier of calf instead of a double accusative construction as in 2 Cor 5.21 tells against making Christ a sin offering here.[207] Regarding an exchange of powers (Sündenmacht), some passages point to the idea that Christ's death allows Christ to defeat death's power, but the context here does not appear to commend that reading although that might be an implication. And finally, regarding Christ as a sinner (Sünder), this does not fit the argument since Paul makes clear that Christ did not 'know' sin.

With those options dismissed, the only one remaining is that Christ was made the 'reality of sin' (Realität der Sünde), which Bieringer subdivides into substitution and representation. The distinctions some make between substitution and representation seem forced, imposing a dichotomy where one is not justified. Addressing, Paul's theology as a whole, Morna Hooker, in particular, argues strongly against substitution in favour of representation.[208] Dunn's more balanced treatment, which affirms both substitution and representation, serves as a helpful rebuttal to Hooker's claims.[209] With both authors, 2 Cor 5.21 plays a small role in determining Paul's overall theology because larger associations between Christ and figures like Adam and the Servant in Isaiah 53 are more explicitly addressed in other passages. Many point to Isaiah 53 as a background for this passage with some warrant, but this is at the level of allusion or echo and thus open for debate.[210] In distinction to 5.14–15, Paul does not emphasise the participatory aspect of death, and so substitution may be more emphasised, but representation need not be ruled out. Before we make further analyis of the first half of the verse, we need to be aware of the second half.

Interpretation of the second half of the verse is no less difficult than the first. The centre of the discussion naturally surrounds the meaning of the 'righteousness of God' (δικαιοσύνη θεοῦ). Since there is little in the context here explicitly describing this righteousness, most argue for its meaning based upon other Jewish texts and other Pauline passages. In Paul, the exact phrase elsewhere occurs only in Romans (1.17; 3.5, 21, 22; 10.3; cf.

---

[206] Cf. also the use of ποιέω with περὶ ἁμαρτίας in Lev 9.7, 22; 14.19; 23.19; Num 6.11, 16; etc.

[207] Accordingly, I view this statement differently from that of Rom 8.3, which follows the LXX pattern.

[208] Hooker, *From Adam*, 13–69, and esp. 17, 26–41.

[209] Dunn, 'Paul's Understanding of the Death of Jesus'.

[210] E.g., Furnish, *II Corinthians*, 351.

Phil 3.9: δικαιοσύνη ἐκ θεοῦ). Based upon those discussions there are three main ways of understanding the phrase.

The first group reads the phrase as a genitive of origin, describing how God justifies believers.[211] Bultmann, in particular, states this position when he argues 'dass die bei Paulus herrschende Bedeutung von δικ. θεοῦ die der Gabe ist, die Gott den Glaubenden schenkt, und dass der Gen. ein Gen. auctoris ist'.[212] Later, regarding 2 Cor 5.21, Bultmann states: 'δικαιοσύνη ist hier gleichbedeutend mit δικαιωθέντες'.[213] In distinction to a mere quality which one possesses, Bultmann argues that this righteousness is a declaration about a relationship.

Käsemann, in response to Bultmann's interpretation which he calls a more anthropologically focused reading, interprets the phrase as a subjective genitive which describes the righteous activity of God. Arguing that Paul took over his conception of the righteousness of God from Jewish tradition, Käsemann defines Paul's use as 'God's sovereignty over the world revealing itself eschatologically in Jesus'.[214] This is not merely a statement about anthropology but about God's activity, so that the gift can never be separated from the Giver. While Käsemann does not explore 2 Cor 5.21 specifically in his discussion of the righteousness of God, he does note: 'The faithful *are* the world as it has been recalled to the sovereignty of God, the company of those who live under the eschatological justice of God, in which company, according to II Cor. 5.21, God's righteousness becomes manifest on earth'.[215] Thus rather than a mere forensic declaration, by believers becoming the righteousness of God they are placed under God's lordship.

Our third group focuses upon God's activity, reading the phrase as a possessive genitive (but with a subjective genitive flavour), which describes God's covenant faithfulness. While Käsemann notes the role of covenant faithfulness in Paul's conception of the righteousness of God, his emphasis is on the whole *world*.[216] N.T. Wright also emphasises God's activity, but he emphasises the continuity with the promises to Israel.[217]

---

[211] E.g., Thrall, *2 Corinthians*, 1:442–44.

[212] Rudolf Bultmann, 'ΔΙΚΑΙΟΣΥΝΗ ΘΕΟΥ', *JBL* 83 (1964): 12–16, at 12.

[213] Ibid. 14n.4.

[214] Käsemann, 'Righteousness of God', 180.

[215] Ibid., 181, emphasis original.

[216] Ibid., 181.

[217] N.T. Wright, 'On Becoming the Righteousness of God: 2 Corinthians 5:21' in *Pauline Theology, Volume II: 1 & 2 Corinthians,* ed. David M. Hay (Minneapolis: Fortress, 1993), 200–8, at 202. cf. A. Katherine Grieb, 'So That in Him We Might Become the "Righteousness of God" (2 Cor 5:21): Some Theological Reflections on the Church Becoming Justice', *ExAud* 22 (2006): 58–80, at 60.

Thus, covenant faithfulness[218] plays a central role in his conception of the righteousness of God. This covenant-world distinction notwithstanding, Wright allows the context of the Paul's ministry to help shape his interpretation. With regard to 2 Cor 5.21, Wright sees a correlation between being a 'minister of the new covenant' and 'become the righteousness of God'. He writes: 'Indeed, we can now suggest that those two phrases are mutually interpretative ways of saying substantially the same thing'.[219] Morna Hooker brings together Käsemann's reading with that of Wright's. While she speaks of living righteously because of this interchange, Hooker mostly emphasizes the ministerial implications. She writes: 'the apostle whose manner of life – as well as his preaching – is conformed to the gospel, and *in* whom the power of God is at work, has become "the righteousness of God"'.[220]

While this interpretation takes seriously Paul's argument about soteriology and ministry, Grieb rightly notes that this interpretation 'does not pick up the rhetorically powerfully [*sic*] contrast within the verse itself that Paul seems to craft deliberately'.[221] That is, the parallelism in the verse calls for a correspondence between the death of Christ and this becoming the righteousness of God. Throughout our discussion of 2 Corinthians 3–5, I have made a case that Paul's apology for his ministry is based upon the reality of the gospel. Thus, I agree with Wright that this verse is not a 'somewhat detached statement of atonement theology', but its affirmations should not be equated with Paul's ministry as quickly as he and Hooker in some ways do.[222] This soteriological statement, like that of 5.14–15 and 5.17, gives theological affirmations from which Paul derives conclusions regarding his ministry.

What then does 'becom[ing] the righteousness of God' refer to? As with our discussion of other soteriological passages, in order to understand the solution we must have a firm grasp on the problem. The parallelism of the verse points directly to the problem of sin (ἁμαρτία). Interestingly, this is the first mention of sin in the letter, and the only other occurrence is in a rhetorical question in 11.7. A close synonym of sin is found in 5.19 – trespasses (παράπτωμα, cf. Rom 5.16). This relational problem, which we

---

[218] Sam K. Williams ('The "Righteousness of God" in Romans', *JBL* 99 [1980]: 241–90) in particular helped promote the understanding of δικαιοσύνη θεοῦ as referring to God's covenant faithfulness, though the idea was in circulation long before him.

[219] Wright, 'Righteousness of God', 206.

[220] Morna D. Hooker, 'On Becoming the Righteousness of God: Another Look at 2 Cor 5:21', *NovT* 50 (2008): 358–75, at 373. Interestingly, she does not mention Wright's essay on the passage in her article.

[221] Grieb, 'Church Becoming Justice', 65.

[222] Wright, 'Righteousness of God', 203.

might characterise as 'condemnation' (cf. 2 Cor 3.9),[223] was resolved by
not counting these trespasses against them. Based upon the proximity in
both meaning and distance we have good evidence to see the resolution of
condemnation in 5.21 as well.

When we consider that Christ's death is the focus of the statement that
'God made him sin' we also gain some clarity. Christ did not become sinful but bore the punishment of sin, which is death (cf. Gal 3.13). Instead
of believers dying for their sins, Christ has. Thus, we see an implicit association between humanity's problem of *mortality* because of the condemnation from sin (cf. Rom 5.12) and God's saving action through Christ's
death. At the same time, Paul made it clear that reconciliation through the
abolishment of condemnation came 'through Christ' (5.18) and 'in Christ'
(5.19). With such a close association between trespasses and sin, we have
good reason to expect that Christ's death also achieves the resolution of
condemnation from sin as well. With mortality (or death) and condemnation seen as the result of sin, Christ's being made sin is a metonymy,
which stands for Christ taking on condemnation and death as the effects of
sin.

With believers becoming the righteousness of God as parallel to Christ
being made sin, should we not then interpret the latter half according to
this parallel? Just as Christ truly bore the effects of sin, believers bear the
effects of righteousness. In that case, becoming the righteousness of God
resolves the problems of condemnation and death, respectively, and is thus
a metonymy for having a restored relationship and experiencing life.
Danker supports this reading, when he writes: 'The resurrection completes
the purpose in that death, and identity in his death makes possible the new
life (cf. Rom. 6:3–5, 11; 8.4–11). This life is called *dikaiosune* in 2 Cor.
5:21 (cf. Rom. 4:25; 5.21; and see 6:9–14)'.[224] Confirmation of this reading comes from the only previous discussion of δικαιοσύνη in the letter to
this point (3.9), where Paul describes the new covenant ministry. In contrast to the old covenant of nullified glory characterised by death and condemnation, the new covenant of permanent glory is characterised by life
and righteousness (3.7–11). Thus, as believers become the righteousness
of God, they experience the new covenant blessings, of which righteousness is central. This righteousness thus consists of a restored relationship
to God through the presence of the Spirit as well as noetic and somatic life.

If this is the case, we can see that 5.21 stands in continuity with the previous two soteriological affirmations in 5.14–15 and 5.17. We noted how
they both correspond to his discussion from chapters 3 and 4 with their use

---

[223] Cf. Wilhelm Michaelis, *TDNT*, 6:172n.12. See p. 122 above for my discussion of
'condemnation' in Romans.

[224] Danker, '2 Corinthians 5:14–21', 114.

of death and life. In addition, we noted above how the treatment of new creation in 5.17 correlates with the new covenant promise of new life through the Spirit. Accordingly, Furnish concludes: This verse [5.21]

emphasizes the reality of the new life opened up for believers through the gift of right-eousness (cf. Phil 3:9, and Thyen 1970: 189). In this way the points about the redemptive effect of Christ's death (5:14–15), the presence of 'new creation' (5:17), and the reality of reconciliation (5:18–19) are effectively summarized and applied to the situation of the individual believer.[225]

As believers become the righteousness of God they experience relational restoration and new life.

Käsemann's warning about separating the gift from the Giver should be heeded, but reading δικαιοσύνη θεοῦ as a genitive of authorship does not divide gift from Giver. Rather, Käsemann's argument against Bultmann creates a false antithesis, like those who make distinctions between participation and justification as acquittal.[226] Paul here combines the two – God's gifts of life and forgiveness only come through Christ for those that are 'in him'. In the same way, only those who are 'in Christ' experience new creation (5.17). As a result, justification cannot be merely imputation or forensic pronouncement but a real experience through participation 'in Christ'.[227] Michael Bird cogently argues that this event can be described as both forensic and participatory:

Given the supremely christocentric ingredient in Paul's formulation of justification it is far more appropriate to speak of *incorporated righteousness* for the righteousness that clothes believers is not that which is somehow abstracted from Christ and projected onto them, but is located exclusively in Christ as the glorified incarnation of God's righteousness.[228]

Therefore, a genitive of origin does not necessarily separate the gift from the Giver. This language of incorporated righteousness is quite helpful in breaking down this false dichotomy. In fact, with this emphasis on par-

---

[225] Furnish, *II Corinthians*, 352.

[226] So Schweitzer, *Mysticism*, 223–26. More recently, Douglas A. Campbell, *The Quest for Paul's Gospel: A Suggested Strategy* (JSNTSup 274; London: T&T Clark, 2005); Campbell, *Deliverance*.

[227] Hooker's (*From Adam*, 5) description of interchange captures this:
It is not that Christ and the believer change places, but rather that Christ, by his involvement in the human situation, is able to transfer believers from one mode of existence to another. Underlying this understanding of redemption is the belief that Christ is 'the last Adam' (1 Cor. 15.45), the true 'image of God', who by sharing fully in humanity's condition – i.e. by being 'in Adam' – opens up the way for men and women to share in his condition, by being 'in Christ'.

[228] Michael F. Bird, *The Saving Righteousness of God: Studies on Paul, Justification and the New Perspective* (Paternoster Biblical Monographs; Milton Keynes, UK: Paternoster, 2007), 85, emphasis original.

ticipation in Paul's language, the gift only comes by encountering the Giver.[229]

We might have expected Paul to say that believers become 'righteous' (δίκαιοι), an adjective, instead of 'righteousness' (δικαιοσύνη), a noun. Paul, because of his qualification that Christ did not know sin, cannot say that Christ became 'sinful' (ἁμαρτωλός), an adjective, but that he became 'sin' (ἁμαρτία), a noun. With the use of a noun for sin, poetic parallelism may have dictated that a noun be used for righteousness. By use of the noun instead of the adjective, Paul is guarding against a mere ascription of value to believers that might be separated from God and Christ. This exchange takes place through union with Christ ('in him'). At the same time, believers do not just become righteous they become the righteousness *of God*, showing that any status or state of being that this represents is mediated from God and not from themselves. Thus, while the experience is focused upon believers it can never be separated from God's activity.[230]

Paul presents a model of (partially) realised eschatology. This is tempered when read in light of the context of chapter 4, but the reality of the Christ event has fundamentally changed history. As a result, the challenge to receive the grace of God in 6.1–2 culminates in the affirmation that '*now* (νῦν) is the acceptable time; see, *now* (νῦν) is the day of salvation' (6.2).

4.3 Conclusion

As we consider the shape of Paul's soteriology in 2 Cor 5.11–6.2, we have seen that he has focused more on the present benefits of salvation. Leaving behind the discussion of present struggles and the future hope of somatic resurrection, Paul now gives general descriptions of Christian life. Despite using general statements, Paul addresses multiple aspects of soteriology. He first refers to heart transformation (5.12) and then discusses moral enablement (5.14–15). With the discussion of new creation, Paul expands the discussion to include a general affirmation about the soteriological process as a whole (5.17). As the dawning of a new age, this new creation draws in new covenant allusions of new life through the Spirit. The latter section of the passage takes a decidedly relational turn with the discussion of reconciliation and righteousness (5.18–6.2). None

---

[229] Perhaps speaking of this as 'giving' rather than 'gift' would better capture Paul's thought. Writing about the exaltation of humans in Barth's theology, McCormack ('Participation in God, Yes', 356) notes that the event should be seen 'in the present tense rather than the past tense; as a giving rather than a giftedness'.

[230] The expression 'righteousness of God' here in 5.21 appears to be used differently from its occurrences in Romans which focus more on God's saving activity, though the participatory character of justification in Romans is similar.

of these appears to be fully accomplished, but Paul also does not point to a future consummation. In distinction, the objective act of reconciliation appears to have been secured by Christ, but humans must still heed the call to be reconciled. In fact, 'now' is the day of salvation.

5. Summary and Conclusion

This analysis of these chapters has been like climbing a mountain. It has been difficult work parsing Paul's argument, but we have reaped the benefit of magnificent vistas spreading out before us. The rhetorical purpose of these chapters is clearly a defence of his ministry, which had been challenged because it did not conform to the outward signs of success expected by the Corinthians. In support of his ministry, Paul not only challenges the Corinthians' conceptions of ministry but their conceptions of the soteriology that undergirds their ministry criteria. A significant difficulty arises when interpreters try to disentangle the discussion of soteriology from ministry without creating false dichotomies. I have argued that key verses which have at times been interpreted as primarily about Paul's ministry (e.g., 3.18; 5.21) are, in fact, soteriological though they surely serve as evidence for the larger argument about ministry.

5.1 Questions

We will now address our specific questions that have guided our study of these chapters. 1) What is the anthropological shape of Pauline soteriology? 2) When do these soteriological changes occur? 3) How does the soteriological change of the human condition come about? 4) How does Paul relate this soteriological change to creation? Since Paul's soteriology in these passages is temporally determined, separating the discussion of the shape of his soteriology and the timing would generate needless repetition so I have combined their discussion.

5.1.1 The Shape of Soteriology and When It Occurs

5.1.1.1 Problems

In order to understand Paul's soteriology best, we must understand the problems which it addresses. As in Romans, Paul presents both inter-personal and intra-personal problems. Regarding the inter-personal, the fundamental problem of sin is that it breaks and perpetuates a break in the human-divine relationship (cf. 5.18–20). This leads to condemnation and death (3.6–9). In addition to the divine-human relational problem, Paul also describes the agency of the 'god of this world' in blinding the minds of unbelievers (4.4). Regarding intra-personal problems, we noted the significance of death, literal and metaphoric, throughout. Just as the body faces corruption (2 Cor 4.16; 5.4; 1 Cor 15.42), God's servants face external troubles metaphorically as an experience of the death (1.8–11; 4.7–12). Closely related with this is the problem of ignorance or blindness. Paul characterises this as being veiled (3.6–18; 4.4), but it also reflects the problem of death associated with the old age (2.14–16; 5.16).

5.1.1.2 Present Salvation

While the future resurrection is central to Paul, his stark exclamation 'now is the acceptable time; see, now is the day of salvation' (6.2) shows the importance of the present reality of salvation. Indeed, 'the old has passed away, and all things have become new' (5.17). This new reality is driven by renewed inter-personal relationships with God that lead to a restoration of the intra-personal human condition. A restored relationship with God and the benefits arising from it are intimately interconnected.

The basis of Paul's soteriology is a restoration in the divine-human relationship. Paul begins our section with a discussion of the new covenant where God has provided humanity a new way of relating to himself (3.1–4.6). By drawing upon the new covenant texts, Paul emphasises the interiority of God's work within believers. That is, the Spirit dwells in them and gives them a new heart. Rather than death and condemnation, believers therefore experience life and righteousness from God (3.7–11). Exploring further this close relationship with God, Paul describes this as an unveiled turning towards the Lord, emphasising the immediate access to God through the Spirit and Christ (3.12–18). Through the metaphors of reconciliation and becoming righteousness, Paul returns to an emphasis on this restored relationship in 5.18–21 when he explores the way God has removed the barrier that sin and trespasses have created between humanity and God. Importantly, Paul characterises this restored relationship with through the category of participation, in that believers are 'in Christ' (5.17, 21).

This restored relationship affects the whole person in the present as God shares his life with believers. Recognising Paul's anthropological distinction between the inner and outer person (4.16) is important. The emphasis of God's current work is upon inward renewal, such that the life-giving work of the Spirit consists of present moral enablement and noetic enlightenment. Paul emphasises the role of heart and minds in these chapters, showing how God provides a new way of perception and liberty from blindness (3.6, 14–16; 4.4, 6; 5.12, 16; Phil 2.2, 5; 3.15, 19). The mental enlightenment and transformative knowledge from the new covenant relationship is the basis of divine moral enablement (e.g., 5.12–15). In Philippians 2 Paul was also acutely aware of God's enabling believers to live according to his moral standard (Phil 2.12–13). Importantly, this inward transformation is characterised as a conformation to Christ's image (2 Cor 3.18).

Central to this transformation into the image of Christ is the embodiment of his death and his life. In the midst of physical suffering and corruption, God's comforts and rescues from bodily danger (1.3–11; 4.7–12). This corresponds to the cruciform sharing in the sufferings of Christ and knowing the power of his resurrection in Phil 3.10–11, which Paul characterises as being conformed to Christ's death. Importantly, the future somatic resurrection is correlated with the present experience of life as moral enablement (2 Cor 3.14–18; Phil 2.1–11; 3.10–11, 20–21).

5.1.1.3 Future Salvation

While suffering and bodily corruption serve as the context that reveals God's life-giving work in the present, these troubles are confined to the current age. The culmination of God's soteriological work comes after death when believers are renewed inwardly *and* outwardly. That is, they will experience bodily incorruption, exemplified by eternal glory that is not yet seen (2 Cor 4.18; 1 Cor 15.42–49; Phil 3.20–21). In all three of the passages we explored, this eternal somatic existence was characterised as heavenly and glorious, showing that believers are somatically drawn up into a divine manner of existence. The old covenant brought a transitory glory (2 Cor 3.10–11), but through the new covenant believers participate in a permanent glory of the resurrected body (4.16–5.5). This resurrection hope is based upon Christ's own resurrection, with which it has an organic relationship (1 Cor 15.42–49; Phil 3.20–21). As believers embody Christ's death and *life*, this will find its culmination through the Spirit-wrought life of the body in the future.

While we noted an anthropological duality within Paul's argument, we also observed that embodiment is central to human existence. We thus determined that Paul's anthropological duality is not as decisive as his temporal duality because the difference in the ages is most determinative. In the future when the temporal duality is overcome, believers will experience life in a unified manner, bringing harmony between the body and mind. The temporal duality of the present and future ages is primary since it drives the discussion, and thus the anthropological duality is secondary and not the ultimate emphasis of Paul's argument.

5.1.2 How It Occurs

The repeated emphasis upon divine agency within these three chapters is notable as Paul goes to great pains to note how God's activity stands as the basis of his work. In particular, Paul makes clear that his show of weakness is in line with God's work in his ministry. Whether it is through God's gift of competence (3.5), reflected glory from God (3.18), or God's work of extraordinary power (4.7), Paul shows that God is the source of the life within his ministry. The important fact about God's power is that his act of raising the dead stands as the basis for all hope in him (1.9; 4.14; cf. Phil 2.9–11). God has shown himself to be faithful to his suffering servant Jesus and able to overcome the power of death. Since he worked that way in the past, believers trust that he will continue to work in the same manner for them.[231]

This work of God is particularly evidenced through the Spirit and Christ. Christ is mentioned in 2.14–17, but Paul emphasises the Spirit's agency is central throughout chapter 3. Specifically, 'the Spirit of the living God' has written letters of commendation on the Corinthians' hearts (3.3), and the rest of the chapter explains the Spirit's life-giving work exclaimed in 3.6, the climax of which is the Spirit-wrought transformation described in 3.18. At the same time, this experience of God as the *Spirit* produces the reflected image of *Christ*.

In 2 Corinthians 4 Christ's agency again rises to prominence, not surprisingly, because Paul explores the implications of death and life in the lives of believers. His image of death and life serves as the model for that of believers. Thus, suffering becomes the place where the death and life of Jesus is manifest (4.10–11). At the same time, Jesus' somatic resurrection is the basis of hope for believers' own experience of resurrection and glory (4.14–18). Christ's agency stands throughout 5.11–21, leading to moral activity (5.14–15), new creation (5.17), reconciliation (5.18–20), and righteousness (5.21). An important signification of those who embody Christ's death and life is that they are 'in Christ' (3.14; 5.17, 21). And, thus, Michael Bird's 'incorporated righteousness' helpfully captures the substance of participation in Christ's life.

While the Spirit is only explicitly mentioned again in 5.5 to give confidence in the hope of resurrection, his role is clear throughout due to Paul's consistent allusions to new covenant themes (e.g., 5.17). The connection of Christ and the Spirit is clear in 1 Cor 15.45 where Christ is associated with the life-giving Spirit. As believers experience the heavenly and spiritual body, they are bearing the image of the man from heaven. Similarly, in Phil 3.20–21 Christ comes from heaven to transform believers bodies so they conform to his own glorious body.

At the heart of this participatory transformation is the use of morphic and image language to describe the conformation of believers to Christ's death and life. This conformation to Christ's image is associated with Christ's death alone (Phil 3.10), his death and resurrection (2 Cor 3.18),

---

[231] Cf. Wright, *Resurrection*, 300–301.

and his resurrection alone (Phil 3.21; 1 Cor 15.49). Paul correlates this conformation to Christ with explicit participation (κοινωνία) language in Phil 3.10 where believers share in his sufferings. He also briefly notes the κοινωνία of the Spirit in Phil 2.1, as well.

5.1.3 Eschatology and Protology

With the use of image language in 3.18 and 4.4, Paul draws from Genesis 1–2. As embodied humans, Christ and believers reveal God. Christ and believers in some sense fulfil what humanity in Adam was supposed to fulfil earlier. Similarly, Paul presents God's revelation of the gospel using creation imagery (4.6), and thus this activity is in continuity with what God has done before. However, when Paul speaks of the resurrection in 2 Cor 5.1–5; 1 Cor 15.42–49; and Phil 3.20–21 using the heaven-earth dialectic, the emphasis is solely on the heavenly aspect in a manner which highlights the discontinuity between the two. Salvation is not just a restoration of earth but an elevation to a greater, even divine, mode of existence. At the same time, we must note that this mode of existence does not necessarily entail an escape from death. With his discussion of new creation in 5.17, Paul's language again highlights discontinuity with the in-breaking of the new age. However, with the allusion to Isaiah 65 which presents a restored earth, the discontinuity should not be overstated.

5.2 Conclusion

In total, Paul's soteriology is about embodying the life of God. The life comes through a transformation wrought by the Spirit by incorporation into the life of Christ. This may be described as glory (3.18), life (4.10–11; 5.14–15), new creation (5.17), or righteousness (5.21), but in each case believers embody the life of Christ through a participatory relationship with Christ and the Spirit. With this emphasis on life culminating in the future, Roetzel argues that Paul employs an eschatological reserve in reaction to his opponents. He writes: 'Against those who claimed that they had overcome the distance between the divine and the human and who argued that Paul's weakness indicated that he has not done so, Paul points out that a gulf remains'.[232] However, this gulf is not traversed only in the eschaton when believers share in the divine glory that suffuses both mind and body, but it is also presently experienced in a way not expected by the Corinthians. Through participation in Christ's death and life presently within the context of somatic suffering, believers experience the divine manner of

---

[232] Calvin J. Roetzel, '"As Dying, and Behold We Live": Death and Resurrection in Paul's Theology', *Interp* 46 (1992): 5–18, at 16.

being modelled by Christ, and this prepares them for that future consummation of life.

Like in Romans 8, we again see life and glory at the heart of the ultimate hope of believers in these three passages. However, the emphasis
upon suffering with Christ, which did not gather a central place for
Irenaeus or Cyril, is even more evident in 2 Cor 4.7–18 and Phil 2.5–11;
3.9–11 than in Romans 8. Also, in 2 Corinthians 3 and Philippians 3 the
place of the law again arises. Importantly, key texts within these passages
emphasise the christo-morphic experience of believers, in which they embody his life and his death. Paul introduces the heaven-earth contrast
when discussing the final state, which is also important to Irenaeus and
Cyril. This speaks of an elevation to a heavenly glory like Christ's, but it
also points towards a discontinuity with the current state, which appears to
be a different emphasis from Irenaeus. With these thoughts in mind, we
will first draw together our overall summary of Paul's soteriology in chapter 7, and then in Part IV we will conclude with a full comparison and
analysis of these soteriological systems.

7. Summary of Paul's Soteriology

1. Introduction

In the previous two chapters, we focused on close readings of Romans 8 (with Galatians 3–4) and 2 Corinthians 3–5 (with 1 Corinthians 15 and Philippians 2–3). Before making larger conclusions about Pauline soteriology with regard to the issue of theosis, a summary of Paul's soteriology would be helpful since the different letters focus on different aspects. This summary will be based on the primary questions we developed in chapter 4. These questions are:

1) What is the anthropological shape of Paul's soteriology? What aspects of the human condition change due to the soteriological encounter with God?

2) When do these soteriological changes occur? Paul's soteriology is frequently characterised as being 'already/not yet', but how can we clarify further when specific aspects of this soteriological experience take place?

3) How does the soteriological change of the human condition come about? What divine and human activities lead to the soteriological changes expected by Paul?

4) How does Paul relate this soteriological change to creation themes? Does Paul view soteriology/eschatology as in continuity or in discontinuity with creation? That is, does Paul's soteriology represent a fulfilment of creation, or does he present his soteriology as something that surpasses creation?

Since the shape and the timing are intimately related in Paul's soteriology, these two aspects are combined in our synthetic summary.

2. Shape and Timing of Pauline Soteriology

As we noted in earlier chapters, understanding the nature of the problem is a primary step in understanding the nature of the solution. As a result, we will first summarise Paul's presentation of the variegated effects of sin (see Table 7.1), both the inter-personal and the intra-personal aspects. While these are not neatly separable categories, we can use them heuristically for our discussion.

Table 7.1: The Effects of Sin

Problem	Romans	2 Corinthians	Excursus Passages
Inter-Personal Condemnation	1.18–32; 8.1–2	3.7–11; 5.19, 21	
Broken Relationships			
With God	1.18–32; 8.5–8	3.9	Phil 3.18–19; Col 2.13–14
With Others		*passim*[1]	Gal 3.26–29; Phil 2.1–4
With Creation	8.18–23	5.17	
Enslavement/ Subjection			
Death	5.12–21; 8.18–23		1 Cor 15.24–28
Sin	6.1–21	5.21	Gal 3.22; 1 Cor 15.17, 56
Law	7.1–6; 8.1–4	3.3–18	Gal 3.23–4.6; 1 Cor 15.56; Phil 3.5–9
Flesh	7.4–6; 8.3–8, 12–13	5.16	Phil 3.3–4; Col 2.11–23
God/Stoicheia of this World		4.4	Gal 4.3, 9; Col 2.8, 15, 20
Intra-Personal Death			
Literal/Somatic	8.9–11, 21	3.7; 4.16; 5.4	1 Cor 15.1–58
Metaphoric	8.1–2, 13, 17–18	4.16	Col 2.11–13
Flesh/Moral Inability	7.4–6; 8.3–8, 12–13	5.16	Phil 3.1–11; Col 2.11–13
Noetic Ignorance/ Anguish	8.5, 15, 26	2.14–16; 3.12–18; 4.4, 8; 5.12, 16	Col 2.8

Regarding the inter-personal aspects, the fundamental problem of sin is that it breaks and perpetuates a break in the human-divine relationship (cf. 2 Cor 5.18–20). Romans describes those who are in the state of sin as

---

[1] The interpersonal problem between Paul and the Corinthians is assumed throughout the passage since Paul is having to make a defence of his ministry.

'hostile to God' and 'unable to please him' (Rom 8.6). Earlier in Romans the foundation of this problem originates from humans' faithlessness and refusal to worship God alone, turning to other gods (Rom 1.18–32). This leads to wrath and judgment from God. In our passages this is reflected in condemnation language (Rom 8.1; 2 Cor 3.9). Humans have also broken relationships with one another and with creation (Rom 8.19–23), but their relationship with God is most central to our texts.

Intimately related to these problems is the work of 'external' agents. In 2 Cor 4.4 the agency of the 'god of this world' in blinding the minds of unbelievers is clear. At the same time, Paul describes the personified agency of Death as a ruler (Romans 5) and the Flesh as one that thwarts obedience (Romans 7–8). As chief of these, Sin itself is a ruler which enslaves humans (Romans 6). The law itself even serves as an enslaving power in line with the στοιχεῖα τοῦ κόσμου (Gal 3.21–4.7; Col 2.8–20). As long as humans are under the sway of the flesh, they can never please God in the context of the law (Rom 7.4–6; 8.3–8). The problem of flesh and disobedience reveals the close interaction between inter- and intrapersonal problems of sin.

Chief among the intra-personal problems of sin, that is the noetic and somatic struggles resulting from sin, is the problem of death. In Romans, in particular, the association between sin and death was central (3.23; 5.12; 8.6, 10, 13). This is primarily a literal description of somatic corruption in the first half of Romans 8, but the problem of suffering serves a similar function in the second half of the chapter. The noetic features of this death are also significant because Paul draws a connection between this death and the inability to submit to God (Rom 8.6–8). This parallel of the literal and metaphoric death is clear in 2 Corinthians 3–5, running throughout. Just as the body faces corruption (2 Cor 4.16; 5.4), God's servants face external troubles as an experience of death (2 Cor 1.8–11; 4.7–12). Closely related with this is the problem of ignorance or blindness. Paul characterises this as being veiled (2 Cor 3.6–18; 4.4), but it also reflects the problem of death associated with the old age (2 Cor 2.14–16; 5.16).

In response to these problems, Paul presents the work of God, Christ, and the Spirit in restoration of inter- and intra-personal harmony (see Table 7.2). Unsurprisingly, this renewal does not remain limited to our heuristic categories but rather unites the relational and personal aspects. For example, with the model of adoption, believers are placed in a new relationship with God, but this also captures the somatic experience of incorruption. Also, glorification denotes both a restored honourable status and the somatic experience of incorruption. With the new covenant, a new way of relating to God coincides with the new life and moral enablement that comes through the Spirit's presence. Similar conclusions are relevant to incorporated righteousness.

Table 7.2: Soteriological Effects

Solution	Romans	2 Corinthians	Excursus Passages
Inter-Personal			
Participation	8.2, 9–11, 14–17, 28–30	3.17–18; 5.14–15, 21	Col 2.6–3.11; Gal 3.26–29; Phil 2.1–2; 3.7–11
Justification	8.1–4, 10, 30	3.9; 5.21	Phil 3.1–11
Liberation	7.4–6; 8.1–2, 15–17, 21	3.17; 4.4–6	Gal 3.22–4.7; 1 Cor 15.54–58
Adoption/Sonship	8.15–17, 18–23, 28–30		Gal 3.22–4.7; Phil 2.14
Glorification	8.17–23, 28–30	3.18; 4.16–18	Col 3.4; 1 Cor 15.40–49; Phil 3.20–21
Reconciliation		5.18–20	
Intra-Personal			
Life	7.4–6, 8.1–4, 6, 10–13, 23	2.14–16	1 Cor 15.1–58; Phil 2.16
Somatic Incorruption	8.17–23, 28–30	3.6, 18; 4.16–5.5, 21	Col 3.4; 1 Cor 15.1–58; Phil 3.10–11, 20–21
Moral Empowerment	7.4–6; 8.1–13	3.3–6, 12–18; 4.7–12; 5.11–15, 17, 21	Phil 2.1–16; 3.10–20; Col 2.11–13
Noetic Enlightenment	8.24–25	2.14–16; 3.12–4.6, 16–18; 5.16–17	Phil 3.15 Col 3.1–3
Rescue		1.7–11; 4.7–12	

Based upon a close divine-human encounter, Paul's soteriology consists, in the present, of a moral enablement and noetic enlightenment in a somatic context of suffering (2 Cor 3.13–4.18; Rom 7.4–6; 8.1–13). This moral enablement is not just for self-fulfilment but it allows believers to please God as they live for God and for Christ (Rom 7.5–6; 2 Cor 5.14–15). While physical suffering and corruption are the expected present context, Paul also notes God's sustaining comfort and his rescue from bodily danger (2 Cor 1.3–11; 4.7–12). The consummation of this soteriology will occur in the future through a bodily resurrection (Rom 8.9–30; 2 Cor 3.6, 18; 4.16–5.5, 21; Col 3.4; 1 Cor 15.12–58; Phil 3.10, 20–21).

During both temporal stages, believers are empowered by the Spirit to grow into conformity with the death and life of Christ. Life then is the most holistic term that characterises this soteriological experience, in that new life relates both to the present and future transformation of believers into the form of Christ. Paul consistently exemplifies this new life as a participation in and transformation according to divine glory (Rom 8.17–30; 2 Cor 3.6–4.7, 16–18; Col 2.11–13; 3.1–4; 1 Cor 15.39–41; Phil 3.20–21). While he primarily reserves this glorification for the somatic experience of incorruption, in 2 Corinthians 3–4 believers experience it as a work of the Spirit for inward transformation as well. Thus, restored inter-personal relationships lead to a restoration of the intra-personal human condition.

Within Paul's soteriological discussion we see both an anthropological duality and a temporal duality, which is most evident in texts like 2 Cor 4.17–18 and Rom 8.5–11. While we might be tempted to see this anthropological duality as most central to Paul's account, Paul's temporal duality is more formative. Believers are presently divided in their christo-form experience of death and life. The mortal body is not presently vivified; rather, life is experienced in the context of mortal flesh as a present renewal of the mind. However, the hope is that this duality that characterises the present age will be overcome in the future so that the life that shines from God as transforming knowledge will infuse the body as well, so that there is unity between the inner and outer as believers experience Christ's glorious life. The temporal duality of the present and future ages is primary since it drives the discussion, and thus the anthropological duality is secondary and not the ultimate emphasis of Paul's argument.

3. How This Soteriology Comes About

The death and resurrection of Christ is where the saving righteousness of God has been revealed and where the power of sin has been overcome. While we might describe this as the 'objective' procurement of salvation for humanity, our focus has been on the 'subjective' application of that salvation within the community of believers through the human-divine encounter. Paul uses a variety of phrases and concepts to explain this divine-human encounter. What is striking is the integration and overlap of language regarding the believer-Christ and believer-Spirit relationships. In Philippians 2–3 we noted explicit use of participation (κοινωνία) language to describe believers' relationship with the Spirit (2.1) and Christ (3.10).

More typical for Paul is the assortment of synonymous phrases like in Rom 8.9–11: 'you are in the Spirit', 'the Spirit is in you', 'have the Spirit', 'of Christ', etc. (cf. Col 2.6–3.11; Gal 3.26–29). We found a similar repetition and variety in all of the passages. This points to the importance of 'participation' for Paul, but it also shows that any one idea or phrase does not serve as its centre. Rather, Paul compounds the imagery like overlapping circles that reveal participation as the centre without any one image fully describing the experience (see Figure 7.1).

Figure 7.1: Overlapping Images of Participation

The fruit of participation in Christ and the Spirit is that believers become like Christ, sharing in both his death and his resurrection. In the present, believers suffer with him and carry around the death of Jesus and therefore experience his life as comfort and enlightenment. The future experience of somatic resurrection is then characterised as sharing in his glory and incorruption (Rom 8.17–30; Col 3.4; 2 Cor 4.17; Phil 3.21; 1 Cor 15.40). Just as he exists in the divine state of glory, this will be the state of believers as well.[2] Carrez captures this when he writes: 'la δόξα est presque toujours une manière paulinienne d'exprimer ce que Dieu communique de son être et de sa vie'.[3] Thus, the experience of glory is not merely the experience of new life but a participation in divine life.

A distinctive aspect of Paul's soteriology is the role the Spirit plays, especially in Romans 8, Galatians 3–4, and 2 Corinthians 3. The Spirit brings life (Rom 8.2, 10; 2 Cor 3.6) and is the instantiation of the divine, glorifying presence (2 Cor 3.17–18). However, it is important to notice that the experience of the Spirit leads to a christoform experience for believers. The life that the Spirit gives results in their being raised like

---

[2] Evans (*Resurrection and the New Testament*, 160) writes: 'The present possession of spirit, which is all there is, is a foretaste and promise of something further, which is the full life of "glory", an eschatological term which comes nearest to denoting the divine life itself'.

[3] Maurice Carrez, *De la Souffrance à la Gloire: De la Δοξα dans la Pensée paulienne* (Neuchâtel: Delachaux & Niestlé, 1964), 6.

Christ (Rom 8.10–11). As believers encounter the Spirit in 2 Cor 3.18, they reflect the image of Christ and are therefore transformed. Likewise, the Spirit's presence is what unites believers to God and makes them adopted sons like Christ (Galatians 3–4; Rom 8.14–17). Thus, the Spirit is central to Paul's portrayal of the believer's experience of the divine, but this experience is christo-telic in nature, such that believers embody the Christ-narrative in death and life.

While believers closely share in divine attributes like life and glory, the Creator-created distinction still remains. In Romans, our discussion of glory fitted within a larger framework based upon the Creator-created distinction. In Rom 1.18–23, God is the one who is incorruptible (ἄφθαρτος) and outside time (ἀΐδιος), and humanity suffers from corruption (φθαρτός) and stands among the things which have been created. The fundamental sin is described as not giving God the worship and glory that he deserved as Creator. Interestingly, concurrent to their refusal to *glorify* God as God was their loss of participation in divine *glory* (Rom 1.18–23; 3.23). After believers returned to proper worship of God, glorifying him like Abraham (Rom 4.20; 15.5–12), they returned to an experience of his glorifying presence, now instantiated through Christ and the Spirit, and thus experienced a participation in divine glory again (Rom 5.2; 8.17–30). Thus, wanting to be like God in an improper manner, they fell from it. However, when they recognised God as the Creator above themselves, as creatures, they actually attained to the true likeness of God. In some sense, believers become like that which they worship. Through affirmation of the Creator-creature distinction, the separation between Creator and the creature is nullified.

This same distinction between humanity and God is clear in 2 Corinthians 3–5 as well. Paul repeatedly notes the divine source of his sufficiency (2 Cor 2.17; 3.3–6, 18; 4.1, 4–12; 5.1, 5, 18–21). A primary example of the divine primacy is in 2 Cor 3.18, where Paul used the mirror metaphor. As believers encountered God, they reflected the glory that came from God, making clear that any glory they experience is only from God. In a similar manner, in 2 Cor 5.21 as believers experience righteousness, this is *God's* righteousness for those *in Christ*. We therefore called it an incorporated righteousness, that is, one achieved through incorporation into Christ.

Accordingly, we can note a couple of key points about Paul's Creator-created cosmology: Paul maintains a fundamental distinction between the Creator and the created, but this distinction does not hinder believers as creatures becoming like God, sharing his righteousness, incorruption, and glory. The two must be held in tension because the Giver becomes the gift.

4. Continuity and Discontinuity with Creation

That Paul uses creation motifs is clear, but he does not dwell on the state of the original creation like the later patristic writers do. This is clear from Paul's two-age duality (this present age vs the future). Were Paul more concerned about the Edenic state, he would work with a three-age system like that found in the *Life of Adam and Eve*. The only prior stage before that current age that Paul mentions is the seemingly timeless act of preordination (Rom 8.29; 1 Cor 2.7) that predates creation. We can draw implications from Paul's statements about Adam's prelapsarian state, but he does not describe it explicitly.

Like the patristic writers, Paul finds image language quite important in his soteriological account. In particular, Paul uses this language as a way to integrate several other soteriological themes. In Rom 8.29–30, the entire soteriological process of suffering and glorification with Christ is described as being 'conformed to the image of [God's] son'. Not only does this capture the intra-personal effects of salvation, but it captures different inter-personal models of relationship, namely, adoption and justification. In 2 Cor 3.18, the transformation of believers into the 'same image', the christological image of God, also serves as a summative account of his soteriology. This passage stands as the climax of the Spirit's life-giving work that includes moral empowerment, noetic enlightenment, and somatic resurrection. This conformation to Christ's image is associated with Christ's death alone (Phil 3.10), his death and resurrection (Rom 8.29–30; 2 Cor 3.18), and his resurrection alone (Phil 3.21; 1 Cor 15.49). As such, this transformation into Christ's image stands as one central way of expressing Paul's soteriology.

This use of image language draws from creation themes in Genesis 1–2 regarding Adam and Eve being made in the image of God. In addition to Adam being associated with 'image' other ancient Jewish traditions also closely associated Adam with glory. While there is good evidence that Paul associates the loss of glory with Adam, the return of glory is always centred around Christ. That is, Paul *explicitly* associates this glory with God and Christ and only *implicitly* with Adam.[4] Paul does not base his theology on notions about Adam's original state. One of Paul's purposes in using Adamic Christology is 'signalled by the contrast between the humanity of Adam and that of Christ .... Nowhere in the Epistles is Adam the perfect man before his sin. Paul knows only the Adam of sin and death.

---

[4] See my 'Immortal Glory'. Cf. Dunn, *Christology*, 106. See Pate as a model of one who often allows Adam to control the discussion instead of Christ: Pate, *Adam Christology*.

Where does Paul look to find man's true nature? He now looks to Christ'.[5]
Thus, in distinction to three texts preserved in Qumran (1QS 4:22–23; CD
3:19–20; 1QH[a] 4:14–15 [17:14–15]) which speak of כול כבוד אדם ('all the
glory of Adam') to describe the eschatological state, for Paul Christ models believers' eschatological state.

An important characterisation of the resurrection state modelled by
Christ is that it is 'heavenly' in distinction to the present 'earthly' state (1
Cor 15.42–49; 2 Cor 5.1–2; Phil 3.20–21). Christ is the heavenly man and
those who follow him will have a heavenly mode of existence as well.
Importantly, heaven is associated with God's presence (note the parallel of
ἐκ θεοῦ and ἐξ οὐρανοῦ in 2 Cor 5.1–2; cf. Phil 3.14). Thus, as believers
are caught up into this heavenly realm, they are transformed into the divine
manner of existence. However, this phrasing borders on becoming too abstract. Paul regularly makes it concrete by describing this divine manner
of existence as a somatic participation in divine incorruption and glory (1
Cor 15.42–43; 2 Cor 4.17–5.5; Phil 3.21), which parallels Paul's other
statements about participation in incorruption and glory in contexts where
the 'heaven' language is not used (2 Cor 3.18; Rom 8.17–30).

While this contrast between the heavenly and earthly seems to present a
strong level of discontinuity with the present state. Several things militate
against a distinct separation between heavenly and earthly states of existence. Although Christ is 'heavenly', Paul also characterises him as an
ἄνθρωπος like Adam (1 Cor 15.21), and he is also called 'the last Adam'
(1 Cor 15.45). Thus, the heavenly state of existence that Christ draws believers into is somatic just as the earthly state of human existence is currently somatic. Also, as Christ comes ἐξ οὐρανοῦ (1 Cor 15.47; Phil 3.20–
21) there is a sense that he is coming to earth to bring earth under heavenly
control.[6] Thus, as his glory transforms the world, this is 'a final amalga-
mation of the earthly and heavenly spheres'.[7] In Christ, the heavenly Last
Adam, the separation between heaven and earth has been bridged. At an
anthropological level, there still exists the strong discontinuity between the
old corruptible existence and the new incorruptible, but when incorruption
arrives unity will also come.

The Pauline letters, like other Jewish apocalyptic texts, have 'an anthropological approach to the created order',[8] but Hahne rightly points out that
Paul's theology integrates anthropological and wider creational redemp-

---

[5] Scroggs, *Last Adam*, 100. Cf. Lincoln, *Paradise Now*, 190.

[6] Lincoln, *Paradise Now*, 108.

[7] Klaus Koch, *The Rediscovery of Apocalyptic* (trans. M. Kohl; London: SCM, 1972),
32. Significantly, Koch lists 'glory' as one of his eight defining characteristics of apocalyptic.

[8] Hahne, *Corruption and Redemption*, 222.

tion. In particular, Romans 8 and 2 Corinthians 5 are focused primarily on anthropological transformation arising from the Christ event; however, Paul situates this within a larger cosmological framework. What is true for one is true for the other. In Romans, where Paul is clearly speaking about 'nature', or non-human creation, he does not describe a cataclysmic conflagration or destruction of creation but rather its redemption. This suggests viewing this as a repair, fixing what was wrong, but creation would remain essentially continuous with what came before. However, in 2 Corinthians 5 Paul's language is much more discontinuous: 'The old has passed away. See! All things have become new' (2 Cor 5.17). In the midst of this discontinuity and continuity, how exactly the new state of existence will turn out is unclear, but we can make two conclusions: 1) the eschatological state will include a transformed non-human creation which will be appropriate for human existence; and 2) the human experience in this context will be modelled after Christ's own heavenly state of existence.

Paul does not provide an either/or perspective on the role of continuity and discontinuity between redemption and creation. Rather, in different contexts he emphasises one aspect or another. Schrage rightly describes his theology as a dialectic.[9] However, the emphasis for Paul is on the eschatological state, and this is the model for understanding life. Bolt rightly notes that we primarily understand creation in light of redemption rather than the other way around when he writes, 'Though creation *ontologically* is prior to redemption, redemption and revelation are *epistemologically* prior to *faith in the Creator God*'.[10] Redemption for Paul is not just a return to creation; rather, redemption fulfils the original creational intent, but it also surpasses it.

Paul provides a rich and full soteriology that addresses both inter- and intra-personal aspects of humanity in the present with fulfilment in the future. With this understanding of his soteriology based upon these representative passages, we can now turn to our larger question of whether and to what extent theosis helpfully captures Paul's presentation of the anthropological dimension of soteriology.

---

[9] Schrage, 'Schöpfung und Neuschöpfung', 249–50. The basis of continuity is God: 'Entscheidend ist nun, dass Gott, der Schöpfer, und Gott, der Neuschöpfer, für Paulus ein und derselbe ist' (246). On the other hand, Schrage also notes that God's work of resurrection is characterised as *ex nihilo* (Rom 4.17), and he later notes: 'Gottes schöpferischer Neubeginn bewirkt einen radikalen Bruch mit dem bisher Gültigen und das Ende des alten Wesens und Wandels' (247).

[10] Bolt, 'Creation and Redemption', 49, emphasis original.

IV. Conclusion

Chapter IV

8. Conclusion

Prompted by modern ecumenical discussions about deification, we have taken steps towards describing in what ways and to what extent we can talk about theosis in Paul, with a specific focus upon the anthropological experience of salvation. Based on the ideas of Gadamer, Jauss, and Bakhtin we are addressing the problem from a history of interpretation point of view by holding a conversation between later interpreters of Paul and Paul himself. We first addressed two Greek patristic interpreters – Irenaeus and Cyril of Alexandria – who used Pauline texts to develop their ideas of deification and then analysed several key Pauline texts, primarily Romans 8 and 2 Corinthians 3–5. Now that we have heard from the three writers, we are in a better position to draw some conclusions about Paul's soteriology in comparison to these later interpreters. However, before exploring the comparison, we will briefly highlight the key points in each soteriological system.

1. Patristic Soteriology

1.1 Irenaeus

While Irenaeus' most direct deification language relates specifically to his use of Psalm 82 and his identification of believers as 'gods' (θεοί) and sons of God, this identification is integrated into his portrayal of the larger soteriological experience of believers, which culminates in a restoration of the image and likeness of God. Since Christ, as the second Adam, became human so that believers could become what he is, believers become like God and are even called gods themselves. By the restoration of the Spirit, believers are restored to God's likeness, which is primarily described as the experience of somatic incorruption. However, intellectual and moral progress is not unimportant to Irenaeus' soteriology. He situates this salvific experience within a restored relationship with God and expresses this restoration through three primary models: adoption, vision of God, and union with God. With his limited use of specific terminology, deification may not be the best summary term for Irenaeus' soteriology, but key aspects of his soteriology do intersect in his deification passages. Pauline themes such as the second Adam, image of God, adoption, immortality, and resurrection are central to Irenaeus' account.

1.2 Cyril

Like Irenaeus, Cyril uses Ps 82.6 to identify believers as gods and sons of God; however, he also incorporates this identification into his discourse about participation in the divine nature from 2 Pet 1.4. For Cyril, deification is participation in the divine attributes such that believers become like God in life and holiness. Believers do not become what God is in his nature, rather they share in these attributes through participation and by grace. They do not participate in the divine in some abstract manner but through the personal presence of Christ through the Spirit, somatically and spiritually. Just as the vivifying and sanctifying presence of the Spirit was lost through the sin of the first Adam, Christ as the second Adam has restored the presence of the Spirit to humanity, returning incorruption and sanctification to them again. In addition to new creation and second Adam themes, the metaphor that Cyril most often uses to describe this process is that of adoption.

1.3 Synthesis

Drawing from (my modified version of) Russell's taxonomy, we noted in chapter 4 that Irenaeus and Cyril's views of deification stand on twin pillars of likeness (*homoiosis*) to God based upon participation (*methexis*) in God.[1] With regard to likeness, they focus specifically upon the image and likeness of God first mentioned in Genesis 1–2 and then later employed through the Pauline texts. With Adam's fall, humanity experienced a broken relationship with God. They lost the protological likeness to God by losing the presence of the Spirit and thus experienced corruption and mortality. Christ, serving as the true image of God and a bridge between humanity and God, restored this relationship. The returning Spirit restores the divine attributes of life and incorruption as well as sanctification. Importantly, since immortality was the marker of divinity in the Greek world, as believers share in immortality, they become like God in a way that easily opened the door to the appellation of gods.[2] Through Christ and the Spirit the protological intent of likeness to God is fulfilled.

---

[1] See p. 102–105. They are generally representative of other Greek writers, but there are also a variety of other themes and emphases that would have arisen if we had focused upon other texts and other writers. For instance, prayer and ascetic struggle has not played the role with these two as others, such as Gregory of Nyssa and the Macarian writings.

[2] See Chp 2, §3.1.2.

As we noted, participation in God served as the basis for this renewal of the image and likeness of God. In particular, it is through a close relationship with God mediated by Christ's uniting of God and humanity and by the Spirit's presence that believers become like God. Irenaeus focused upon adoption, vision of God and union with God as three primary models of this relationship, whereas Cyril focused directly upon the language of participation and adoption. Adoption language showed up most frequently in specific deification passages: as believers are called gods, they are also termed adopted sons of God, by grace and not by nature.[3] With this grace-nature distinction, the Creator-created distinction is firmly preserved. In fact, the powerful, and sometimes unqualified, affirmation about believers being gods is built strongly upon a distinction between Creator and the created and a system of relational participation.

With these two pillars in mind, we can therefore describe deification as the process of restoring the image and likeness of God, primarily experienced as incorruption and sanctification, through a participatory relationship with God mediated by Christ and the Spirit. Through the Son and the Spirit believers become adopted sons of God, even gods, by grace and not by nature, because they participate in divine attributes. Accordingly, we characterised this ontological transformation as attributive deification in contrast to essential deification. That is, since Irenaeus and Cyril maintain a fundamental Creator-created distinction as well as the distinct agency of the Spirit, deified believers do not consubstantually or connaturally share in the divine essence; rather, deified believers are ontologically transformed by the personal presence of the Spirit and therefore experience the divine attributes. Importantly, this excludes any hint of absorption, a problem which many Western readers anticipate when they hear the language of deification but which has no basis due to the theological structure.[4] While exegesis of Ps 82.6 served as the formal basis of this affirmation of believers as gods, the association between life and sonship was primarily supported using Pauline texts, especially, 1 Corinthians 15; Romans 8; Galatians 4; and 2 Corinthians 5.

2. Pauline Soteriology

From our study of how Irenaeus and Cyril employed Pauline texts for their development of deification themes, we developed four primary questions that guided our study of Paul:

---

[3] Irenaeus integrated adoption into his deification language so closely that he even treated adoption as synonymous with the gift of incorruption.

[4] See Chp 4, §1.4.

1) What is the anthropological shape of Paul's soteriology?

2) When do these soteriological changes occur?

3) How do these soteriological changes of the human condition come about?

4) How does this transformation of the human condition relate to creation?

Guided by these four questions we analysed several key texts in the Pauline corpus: primarily Romans 8 and 2 Corinthians 3–5 and secondarily Colossians 2, Galatians 3–4, 1 Corinthians 15, and Philippians 2–3.

Using a variety of models and metaphors, Paul's soteriology addresses intra- and inter-personal problems. Describing the restored relationship with God as justification, adoption, and reconciliation, among other terms, believers experience an intimate, even participatory, relationship with God. Paul uses a variety of phrases (like 'in Christ', 'the Spirit in you', etc.) to describe this, but the variety shows that none by itself captures the totality of the participatory relationship. On the basis of this close relationship with Christ and the Spirit, believers are transformed into the image of Christ. This conformation to Christ's image is associated with Christ's death alone (Phil 3.10), his death and resurrection (Rom 8.29–30; 2 Cor 3.18), and his resurrection alone (Phil 3.21; 1 Cor 15.49). The primary anthropological experience is new life, which is also specified as noetic enlightenment, moral enablement, and somatic resurrection. This is often associated with a participation in heavenly glory. In particular, Paul is much more concerned with the heavenly Christ as the model for new humanity than with Adam. The use of heaven and earth language in the letters shows that his soteriology maintains a tension between continuity and discontinuity with creation.

3. Analysis and Conclusions

With their different roles, rhetorical intentions, and historical contexts, we should not be critical of Irenaeus and Cyril because they do not merely say the same things as Paul. At the same time, their different situations do not preclude us from noting the commonalities and distinctive emphases that characterise these writers.

3.1 Common Emphases

While there are several areas of notable overlap, I will focus on three: the experience of life, the image of God, and a triune divine relationship.

3.1.1 Life, Incorruption, and Glory

The centre of the anthropological dimension of soteriology within each of these three authors can be summed up with the term *life*. While their theological anthropologies are not identical, all three work with an outer-inner, or body-mind, duality.[5] Therefore, they see life at work within believers according to these two aspects. The culmination of salvation for all three is the future somatic experience of resurrection, characterised as immortality and incorruption and adoption as sons of God. Significantly, Irenaeus and Paul also describe this as an experience of divine glory.

As the culmination of salvation, this somatic incorruption is not unrelated to the present experience of life, which includes moral enablement and noetic enlightenment. Paul, in particular, focuses on present moral enablement as correlated to God's act in resurrecting Christ, but this renewed life is also associated with noetic enlightenment. Importantly, this present moral enablement and noetic enlightenment is associated with participation in divine glory in 2 Corinthians 3–4 and thus correlated to the somatic experience of glory in 2 Cor 4.16–5.5. In Irenaeus we noted clear aspects related to the moral enablement and noetic enlightenment especially with regard to the progression of believers towards perfection, but his polemical context led him to focus primarily upon the future somatic, even carnal, experience of immortality. Cyril's works, on the other hand, presented what might be described as a more balanced emphasis on present and future life. In particular, he correlated the experience of sanctification and immortality as the key aspects of soteriology.

Importantly, the use of immortality, glory, and sons of God language to describe this salvific process gives overtones of humans being drawn into the divine sphere.[6] Immortality, especially in the Greek world, was *the* decisive marker of divine status.[7] For our writers, this immortality is not native to the soul, but God grants incorrupt life to the whole person, body and soul. When God's immortal mode of being is communicated through Christ and the Spirit to believers, they are entering the realm of the divine.

At the same time, the use of glory language, when used in contexts beyond that of honour discourse, was primarily associated with God's being and presence in Jewish texts. Paul follows other Jewish traditions that associate the eschatological state as one of glory, capturing both sociological

---

[5] Irenaeus, at times, appears to work with a trichotomous view of humans, where they have a body, soul, and spirit, but the spirit is closely correlated with the Spirit of God, such that it becomes difficult to distinguish the two.

[6] Life (e.g., Rom 6.23; 9.26; 2 Cor 3.3; 6.16), glory (e.g., Rom 1.23; 3.23; 5.2; 2 Cor 4.6), and immortality (e.g., Rom 1.20, 23) are directly associated with God's being and presence in Paul's letters.

[7] Cf. Chp 2, §3.1.2.

status and an ontological state of incorruption. This language too draws believers into a heavenly manner of being like that of God. While Paul is not the first to associate glory and immortality, he surely exploits this connection as he describes the ultimate state of believers with combined terminology that bridges the divine-human gap. Importantly, Irenaeus also correlated glory and immortality as his eschatological hope for believers. Cyril associates human participation in the attributes of God such as light and life as a participation in the divine presence.

An important connection with this is the use of sons of God language. As we saw in Romans 8, Paul identified glorification and the experience of incorruption with adoption as sons of God. With this glory-immortality-adoption hope, Paul brings together both Jewish and Greco-Roman themes, showing that as a Hellenistic Jew Paul seamlessly integrates both together. Likewise, reading Ps 82.6 in light of Romans 8 and Galatians 4, Irenaeus and Cyril repeatedly associate adoption as sons of God with the deifying experience of incorruption. Therefore, with this common expectation of the experience of divine life as immortality, glory, and adoption, believers are drawn into a divine sphere of existence.

3.1.2 Image of God

As a summary of what this life means, all three writers describe the consummation of true humanity in terms of the restoration of the image of God. As one of the twin pillars in their deification constructs, Irenaeus and Cyril both capture likeness to God through this language.[8] Important for both is their explicit and well-developed theology of Adam and the fall. Drawing from Genesis 1–2, Irenaeus and Cyril use the image-likeness pair to describe the protological state of humanity and the creational intent of similarity to God, particularly in life and sanctification. However, Adam sinned, and with the Spirit's departure humans were cursed with death. As the divine human, Christ then reveals the true image of God, and he restores the presence of the Spirit, who establishes life and sanctification. Thus, the image unites protology and teleology, with Christ as the model for both and the Spirit as the primary agent.

In Paul, image language can refer to a creational cosmology (1 Cor 11.1–7), but more often it refers to the telos of humanity as believers are conformed to or transformed into the image of Christ. In conjunction with the use of εἰκών, Paul uses a variety of 'morphic' terms to describe the way believers are conformed to Christ. Whereas for our patristic writers,

---

[8] The two most often use image and likeness as a hendiadys, although Irenaeus is noted for making a distinction between the two, especially in *AH* 5.

the image of God in Christ is expressed in the sharing of his life, for Paul this image is an embodiment of both Christ's death and his life.

We noted the significant role of the Spirit in all three because it is through the Spirit that believers are transformed into this image of Christ. Importantly, for all three Christ as the *heavenly* man serves as the model for humanity and draws them up into a divine state of existence characterised by immortal glory. Consequently, the three share a common way of speaking about the fulfilment of humanity as being christo-telically focused by means of the Spirit, but Paul incorporates a distinct present emphasis on sharing in Christ's death as well.

3.1.3 Participatory Triune Divine Encounter

An important aspect of their soteriologies is that believers experience this life through a close relationship and encounter with God. Two key aspects of this encounter with God are 1) a close interaction between believers and the triune divinity and 2) a clear distinction between the Creator and created.

While there is clearly development and clarification with regard to the triune nature of divinity from the time of Paul through to Cyril, we see a genetic connection between Paul's presentation of the divine-human encounter and that of later interpreters. The first correspondence is the distinctly triune nature of this divine interaction.

Our purpose here is not to demonstrate that Paul affirmed the deity of Christ and the Spirit, but we can note that they are both presented in Paul as mediators of divine action.[9] For instance, Christ is the heavenly saviour (1 Cor 15.49; Phil 3.20), through whom all things exist (1 Cor 8.6) and through whom God reconciles the world (2 Cor 5.18–19).[10] While we have what seems like a clear indication of Christ's pre-existence in Paul (Rom

---

[9] Dunn (*Christology*, 98–128) stands as representative of those who argue for the affirmation of Christ's divinity as a later development. On the other hand, Hurtado, Watson, and Fee, among others, have more recently detailed several reasons for seeing this affirmation in Paul's letters: Larry W. Hurtado, *Lord Jesus Christ: Devotion to Jesus in Earliest Christianity* (Grand Rapids: Eerdmans, 2003), 79–153; Francis Watson, 'The Triune Divine Identity: Reflections on Pauline God-language, in Disagreement with J.D.G. Dunn', *JSNT* 80 (2000): 99–124; Gordon D. Fee, *Pauline Christology: An Exegetical-Theological Study* (Peabody, MA: Hendrickson, 2007), 481–99.

[10] Adela Yarbro Collins and John Collins, *King and Messiah as Son of God: Divine, Human, and Angelic Messianic Figures in Biblical and Related Literature* (Grand Rapids: Eerdmans, 2008). They describe a difference between 'functional' and 'ontic' divinity. While this later tradition of Jesus' divinity may appear to be a later accretion, the idea of Jesus as the 'Son of God' is particularly fruitful as a first century basis of Jesus' divinity, which also has implications for the correspondence of deification and believers being sons of God.

8.3; Phil 2.6), it is his post-resurrection state as the 'heavenly' man that draws believers into this heavenly state of being that is more central for Paul.[11] Consequently, Hays writes: 'being united with Christ is salvific because to share his life is to share in the life of God'.[12] In addition to Jesus being associated with Yahweh in Phil 2.11, the strongest evidence is that of Col 2.9–10 which speaks of 'all the fullness of deity' dwelling in Christ. At the same time, the Spirit who is the Lord/Yahweh (2 Cor 3.17–18) is the Spirit *of God* who gives life (2 Cor 3.6; Rom 8.11) and the Spirit *of God* who makes believers children *of God* (Rom 8.14).[13] Accordingly, Christ and the Spirit serve as mediators of God to humanity and mediators of participation in the divine, that is, participation in divine attributes.

Thus, Paul does not explicitly clarify the relationship between God (the Father), Christ the Son, and the Holy Spirit, but Christ and the Spirit are agents that mediate access to God and participation in divine attributes. Irenaeus, on the other hand, explicitly notes that Jesus is God, but he also coordinates the work of the Spirit with that of Christ, in that together they are the two hands of God. Cyril explicitly affirms the deity of Father, Son, and Spirit. Even with this diversity with regard to their explicit dogmatic confession, the similarity of the functional soteriology is clear: God, Christ, and the Spirit work in tandem to achieve the salvation of believers. All three note that Christ's incarnation, death and resurrection unite humanity with God, and that the Spirit actualises this relationship and gives life to believers.

Not only do each describe triune divine activity in the salvation of humanity, but importantly they each also describe this as a participatory relationship. The primary difference between Paul and our patristic writers, in this regard, is the nature of explicit language. Paul does use some explicit participation language (e.g., Phil 2.1; 3.10), but he primarily makes use of a variety of prepositional phrases and oblique cases to describe the divine-human relationship. The variety and distribution shows the importance of participation for Paul but also that no one phrase holds the centre for him. Both Irenaeus and Cyril move away from this use of prepositional phrases, presumably because of its ambiguity. In fact, they resolve the ambiguity in Paul's letters by using the terminology of union, communion, and participation regularly. Even with these obvious developments and the differ-

---

[11] In fact, Christ is more often the one explicitly associated with heaven than God (Lincoln, *Paradise Now*, 180).

[12] Richard B. Hays, *The Faith of Jesus Christ*, xxxiii. Cf. idem., 'The God of Mercy Who Rescues Us from the Present Evil Age: Romans and Galatians' in *The Forgotten God: Perspectives in Biblical Theology*, A. Andrew Das and Frank J. Matera, eds. (Louisville: Westminster John Knox, 2002), 123-143, at 125, 135.

[13] Fee, *Empowering Presence*, 827–45.

ent emphases that arise from a change in terminology, 'participation' plays the same structural role within the soteriology of each. That is, divine activity is not merely external but internal, within believers through the presence of Christ and the Spirit.

Importantly, for all three this human participation in the divine does not deny a fundamental distinction between the Creator and created. Responding to Gnosticism and Arianism, respectively, both Irenaeus and Cyril explicitly affirm the Creator-created distinction because of the dogmatic debates of their times. This distinction is also clear in Paul's letters, where the fundamental sin of humanity is not respecting God as the creator. But, importantly, as believers return to proper worship, they become like the one they worship. As they all see creation as *ex nihilo*, this means that there is not an original divine-human ontological association (as with essential-natural deification). As a result, a common aspect of their soteriology is that believers are drawn close to God in participatory relationships but they always remain distinct from him. All three find adoption terminology useful because it maintains this distinction.

3.2 Distinct Pauline Emphases: Law and Suffering

As we saw in the introduction, Gadamer, Jauss, and Skinner emphasise the fact that each writing stands as an answer to (often implicit) questions arising from its author's context. Our patristic writers share much in common with Paul's soteriology but they do not share all the same questions as Paul, and there are two distinct emphases, among others, in the Pauline letters that do not play as significant a role in these later writers: law and suffering.

3.2.1 Law and Righteousness

In their contextual setting, Irenaeus and Cyril fought battles related to the nature of God and Christ, whereas with his close relationship to Judaism Paul is very concerned about matters relating to the law. If we remember two of the key thesis statements for the main passages we addressed (Romans 8 and 2 Corinthians 3–5), the place of the law becomes apparent:

Rom 7.5–6: 'While we were living in the flesh, our sinful passions, aroused by the law, were at work in our members to bear fruit for death. But now we are discharged from the law, dead to that which held us captive, so that we are slaves not under the old written code but in the new life of the Spirit'.

2 Cor 3.6: God 'made us competent to be ministers of the new covenant, not of the letter but of the Spirit; for the letter kills, but the Spirit gives life'.

We see that the death–life theme so central to Paul and the patristic writers is inherently tied to the issue of law for Paul. Along with these passages where the law and the letter are significant, we can easily see the corresponding use of righteousness language in Rom 8.1–11, 30; 2 Cor 3.7–11; 5.21; and Phil 3.1–11 in similar contexts. Because of the problem of the flesh, humans are incapable of true moral behaviour and face condemnation before God. In response, Christ and the Spirit break the power of sin and the flesh, and believers are justified and experience new life. The centrality of righteousness language to Paul's soteriology is clear. In Romans the 'righteousness of God' in Romans is a revelation of God's saving work, and in 2 Cor 5.21 it is an affirmation of human participation in acquittal and new life through incorporation into Christ.

Irenaeus and Cyril are concerned with the relationship between Christianity and Judaism, the new covenant and the old covenant.[14] They even address the freedom from the problem of slavery and inability in the context of the flesh and law (e.g., *AH* 3.18.7; *In Jo.* 8.32–35, 1:623–29). However, our two writers employ righteousness language differently from Paul and one another. Irenaeus does not often speak of justification by faith, but he does seem to associate righteousness, at least in some cases, with one's status at the final judgment and the gift of incorruption.[15] Cyril, on the other hand, employs justification language more often and appears to develop it further. He regularly contrasts justification with condemnation and characterises it as a forgiveness of sins.[16] However, he also associates justification with 'freedom' and a purification from sin brought about by participation in Christ and the Spirit, which allows believers to embody the divine attributes of moral righteousness and holiness. Importantly, Cyril contrasts this with the Jewish attempt to attain righteousness through the law.

Through these admittedly preliminary sketches, we can note some distinct overlap in their conceptions of the forensic context of righteousness language. The combination of forensic and participatory conceptions of justification in Cyril warrants further investigation. On the other hand, righteousness and justification seem to play a larger role for Paul, especially in light of his context of situating Christianity vis-à-vis Judaism. The anthropological hope for Paul and these Greek interpreters is quite similar with the common emphasis on moral and somatic life through an intimate divine-human encounter. However, by emphasising different metaphors and models to describe this soteriological process, they accentuate different aspects. Thus, we must not underestimate the effect that selection or exclusion of certain language can have. The de-emphasis of

---

[14] Noormann, *Irenäus*, 379–426; Wilken, *Judaism*.

[15] E.g., *AH* 1.10.1; 2.29.2; 4.6.5.

[16] E.g., *In Jo.* 7.24, 1:492–510; 14.4, 2:239–40.

righteousness terminology can be correlated with a neglect of some related ideas, especially by those who follow in particular traditions.[17]

3.2.2 Suffering

In our Pauline texts we found striking comments on the role of suffering in believers' present lives. Suffering is not merely an instantiation of corruption from which the gift of eschatological incorruption will bring release (Rom 8.18–23). It also allows believers to embody the narrative of Christ. This metaphorical death with Christ is regularly associated with a corresponding experience of life as the result or outcome (see Table 8.1). We see the intimate connection between present suffering and life experienced in the present and the future. Rather than merely the present state of life, Paul infuses these difficulties with value because they are an embodiment of the Christ narrative. Just as Christ passed through death before being raised from the dead, believers too die with Christ in order to share in his life.

Table 8.1: Suffering and Life

Rom 8.17	we suffer with Christ	in order that (ἵνα)	we may also be glorified with him
2 Cor 4.10	carrying around the death of Jesus in the body	in order that (ἵνα)	the life of Jesus may also be visible in our bodies
2 Cor 4.11	being given up to death for Jesus' sake	in order that (ἵνα)	the life of Jesus may be visible in our mortal flesh
2 Cor 4.17	this slight momentary affliction	is preparing us for	an eternal weight of glory beyond all measure
Phil 3.10–11	sharing in his sufferings by being conformed to his death	if somehow (εἴ πως)	I may attain the resurrection from the dead

This dying with Christ is not unknown to Irenaeus and Cyril.[18] For instance, Irenaeus speaks of martyrs who follow Christ in their death (e.g.,

---

[17] This bifurcation can be evidenced in the later emphasis on guilt and justification in the Western traditions and corruption and theosis in Eastern traditions. For discussion of the East-West emphases of guilt versus death, see especially, Donald Fairbairn, *Eastern Orthodoxy Through Western Eyes* (Louisville: Westminster John Knox, 2002), 79–95. Cf. Juoko Martikainen, 'Man's Salvation: Deification or Justification?', *Sobernost* 7 (1976): 180–92, at 189–90.

[18] Nevertheless, this motif appears to be more prominent in writers that emphasise ascetic exercise and purification of the soul.

AH 3.12.10,13; 3.18.5). Cyril, on the other hand, speaks of the circumcision of the Spirit and ascetic practice which brings purification (e.g., *In Jo.* 7.24, 1:500–03; *In Luc.* 2.21–24, 1:21–22). He also addresses asceticism in discussion of losing one's life for Christ's sake (e.g., *In Jo.* 12.25–26, 2:148–49). These different treatments of external and internal suffering are not necessarily unlike the sufferings described by Paul, but their relative infrequency in these works makes Paul distinctive. In addition, these sufferings are not separated from Christ, but Paul makes conformation to Christ's suffering and death as central as conformation to his resurrection life. Accordingly, a description of Paul's soteriology must include this important aspect of the present experience of believers.

3.3 Conclusions

We recognise that Paul and his later interpreters have significant overlaps and distinctive emphases based upon their different ideologies, contexts, and rhetorical purposes. As a simple illustration of the similarities and differences, see Figure 8.1. The three writers share a larger soteriological structure of experiencing incorrupt life as conformation to Christ's image through participation in the divine. What distinguishes the patristic writers from Paul is their explicit ascription of deity to Christ (Irenaeus and Cyril) and to the Spirit (Cyril). Also, while Paul makes use of Adam themes, Irenaeus and Cyril flesh these out into a larger narrative. On the other hand, Paul frames his theology in light of law and justification and emphasises conformation to Christ's suffering as well as his life.

Figure 8.1: Comparison of Patristic Notions
of Deification and Pauline Soteriology

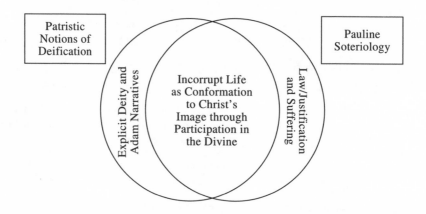

With these similarities and differences in mind, we can now address the aim of the study which is to explore whether and to what extent theosis helpfully captures Paul's presentation of the anthropological dimension of soteriology. That is, does this admittedly later, and thus anachronistic, notion help us to read Paul in a way that draws out and connects aspects of his theology that Western readers have routinely missed or underplayed?

Based on Col 2.9–10 alone, we would not be unjustified for arguing that Paul taught a form of deification, in that the deity that dwells in Christ also fills and transforms believers. However, for a more substantial conclusion we should return to the three criteria of 'sameness' Yeago listed for comparing *judgments* despite differences in *concepts*.[19] (Judgments are the basic logic and content of a position, while concepts are the language and terminology used to express judgments.) To argue for similarity in the judgments, there must be similarity 1) in the logical subject, 2) in what is predicated about the subject, and 3) in the point of the affirmations. Based on our study we can note the following:

1) The logical subject is the same between the three writers. All three concern themselves with God's activity to save humanity from the effects of sin. Therefore, the logical subject consisting of the salvation of believers is equivalent.

2) The logical predicate is the same between the three writers. The basis of this equivalence is displayed in the overlapping area of the Venn diagram above (see Figure 8.1). That is, all three argue that soteriology entails an experience of incorrupt life as conformation to Christ's image through participation in the divine. This corresponds directly to the definition for deification which we established in Part II of our study: Deification, for Irenaeus and Cyril, is the process of restoring likeness to God, primarily experienced as incorruption and sanctification, through a participatory relationship with God mediated by Christ and the Spirit. Through the Son and the Spirit believers become adopted sons of God, even gods, by grace and not by nature, because they participate in divine attributes (and not in the divine essence). This entails an ontological transformation, but we characterised this form of deification as attributive deification in distinction to essential deification due to the relational nature of the divine-human interaction with the Spirit. Like the patristic writers, Paul argues for an ontological transformation that entails a participation in the divine attributes not in the divine essence.

The primary difference is the different conceptual language of the appellation 'gods' by Irenaeus and Cyril. Does then the explicit affirmation of believers as 'gods' depend on an explicit affirmation of Jesus (and the

---

[19] See p. 21–22.

Spirit) as God, as Russell argued?[20] Since, as we noted above, Christ and the Spirit serve as mediators of God to humanity and thus mediators of participation in the divine. Since the patristic writers nor Paul argue for a sharing in the divine essence, as with essential deification, the explicit affirmation of deity is not necessary. Obviously, if Paul considered Christ and the Spirit to be divine as some argue (and with whom I agree),[21] the bridge between Paul's theology and later views becomes much shorter. Nevertheless, with a shared focus on attributes rather than essence this explicit affirmation about deity does not affect the equivalence of their predication about soteriology.

3) In spite of their different contexts and rhetorical purposes, all three are attempting to articulate the culmination of human flourishing in light of the divine-human encounter as the point of their soteriologies.

Since we demonstrated the equivalence with regard to all three criteria, we can conclude that the anthropological dimension of Paul's soteriology is equivalent to attributive deification as described by Irenaeus and Cyril. We can, therefore, affirm that attributive deification, as described by Irenaeus and Cyril, aptly describes the anthropological dimension of Paul's soteriology.[22] In light of this, we remember Bakhtin's statement about meaning potential: 'semantic phenomena can exist in concealed form, potentially, and be revealed only in semantic cultural contexts of subsequent epochs that are favourable for such disclosure'.[23] Deification is the revelation from subsequent epochs that helps us to understand better the anthropological dimension of Paul's soteriology.

At the same time, while deification, or theosis, can generally serve as a helpful description of Paul's soteriology, perhaps *christosis* is a better term to describe Paul's specific soteriological emphasis for two reasons.[24] The first is substantive, and the second is more pragmatic.

---

[20] Russell, *Deification*, 85.

[21] See footnote 9 above.

[22] In the Introduction, we noted Hallonsten's ('Theosis', 285–86) critique against overestimating the similarities of soteriological systems in order to make them agree. He noted specifically the need for a theological anthropology informed by the image of God and for participation as a central mode of relationship, both of which are evident in Paul.

[23] Bakhtin, 'Response', at 5.

[24] Nellas, Finlan, and Bouteneff, among others, speak of 'Christification': Panayiotis Nellas, *Deification in Christ: Orthodox Perspectives on the Nature of the Human Person* (trans. Norman Russell; Crestwood: St Vladimir's Seminary Press, 1997), 115–59; Finlan, '*Theosis* in Paul?', 71; Peter Bouteneff, 'Christ and Salvation' in *The Cambridge Companion to Orthodox Christian Theology,* eds. Mary Cunningham and Elizabeth Theokritoff (Cambridge: Cambridge University Press, 2008), 93–106, at 104. Lot-Borodine also notes this language in the Macarian writings: Myrrha Lot-Borodine, *La déification de l'homme: selon la doctrine des Pères grecs* (Cerf: Paris, 1970), 167. See BDF §109, which describes the –ωσις suffix as making an abstract noun from a verb.

The first reason for preferencing christosis is due to the particularly christo-form nature of the experience. Irenaeus and Cyril share Paul's emphasis on conformation to Christ's image, which includes a holistic – noetic, moral, and somatic – transformation of the human modelled around Christ's restoration of humanity. However, a significant aspect Paul's account of this transformation is that it is an embodiment of not just the life of Christ but also his death. We noted the importance of the 'morphic' language to describe this: This conformation to Christ's image is associated with Christ's death alone (Phil 3.10), his death and resurrection (Rom 8.29–30; 2 Cor 3.18), and his resurrection alone (Phil 3.21; 1 Cor 15.49).

While the shape of Pauline soteriology is specifically christo-form, a possible weakness of using the term christosis is its possible overemphasis on Christ and underemphasis on the necessary and unique roles of God (the Father) and the Holy Spirit. For instance, Paul repeatedly emphasises the agency of God in empowering and revealing. The distinctive role of the Spirit permeates our passages, especially in Romans 8, Galatians 3–4, and 2 Corinthians 3. The Spirit brings life and is the instantiation of the divine presence. However, it is important to notice that the experience of the Spirit leads to a christoform experience for believers. As believers encounter the Spirit in 2 Cor 3.18, they reflect the image of Christ as they are transformed. The life that the Spirit gives results in their being raised like Christ (Rom 8.10–11). Believers are adopted sons of God through the Spirit's presence, such that they cry 'Abba, Father' (Galatians 3–4; Rom 8.14–17). At the same time, Paul primarily compares believers to Christ as the Son and heir so that they are conformed to his image as Son (e.g., Gal 4.4–7; Rom 8.29). The Spirit is central to Paul's portrayal of the believer's experience of the divine, but this experience is christo-telic in nature, such that believers embody the Christ-narrative in death and life through the Spirit. Consequently, christosis properly captures this christo-telic emphasis, but it cannot be separated from conceptions of the triune divine encounter.[25] One cannot separate christosis from theosis (or Christ from God).[26] Viewing χριστός in light of its original meaning of 'being

---

Just as θέωσις is the abstract noun representing the process of making one divine from θεόω, χρίστωσις is the abstract noun from the implied verb χριστόω (χρίω), to make one a christ.

[25] My overall proposal draws from Schweitzer (and Sanders), but I disagree with the distinction that Schweitzer makes between an 'in God' and an 'in Christ' mysticism because it unnecessarily bifurcates Christ and God in Paul's theology. Cf. Schweitzer, *Mysticism*, 3–6.

[26] Speaking of the 'relational and actualistic accounts of divine identity' Francis Watson ('The Triune Divine Identity', 115) writes: 'Jesus is 'son' (and God is 'father') not in abstraction but, supremely and definitively, in and through his death and resurrection'. Based upon Watson's observation of the correlation between 'son' and 'image' language

anointed', just as Jesus Χριστός is a person elected by God and anointed by the Spirit to lead a cruciform and anastasiform life, believers too are called by God and anointed by the Spirit (cf. 2 Cor 1.21–22) to be conformed to the image of the dying and rising Christ.[27] Thus, christosis captures the christo-telic nature of Paul's soteriology, but this can only be properly understood in the context of the work of God and the Spirit.[28]

The second reason for preferring christosis over theosis relates to the 'meaning' of the term theosis. Since immortality and divinity were inseparable in the ancient world, the association between theosis or theopoiesis and immortality was clear. However, this association no longer remains in the modern mind, and many people do not easily understand this important connection and can be misled by the connotations the term theosis engenders. A related terminological problem is the fact that theosis encompasses a range of ideas. Russell noted two distinct traditions of use in the patristic era, and more development occurred with the late Byzantine theologian Gregory Palamas and others through the modern age. This diversity makes it difficult in some discussions to distinguish theosis as a modern term from theosis as a historical term.[29] As a result, the term theosis can be ambiguous with regard to its referent because of its varied use in ancient and modern contexts. As a relatively new term christosis has less baggage and allows us to focus on the christo-form nature of Pauline soteriology without the potential confusion of theosis.

This is not to say that deification, or theosis, should be avoided because christosis can only be properly understood when it is properly situated under a larger umbrella of theosis.[30] However, no single term will be suffi-

---

in Paul's thought, we could easily say that 'Jesus is *image* not in abstraction but, supremely and definitively, in and through his death and resurrection'.

[27] Cf. Thomas D. Stegman, *The Character of Jesus: The Linchpin to Paul's Argument in 2 Corinthians* (Analecta Biblica 158; Rome: Editrice Pontificio Istituto Biblico, 2005), 218–33.

[28] By choosing just 'christosis' I am resisting the urge to add modifiers because of the diminishing marginal utility of additional terms. For example, while I highly respect Campbell's (*The Quest for Paul's Gospel* and *Deliverance*) discussion of Paul's soteriology and my own construction has an affinity to his, the acronym PPME and the phrase it represents (pneumatological participatory matyrological eschatology) is a little unwieldy due to its length. I intend that christosis will capture (roughly) the same ideas but with just one word.

[29] Another difficulty associated theosis is the issue of synergism. Western concerns about merit and grace were not an issue for Irenaeus and Cyril, but this issue repeatedly returns in modern discussions of the topic. See p. 268 below.

[30] Although I make a terminological distinction which seems similar to the division between the Christotokos and the Theotokos that served as the foundation of the fifth century Christological debates, I am explicitly not basing notions of christosis on a division between Christ's humanity and divinity.

cient for fully encompassing Pauline soteriology because he uses diverse terminology and metaphors to describe his theology. Accordingly, christosis cannot be the only term we use to describe Pauline soteriology any more than justification can, but at the same time deification and christosis would not be inadequate terminology for describing Pauline soteriology. As believers participate in the divine form of life, particularly noted as glory, through conformation to Christ and by the presence of the Spirit they become like God. Nevertheless, Paul's specific contribution is a specifically christo-telic and christo-morphic soteriology, and, thus, christosis helps sharpen the analysis of this dimension of his theology.

4. Significance and Implications

While I propose a thesis similar to that of Finlan, Litwa, and Gorman, this study advances the discussion by historically situating what we mean by deification. In particular, Paul's soteriology if it is to be characterised as deification, it must be characterised as attributive deification in distinction to essential deification. That is, believers remain ontologically separate from the divine primarily due to a distinction between the Creator and the created, but humans are ontologically changed as they share in particular divine attributes such as immortality. One primary distinction between supernatural essential deification and attributive deification is the nature of *pneuma*. With supernatural essential deification, the pneuma is the divine material in which believers come to share and by which they are constituted, as Litwa argues. In contrast, attributive deification maintains the agency of the Spirit as one who mediates the divine presence and always remains distinct from believers who nonetheless come to take on a pneumatic body.

This comprehensive reassessment of Pauline soteriology is of significance to other discussions, particularly those related to justification. Gorman's study shows this need as he attempts to redefine justification in order to make it fit squarely with his views of theosis. He reflects a larger debate between those trying to situate participation and justification in Pauline soteriology. Schweitzer and Sanders have argued that participation is primary and that justification is secondary.[31] Campbell, following their lead, removes traditional forms of justification and interprets justification solely in terms of a participatory liberation.[32] (Indeed, he sets his

---

[31] Schweitzer, *Mysticism*; E. P. Sanders, *Paul and Palestinian Judaism: A Comparison of Patterns of Religion* (Minneapolis: Fortress, 1977).

[32] Campbell, *Deliverance*.

soteriological reading in the context of theosis.[33]) On the other hand, many
are wary of confusing justification with moral transformation and therefore
treat it as merely a forensic declaration. Westerholm, for example, does
not argue against participation in his excellent study of justification but
effectively minimises its position by only giving a brief nod to Hooker's
interchange language.[34] In our reading, this is an unnecessary bifurcation
of the two, although participation does capture a larger aspect of Paul's
soteriology, in which justification plays a major role. Michael Bird's terminology of 'incorporated righteousness' rightly helps bring the two concepts together.[35]

This also heads off simplistic reactions to Eastern 'synergism'. If the
experience of the divine attributes is always dependent upon participation
in Christ through the Spirit, there is never a time when a believer creates
their own life, glory, or righteousness as if they were simply an independent agent apart from God. All these divine attributes are experienced because the gift is only accessed through participation in the Giver. As with
the assumed problem of absorption, when synergism is considered in this
wholistic context, the straw-man characterisations fall by the wayside.
Differences will and do exist in some conceptions about divine and human
agency in Paul and Eastern theology, but the idea of the human as merely
an indepedent agent is excluded from both positions.

Since my reading offers support for the importance of participation in
Paul's soteriology, it builds upon Sanders' study, but does not support his
separation of justification and participation. However, even as a strong
proponent of a participationist eschatology, Sanders confesses that he does
not have a category into which to fit Paul's language when he writes:

It seems to me best to understand Paul as saying what he meant and meaning what he
said: Christians really are one body and Spirit with Christ, the form of the present world
really is passing away, Christians really are being changed from one stage of glory to
another, the end really will come and those who are in Christ will really be transformed.
But what does this mean? How are we to understand it? We seem to lack a category of
'reality' – real participation in Christ, real possession of the Spirit – which lies between
naïve cosmological speculation and belief in magical transference on the one hand and a
revised self-understanding on the other. I must confess that I do not have a new category
of perception to propose here. This does not mean, however, that Paul did not have
one.[36]

Perhaps, then, christosis with its emphasis upon embodying the death and
life of Christ through participation in the triune divinity takes steps to-

---

[33] Ibid., 211, 265.

[34] Stephen Westerholm, *Perspectives Old and New on Paul: The 'Lutheran' Paul and
His Critics* (Grand Rapids: Eerdmans, 2004), 277–78.

[35] Bird, *Saving Righteousness*, 60–87.

[36] Sanders, *Paul and Palestinian Judaism*, 522–23.

wards providing the categories in which to understand Paul's participation-ist eschatology in which the Giver is also the gift.[37] This could be a thesis in itself, so we must leave this for further studies.

In addition to the field of Pauline soteriology, this study helps show the relevance of the history of interpretation for study of biblical texts. In particular, this study reinforces recent challenges to the hegemony of traditional historical-critical exegesis because it shows how this methodology can ignore aspects of texts which are unimportant for the Western tradition from which it arises. Gadamer and Jauss remind us that we search texts and write essays to answer modern questions. To the extent that we allow these modern questions to determine our readings, the questions and answers from the texts may be ignored. We need, as Jauss noted, something to see these master works from a fresh perspective so that we do not merely recycle interpretations handed down by our own interpretive context. Paul's language is multivalent and open to many interpretations, and other points of view offered by historical interpreters from different temporal and cultural settings offer a window onto these different views. These points of view should not limit our reading of the text any more than our current intellectual tradition should limit our readings. Rather they serve as heuristic devices to open doors to forgotten possibilities.

In our own study, we found that analysing Irenaeus and Cyril helped us to view Pauline texts freshly and to see the striking overlaps with their views of deification. This statement by Bakhtin captures how the life of this reading was not destined to be lost, but rather through the study of Paul's interpreters, we would find it again:

There is neither a first nor a last word and there are no limits to the dialogic context .... Even *past* meanings, that is, those born in the dialogue of past centuries, can never be stable (finalized, ended once and for all) – they will always change (be renewed) in the process of subsequent, future development of dialogue. At any moment in the development of the dialogue there are immense, boundless masses of forgotten contextual meanings, but at certain moments of the dialogue's subsequent development along the way they are recalled and invigorated in renewed form (in a new context). Nothing is absolutely dead: every meaning will have its homecoming festival.[38]

This reading of participation in Paul has been invigorated in a renewed form through the lens of deification in Irenaeus and Cyril.

---

[37] I would thus argue that Richard Hays' commendation of the Greek patristic writers to help understand participation in Paul's soteriology is justified: Hays, *The Faith of Jesus Christ*, xxxii.

[38] Bakhtin, 'Toward a Methodology', 170.

5. Further Study

While I have addressed certain key texts in Paul's letters, this initial study is by no means sufficient for a fully worked out Pauline soteriology with regard to deification. Obviously, the texts we only briefly covered in the excursus should gain more attention, and other theotic texts such as Eph 3.18–19 are yet to be explored. Outside the Pauline letters, numerous NT passages such as 1 John 3 also reflect the issues we have explored. In addition, 4Q Instruction also has some interesting parallels.[39]

With a balanced emphasis between the problems of condemnation and mortality in Paul's theology, the importance of resurrection – Christ's and believers' – becomes clearer, such that the sole focus should not be on Christ's death and merely on the problem of condemnation. The recent contributions by Daniel Kirk and Michael Bird are helpful in this regard, but more work can be done to explore the role of Christ's resurrection in atonement.[40] On the side of believers' experience the relationship between justification and new life/resurrection is clear in Paul's letters but gets little attention because of the emphasis upon present justification. Also, more attention has been given to the topic of glory and its important association with resurrection as of late, but renewed attention to the literary context of the individual letters and to the social and theological contexts would help move the discussion further along.

Since our study focused upon the anthropological dimension of soteriology, many questions remain unexplored regarding atonement and deification in the Pauline texts. I focused primarily on individuals, but Paul is clearly interested in the role of the church as the body of Christ. In addition, I briefly addressed the question of whether explicit affirmations about the divinity of Christ and the Spirit are necessary for the deification of the believer, but this area is ripe for further investigation in Paul's letters. Morna Hooker's work on interchange and Daniel Powers work on participation give a good basis for further study, but further work in light of deification themes would be helpful.[41] Unfortunately, both Hooker and Powers reject notions of substitution in Paul's letters, and perhaps a comparative study with Cyril, who balances cultic and participationist atonement ideas, would give further light on how these fit together in Paul's theology.

---

[39] In particular, the latter sections of 4Q417 and 4Q418 are interesting, but the background of glory and inheritance runs throughout all the texts in that group.

[40] Kirk, *Unlocking Romans*; Bird, *Saving Righteousness*, 40–59.

[41] Hooker, *From Adam*; Daniel G. Powers, *Salvation through Participation: An Examination of the Notion of the Believers' Corporate Unity with Christ in Early Christian Soteriology* (Leuven: Peeters, 2001).

We addressed the Pauline texts from the vantage point of Paul's later interpreters, but the strength of our reading must also be tested by those readings that approach Paul from a history of religions background because it is only from this perspective that the questions to which Paul was responding will become most clear. More studies like that of Byrne and Fletcher-Louis that attempt to draw together various deification themes like immortality, glory, likeness, adoption/sonship, and participation would be welcome.[42] Many studies look at these aspects individually, but more holistic accounts would better situate Paul within his historical context. At the same time, these studies would fit well with recent re-evaluations of monotheism and the place of divine or semi-divine mediatorial figures.[43] For instance, as we consider a soteriology that expects believers to be glorified and semi-divine, this has direct correlation to ancient conceptions of angelic figures.

While there is a need to test this thesis against other sources antecedent to and contemporary with Paul, there is a much greater need for more studies focusing on history of interpretation. At this moment when biblical scholars are becoming more interested in the history of interpretation, those studying patristics are focusing more upon the history of doctrine as a history of biblical interpretation. More tools and resources are also becoming available for use in both fields. For instance, the recent spate of translations of other fourth and fifth century commentaries will open doors to new areas of investigation. At the same time, other works have been virtually ignored. For example, Cyril's commentaries on Romans, 1 and 2 Corinthians have yet to be translated and have received little, if any, real attention. I hope to fill this particular lacuna myself. In addition, writings from the 'Gnostic' and Mystical traditions would provide a lens very distinct from that of Irenaeus and Cyril, and these would help sharpen the conclusions made here.

6. Final Reflections

In our goal to explore whether and to what extent theosis helpfully captures Paul's presentation of the anthropological dimension of soteriology, we held a conversation between Paul and two of his later patristic inter-

---

[42] Byrne, *'Sons'*; Crispin H.T. Fletcher-Louis, *All the Glory of Adam: Liturgical Anthropology in the Dead Sea Scrolls* (Leiden: Brill, 2002).

[43] E.g., Andrew Chester, 'Jewish Messianic Expectations and Mediatorial Figures and Pauline Christology' in *Paulus und das antike Judentum,* eds. Martin Hengel and Ulrich Heckel (Tübingen: Mohr Siebeck, 1991), 17–89; William Horbury, 'Jewish and Christian Monotheism in the Herodian Age' in *Early Jewish and Christian Monotheism,* ed. Loren T. Stuckenbruck and Wendy E.S. North (London: T&T Clark), 16–44, at 31–40.

preters. These later interpreters were not seen as a series of misreadings of Paul and developments away from him but as an aid to better understanding of his texts. Indeed, the questions raised by the patristic use of texts like these have opened our eyes to fresh ways of seeing Pauline themes. Because of the significant parallels with Irenaeus' and Cyril's views of deification, we determined that deification is an apt description of the anthropological dimension of Paul's soteriology. However, christosis serves as a better description because believers are formed into Christ's image in death and life through a participatory triune divine encounter. Accordingly, believers are adopted as sons of God and experience immortal glory like Christ through the Spirit.

While this study is primarily focused on ancient texts, its relevance to current theological and ecumenical discussions is obvious. Further conversations between Eastern and Western theologians are increasingly welcome, and, hopefully, this study will stimulate further discussion, showing that the Pauline texts are patient of readings from both traditions.

Bibliography

Primary Sources

Cyril of Alexandria. *A Commentary Upon the Gospel According to St. Luke by St. Cyril.* Translated by R. Payne Smith. 2 vols. Oxford: Oxford University Press, 1859.

–. *Commentary on the Gospel According to St. John (I–VIII).* Translated by P.E. Pusey. Library of the Fathers of the Church 43. Oxford: James Parker, 1874.

–. *Commentary on the Gospel According to St. John (IX–XXI).* Translated by T. Randell. Library of the Fathers of the Church 48. Oxford: Walter Smith, 1885.

–. *Deux Dialogues Christologiques.* Translated by G.M. de Durand. SC 97. Edited by G.M. de Durand. Paris: Cerf, 1964.

–. *Lettres Festales, 1–6.* Edited and Translated by P. Évieux. SC 372. Paris: Cerf, 1991.

–. *On the Unity of Christ.* Translated by John McGuckin. Crestwood, NY: St. Vladimir's Seminary Press, 1995.

–. *Sancti Patris Nostri Cyrilli Archiepiscopi Alexandrini in D. Joannis Evangelium.* 3 vols. Edited by P.E. Pusey. Bruxelles: Culture et Civilisation, 1965 [1872].

Irenaeus. "Against Heresies, Books 1–5 and Fragments." Pages in *The Ante-Nicene Fathers. Vol. 1, The Apostolic Fathers with Justin Martyr and Irenaeus.* Edinburgh: T&T Clark, 1885–1887.

–. *Against Heresies: On the Detection and Refutation of the Knowledge Falsely So Called.* Translated by Robert McQueen Grant. New York: Routledge, 1997.

–. *Contre les hérésies, Livre I.* Edited by A. Rousseau and L. Doutreleau. 2 vols., SC 263, 264. Paris: Cerf, 1979.

–. *Contre les hérésies, Livre II.* Edited by A. Rousseau and L. Doutreleau. 2 vols., SC 293, 294. Paris: Cerf, 1982.

–. *Contre les hérésies, Livre III.* Edited by A. Rousseau and L. Doutreleau. 2 vols., SC 210, 211. Paris: Cerf, 1974.

–. *Contre les hérésies, Livre IV.* Edited by A. Rousseau. 2 vols., SC 100.1, 100.2. Paris: Cerf, 1965.

–. *Contre les hérésies, Livre V.* Edited by A. Rousseau, L. Doutreleau, and C. Mercier. 2 vols., SC 152, 153. Paris: Cerf, 1969.

–. *On the Apostolic Preaching.* Translated by John Behr. Crestwood, NY: St. Vladimir's Seminary Press, 1997.

Gregory of Nyssa. *The Life of Moses.* Translated by Abraham J. Malherbe and Everett Ferguson. New York: Paulist, 1978.

Pseudo Dionysius. *The Complete Works.* Translated by Colm Luibheid. Classics of Western Spirituality. New York: Paulist, 1987.

Secondary Sources

Aasgaard, Reidar. *'My Beloved Brothers and Sisters!':* *Christian Siblingship in Paul.* JSNTSup 265. London: T&T Clark, 2004.

Abineau, Michael. 'Incorruptibilité et Divinisation selon Saint Irénée'. *RSR* 44 (1956): 25–52.

Adams, Edward. *Constructing the World: A Study in Paul's Cosmological Language.* Studies in the New Testament and Its World. Edinburgh: T&T Clark, 2000.

–. 'Paul's Story of God and Creation: The Story of How God Fulfils His Purposes in Creation', Pages 19–43 in *Narrative Dynamics in Paul: A Critical Assessment.* Edited by Bruce W. Longenecker. London: Westminster John Knox, 2002.

Aletti, Jean-Noël. 'Romans 8: The Incarnation and its Redemptive Impact', Pages 93–115 in *The Incarnation: An Interdisciplinary Symposium on the Incarnation of the Son of God.* Edited by Stephen Davis, Daniel Kendall, and Gerald O'Collins. Oxford: Oxford University Press, 2002.

Allenbach, Jean. *Des origines à Clément d'Alexandrie et Turtullien.* Vol. 1, BiPa. CNRS, 1975–.

Anatolios, Khaled. 'The Influence of Irenaeus on Athanasius', Pages 463–76 in *Studia Patristica: XXXVI.* Edited by M.F. Wiles and E.J. Yarnold. Leuven: Peeters, 2001.

Angstenberger, Pius. *Der reiche und der arme Christus: Die Rezeptionsgeschichte von 2 Kor 8,9 zwischen dem 2. und 6. Jahrhundert.* Bonn: Borengässer, 1997.

Aulén, Gustaf. *Christus Victor: An Historical Study of the Three Main Types of the Idea of the Atonement.* Translated by A.G. Hebert. London: SPCK, 1931.

Aune, David E. 'Anthropological Duality in the Eschatology of 2 Cor 4:16–5:10', Pages 215–239 in *Paul Beyond the Judaism/Hellenism Divide.* Edited by Troels Engberg-Pedersen, Louisville: Westminster John Knox Press, 2001.

Ayres, Lewis. *Nicaea and Its Legacy: An Approach to Fourth-Century Trinitarian Theology.* Oxford: Oxford University Press, 2006.

Back, Frances. *Verwandlung durch Offenbarung bei Paulus: Eine religionsgeschichtlich-exegetische Untersuchung zu 2 Kor 2,14–4,6.* WUNT 2/153. Tübingen: Mohr Siebeck, 2002.

Bakhtin, Mikhail M. 'Response to a Question from the *Novy Mir* Editorial Staff', Pages 1–9 in *Speech Genres and Other Late Essays.* Edited by Caryl Emerson and Michael Holquist. Translated by Vern W. McGee. Austin: University of Texas Press, 1986.

–. 'Toward a Methodology for the Human Sciences', Pages 159–72 in *Speech Genres and Other Late Essays.* Edited by Caryl Emerson and Michael Holquist. Translated by Vern W. McGee. Austin: University of Texas Press, 1986.

Balás, David L. 'The Use and Interpretation of Paul in Irenaeus's Five Books *Adversus haereses*'. *SecCent* 9 (1992): 27–39.

Balz, Horst R. *Heilsvertrauen und Welterfahrung: Strukturen der paulinischen Eschatologie nach Römer 8,18–39.* München: Chr. Kaiser, 1971.

Bammel, E. 'Gottes ΔIAΘHKH (Gal. III.15–17) und das jüdische Rechtsdenken'. *NTS* 6 (1959–60): 313–19.

Barclay, John M.G. *Colossians and Philemon.* London: T&T Clark, 2004.

–. *Obeying the Truth: Paul's Ethics in Galatians.* Edinburgh: T&T Clark, 1988.

Barnett, Paul. *The Second Episitle to the Corinthians.* NICNT. Grand Rapids: Eerdmans, 1997.

Barr, James. *The Semantics of Biblical Language.* London: Oxford University Press, 1961.

Barrett, C.K. *The First Epistle to the Corinthians.* 2nd ed., BNTC. London: A & C Black, 1971.

–. *The Second Epistle to the Corinthians.* BNTC. London: A & C Black, 1973.

Barth, Karl. 'The Preface to the Second Edition', in *The Epistle to the Romans.* Translated by Edwyn C. Hoskyns. London: Oxford University Press, 1933.

Bash, Anthony. *Ambassadors for Christ.* WUNT 2/92. Tübingen: Mohr Siebeck, 1997.

Behr, John. *Asceticism and Anthropology in Irenaeus and Clement.* Oxford: Oxford University Press, 2000.

Beker, J. Christiaan. 'Suffering and Triumph in Paul's Letter to the Romans'. *HBT* 7 (1985): 105–119.

Belleville, Linda L. *Reflections of Glory: Paul's Polemical Use of the Moses-Doxa Tradition in 2 Corinthians 3.1–18.* JSNTSup 52. Sheffield: JSOT Press, 1991.

–. 'Paul's Polemic and Theology of the Spirit in Second Corinthians'. *CBQ* 58 (1996): 281–304.

Bermejo, A.M. *The Indwelling of the Holy Spirit according to Cyril of Alexandria.* Ona: Facultad de Teologia, 1963.

Bertone, John A. *"The Law of the Spirit": Experience of the Spirit and Displacement of the Law in Romans 8:1–16.* Studies in Biblical Literature 86. Berlin: Peter Lang, 2005.

Best, Ernest. *One Body in Christ.* London: SPCK, 1955.

Betz, Hans Dieter. 'The Concept of the 'Inner Human Being' (ὁ ἔσω ἄνθρωπος) in the Anthropology of Paul'. *NTS* 46 (2000): 315–41.

Bieringer, Reimund. 'Sünde und Gerechtigkeit in 2 Korinther 5,21', Pages 461–514 in *Studies on 2 Corinthians.* Edited by Reimund Bieringer and Jan Lambrecht. Leuven: Leuven University Press, 1994.

Bilaniuk, Petro B.T. 'The Mystery of Theosis or Divinization', Pages 337–359 in *The Heritage of the Early Church.* Edited by David Neiman and Margaret Schatkin. Orientalia Christiana Analecta 195. Rome: Pont. Institutum Studiorum Orientalium, 1973.

Bindemann, Walther. *Die Hoffnung der Schöpfung: Römer 8,18–27 und die Frage einer Theologie der Befreiung von Mensch und Natur.* Neukirchen-Vluyn: Neukirchener, 1983.

Bird, Michael F. *The Saving Righteousness of God: Studies on Paul, Justification and the New Perspective.* Paternoster Biblical Monographs. Milton Keynes, UK: Paternoster, 2007.

Black, C. Clifton. 'Pauline Perspectives on Death in Romans 5–8'. *JBL* 103 (1984): 413–433.

Blackwell, Ben C. 'Immortal Glory and the Problem of Death in Romans 3:23'. *JSNT* 32 (2010): 285–308.

–. 'Paul and Irenaeus', Pages 190–206 in *Paul in the Second Century.* Edited by Michael F. Bird and Joseph R. Dodson. LNTS 412. London: T&T Clark, 2011.

Blanchette, O. 'Saint Cyril of Alexandria's Idea of the Redemption'. *ScEccl* 16 (1964): 455–480.

Bockmuehl, Markus. 'A Commentator's Approach to the "Effective History" of Philippians'. *JSNT* 60 (1995): 57–88.

–. *Seeing the Word: Refocusing New Testament Study.* Studies in Theological Interpretation. Grand Rapids: Baker, 2006.

–. *The Epistle to the Philippians.* BNTC. London: A & C Black, 1997.

Boersma, Hans. 'Accommodation to What? Univocity of Being, Pure Nature, and the Anthropology of St Irenaeus'. *IJST* 8 (2006): 266–93.

Bogdasavich, M. 'The Idea of Pleroma in the Epistles to the Colossians and Ephesians', *The Downside Review* 83 (1965): 118–30.

Bolt, John. 'The Relation Between Creation and Redemption in Romans 8:18–27'. *CTJ* 30 (1995): 34–51.

Boulnois, Marie-Odile. 'Le souffle et l'Esprit: Exégèses patristiques de l'insufflation originelle de Gen. 2,7 en lien avec celle de *Jn* 20,22'. *RechAug* 24 (1989): 3–37.

–. *Le Paradoxe trinitaire chez Cyrille d'Alexandrie.* Paris: Institut d'Études Augustiniennes, 1994.

Bousset, Wilhelm. *Kyrios Christos.* Translated by John E. Seely. Nashville: Abingdon, 1970.

Bouteneff, Peter. 'Christ and Salvation', Pages 93–106 in *The Cambridge Companion to Orthodox Christian Theology.* Edited by Mary Cunningham and Elizabeth Theokritoff. Cambridge: Cambridge University Press, 2008.

Branick, Vincent. 'The Sinful Flesh of the Son of God (Rom 8:3): A Key Image of Pauline Theology'. *CBQ* 47 (1985): 246–62.

Briones, David. 'Mutual Brokers of Grace: A Study in 2 Corinthians 1.3–11'. *NTS* 56 (2010): 536–56.

Bultmann, Rudolf. *Theology of the New Testament.* Translated by Kendrick Grobel. 2 vols. London: SCM, 1952.

–. 'ΔΙΚΑΙΟΣΥΝΗ ΘΕΟΥ'. *JBL* 83 (1964): 12–16.

–. 'Is Exegesis Without Presuppositions Possible?', Pages 145–53 in *New Testament and Mythology and Other Basic Theological Writings.* Edited by Schubert M. Ogden. Translated by Schubert M. Ogden. Philadelphia: Fortress, 1984.

–. *The Second Letter to the Corinthians.* Translated by Roy A. Harrisville. Minneapolis: Augsburg, 1985.

Burghardt, Walter J. *The Image of God in Man According to Cyril of Alexandria.* Washington: Catholic University of America Press, 1957.

Burke, Trevor. *Adopted into God's Family: Exploring a Pauline Metaphor.* NSBT 22. Downers Grove: Intervarsity, 2006.

Byrne, Brendan. *'Sons of God' – 'Seed of Abraham'.* AnBib 83. Rome: Biblical Institute Press, 1979.

–. *Romans.* SP 6. Collegeville, MN: Liturgical Press, 1996.

–. 'Christ's Pre-Existence in Pauline Soteriology'. *TS* 58 (1997): 308–30.

Cairns, David. *The Image of God in Man.* London: SCM, 1953.

Campbell, Douglas A. 'The Story of Jesus in Romans and Galatians', Pages 97–124 in *Narrative Dynamics in Paul: A Critical Assessment.* Edited by Bruce W. Longenecker. London: Westminster John Knox, 2002.

–. *The Deliverance of God: An Apocalyptic Rereading of Justification in Paul.* Grand Rapids: Eerdmans, 2009.

–. *The Quest for Paul's Gospel: A Suggested Strategy.* JSNTSup 274. London: T&T Clark, 2005.

Canlis, Julie. 'Being Made Human: The Significance of Creation for Irenaeus' Doctrine of Participation'. *SJT* 58 (2005): 434–54.

Carrez, Maurice. *De la Souffrance à la Gloire: De la Δοξα dans la Pensée paulienne.* Neuchâtel: Delachaux & Niestlé, 1964.

Chadwick, Henry. 'Eucharist and Christology in the Nestorian Controversy'. *JTS* 2 (1951): 145–64.

Chester, Andrew. 'Jewish Messianic Expectations and Mediatorial Figures and Pauline Christology', Pages 17–89 in *Paulus und das antike Judentum.* Edited by Martin Hengel and Ulrich Heckel. WUNT 58. Tübingen: Mohr Siebeck, 1991.

–. 'Resurrection and Transformation', Pages 47–77 in *Auferstehung – Resurrection: The Fourth Durham-Tübingen Research Symposium: Resurrection, Transfiguration and Exaltation in Old Testament, Ancient Judaism and Early Christianity.* Edited by Friedrich Avemarie and Hermann Lichtenberger. WUNT 135. Tübingen: Mohr Siebeck, 2001.

Choufrine, Arkadi. *Gnosis, Theophany, Theosis: Studies in Clement of Alexandria's Appropriation of his Background.* Patristic Studies 5. New York: Peter Lang, 2002.

Collange, J.-F. *Énigmes de la deuxième épître de Paul aux Corinthiens: Etude exégétique de 2 Cor. 2:14–7:4.* SNTSMS 18. Cambridge: Cambridge University Press, 1972.

Cranfield, C.E.B. *Romans.* 2 vols., ICC. Edinburgh: T&T Clark, 1975.

–. 'Some Comments on Professor J.D.G. Dunn's *Christology in the Making*', Pages 267–80 in *The Glory of Christ in the New Testament: Studies in Christology.* Edited by L.D. Hurst and N.T. Wright. Oxford: Clarendon, 1987.

Danker, Frederick W. 'Exegesis of 2 Corinthians 5:14–21', Pages 105–126 in *Interpreting 2 Corinthians 5:14–21.* Edited by Jack P. Lewis. Lampeter: Edwin Mellen, 1989.

Dassmann, Ernst. *Der Stachel im Fleisch: Paulus in der frühchristlichen Literatur bis Irenäus.* Münster: Aschendorff, 1979.

Davis, Ellen F. and Richard B. Hays, eds. 'Nine Theses on the Interpretation of Scripture', Pages 1–8 in *The Art of Reading Scripture.* Grand Rapids: Eerdmans, 2003.

de Andia, Ysabel. *Homo vivens: incorruptibilité et divinisation de l'homme selon Irénée de Lyon.* Paris: Études Augustiniennes, 1986.

de Durand, G.M. *Cyrille d'Alexandrie: Deux Dialogues Christologiques.* SC 97. Paris: Cerf, 1964.

Donfried, Karl P. *The Romans Debate.* rev. and exp. ed. Peabody, MA: Hendrickson, 1991.

Donovan, Mary Ann. 'Alive to the Glory of God: A Key Insight in St Irenaeus'. *TS* 49 (1988): 283–97.

Duff, Paul B. 'Transformed 'from Glory to Glory': Paul's Appeal to the Experience of His Readers in 2 Corinthians 3:18'. *JBL* 127 (2008): 759–780.

Dunn, James D.G. '2 Corinthians 3.17 – 'The Lord is the Spirit''. *JTSns* 21 (1970): 309–20.

–. 'Adam in Paul', Pages 120–135 in *The Pseudepigrapha and Christian Origins.* Edited by Gerbern S. Oegema and James H. Charlesworth. London: T&T Clark, 2008.

–. 'Christ, Adam, and Preexistence', Pages 74–83 in *Where Christology Began: Essays on Philippians 2.* Edited by Ralph P. Martin and B.J. Dodd. Louisville: Westminster John Knox, 1998.

–. *Christology in the Making.* 2nd ed. London: SCM, 1989.

–. 'Jesus the Judge: Further Thoughts on Paul's Christology and Soteriology', Pages 34–54 in *Convergence of Theology*, eds. Daniel Kendall and Stephen T. Davis. New York: Paulist, 2001.

–. 'Paul's Understanding of the Death of Jesus', Pages 35–56 in *Sacrifice and Redemption: Durham Essays in Theology.* Edited by S.W. Sykes. Cambridge: Cambridge University Press, 1991.

–. *Romans.* 2 vols., WBC 38A–B. Dallas: Word, 1988.

–. *The Epistles to the Colossians and to Philemon.* NIGTC. Grand Rapids: Eerdmans, 1996.

Dupont, Jacques. 'Le Chrétien, Miroir de la Gloire divine d'après II Cor. III,18'. *RB* 56 (1949): 392–411.

Eastman, Susan. 'Whose Apocalypse? The Identity of the Sons of God in Romans 8.19'. *JBL* 121 (2002): 263–77.

Ellis, E. Earle. '2 Corinthians 5:1–10 in Pauline Eschatology'. *NTS* 6 (1960): 211–224.

Engberg-Pedersen, Troels. *Cosmology and Self in the Apostle Paul: The Material Spirit.* Oxford: Oxford University Press, 2010.

–. *Paul and the Stoics.* Edinburgh: T&T Clark, 2000.

–. 'The Material Spirit: Cosmology and Ethics in Paul'. *NTS* 55 (2009): 179–97.

Evans, C.F. *Resurrection and the New Testament.* London: SCM, 1970.

Fairbairn, Donald. *Eastern Orthodoxy Through Western Eyes.* Louisville: Westminster John Knox, 2002.

–. *Grace and Christology in the Early Church.* Oxford: Oxford University Press, 2003.

–. 'Patristic Exegesis and Theology: The Cart and the Horse', *WTJ* 69 (2007): 1-19.

–. 'Patristic Soteriology: Three Trajectories'. *JETS* 50 (2007): 289–310.

Fantino, Jacques. *L'homme image de Dieu: Chez Saint Irenée de Lyon.* Paris: Cerf, 1986.

Farag, Lois M. *St. Cyril of Alexandria, A New Testament Exegete: His Commentary on the Gospel of John.* Gorgias Dissertations 29. Piscataway, NJ: Gorgias, 2007.

Fatehi, Mehrdad. *The Spirit's Relation to the Risen Lord in Paul.* WUNT 2/128. Tübingen: Mohr Siebeck, 2000.

Fay, Ron C. 'Was Paul a Trinitarian? A Look at Romans 8', Pages 327–345 in *Paul and His Theology.* Edited by Stanley E. Porter. Pauline Studies 3. Leiden: Brill, 2006.

Fee, Gordon D. *God's Empowering Presence: The Holy Spirit in the Letters of Paul.* Peabody, MA: Hendrickson, 1994.

–. *Pauline Christology: An Exegetical-Theological Study.* Peabody, MA: Hendrickson, 2007.

–. *Paul's Letter to the Philippians.* NICNT. Grand Rapids: Eerdmans, 1995.

Feuillet, André. 'Les attaches bibliques des antithèses pauliniennes dans la première partie de l'Épître aux Romains (1–8)', Pages 323–49 in *Mélanges Bibliques.* Edited by Albert Descamps and André de Halleux. Gembloux: Duculot, 1970.

Finch, Jeffrey. 'Irenaeus on the Christological Basis of Human Divinization', Pages 86–103 in *Theosis: Deification in Christian Theology.* Edited by Stephen Finlan and Vladimir Kharlamov. PTMS. Eugene, OR: Pickwick, 2006.

Finlan, Stephen. 'Second Peter's Notion of Divine Participation', Pages 32–50 in *Theosis: Deification in Christian Theology.* Edited by Stephen Finlan and Vladimir Kharlamov. PTMS. Eugene, OR: Pickwick, 2006.

–. 'Can We Speak of *Theosis* in Paul?', Pages 68–80 in *Partakers of the Divine Nature: The History and Development of Deification in the Christian Traditions.* Edited by Michael J. Christensen and Jeffery A. Wittung. Grand Rapids: Baker, 2008.

Fitzgerald, John T. *Cracks in an Earthen Vessel: An Examination of the Catalogues of Hardships in the Corinthian Correspondence.* SBLDS. Atlanta: Scholars, 1988.

Fitzmyer, Joseph A. '"To Know Him and the Power of His Resurrection" (Phil 3.10)', Pages 411–25 in *Mélanges Bibliques.* Edited by Albert Descamps and André de Halleux. Gembloux: Ducolot, 1970.

Fletcher-Louis, Crispin H.T. *All the Glory of Adam: Liturgical Anthropology in the Dead Sea Scrolls.* Leiden: Brill, 2002.

Fowl, Stephen. *Engaging Scripture.* Oxford: Blackwell, 1998.

Friesen, Steven J. *Twice Neokoros: Ephesus, Asia and the Cult of the Flavian Imperial Family.* Leiden: Brill, 1993.

Furnish, Victor Paul. *II Corinthians.* AB 32A. New York: Doubleday, 1984.

Gadamer, Hans-Georg. *Wahrheit und Methode: Grundzüge einer philosophischen Hermeneutik.* 2nd ed. Tübingen: JCB Mohr, 1975.

–. *Truth and Method.* Translated by J. Weinsheimer and D.G. Marshall. 2nd rev ed. London: Sheed & Ward, 1989.

Gebremedhin, Ezra. *Life-Giving Blessing: An Inquiry into the Eucharistic Doctrine of Cyril of Alexandria.* Uppsala: Borgströms, 1977.

Geerard, M. and F. Glorie, eds. *Clavis Patrum Graecorum.* Turnhout: Brepols, 1979.

Georgi, Dieter. *The Opponents of Paul in Second Corinthians.* Philadelphia: Fortress, 1986.

Gibbs, John G. *Creation and Redemption: A Study in Pauline Theology.* NovTSup 26. Leiden: Brill, 1971.

Gieniusz, Andrzej. *Romans 8:18–30: "Suffering Does Not Thwart the Future Glory".* Atlanta: Scholars Press, 1999.

Gignilliat, Mark. 'A Servant Follower of the Servant: Paul's Eschatological Reading of Isaiah 40–66 in 2 Corinthians 5:14–6:10'. *HBT* 26 (2004): 98–124.

Gorman, Michael J. *Cruciformity: Paul's Narrative Spirituality of the Cross.* Grand Rapids: Eerdmans, 2001.

–. *Inhabiting the Cruciform God: Kenosis, Justification, and Theosis in Paul's Narrative Soteriology.* Grand Rapids: Eerdmans, 2009.

–. 'Romans: The First Christian Treatise on Theosis', *JTI* 5 (2011):13–34.

Gradel, Ittai. *Emperor Worship and Roman Religion.* Oxford: OUP, 2002.

Grant, R.M. *Gnosticism: An Anthology.* London: Collins, 1961.

Grieb, A. Katherine. 'So That in Him We Might Become the "Righteousness of God" (2 Cor 5:21): Some Theological Reflections on the Church Becoming Justice'. *ExAud* 22 (2006): 58–80.

Grillmeier, Aloys. *Christ in Christian Tradition.* Translated by John Bowden. 2nd rev. ed. London: Mowbrays, 1975.

Gross, Jules. *The Divinization of the Christian According to the Greek Fathers.* Translated by Paul A. Onica. Anaheim: A&C Press, 2002.

Gundry, Robert H. *Sōma in Biblical Theology: With Emphasis on Pauline Theology.* Cambridge: Cambridge University Press, 1976.

Güttgemanns, Erhardt. *Der leidende Apostel und sein Herr.* FRLANT 90. Göttingen: Vandenhoeck & Ruprecht, 1966.

Habets, Myk. '"Reformed Theosis?": A Response to Gannon Murphy', *Theology Today* 65 (2009): 489-498.

Hafemann, Scott J. *Paul, Moses, and the History of Israel: The Letter/Spirit Contrast and the Argument from Scripture in 2 Corinthians 3.* Peabody, MA: Hendrickson, 1996.

Hahne, Harry Alan. *The Corruption and Redemption of Creation: Nature in Romans 8.19–22 and Jewish Apocalyptic Literature.* LNTS 336. London: T&T Clark, 2006.

Hallonsten, Gösta. '*Theosis* in Recent Research: A Renewal of Interest and a Need for Clarity', Pages 281–93 in *Partakers of the Divine Nature: The History and Development of Deification in the Christian Traditions.* Edited by Michael J. Christensen and Jeffery A. Wittung. Grand Rapids: Baker, 2008.

Harnack, Adolf. *History of Dogma.* Translated by Neil Buchanan. 7 vols. New York: Dover, 1961.

Harris, Murray J. *The Second Episitle of Paul to the Corinthians.* NIGTC. Grand Rapids: Eerdmans, 2005.

Hart, Trevor A. 'Irenaeus, Recapitulation and Physical Redemption', Pages 152–181 in *Christ in Our Place.* Edited by Trevor A. Hart and Daniel P. Thimell. Allison Park: Pickwick, 1989.

Harvey, A.E. *Renewal Through Suffering: A Study of 2 Corinthians.* Edinburgh: T&T Clark, 1996.

Hawthorne, Gerald F. and Ralph P. Martin. *Philippians*. WBC 43. Nashville: Thomas Nelson, 2004.

Hay, David M. 'All the Fullness of God: Concepts of Deity in Colossians and Ephesians', Pages 163–79 in *The Forgotten God: Perspectives in Biblical Theology*. Edited by A. Andrew Das and Frank J. Matera. Louisville: WJK, 2002.

–. *Colossians*. ANTC. Nashville: Abingdon, 2000.

Hays, Richard B. *Echoes of Scripture in the Letters of Paul*. New Haven: Yale University Press, 1989.

–. *First Corinthians*. Interpretation. Louisville: John Knox, 1997.

–. *The Faith of Jesus Christ: The Narrative Substructure of Galatians 3:1–4:11*. 2nd ed. Grand Rapids: Eerdmans, 2002.

–. 'The God of Mercy Who Rescues Us from the Present Evil Age: Romans and Galatians', Pages 123–143 in *The Forgotten God: Perspectives in Biblical Theology*. Edited by A. Andrew Das and Frank J. Matera. Louisville: Westminster John Knox, 2002.

Hester, James C. *Paul's Concept of Inheritance: A Contribution to the Understanding of Heilsgeschichte*. Edinburgh: Oliver & Boyd, 1968.

Hodgson, Robert. 'Paul the Apostle and First Century Tribulation Lists'. *ZNW* 74 (1983): 59–80.

Hooker, Morna D. 'Chalcedon and the New Testament', Pages 73–93 in *The Making and Remaking of Christian Doctrine: Essays in Honour of Maurice Wiles*. Edited by Sarah Coakley and David A. Pailin. Oxford: Clarendon Press, 1993.

–. 'Beyond Things That Are Written? St Paul's Use of Scripture', Pages 139–154 in *From Adam to Christ*. Eugene, OR: Wipf & Stock, 2008.

–. *From Adam to Christ*. Eugene, OR: Wipf & Stock, 2008.

–. 'Interchange and Atonement', Pages 26–41 in *From Adam to Christ*. Eugene, OR: Wipf & Stock, 2008.

–. 'Interchange in Christ', Pages 13–25 in *From Adam to Christ*. Eugene, OR: Wipf & Stock, 2008.

–. 'On Becoming the Righteousness of God: Another Look at 2 Cor 5:21'. *NovT* 50 (2008): 358–75.

Horbury, William. 'Jewish and Christian Monotheism in the Herodian Age', Pages 16–44 in *Early Jewish and Christian Monotheism*. Edited by Loren T. Stuckenbruck and Wendy E.S. North. London: T&T Clark.

Horn, Friedrich Wilhelm. *Das Angeld des Geistes: Studien zur paulinischen Pneumatologie*. Göttingen: Vandenhoeck & Ruprecht, 1992.

Hubbard, Moyer V. *New Creation in Paul's Letters and Thought*. SNTSMS 119. Cambridge: Cambridge University Press, 2002.

Hugedé, Norbert. *La métaphore du miroir dans les Epîtres de saint Paul aux Corinthiens*. Neuchatel: Delachaux et Niestlé, 1957.

Hurtado, Larry W. *Lord Jesus Christ: Devotion to Jesus in Earliest Christianity*. Grand Rapids: Eerdmans, 2003.

Janssens, L. 'Notre Filiation divine d'après Saint Cyrille d'Alexandrie'. *ETL* 15 (1938): 233–78.

Jauss, Hans Robert. 'Goethe's and Valéry's *Faust*: On the Hermeneutics of Question and Answer', Pages 110–38 in *Toward an Aesthetic of Reception*. Translated by Timothy Bahti. Minneapolis: University of Minnesota Press, 1982.

–. 'Horizon Structure and Dialogicity', Pages 197–231 in *Question and Answer: Forms of Dialogic Understanding*. Translated by Michael Hays. Minneapolis: University of Minnesota Press, 1989.

–. 'Literary History as a Challenge to Literary Theory', Pages 3–45 in *Toward an Aesthetic of Reception*. Translated by Timothy Bahti. Minneapolis: Univ of Minnesota Press, 1982.

Jervell, Jacob. *Imago Dei: Gen. 1.26f. im Spätjudentum, in der Gnosis und in den paulinischen Briefen*. Göttingen: Vandenhoeck & Ruprecht, 1960.

Jervis, L. Ann. *At the Heart of the Gospel: Suffering in the Earliest Christian Message*. Cambridge: Eerdmans, 2007.

Jewett, Robert. *Paul's Anthropological Terms: A Study of Their Use in Conflict Settings*. Leiden: Brill, 1971.

–. *Romans: A Commentary*. Hermeneia. Minneapolis: Fortress, 2007.

Kärkkäinen, Veli-Matti. *One with God: Salvation as Deification and Justification*. Collegeville, MN: Liturgical Press, 2004.

Käsemann, Ernst. *Commentary on Romans*. Translated by Geoffrey William Bromiley. Grand Rapids: Eerdmans, 1980.

–. 'On Paul's Anthropology', Pages 1–31 in *Perspectives on Paul*. London: SCM, 1971.

–. 'The Cry for Liberty in the Worship of the Church', Pages 122–37 in *Perspectives on Paul*. London: SCM, 1971.

–. 'The "Righteousness of God" in Paul', Pages 168–82 in *New Testament Questions of Today*. Translated by W. J. Montague. Philadelphia: Fortress, 1979.

–. 'The Saving Significance of the Death of Jesus in Paul', Pages 32–59 in *Perspectives on Paul*. London: SCM, 1971.

Kaufman, John. 'Becoming Divine, Becoming Human: Deification Themes in Irenaeus of Lyons'. Ph.D. diss., MF Norwegian School of Theology, 2009.

Keating, Daniel A. 'The Baptism of Jesus in Cyril of Alexandria: The Re-creation of the Human Race'. *ProEccl* 8 (1999): 201–22.

–. *The Appropriation of Divine Life in Cyril of Alexandria*. Oxford: Oxford University Press, 2004.

–. *Deification and Grace*. Naples, FL: Sapientia, 2007.

Keck, Leander E. 'The Law And 'The Law of Sin and Death' (Romans 8:1–4): Reflections on the Spirit and Ethics in Paul', Pages 41–57 in *The Divine Helmsman: Studies on God's Control of Human Events, Presented to Lou H. Silberman*. Edited by J.L. Crenshaw and S. Sandmel. New York: KTAV, 1980.

Keesmaat, Sylvia. *Paul and His Story: (Re)Interpreting the Exodus Tradition*. JSNTSup 181. Sheffield: Sheffield Academic, 1999.

Kehnscherper, Günter. 'Romans 8:19 – On Pauline Belief and Creation', Pages 233–243 in *Studia Biblica 1978*. Edited by E. Livingstone. JSNTSup 3. Sheffield: JSOT Press, 1978.

Kim, Seyoon. *The Origin of Paul's Gospel*. Grand Rapids: Eerdmans, 1982.

Kirk, J.R. Daniel. 'Reconsidering *Dikaiōma* in Romans 5:16'. *JBL* 126 (2007): 787–92.

–. *Unlocking Romans: Resurrection and the Justification of God*. Grand Rapids: Eerdmans, 2008.

Knox, John. *Life in Christ Jesus: Reflections on Romans 5–8*. New York: Seabury, 1961.

Koch, Klaus. *The Rediscovery of Apocalyptic*. Translated by M. Kohl. London: SCM, 1972.

Koen, Lars. *The Saving Passion: Incarnational and Soteriological Thought in Cyril of Alexandria's Commentary on the Gospel according to John*. Uppsala: Graphic Systems, 1991.

Kruse, Colin G. 'Paul, the Law, and the Spirit', Pages 109–130 in *Paul and His Theology*. Edited by Stanley E. Porter. Pauline Studies 3. Leiden: Brill, 2006.

Kuss, Otto. *Der Römerbrief*. 3 vols. Regensburg: F. Pustet, 1963–1978.

Lambrecht, Jan. 'Transformation in 2 Cor 3:18'. *Bib* 64 (1983): 243–254.

–. 'The Nekrōsis of Jesus: Ministry and Suffering in 2 Cor 4,7–15', Pages 120–143 in *L'Apôtre Paul*. Edited by A. Vanhoye. Leuven: Leuven University, 1986.

–. *Second Corinthians*. SP 8. Collegeville, MN: Liturgical, 1999.

Langevin, G. 'La Thème de l'Incorruptibilité dans le Commentaire de Saint Cyrille d'Alexandrie sur l'Evangile Selon Saint Jean'. *ScEccl* 8 (1956): 295–316.

Levison, John R. *Portraits of Adam in Early Judaism: From Sirach to 2 Baruch*. JSPSup 1. Sheffield: JSOT Press, 1988.

Lewis, Jack P. 'Exegesis of 2 Corinthians 5:14–21', Pages 129–41 in *Interpreting 2 Corinthians 5:14–21: An Exercise in Hermeneutics*. Edited by Jack P. Lewis. Lampeter: Edwin Mellen, 1989.

Lincoln, Andrew T. *Paradise Now and Not Yet: Studies in the Role of the Heavenly Dimension in Paul's Thought with Special Reference to His Eschatology*. SNTSMS 43. Cambridge: Cambridge University Press, 1991.

Lindbeck, George. *The Nature of Doctrine: Religion and Theology in a Postliberal Age*. London: SPCK, 1984.

Lindemann, Andreas. *Paulus im ältesten Christentum: Das Bild des Apostels und die Rezeption der paulinischen Theologie in der frühchristlichen Literatur bis Marcion*. BHT 58. Tübingen: Mohr Siebeck, 1979.

Lindgård, Fredrik. *Paul's Line of Thought in 2 Corinthians 4:16–5:10*. WUNT 2/189. Tübingen: Mohr Siebeck, 2005.

Litwa, M. David. '2 Corinthians 3:18 and Its Implications for *Theosis*'. *JTI* 2 (2008): 117–133.

Loewe, William P. 'Irenaeus' Soteriology: *Christus Victor* Revisited'. *AThR* 67 (1985): 1–15.

Longenecker, Richard. *Galatians*. WBC 41. Waco: Word, 1990.

Lorenzen, Stefanie. *Das paulinische Eikon-Konzept: Semantische Analysen zur Sapientia Salomonis, zu Philo und den Paulusbriefen*. WUNT 2/250. Tübingen: Mohr Siebeck, 2008.

Lot-Borodine, Myrrha. *La déification de l'homme: selon la doctrine des Pères grecs*. Cerf: Paris, 1970.

Louth, Andrew. *Discerning the Mystery: An Essay on the Nature of Theology* Oxford: Oxford University Press, 1983.

–. 'The Place of *Theosis* in Orthodox Theology', Pages 32–44 in *Partakers of the Divine Nature: The History and Development of Deification in the Christian Traditions*. Edited by Michael J. Christensen and Jeffery A. Wittung. Grand Rapids: Baker, 2008.

–. *The Origins of the Christian Mystical Tradition: From Plato to Denys*. 2nd ed. Oxford: Oxford University Press, 2007.

Luz, Ulrich. *Das Evangelium nach Matthäus*. 3 vols., EKK 1. Zürich: Benzinger, 1985.

–. *Matthew 1–7: A Commentary*. Translated by Wilhelm Linss. Minneapolis: Augsburg, 1989.

–. *Matthew in History: Interpretation, Influence, and Effects*. Minneapolis: Fortress, 1994.

Lyall, Francis. 'Roman Law in the Writings of Paul: Adoption'. *JBL* 88 (1969): 458–66.

Marshall, B. 'Justification as Declaration and Deification'. *IJST* 4 (2002): 3–28.

Martikainen, Juoko. 'Man's Salvation: Deification or Justification?'. *Sobernost* 7 (1976): 180–92.

Martin, Ralph P. *2 Corinthians*. WBC 40. Waco: Word, 1986.

Martyn, J. Louis. *Galatians: A New Translation with Introduction and Commentary*. AB 33A. New York: Doubleday, 1997.

–. *Theological Issues in the Letters of Paul.* Nashville, TN: Abingdon, 1997.

Maston, Jason. *Divine and Human Agency in Second Temple Judaism and Paul.* WUNT 2/297. Tübingen: Mohr Siebeck, 2010.

Matera, Frank J. *Galatians.* SP 9. Collegeville, MN: Liturgical, 1992.

Matthews, Bradley J. 'A Theology of Christian Maturity with Special Reference to Ephesians and Colossians'. Ph.D. Thesis. University of Durham, 2008.

McCormack, Bruce. 'Participation in God, Yes, Deification, No: Two Modern Protestant Responses to an Ancient Question', Pages 347–74 in *Denkwürdiges Geheimnis: Beiträge zur Gotteslehre. Festschrift für Eberhard Jüngel zum 70. Geburtstag.* Edited by Ingolf U. Dalferth, Johannes Fischer, and Hans-Peter Großhans. Tübingen: Mohr Siebeck, 2004.

McGuckin, John A. *St. Cyril of Alexandria and the Christological Controversy.* Crestwood, NY: St. Vladimir's Seminary Press, 2004.

McInerney, J.L. 'Soteriological Commonplaces in Cyril of Alexandria's Commentary on the Gospel of John', Pages 179–185 in *Disciplina Nostra.* Edited by D.F. Winslow. Philadelphia: Patristic Foundation, 1979.

Mead, Richard T. 'Exegesis of 2 Corinthians 5:14–21', Pages 143–62 in *Interpreting 2 Corinthians 5:14–21.* Edited by Jack P. Lewis. Lampeter: Edwin Mellen, 1989.

Meeks, Wayne A. 'Why Study the New Testament'. *NTS* 51 (2005): 155–70.

Mell, Ulrich. *Neue Schöpfung.* Berlin: Walter de Gruyter, 1989.

Metzger, Bruce M. *A Textual Commentary on the Greek New Testament.* 2nd ed. Stuttgart: Deutsche Bibelgesellschaft, 1994.

Minns, Denis. *Irenaeus.* Washington, DC: Georgetown University Press, 1994.

Moo, Douglas J. *The Epistle to the Romans.* NICNT. Cambridge: Eerdmans, 1996.

Mosser, Carl. 'The Earliest Patristic Interpretations of Psalm 82, Jewish Antecedents, and the Origin of Christian Deification'. *JTSns* 56 (2005): 30–74.

Moule, C.F.D. '2 Cor 3.18b, καθάπερ ἀπὸ κυρίου πνεύματος', Pages 231–237 in *Neues Testament und Geschichte.* Edited by Heinrich Baltensweiler and Bo Reicke. Tübingen: Mohr Siebeck, 1972.

–. 'Death "to Sin", "to Law", and "to the World": A Note on Certain Datives', Pages 367–75 in *Mélanges Bibliques.* Edited by Albert Descamps and André de Halleux. Gembloux: Ducolot, 1970.

–. '"Fullness" and "Fill" in the New Testament', *SJT* 4 (1951): 78–86.

–. 'Review of *Chistology in the Making*'. *JTSns* 33 (1982): 258–63.

Münch-Labacher, Gudrun. *Naturhaftes und geschichtliches Denken bei Cyrill von Alexandrien: Die verschiedenen Betrachtungsweisen der Heilsverwirklichung in seinem Johannes-Kommentar.* Hereditas 10. Bonn: Borengässer, 1996.

Murphy-O'Connor, Jerome. 'Faith and Resurrection in 2 Cor 4:13–14'. *RB* 95 (1988): 543–550.

Nash, H.S. 'θειότης – θεότης, Rom. i.20; Col. ii.9', *JBL* 18 (1899): 1–34.

Nellas, Panayiotis. *Deification in Christ: Orthodox Perspectives on the Nature of the Human Person.* Translated by Norman Russell. Crestwood: St Vladimir's Seminary Press, 1997.

Newman, Carey C. *Paul's Glory-Christology: Tradition and Rhetoric.* NovTSup 69. Leiden: Brill, 1992.

–. 'Resurrection as Glory: Divine Presence and Christian Origins', Pages 59–89 in *The Resurrection – An Interdisciplinary Symposium on the Resurrection of Jesus.* Edited by Stephen T. Davis, Daniel Kendall, and Gerald O'Collins. Oxford: Oxford University Press, 1998.

Nguyen, V. Henry T. *Identity in Corinth: A Comparative Study of 2 Corinthians, Epictetus and Valerius Maximus.* WUNT 2/243. Tübingen: Mohr Siebeck, 2008.

Nicholls, Rachel. *Walking on the Water: Reading Mt. 14:22–33 in the Light of Its Wirkungsgeschichte.* Biblical Interpretation 90. Leiden: Brill, 2008.

Nielsen, Jan Tjeerd. *Adam and Christ in the Theology of Irenaeus of Lyons.* Assen, Netherlands: Van Gorcum, 1968.

Nispel, Mark D. 'Christian Deification and the Early *Testimonia*'. *VC* 53 (1999): 289–304.

Noormann, Rolf. *Irenäus als Paulusinterpret: zur Rezeption und Wirkung der paulinischen und deuteropaulinischen Briefe im Werk des Irenäus von Lyon.* WUNT 2/66. Tübingen: Mohr Siebeck, 1994.

Norris, Richard A. 'Irenaeus' Use of Paul in his Polemic against the Gnostics', Pages 79–98 in *Paul and the Legacies of Paul.* Edited by William S. Babcock. Dallas: Southern Methodist University Press, 1990.

Nygren, Anders. *Commentary on Romans.* Translated by Carl C. Rasmussen. London: SCM Press, 1952.

O'Brien, Peter T. *Colossians-Philemon.* WBC 44. Waco: Word, 1982.

–. *The Epistle to the Philippians.* NIGTC. Carlisle, UK: Paternoster, 1991.

O'Keefe, John J. 'Impassible Suffering? Divine Passion and Fifth-Century Christology'. *TS* 58 (1997): 39–60.

Osborn, Eric F. *Irenaeus of Lyons.* Cambridge: Cambridge University Press, 2001.

Osten-Sacken, Peter von der. *Römer 8 als Beispiel paulinischer Soteriologie.* FRLANT. Göttingen: Vandenhoeck & Ruprecht, 1975.

Pagels, Elaine. *The Gnostic Paul: Gnostic Exegesis of the Pauline Letters.* Philadelphia: Fortress, 1975.

Passmore, John. *The Perfectibility of Man.* London: Duckworth, 1970.

Pate, C. Marvin. *Adam Christology as the Exegetical and Theological Substructure of 2 Corinthians 4.7–5.21.* Lanham, MD: University Press of America, 1991.

Paulsen, Henning. *Uberlieferung und Auslegung in Römer 8.* Neukirchen-Vluyn: Neukirchener Verlag, 1974.

Pokorný, Petr. *Colossians: A Commentary.* Peabody: Hendrickson, 1991.

Powers, Daniel G. *Salvation through Participation: An Examination of the Notion of the Believers' Corporate Unity with Christ in Early Christian Soteriology.* Leuven: Peeters, 2001.

Price, S.R.F. 'Gods and Emperors: The Greek Language of The Roman Imperial Cult', *JHS* 104 (1984): 79-95.

Purves, James G.M. 'The Spirit and the Imago Dei: Reviewing the Anthropology of Irenaeus of Lyons'. *EvQ* 68 (1996): 99–120.

Rabens, Volker. *The Holy Spirit and Ethics in Paul: Transformation and Empowering for Religious-Ethical Life.* WUNT 2/283. Tübingen: Mohr Siebeck, 2010.

Räisänen, Heikki. 'The Effective "History" of the Bible : A Challenge to Biblical Scholarship?'. *SJT* 45 (1992): 303–324.

Reed, J.T. *A Discourse Analysis of Philippians: Method and Rhetoric in the Debate over Literary Integrity.* JSNTSup 136. Sheffield: Sheffield Academic, 1997.

Reitzenstein, Richard. *Hellenistic Mystery-Religions: Their Basic Ideas and Significance.* Translated by John E. Steely. Eugene, OR: Pickwick, 1978.

Renwick, David A. *Paul, the Temple, and the Presence of God.* Atlanta: Scholars Press, 1991.

Robinson, John A.T. *The Body.* London: SCM, 1952.

Roetzel, Calvin J. "'As Dying, and Behold We Live": Death and Resurrection in Paul's Theology'. *Interp* 46 (1992): 5–18.

–. 'Paul in the Second Century', Pages 227–41 in *The Cambridge Companion to St. Paul*. Edited by James D.G. Dunn. Cambridge: Cambridge University Press, 2003.

Rowe, C. Kavin. 'New Testament Iconography? Situating Paul in the Absence of Material Evidence', Pages 289–312 in *Picturing the New Testament*. Edited by Annette Weissenrieder, Friederike Wendt, and Petra von Gemünden. WUNT 2/193. Tübingen: Mohr Siebeck, 2005.

Russell, Norman. "'Partakers of the Divine Nature' (2 Peter 1:4) in the Byzantine Tradition', Pages 51–67 in *ΚΑΘΗΓΗΤΡΙΑ: Essays Presented to Joan Hussey for her 80th birthday*. Edited by J. Chysostomides. Athens: Porphyrogenitus, 1988.

–. *The Doctrine of Deification in the Greek Patristic Tradition*. Oxford: Oxford University Press, 2004.

Sanders, E. P. *Paul and Palestinian Judaism: A Comparison of Patterns of Religion*. Minneapolis: Fortress, 1977.

Savage, Timothy B. *Power Through Weakness: Paul's Understanding of Christian Ministry in 2 Corinthians*. SNTSMS 86. Cambridge: Cambridge University Press, 1996.

Schlatter, Adolf von. *Romans: The Righteousness of God*. Translated by Siegfried S. Schatzmann. Peabody, MA: Hendrickson, 1995.

Schneemelcher, Wilhelm. 'Paulus in der griechischen Kirche des zweiten Jahrhunderts'. *ZKG* 75 (1964): 1–20.

Schrage, Wolfgang. 'Leid, Kreuz und Eschaton. Die Peristasenkataloge als Merkmake paulinischer *theologia crucis* und Eschatologie'. *EvT* 34 (1974): 141–75.

–. 'Schöpfung und Neuschöpfung in Kontinuität und Diskontinuität bei Paulus'. *EvT* 65 (2005): 245–259.

Schweitzer, Albert. *The Mysticism of Paul the Apostle*. Translated by William Montgomery. Baltimore: Johns Hopkins, 1998.

Schweizer, Eduard. 'What Do We Really Mean When We Say "God sent his son ..."?', Pages 298–312 in *Faith and History: Essays in Honor of Paul W. Meyer*. Edited by John T. Carroll, Charles H. Cosgrove, and E. Elizabeth Johnson. Atlanta: Scholars Press, 1990.

Scott, James M. *Adoption as Sons of God: An Exegetical Investigation into the Background of ΥΙΟΘΕΣΙΑ in the Pauline Corpus*. WUNT 2/48. Tübingen: Mohr Siebeck, 1992.

Scroggs, Robin. *The Last Adam: A Study in Pauline Anthropology*. Oxford: Blackwell, 1966.

Seifrid, Mark A. *Christ Our Righteousness: Paul's Theology of Justification*. Downers Grove: InterVarsity Press, 2000.

Simonetti, Manlio. *Biblical Interpretation in the Early Church: An Historical Introduction to Patristic Exegesis*. Translated by John A. Hughes. Edinburgh: T&T Clark, 1994.

Skinner, Quentin. 'Meaning and understanding in the history of ideas', Pages 57–89 in *Visions of Politics. Volume I: Regarding Method*. Cambridge: Cambridge University Press, 2002.

Sprinkle, Preston. 'The Afterlife in Romans: Understanding Paul's Glory Motif in Light of the Apocalypse of Moses and 2 Baruch', Pages 201–33 in *Lebendige Hoffnung – ewiger Tod?!: Jenseitsvorstellungen im Hellenismus, Judentum, und Christentum*. Edited by Michael Labahn and Manfred Lang. Leipzig: Evangelische Verlagsanstalt, 2007.

Stanley, David M. 'Paul's Interest in the Early Chapters of Genesis', Pages 241–252 in *Studiorum Paulinorum.* Rome: Pontifico Instituto Biblico, 1963.

Starr, James. 'Does 2 Peter 1:4 Speak of Deification?', Pages 81–92 in *Partakers of the Divine Nature: The History and Development of Deification in the Christian Traditions.* Edited by Michael J. Christensen and Jeffery A. Wittung. Grand Rapids: Baker, 2008.

Steenberg, M.C. *Irenaeus on Creation: The Cosmic Christ and the Saga of Redemption.* SuppVC 91. Leiden: Brill, 2008.

Stegman, Thomas D. *The Character of Jesus: The Linchpin to Paul's Argument in 2 Corinthians.* Analecta Biblica 158. Rome: Editrice Pontificio Istituto Biblico, 2005.

Steinmetz, David C. 'Uncovering a Second Narrative: Detective Fiction and the Construction of Historical Method', Pages 54–68 in *The Art of Reading Scripture.* Edited by Ellen F. Davis and Richard B. Hays. Grand Rapids: Eerdmans, 2003.

Stuhlmacher, Peter. 'Erwägungen zum ontologische Character der καινή κτίσις bei Paulus'. *EvT* 27 (1967): 1–35.

–. 'The Theme of Romans', Pages 333–345 in *The Romans Debate.* Edited by Karl P. Donfried. Edinburgh: T&T Clark, 1991.

–. *Paul's Letter to the Romans: A Commentary.* Louisville: Westminster John Knox, 1994.

Sumney, Jerry L. *Identifying Paul's Opponents: The Question of Method in 2 Corinthians.* JSNTSup 40. Sheffield: JSOT Press, 1990.

Tannehill, Robert C. *Dying and Rising with Christ: A Study in Pauline Theology.* Eugene, OR: Wipf & Stock, 2006.

Thiselton, Anthony C. *The Two Horizons: New Testament Hermeneutics and Philosophical Description.* Exeter: Paternoster, 1980.

–. *The First Epistle to the Corinthians.* NIGTC. Cambridge: Eerdmans, 2000.

Thrall, Margaret E. *2 Corinthians.* 2 vols., ICC. London: T&T Clark, 1994.

Thunberg, Lars. *Microcosm and Mediator: The Theological Anthropology of Maximus the Confessor.* Lund: Gleerup, 1965.

Thüsing, Wilhelm. *Per Christum in Deum: Gott und Christus in der paulinischen Soteriologie.* 3 ed. Münster: Aschendorff, 1986.

van Kooten, George. *Paul's Anthropology in Context: The Image of God, Assimilation to God, and Tripartite Man in Ancient Judaism, Ancient Philosophy and Early Christianity.* WUNT 232. Tübingen: Mohr Siebeck, 2008.

van Unnik, W.C. ''With Unveiled Face', An Exegesis of 2 Corinthians 3.12–18'. *NTS* 6 (1963): 153–69.

Vogel, Jeff. 'The Haste of Sin, the Slowness of Salvation: An Interpretation of Irenaeus on the Fall and Redemption'. *AThR* 89 (2007): 443–59.

Vogel, Manuel. *Commentatio mortis: 2Kor 5,1–10 auf dem Hintergrund antiker ars moriendi.* FRLANT 214. Göttingen: Vandenhoeck & Ruprecht, 2006.

Vollenweider, Samuel. *Freiheit als neue Schöpfung: Eine Untersuchung zur Eleutheria bei Paulus und in seiner Umwelt.* Göttingen: Vandenhoeck & Ruprecht, 1989.

Wallace, Daniel B. *Greek Grammar Beyond the Basics: An Exegetical Syntax of the New Testament.* Grand Rapids: Zondervan, 1996.

Walters, James C. 'Paul, Adoption, and Inheritance', Pages 42–76 in *Paul in the Greco-Roman World.* Edited by J. Paul Sampley. Harrisburg: Trinity Press, 2003.

Wasserman, Emma. 'Paul among the Philosophers: The Case of Sin in Romans 6–8'. *JSNT* 30 (2008): 387–415.

Watson, D.F. 'A Rhetorical Analysis of Philippians and its Implications for the Unity Question'. *NovT* 30 (1988): 57–88.

Watson, Francis. '2 Cor. 10–13 and Paul's Painful Letter to the Corinthians', *JTSns* 35 (1984): 324–46.

–. *Paul and the Hermeneutics of Faith.* London: T&T Clark, 2004.

–. 'The Triune Divine Identity: Reflections on Pauline God-language, in Disagreement with J.D.G. Dunn'. *JSNT* 80 (2000): 99–124.

Watts Henderson, Suzanne. 'God's Fullness in Bodily Form: Christ and Church in Colossians', 118 *ET* (2007): 169-73.

Wedderburn, A. J. M. 'Adam in Paul's Letter to the Romans', Pages 413–30 in *Studia Biblica 1978*. Edited by E. Livingstone. JSNTSup 3. Sheffield: JSOT Press, 1978.

–. 'Theology of Colossians' Pages 1–71 in *The Theology of the Later Pauline Letters*. Edited by Andrew T. Lincoln and A.J.M Wedderburn. Cambridge: CUP, 1993.

Weigl, Eduard. *Die Heilslehre des heiligen Cyril von Alexandrien.* Mainz: Kirchenheim, 1905.

Werner, Johannes. *Der Paulinismus des Irenaeus.* TU 6.2. Leipzig: J.C. Hinrichs, 1889.

Wessel, Susan. *Cyril of Alexandria and the Nestorian Controversy: The Making of a Saint and of a Heretic.* Oxford: Oxford University Press, 2004.

Westerholm, Stephen. *Perspectives Old and New on Paul: The 'Lutheran' Paul and His Critics.* Grand Rapids: Eerdmans, 2004.

Wilckens, Ulrich. *Der Brief an die Römer.* 3 vols., EKK. Neukirchen-Vluyn: Neukirchener, 1978.

Wilken, Robert L. 'Exegesis and the History of Theology: Reflections on the Adam-Christ Typology in Cyril of Alexandria'. *CH* 25 (1966): 139–56.

–. *Judaism and the Early Christian Mind: A Study of Cyril of Alexandria's Exegesis and Theology.* New Haven: Yale University Press, 1971.

–. 'St Cyril of Alexandria: The Mystery of Christ in the Bible'. *ProEccl* 4 (1995): 454–78.

Williams, Michael Allen. *Rethinking "Gnosticism".* Princeton: Princeton University Press, 1996.

Williams, Sam K. 'The "Righteousness of God" in Romans'. *JBL* 99 (1980): 241–90.

–. 'Justification and the Spirit in Galatians'. *JSNT* 29 (1987): 91–100.

Windisch, Hans. *Der zweite Korintherbief.* 9. ed., KEK. Göttingen: Vandenhoeck & Ruprecht, 1924.

Winger, Michael. *By What Law?: The Meaning of Nomos in the Letters of Paul.* SBLDS 128. Atlanta: Scholars, 1992.

Wingren, Gustaf. *Man and the Incarnation: A Study in the Biblical Theology of Irenaeus.* Edinburgh: Oliver & Boyd, 1959.

Wrede, William. *Paul.* Eugene, OR: Wipf & Stock, 2001.

Wright, N.T. 'Jesus Christ is Lord: Philippians 2.5–11', Pages 56–98 in *The Climax of the Covenant.* Minneapolis: Fortress, 1991.

–. 'On Becoming the Righteousness of God: 2 Corinthians 5:21', Pages 200–8 in *Pauline Theology, Volume II: 1 & 2 Corinthians.* Edited by David M. Hay. Minneapolis: Fortress, 1993.

–. 'Reflected Glory: 2 Corinthians 3:18', Pages 175–92 in *Climax of the Covenant.* Minneapolis: Fortress, 1992.

–. *Romans.* NIB 10. Nashville: Abingdon, 2002.

–. *The New Testament and the People of God.* Minneapolis: Fortress, 1992.

–. *The Resurrection of the Son of God.* London: SPCK, 2003.

–. 'The Vindication of the Law: Narrative Analysis and Romans 8.1–11', Pages 193–219 in *Climax of the Covenant: Christ and the Law in Pauline Theology.* Minneapolis: Fortress, 1992.

Yarbro Collins, Adela and John Collins. *King and Messiah as Son of God: Divine, Human, and Angelic Messianic Figures in Biblical and Related Literature.* Grand Rapids: Eerdmans, 2008.

Yates, John W. *The Spirit and Creation in Paul.* WUNT 2/251. Tübingen: Mohr Siebeck, 2008.

Yeago, David S. 'The New Testament and the Nicene Dogma: A Contribution to the Recovery of Theological Exegesis'. *ProEccl* 3 (1994): 152–64.

Young, Frances. '"Creatio ex Nihilo": A Context for the Emergence of the Christian Doctrine of Creation'. *SJT* 44 (1991): 139–51.

Young, Frances and David F. Ford. *Meaning and Truth in 2 Corinthians.* SPCK: London, 1987.

Ziesler, J. A. 'The Just Requirement of the Law (Romans 8:4)'. *ABR* 35 (1987): 77–82.

Index of Ancient Sources

Old Testament and Deuterocanonical Texts

New Testament

Ancient Jewish Literature

Greco-Roman Texts

Patristic Texts

Index of Modern Authors

Index of Subjects

Wissenschaftliche Untersuchungen zum Neuen Testament

Alphabetical Index of the First and Second Series

Becker, Eve-Marie and *Peter Pilhofer* (Ed.): Biographie und Persönlichkeit des Paulus. 2005. *Vol. 187.*
– and *Anders Runesson* (Ed.): Mark and Matthew I. 2011. *Vol. 271.*
Becker, Michael: Wunder und Wundertäter im frührabbinischen Judentum. 2002. *Vol. II/144.*
Becker, Michael and *Markus Öhler* (Ed.): Apokalyptik als Herausforderung neutestamentlicher Theologie. 2006. *Vol. II/214.*
Bell, Richard H.: Deliver Us from Evil. 2007. *Vol. 216.*
– The Irrevocable Call of God. 2005. *Vol. 184.*
– No One Seeks for God. 1998. *Vol. 106.*
– Provoked to Jealousy. 1994. *Vol. II/63.*
Bennema, Cornelis: The Power of Saving Wisdom. 2002. *Vol. II/148.*
Bergman, Jan: see *Kieffer, René*
Bergmeier, Roland: Das Gesetz im Römerbrief und andere Studien zum Neuen Testament. 2000. *Vol. 121.*
Bernett, Monika: Der Kaiserkult in Judäa unter den Herodiern und Römern. 2007. *Vol. 203.*
Betz, Otto: Jesus, der Messias Israels. 1987. *Vol. 42.*
– Jesus, der Herr der Kirche. 1990. *Vol. 52.*
Beyschlag, Karlmann: Simon Magus und die christliche Gnosis. 1974. *Vol. 16.*
Bieringer, Reimund: see *Koester, Craig.*
Bittner, Wolfgang J.: Jesu Zeichen im Johannesevangelium. 1987. *Vol. II/26.*
Bjerkelund, Carl J.: Tauta Egeneto. 1987. *Vol. 40.*
Blackburn, Barry Lee: Theios Aner and the Markan Miracle Traditions. 1991. *Vol. II/40.*
Blackwell, Ben C.: Christosis. 2011. *Vol. II/314.*
Blanton IV, Thomas R.: Constructing a New Covenant. 2007. *Vol. II/233.*
Bock, Darrell L.: Blasphemy and Exaltation in Judaism and the Final Examination of Jesus. 1998. *Vol. II/106.*
– and *Robert L. Webb* (Ed.): Key Events in the Life of the Historical Jesus. 2009. *Vol. 247.*
Bockmuehl, Markus: The Remembered Peter. 2010. *Vol. 262.*
– Revelation and Mystery in Ancient Judaism and Pauline Christianity. 1990. *Vol. II/36.*
Bøe, Sverre: Cross-Bearing in Luke. 2010. *Vol. II/278.*
– Gog and Magog. 2001. *Vol. II/135.*
Böhlig, Alexander: Gnosis und Synkretismus. Vol. 1 1989. *Vol. 47* – Vol. 2 1989. *Vol. 48.*
Böhm, Martina: Samarien und die Samaritai bei Lukas. 1999. *Vol. II/111.*
Börstinghaus, Jens: Sturmfahrt und Schiffbruch. 2010. *Vol. II/274.*

Böttrich, Christfried: Weltweisheit – Menschheitsethik – Urkult. 1992. *Vol. II/50.*
– and *Herzer, Jens* (Ed.): Josephus und das Neue Testament. 2007. *Vol. 209.*
Bolyki, János: Jesu Tischgemeinschaften. 1997. *Vol. II/96.*
Bosman, Philip: Conscience in Philo and Paul. 2003. *Vol. II/166.*
Bovon, François: New Testament and Christian Apocrypha. 2009. *Vol. 237.*
– Studies in Early Christianity. 2003. *Vol. 161.*
Brändl, Martin: Der Agon bei Paulus. 2006. *Vol. II/222.*
Braun, Heike: Geschichte des Gottesvolkes und christliche Identität. 2010. *Vol. II/279.*
Breytenbach, Cilliers: see *Frey, Jörg.*
Broadhead, Edwin K.: Jewish Ways of Following Jesus Redrawing the Religious Map of Antiquity. 2010. *Vol. 266.*
Brocke, Christoph vom: Thessaloniki – Stadt des Kassander und Gemeinde des Paulus. 2001. *Vol. II/125.*
Brunson, Andrew: Psalm 118 in the Gospel of John. 2003. *Vol. II/158.*
Büchli, Jörg: Der Poimandres – ein paganisiertes Evangelium. 1987. *Vol. II/27.*
Bühner, Jan A.: Der Gesandte und sein Weg im 4. Evangelium. 1977. *Vol. II/2.*
Burchard, Christoph: Untersuchungen zu Joseph und Aseneth. 1965. *Vol. 8.*
– Studien zur Theologie, Sprache und Umwelt des Neuen Testaments. Ed. by D. Sänger. 1998. *Vol. 107.*
Burnett, Richard: Karl Barth's Theological Exegesis. 2001. *Vol. II/145.*
Byron, John: Slavery Metaphors in Early Judaism and Pauline Christianity. 2003. *Vol. II/162.*
Byrskog, Samuel: Story as History – History as Story. 2000. *Vol. 123.*
Cancik, Hubert (Ed.): Markus-Philologie. 1984. *Vol. 33.*
Capes, David B.: Old Testament Yaweh Texts in Paul's Christology. 1992. *Vol. II/47.*
Caragounis, Chrys C.: The Development of Greek and the New Testament. 2004. *Vol. 167.*
– The Son of Man. 1986. *Vol. 38.*
– see *Fridrichsen, Anton.*
Carleton Paget, James: The Epistle of Barnabas. 1994. *Vol. II/64.*
– Jews, Christians and Jewish Christians in Antiquity. 2010. *Vol. 251.*
Carson, D.A., O'Brien, Peter T. and *Mark Seifrid* (Ed.): Justification and Variegated Nomism.

Vol. 1: The Complexities of Second Temple Judaism. 2001. *Vol. II/140.*

Vol. 2: The Paradoxes of Paul. 2004. *Vol. II/181.*

Caulley, Thomas Scott und *Hermann Lichtenberger* (Ed.): Die Septuaginta und das frühe Christentum – The Septuagint and Christian Origins. 2011. *Vol. 277.*

– see *Lichtenberger, Hermann.*

Chae, Young Sam: Jesus as the Eschatological Davidic Shepherd. 2006. *Vol. II/216.*

Chapman, David W.: Ancient Jewish and Christian Perceptions of Crucifixion. 2008. *Vol. II/244.*

Chester, Andrew: Messiah and Exaltation. 2007. *Vol. 207.*

Chibici-Revneanu, Nicole: Die Herrlichkeit des Verherrlichten. 2007. *Vol. II/231.*

Ciampa, Roy E.: The Presence and Function of Scripture in Galatians 1 and 2. 1998. *Vol. II/102.*

Classen, Carl Joachim: Rhetorical Criticsm of the New Testament. 2000. *Vol. 128.*

Claußen, Carsten (Ed.): see *Frey, Jörg.*

Colpe, Carsten: Griechen – Byzantiner – Semiten – Muslime. 2008. *Vol. 221.*

– Iranier – Aramäer – Hebräer – Hellenen. 2003. *Vol. 154.*

Cook, John G.: Roman Attitudes Towards the Christians. 2010. *Vol. 261.*

Coote, Robert B. (Ed.): see *Weissenrieder, Annette.*

Coppins, Wayne: The Interpretation of Freedom in the Letters of Paul. 2009. *Vol. II/261.*

Crump, David: Jesus the Intercessor. 1992. *Vol. II/49.*

Dahl, Nils Alstrup: Studies in Ephesians. 2000. *Vol. 131.*

Daise, Michael A.: Feasts in John. 2007. *Vol. II/229.*

Deines, Roland: Die Gerechtigkeit der Tora im Reich des Messias. 2004. *Vol. 177.*

– Jüdische Steingefäße und pharisäische Frömmigkeit. 1993. *Vol. II/52.*

– Die Pharisäer. 1997. *Vol. 101.*

Deines, Roland, Jens Herzer and *Karl-Wilhelm Niebuhr* (Ed.): Neues Testament und hellenistisch-jüdische Alltagskultur. III. Internationales Symposium zum Corpus Judaeo-Hellenisticum Novi Testamenti. 21.–24. Mai 2009 in Leipzig. 2011. *Vol. 274.*

– and *Karl-Wilhelm Niebuhr* (Ed.): Philo und das Neue Testament. 2004. *Vol. 172.*

Dennis, John A.: Jesus' Death and the Gathering of True Israel. 2006. *Vol. 217.*

Dettwiler, Andreas and *Jean Zumstein* (Ed.): Kreuzestheologie im Neuen Testament. 2002. *Vol. 151.*

Dickson, John P.: Mission-Commitment in Ancient Judaism and in the Pauline Communities. 2003. *Vol. II/159.*

Dietzfelbinger, Christian: Der Abschied des Kommenden. 1997. *Vol. 95.*

Dimitrov, Ivan Z., James D.G. Dunn, Ulrich Luz and *Karl-Wilhelm Niebuhr* (Ed.): Das Alte Testament als christliche Bibel in orthodoxer und westlicher Sicht. 2004. *Vol. 174.*

Dobbeler, Axel von: Glaube als Teilhabe. 1987. *Vol. II/22.*

Docherty, Susan E.: The Use of the Old Testament in Hebrews. 2009. *Vol. II/260.*

Dochhorn, Jan: Schriftgelehrte Prophetie. 2010. *Vol. 268.*

Downs, David J.: The Offering of the Gentiles. 2008. *Vol. II/248.*

Dryden, J. de Waal: Theology and Ethics in 1 Peter. 2006. *Vol. II/209.*

Dübbers, Michael: Christologie und Existenz im Kolosserbrief. 2005. *Vol. II/191.*

Dunn, James D.G.: The New Perspective on Paul. 2005. *Vol. 185.*

Dunn , James D.G. (Ed.): Jews and Christians. 1992. *Vol. 66.*

– Paul and the Mosaic Law. 1996. *Vol. 89.*

– see *Dimitrov, Ivan Z.*

–, *Hans Klein, Ulrich Luz,* and *Vasile Mihoc* (Ed.): Auslegung der Bibel in orthodoxer und westlicher Perspektive. 2000. *Vol. 130.*

Ebel, Eva: Die Attraktivität früher christlicher Gemeinden. 2004. *Vol. II/178.*

Ebertz, Michael N.: Das Charisma des Gekreuzigten. 1987. *Vol. 45.*

Eckstein, Hans-Joachim: Der Begriff Syneidesis bei Paulus. 1983. *Vol. II/10.*

– Verheißung und Gesetz. 1996. *Vol. 86.*

–, *Christoph Landmesser* und *Hermann Lichtenberger* (Ed.): Eschatologie – Eschatology. The Sixth Durham-Tübingen Research Symposium. 2011. *Vol. 272.*

Ego, Beate: Im Himmel wie auf Erden. 1989. *Vol. II/34.*

Ego, Beate, Armin Lange and *Peter Pilhofer* (Ed.): Gemeinde ohne Tempel – Community without Temple. 1999. *Vol. 118.*

– and *Helmut Merkel* (Ed.): Religiöses Lernen in der biblischen, frühjüdischen und frühchristlichen Überlieferung. 2005. *Vol. 180.*

Eisele, Wilfried: Welcher Thomas? 2010. *Vol. 259.*

Eisen, Ute E.: see *Paulsen, Henning.*

Elledge, C.D.: Life after Death in Early Judaism. 2006. *Vol. II/208.*

Ellis, E. Earle: Prophecy and Hermeneutic in Early Christianity. 1978. *Vol. 18.*
- The Old Testament in Early Christianity. 1991. *Vol. 54.*

Elmer, Ian J.: Paul, Jerusalem and the Judaisers. 2009. *Vol. II/258.*

Endo, Masanobu: Creation and Christology. 2002. *Vol. 149.*

Ennulat, Andreas: Die 'Minor Agreements'. 1994. *Vol. II/62.*

Ensor, Peter W.: Jesus and His 'Works'. 1996. *Vol. II/85.*

Eskola, Timo: Messiah and the Throne. 2001. *Vol. II/142.*
- Theodicy and Predestination in Pauline Soteriology. 1998. *Vol. II/100.*

Farelly, Nicolas: The Disciples in the Fourth Gospel. 2010. *Vol. II/290.*

Fatehi, Mehrdad: The Spirit's Relation to the Risen Lord in Paul. 2000. *Vol. II/128.*

Feldmeier, Reinhard: Die Krisis des Gottessohnes. 1987. *Vol. II/21.*
- Die Christen als Fremde. 1992. *Vol. 64.*

Feldmeier, Reinhard and *Ulrich Heckel* (Ed.): Die Heiden. 1994. *Vol. 70.*

Felsch, Dorit: Die Feste im Johannesevangelium. 2011. *Vol. II/308.*

Finnern, Sönke: Narratologie und biblische Exegese. 2010. *Vol. II/285.*

Fletcher-Louis, Crispin H.T.: Luke-Acts: Angels, Christology and Soteriology. 1997. *Vol. II/94.*

Förster, Niclas: Marcus Magus. 1999. *Vol. 114.*

Forbes, Christopher Brian: Prophecy and Inspired Speech in Early Christianity and its Hellenistic Environment. 1995. *Vol. II/75.*

Fornberg, Tord: see *Fridrichsen, Anton.*

Fossum, Jarl E.: The Name of God and the Angel of the Lord. 1985. *Vol. 36.*

Foster, Paul: Community, Law and Mission in Matthew's Gospel. *Vol. II/177.*

Fotopoulos, John: Food Offered to Idols in Roman Corinth. 2003. *Vol. II/151.*

Frank, Nicole: Der Kolosserbrief im Kontext des paulinischen Erbes. 2009. *Vol. II/271.*

Frenschkowski, Marco: Offenbarung und Epiphanie. Vol. 1 1995. *Vol. II/79* – Vol. 2 1997. *Vol. II/80.*

Frey, Jörg: Eugen Drewermann und die biblische Exegese. 1995. *Vol. II/71.*
- Die johanneische Eschatologie. Vol. I. 1997. *Vol. 96.* – Vol. II. 1998. *Vol. 110.* – Vol. III. 2000. *Vol. 117.*

Frey, Jörg, Carsten Claußen and *Nadine Kessler* (Ed.): Qumran und die Archäologie. 2011. *Vol. 278.*

- and *Cilliers Breytenbach* (Ed.): Aufgabe und Durchführung einer Theologie des Neuen Testaments. 2007. *Vol. 205.*
- *Jens Herzer, Martina Janßen* and *Clare K. Rothschild* (Ed.): Pseudepigraphie und Verfasserfiktion in frühchristlichen Briefen. 2009. *Vol. 246.*
- *Stefan Krauter* and *Hermann Lichtenberger* (Ed.): Heil und Geschichte. 2009. *Vol. 248.*
- and *Udo Schnelle (Ed.):* Kontexte des Johannesevangeliums. 2004. *Vol. 175.*
- and *Jens Schröter* (Ed.): Deutungen des Todes Jesu im Neuen Testament. 2005. *Vol. 181.*
- Jesus in apokryphen Evangelienüberlieferungen. 2010. *Vol. 254.*
- -, *Jan G. van der Watt,* and *Ruben Zimmermann* (Ed.): Imagery in the Gospel of John. 2006. *Vol. 200.*

Freyne, Sean: Galilee and Gospel. 2000. *Vol. 125.*

Fridrichsen, Anton: Exegetical Writings. Edited by C.C. Caragounis and T. Fornberg. 1994. *Vol. 76.*

Gadenz, Pablo T.: Called from the Jews and from the Gentiles. 2009. *Vol. II/267.*

Gäbel, Georg: Die Kulttheologie des Hebräerbriefes. 2006. *Vol. II/212.*

Gäckle, Volker: Die Starken und die Schwachen in Korinth und in Rom. 2005. *Vol. 200.*

Garlington, Don B.: 'The Obedience of Faith'. 1991. *Vol. II/38.*
- Faith, Obedience, and Perseverance. 1994. *Vol. 79.*

Garnet, Paul: Salvation and Atonement in the Qumran Scrolls. 1977. *Vol. II/3.*

Gemünden, Petra von (Ed.): see *Weissenrieder, Annette.*

Gese, Michael: Das Vermächtnis des Apostels. 1997. *Vol. II/99.*

Gheorghita, Radu: The Role of the Septuagint in Hebrews. 2003. *Vol. II/160.*

Gordley, Matthew E.: The Colossian Hymn in Context. 2007. *Vol. II/228.*
- Teaching through Song in Antiquity. 2011. *Vol. II/302.*

Gräbe, Petrus J.: The Power of God in Paul's Letters. 2000, ²2008. *Vol. II/123.*

Gräßer, Erich: Der Alte Bund im Neuen. 1985. *Vol. 35.*
- Forschungen zur Apostelgeschichte. 2001. *Vol. 137.*

Grappe, Christian (Ed.): Le Repas de Dieu / Das Mahl Gottes. 2004. *Vol. 169.*

Gray, Timothy C.: The Temple in the Gospel of Mark. 2008. *Vol. II/242.*

Green, Joel B.: The Death of Jesus. 1988. *Vol. II/33.*

Gregg, Brian Han: The Historical Jesus and the Final Judgment Sayings in Q. 2005. *Vol. II/207.*

Gregory, Andrew: The Reception of Luke and Acts in the Period before Irenaeus. 2003. *Vol. II/169.*

Grindheim, Sigurd: The Crux of Election. 2005. *Vol. II/202.*

Gundry, Robert H.: The Old is Better. 2005. *Vol. 178.*

Gundry Volf, Judith M.: Paul and Perseverance. 1990. *Vol. II/37.*

Häußer, Detlef: Christusbekenntnis und Jesus-überlieferung bei Paulus. 2006. *Vol. 210.*

Hafemann, Scott J.: Suffering and the Spirit. 1986. *Vol. II/19.*

– Paul, Moses, and the History of Israel. 1995. *Vol. 81.*

Hahn, Ferdinand: Studien zum Neuen Testament.
Vol. I: Grundsatzfragen, Jesusforschung, Evangelien. 2006. *Vol. 191.*
Vol. II: Bekenntnisbildung und Theologie in urchristlicher Zeit. 2006. *Vol. 192.*

Hahn, Johannes (Ed.): Zerstörungen des Jerusalemer Tempels. 2002. *Vol. 147.*

Hamid-Khani, Saeed: Relevation and Concealment of Christ. 2000. *Vol. II/120.*

Hannah, Darrel D.: Michael and Christ. 1999. *Vol. II/109.*

Hardin, Justin K.: Galatians and the Imperial Cult? 2007. *Vol. II /237.*

Harrison, James R.: Paul and the Imperial Authorities at Thessolanica and Rome. 2011. *Vol. 273.*

– Paul's Language of Grace in Its Graeco-Roman Context. 2003. *Vol. II/172.*

Hartman, Lars: Text-Centered New Testament Studies. Ed. von D. Hellholm. 1997. *Vol. 102.*

Hartog, Paul: Polycarp and the New Testament. 2001. *Vol. II/134.*

Hasselbrook, David S.: Studies in New Testament Lexicography. 2011. *Vol. II/303.*

Hays, Christopher M.: Luke's Wealth Ethics. 2010. *Vol. 275.*

Heckel, Theo K.: Der Innere Mensch. 1993. *Vol. II/53.*

– Vom Evangelium des Markus zum viergestaltigen Evangelium. 1999. *Vol. 120.*

Heckel, Ulrich: Kraft in Schwachheit. 1993. *Vol. II/56.*

– Der Segen im Neuen Testament. 2002. *Vol. 150.*

– see *Feldmeier, Reinhard.*

– see *Hengel, Martin.*

Heemstra, Marius: The Fiscus Judaicus and the Parting of the Ways. 2010. *Vol. II/277.*

Heiligenthal, Roman: Werke als Zeichen. 1983. *Vol. II/9.*

Heininger, Bernhard: Die Inkulturation des Christentums. 2010. *Vol. 255.*

Heliso, Desta: Pistis and the Righteous One. 2007. *Vol. II/235.*

Hellholm, D.: see *Hartman, Lars.*

Hemer, Colin J.: The Book of Acts in the Setting of Hellenistic History. 1989. *Vol. 49.*

Henderson, Timothy P.: The Gospel of Peter and Early Christian Apologetics. 2011. *Vol. II/301.*

Hengel, Martin: Jesus und die Evangelien. Kleine Schriften V. 2007. *Vol. 211.*

– Die johanneische Frage. 1993. *Vol. 67.*

– Judaica et Hellenistica. Kleine Schriften I. 1996. *Vol. 90.*

– Judaica, Hellenistica et Christiana. Kleine Schriften II. 1999. *Vol. 109.*

– Judentum und Hellenismus. 1969, ³1988. *Vol. 10.*

– Paulus und Jakobus. Kleine Schriften III. 2002. *Vol. 141.*

– Studien zur Christologie. Kleine Schriften IV. 2006. *Vol. 201.*

– Studien zum Urchristentum. Kleine Schriften VI. 2008. *Vol. 234.*

– Theologische, historische und biographische Skizzen. Kleine Schriften VII. 2010. *Vol. 253.*

– and *Anna Maria Schwemer:* Paulus zwischen Damaskus und Antiochien. 1998. *Vol. 108.*

– Der messianische Anspruch Jesu und die Anfänge der Christologie. 2001. *Vol. 138.*

– Die vier Evangelien und das eine Evangelium von Jesus Christus. 2008. *Vol. 224.*

Hengel, Martin and *Ulrich Heckel* (Ed.): Paulus und das antike Judentum. 1991. *Vol. 58.*

– and *Hermut Löhr* (Ed.): Schriftauslegung im antiken Judentum und im Urchristentum. 1994. *Vol. 73.*

– and *Anna Maria Schwemer* (Ed.): Königsherrschaft Gottes und himmlischer Kult. 1991. *Vol. 55.*

– Die Septuaginta. 1994. *Vol. 72.*

–, *Siegfried Mittmann* and *Anna Maria Schwemer* (Ed.): La Cité de Dieu / Die Stadt Gottes. 2000. *Vol. 129.*

Hentschel, Anni: Diakonia im Neuen Testament. 2007. *Vol. 226.*

Hernández Jr., Juan: Scribal Habits and Theological Influence in the Apocalypse. 2006. *Vol. II/218.*

Kleinknecht, Karl Th.: Der leidende Gerechtfertigte. 1984, ²1988. *Vol. II/13.*

Klinghardt, Matthias: Gesetz und Volk Gottes. 1988. *Vol. II/32.*

Kloppenborg, John S.: The Tenants in the Vineyard. 2006, student edition 2010. *Vol. 195.*

Koch, Michael: Drachenkampf und Sonnenfrau. 2004. *Vol. II/184.*

Koch, Stefan: Rechtliche Regelung von Konflikten im frühen Christentum. 2004. *Vol. II/174.*

Köhler, Wolf-Dietrich: Rezeption des Matthäusevangeliums in der Zeit vor Irenäus. 1987. *Vol. II/24.*

Köhn, Andreas: Der Neutestamentler Ernst Lohmeyer. 2004. *Vol. II/180.*

Koester, Craig and *Reimund Bieringer* (Ed.): The Resurrection of Jesus in the Gospel of John. 2008. *Vol. 222.*

Konradt, Matthias: Israel, Kirche und die Völker im Matthäusevangelium. 2007. *Vol. 215.*

Kooten, George H. van: Cosmic Christology in Paul and the Pauline School. 2003. *Vol. II/171.*

– Paul's Anthropology in Context. 2008. *Vol. 232.*

Korn, Manfred: Die Geschichte Jesu in veränderter Zeit. 1993. *Vol. II/51.*

Koskenniemi, Erkki: Apollonios von Tyana in der neutestamentlichen Exegese. 1994. *Vol. II/61.*

– The Old Testament Miracle-Workers in Early Judaism. 2005. *Vol. II/206.*

Kraus, Thomas J.: Sprache, Stil und historischer Ort des zweiten Petrusbriefes. 2001. *Vol. II/136.*

Kraus, Wolfgang: Das Volk Gottes. 1996. *Vol. 85.*

– see *Karrer, Martin.*

– see *Walter, Nikolaus.*

– and *Martin Karrer* (Hrsg.): Die Septuaginta – Texte, Theologien, Einflüsse. 2010. *Bd. 252.*

– and *Karl-Wilhelm Niebuhr* (Ed.): Frühjudentum und Neues Testament im Horizont Biblischer Theologie. 2003. *Vol. 162.*

Krauter, Stefan: Studien zu Röm 13,1-7. 2009. *Vol. 243.*

– see *Frey, Jörg.*

Kreplin, Matthias: Das Selbstverständnis Jesu. 2001. *Vol. II/141.*

Kuhn, Karl G.: Achtzehngebet und Vaterunser und der Reim. 1950. *Vol. 1.*

Kvalbein, Hans: see *Ådna, Jostein.*

Kwon, Yon-Gyong: Eschatology in Galatians. 2004. *Vol. II/183.*

Laansma, Jon: I Will Give You Rest. 1997. *Vol. II/98.*

Labahn, Michael: Offenbarung in Zeichen und Wort. 2000. *Vol. II/117.*

Lambers-Petry, Doris: see *Tomson, Peter J.*

Lampe, Peter: Die stadtrömischen Christen in den ersten beiden Jahrhunderten. 1987, ²1989. *Vol. II/18.*

Landmesser, Christof: Wahrheit als Grundbegriff neutestamentlicher Wissenschaft. 1999. *Vol. 113.*

– Jüngerberufung und Zuwendung zu Gott. 2000. *Vol. 133.*

– see *Eckstein, Hans-Joachim.*

Lange, Armin: see *Ego, Beate.*

Lau, Andrew: Manifest in Flesh. 1996. *Vol. II/86.*

Lawrence, Louise: An Ethnography of the Gospel of Matthew. 2003. *Vol. II/165.*

Lee, Aquila H.I.: From Messiah to Preexistent Son. 2005. *Vol. II/192.*

Lee, Pilchan: The New Jerusalem in the Book of Relevation. 2000. *Vol. II/129.*

Lee, Sang M.: The Cosmic Drama of Salvation. 2010. *Vol. II/276.*

Lee, Simon S.: Jesus' Transfiguration and the Believers' Transformation. 2009. *Vol. II/265.*

Lichtenberger, Hermann: Das Ich Adams und das Ich der Menschheit. 2004. *Vol. 164.*

– see *Avemarie, Friedrich.*

– see *Eckstein, Hans-Joachim.*

– see *Frey, Jörg.*

– and *Thomas Scott Caulley* (Ed.): Die Septuaginta und das frühe Christentum – The Septuagint and Christian Origins. 2011. *Vol. 277.*

Lierman, John: The New Testament Moses. 2004. *Vol. II/173.*

– (Ed.): Challenging Perspectives on the Gospel of John. 2006. *Vol. II/219.*

Lieu, Samuel N.C.: Manichaeism in the Later Roman Empire and Medieval China. ²1992. *Vol. 63.*

Lindemann, Andreas: Die Evangelien und die Apostelgeschichte. 2009. *Vol. 241.*

Lincicum, David: Paul and the Early Jewish Encounter with Deuteronomy. 2010. *Vol. II/284.*

Lindgård, Fredrik: Paul's Line of Thought in 2 Corinthians 4:16–5:10. 2004. *Vol. II/189.*

Livesey, Nina E.: Circumcision as a Malleable Symbol. 2010. *Vol. II/295.*

Loader, William R.G.: Jesus' Attitude Towards the Law. 1997. *Vol. II/97.*

Löhr, Gebhard: Verherrlichung Gottes durch Philosophie. 1997. *Vol. 97.*

Löhr, Hermut: Studien zum frühchristlichen und frühjüdischen Gebet. 2003. *Vol. 160.*
– see *Hengel, Martin.*
Löhr, Winrich Alfried: Basilides und seine Schule. 1995. *Vol. 83.*
Lorenzen, Stefanie: Das paulinische Eikon-Konzept. 2008. *Vol. II/250.*
Luomanen, Petri: Entering the Kingdom of Heaven. 1998. *Vol. II/101.*
Luz, Ulrich: see *Alexeev, Anatoly A.*
– see *Dunn, James D.G.*
Mackay, Ian D.: John's Raltionship with Mark. 2004. *Vol. II/182.*
Mackie, Scott D.: Eschatology and Exhortation in the Epistle to the Hebrews. 2006. *Vol. II/223.*
Magda, Ksenija: Paul's Territoriality and Mission Strategy. 2009. *Vol. II/266.*
Maier, Gerhard: Mensch und freier Wille. 1971. *Vol. 12.*
– Die Johannesoffenbarung und die Kirche. 1981. *Vol. 25.*
Markschies, Christoph: Valentinus Gnosticus? 1992. *Vol. 65.*
Marshall, Jonathan: Jesus, Patrons, and Benefactors. 2009. *Vol. II/259.*
Marshall, Peter: Enmity in Corinth: Social Conventions in Paul's Relations with the Corinthians. 1987. *Vol. II/23.*
Martin, Dale B.: see *Zangenberg, Jürgen.*
Maston, Jason: Divine and Human Agency in Second Temple Judaism and Paul. 2010. *Vol. II/297.*
Mayer, Annemarie: Sprache der Einheit im Epheserbrief und in der Ökumene. 2002. *Vol. II/150.*
Mayordomo, Moisés: Argumentiert Paulus logisch? 2005. *Vol. 188.*
McDonough, Sean M.: YHWH at Patmos: Rev. 1:4 in its Hellenistic and Early Jewish Setting. 1999. *Vol. II/107.*
McDowell, Markus: Prayers of Jewish Women. 2006. *Vol. II/211.*
McGlynn, Moyna: Divine Judgement and Divine Benevolence in the Book of Wisdom. 2001. *Vol. II/139.*
McNamara, Martin: Targum and New Testament. 2011. *Vol. 279.*
Meade, David G.: Pseudonymity and Canon. 1986. *Vol. 39.*
Meadors, Edward P.: Jesus the Messianic Herald of Salvation. 1995. *Vol. II/72.*
Meißner, Stefan: Die Heimholung des Ketzers. 1996. *Vol. II/87.*
Mell, Ulrich: Die „anderen" Winzer. 1994. *Vol. 77.*
– see *Sänger, Dieter.*

Mengel, Berthold: Studien zum Philipperbrief. 1982. *Vol. II/8.*
Merkel, Helmut: Die Widersprüche zwischen den Evangelien. 1971. *Vol. 13.*
– see *Ego, Beate.*
Merklein, Helmut: Studien zu Jesus und Paulus. Vol. 1 1987. *Vol. 43.* – Vol. 2 1998. *Vol. 105.*
Merkt, Andreas: see *Nicklas, Tobias*
Metzdorf, Christina: Die Tempelaktion Jesu. 2003. *Vol. II/168.*
Metzler, Karin: Der griechische Begriff des Verzeihens. 1991. *Vol. II/44.*
Metzner, Rainer: Die Rezeption des Matthäusevangeliums im 1. Petrusbrief. 1995. *Vol. II/74.*
– Das Verständnis der Sünde im Johannesevangelium. 2000. *Vol. 122.*
Mihoc, Vasile: see *Dunn, James D.G.*
– see *Klein, Hans.*
Mineshige, Kiyoshi: Besitzverzicht und Almosen bei Lukas. 2003. *Vol. II/163.*
Mittmann, Siegfried: see *Hengel, Martin.*
Mittmann-Richert, Ulrike: Magnifikat und Benediktus. 1996. *Vol. II/90.*
– Der Sühnetod des Gottesknechts. 2008. *Vol. 220.*
Miura, Yuzuru: David in Luke-Acts. 2007. *Vol. II/232.*
Moll, Sebastian: The Arch-Heretic Marcion. 2010. *Vol. 250.*
Morales, Rodrigo J.: The Spirit and the Restorat. 2010. *Vol. 282.*
Mournet, Terence C.: Oral Tradition and Literary Dependency. 2005. *Vol. II/195.*
Mußner, Franz: Jesus von Nazareth im Umfeld Israels und der Urkirche. Ed. von M. Theobald. 1998. *Vol. 111.*
Mutschler, Bernhard: Das Corpus Johanneum bei Irenäus von Lyon. 2005. *Vol. 189.*
– Glaube in den Pastoralbriefen. 2010. *Vol. 256.*
Myers, Susan E.: Spirit Epicleses in the Acts of Thomas. 2010. *Vol. 281.*
Nguyen, V. Henry T.: Christian Identity in Corinth. 2008. *Vol. II/243.*
Nicklas, Tobias, Andreas Merkt und *Joseph Verheyden* (Ed.): Gelitten – Gestorben – Auferstanden. 2010. *Vol. II/273.*
– see *Verheyden, Joseph*
Niebuhr, Karl-Wilhelm: Gesetz and Paränese. 1987. *Vol. II/28.*
– Heidenapostel aus Israel. 1992. *Vol. 62.*
– see *Deines, Roland.*
– see *Dimitrov, Ivan Z.*
– see *Klein, Hans.*
– see *Kraus, Wolfgang.*

Nielsen, Anders E.: "Until it is Fullfilled". 2000. *Vol. II/126.*

Nielsen, Jesper Tang: Die kognitive Dimension des Kreuzes. 2009. *Vol. II/263.*

Nissen, Andreas: Gott und der Nächste im antiken Judentum. 1974. *Vol. 15.*

Noack, Christian: Gottesbewußtsein. 2000. *Vol. II/116.*

Noormann, Rolf: Irenäus als Paulusinterpret. 1994. *Vol. II/66.*

Norin, Stig: see *Hultgård, Anders.*

Novakovic, Lidija: Messiah, the Healer of the Sick. 2003. *Vol. II/170.*

Obermann, Andreas: Die christologische Erfüllung der Schrift im Johannesevangelium. 1996. *Vol. II/83.*

Öhler, Markus: Barnabas. 2003. *Vol. 156.*
– see *Becker, Michael.*
– (Ed.): Aposteldekret und antikes Vereinswesen. 2011. *Vol. 280.*

Okure, Teresa: The Johannine Approach to Mission. 1988. *Vol. II/31.*

Onuki, Takashi: Heil und Erlösung. 2004. *Vol. 165.*

Oropeza, B. J.: Paul and Apostasy. 2000. *Vol. II/115.*

Ostmeyer, Karl-Heinrich: Kommunikation mit Gott und Christus. 2006. *Vol. 197.*
– Taufe und Typos. 2000. *Vol. II/118.*

Pao, David W.: Acts and the Isaianic New Exodus. 2000. *Vol. II/130.*

Park, Eung Chun: The Mission Discourse in Matthew's Interpretation. 1995. *Vol. II/81.*

Park, Joseph S.: Conceptions of Afterlife in Jewish Insriptions. 2000. *Vol. II/121.*

Parsenios, George L.: Rhetoric and Drama in the Johannine Lawsuit Motif. 2010. *Vol. 258.*

Pate, C. Marvin: The Reverse of the Curse. 2000. *Vol. II/114.*

Paulsen, Henning: Studien zur Literatur und Geschichte des frühen Christentums. Ed. von Ute E. Eisen. 1997. *Vol. 99.*

Pearce, Sarah J.K.: The Land of the Body. 2007. *Vol. 208.*

Peres, Imre: Griechische Grabinschriften und neutestamentliche Eschatologie. 2003. *Vol. 157.*

Perry, Peter S.: The Rhetoric of Digressions. 2009. *Vol. II/268.*

Pierce, Chad T.: Spirits and the Proclamation of Christ. 2011. *Vol. II/305.*

Philip, Finny: The Origins of Pauline Pneumatology. 2005. *Vol. II/194.*

Philonenko, Marc (Ed.): Le Trône de Dieu. 1993. *Vol. 69.*

Pilhofer, Peter: Presbyteron Kreitton. 1990. *Vol. II/39.*
– Philippi. Vol. 1 1995. *Vol. 87.* – Vol. 2 [2]2009. *Vol. 119.*
– Die frühen Christen und ihre Welt. 2002. *Vol. 145.*
– see *Becker, Eve-Marie.*
– see *Ego, Beate.*

Pitre, Brant: Jesus, the Tribulation, and the End of the Exile. 2005. *Vol. II/204.*

Plümacher, Eckhard: Geschichte und Geschichten. 2004. *Vol. 170.*

Pöhlmann, Wolfgang: Der Verlorene Sohn und das Haus. 1993. *Vol. 68.*

Poirier, John C.: The Tongues of Angels. 2010. *Vol. II/287.*

Pokorný, Petr and *Josef B. Souček:* Bibelauslegung als Theologie. 1997. *Vol. 100.*
– and *Jan Roskovec* (Ed.): Philosophical Hermeneutics and Biblical Exegesis. 2002. *Vol. 153.*

Popkes, Enno Edzard: Das Menschenbild des Thomasevangeliums. 2007. *Vol. 206.*
– Die Theologie der Liebe Gottes in den johanneischen Schriften. 2005. *Vol. II/197.*

Porter, Stanley E.: The Paul of Acts. 1999. *Vol. 115.*

Prieur, Alexander: Die Verkündigung der Gottesherrschaft. 1996. *Vol. II/89.*

Probst, Hermann: Paulus und der Brief. 1991. *Vol. II/45.*

Puig i Tàrrech, Armand: Jesus: An Uncommon Journey. 2010. *Vol. II/288.*

Rabens, Volker: The Holy Spirit and Ethics in Paul. 2010. *Vol. II/283.*

Räisänen, Heikki: Paul and the Law. 1983, [2]1987. *Vol. 29.*

Rehkopf, Friedrich: Die lukanische Sonderquelle. 1959. *Vol. 5.*

Rein, Matthias: Die Heilung des Blindgeborenen (Joh 9). 1995. *Vol. II/73.*

Reinmuth, Eckart: Pseudo-Philo und Lukas. 1994. *Vol. 74.*

Reiser, Marius: Bibelkritik und Auslegung der Heiligen Schrift. 2007. *Vol. 217.*
– Syntax und Stil des Markusevangeliums. 1984. *Vol. II/11.*

Reynolds, Benjamin E.: The Apocalyptic Son of Man in the Gospel of John. 2008. *Vol. II/249.*

Rhodes, James N.: The Epistle of Barnabas and the Deuteronomic Tradition. 2004. *Vol. II/188.*

Richards, E. Randolph: The Secretary in the Letters of Paul. 1991. *Vol. II/42.*

Riesner, Rainer: Jesus als Lehrer. 1981, [3]1988. *Vol. II/7.*

– Die Frühzeit des Apostels Paulus. 1994. *Vol. 71.*

Rissi, Mathias: Die Theologie des Hebräerbriefs. 1987. *Vol. 41.*

Röcker, Fritz W.: Belial und Katechon. 2009. *Vol. II/262.*

Röhser, Günter: Metaphorik und Personifikation der Sünde. 1987. *Vol. II/25.*

Rose, Christian: Theologie als Erzählung im Markusevangelium. 2007. *Vol. II/236.*

– Die Wolke der Zeugen. 1994. *Vol. II/60.*

Roskovec, Jan: see Pokorný, Petr.

Rothschild, Clare K.: Baptist Traditions and Q. 2005. *Vol. 190.*

– Hebrews as Pseudepigraphon. 2009. *Vol. 235.*

– Luke Acts and the Rhetoric of History. 2004. *Vol. II/175.*

– see Frey, Jörg.

Rudolph, David J.: A Jew to the Jews. 2011. *Vol. II/304.*

Rüegger, Hans-Ulrich: Verstehen, was Markus erzählt. 2002. *Vol. II/155.*

Rüger, Hans Peter: Die Weisheitsschrift aus der Kairoer Geniza. 1991. *Vol. 53.*

Ruf, Martin G.: Die heiligen Propheten, eure Apostel und ich. 2011. *Vol. II/300.*

Runesson, Anders: see Becker, Eve-Marie.

Sänger, Dieter: Antikes Judentum und die Mysterien. 1980. *Vol. II/5.*

– Die Verkündigung des Gekreuzigten und Israel. 1994. *Vol. 75.*

– see Burchard, Christoph

– and Ulrich Mell (Ed.): Paulus und Johannes. 2006. *Vol. 198.*

Salier, Willis Hedley: The Rhetorical Impact of the Semeia in the Gospel of John. 2004. *Vol. II/186.*

Salzmann, Jörg Christian: Lehren und Ermahnen. 1994. *Vol. II/59.*

Samuelsson, Gunnar: Crucifixion in Antiquity. 2011. *Vol. II/310.*

Sandnes, Karl Olav: Paul – One of the Prophets? 1991. *Vol. II/43.*

Sato, Migaku: Q und Prophetie. 1988. *Vol. II/29.*

Schäfer, Ruth: Paulus bis zum Apostelkonzil. 2004. *Vol. II/179.*

Schaper, Joachim: Eschatology in the Greek Psalter. 1995. *Vol. II/76.*

Schimanowski, Gottfried: Die himmlische Liturgie in der Apokalypse des Johannes. 2002. *Vol. II/154.*

– Weisheit und Messias. 1985. *Vol. II/17.*

Schlichting, Günter: Ein jüdisches Leben Jesu. 1982. *Vol. 24.*

Schließer, Benjamin: Abraham's Faith in Romans 4. 2007. *Vol. II/224.*

Schnabel, Eckhard J.: Law and Wisdom from Ben Sira to Paul. 1985. *Vol. II/16.*

Schnelle, Udo: see Frey, Jörg.

Schröter, Jens: Von Jesus zum Neuen Testament. 2007. *Vol. 204.*

– see Frey, Jörg.

Schutter, William L.: Hermeneutic and Composition in I Peter. 1989. *Vol. II/30.*

Schwartz, Daniel R.: Studies in the Jewish Background of Christianity. 1992. *Vol. 60.*

Schwemer, Anna Maria: see Hengel, Martin

Scott, Ian W.: Implicit Epistemology in the Letters of Paul. 2005. *Vol. II/205.*

Scott, James M.: Adoption as Sons of God. 1992. *Vol. II/48.*

– Paul and the Nations. 1995. *Vol. 84.*

Shi, Wenhua: Paul's Message of the Cross as Body Language. 2008. *Vol. II/254.*

Shum, Shiu-Lun: Paul's Use of Isaiah in Romans. 2002. *Vol. II/156.*

Siegert, Folker: Drei hellenistisch-jüdische Predigten. Teil I 1980. *Vol. 20* – Teil II 1992. *Vol. 61.*

– Nag-Hammadi-Register. 1982. *Vol. 26.*

– Argumentation bei Paulus. 1985. *Vol. 34.*

– Philon von Alexandrien. 1988. *Vol. 46.*

Siggelkow-Berner, Birke: Die jüdischen Feste im Bellum Judaicum des Flavius Josephus. 2011. *Vol. II/306.*

Simon, Marcel: Le christianisme antique et son contexte religieux I/II. 1981. *Vol. 23.*

Smit, Peter-Ben: Fellowship and Food in the Kingdom. 2008. *Vol. II/234.*

Smith, Julien: Christ the Ideal King. 2011. *Vol. II/313.*

Snodgrass, Klyne: The Parable of the Wicked Tenants. 1983. *Vol. 27.*

Söding, Thomas: Das Wort vom Kreuz. 1997. *Vol. 93.*

– see Thüsing, Wilhelm.

Sommer, Urs: Die Passionsgeschichte des Markusevangeliums. 1993. *Vol. II/58.*

Sorensen, Eric: Possession and Exorcism in the New Testament and Early Christianity. 2002. *Vol. II/157.*

Souček, Josef B.: see Pokorný, Petr.

Southall, David J.: Rediscovering Righteousness in Romans. 2008. *Vol. 240.*

Spangenberg, Volker: Herrlichkeit des Neuen Bundes. 1993. *Vol. II/55.*

Spanje, T.E. van: Inconsistency in Paul? 1999. *Vol. II/110.*

Speyer, Wolfgang: Frühes Christentum im antiken Strahlungsfeld. Vol. I: 1989. *Vol. 50.*

– Vol. II: 1999. *Vol. 116.*

– Vol. III: 2007. *Vol. 213.*

Spittler, Janet E.: Animals in the Apocryphal Acts of the Apostles. 2008. *Vol. II/247.*
Sprinkle, Preston: Law and Life. 2008. *Vol. II/241.*
Stadelmann, Helge: Ben Sira als Schriftgelehrter. 1980. *Vol. II/6.*
Stein, Hans Joachim: Frühchristliche Mahlfeiern. 2008. *Vol. II/255.*
Stenschke, Christoph W.: Luke's Portrait of Gentiles Prior to Their Coming to Faith. *Vol. II/108.*
Stephens, Mark B.: Annihilation or Renewal? 2011. *Vol. II/307.*
Sterck-Degueldre, Jean-Pierre: Eine Frau namens Lydia. 2004. *Vol. II/176.*
Stettler, Christian: Der Kolosserhymnus. 2000. *Vol. II/131.*
– Das letzte Gericht. 2011. *Vol. II/299.*
Stettler, Hanna: Die Christologie der Pastoralbriefe. 1998. *Vol. II/105.*
Stökl Ben Ezra, Daniel: The Impact of Yom Kippur on Early Christianity. 2003. *Vol. 163.*
Strobel, August: Die Stunde der Wahrheit. 1980. *Vol. 21.*
Stroumsa, Guy G.: Barbarian Philosophy. 1999. *Vol. 112.*
Stuckenbruck, Loren T.: Angel Veneration and Christology. 1995. *Vol. II/70.*
–, *Stephen C. Barton* and *Benjamin G. Wold* (Ed.): Memory in the Bible and Antiquity. 2007. *Vol. 212.*
Stuhlmacher, Peter (Ed.): Das Evangelium und die Evangelien. 1983. *Vol. 28.*
– Biblische Theologie und Evangelium. 2002. *Vol. 146.*
Sung, Chong-Hyon: Vergebung der Sünden. 1993. *Vol. II/57.*
Svendsen, Stefan N.: Allegory Transformed. 2009. *Vol. II/269.*
Tajra, Harry W.: The Trial of St. Paul. 1989. *Vol. II/35.*
– The Martyrdom of St.Paul. 1994. *Vol. II/67.*
Tellbe, Mikael: Christ-Believers in Ephesus. 2009. *Vol. 242.*
Theißen, Gerd: Studien zur Soziologie des Urchristentums. 1979, ³1989. *Vol. 19.*
Theobald, Michael: Studien zum Corpus Iohanneum. 2010. *Vol. 267.*
– Studien zum Römerbrief. 2001. *Vol. 136.*
– see *Mußner, Franz.*
Thornton, Claus-Jürgen: Der Zeuge des Zeugen. 1991. *Vol. 56.*
Thüsing, Wilhelm: Studien zur neutestamentlichen Theologie. Ed. von Thomas Söding. 1995. *Vol. 82.*
Thurén, Lauri: Derhethorizing Paul. 2000. *Vol. 124.*

Thyen, Hartwig: Studien zum Corpus Iohanneum. 2007. *Vol. 214.*
Tibbs, Clint: Religious Experience of the Pneuma. 2007. *Vol. II/230.*
Toit, David S. du: Theios Anthropos. 1997. *Vol. II/91.*
Tolmie, D. Francois: Persuading the Galatians. 2005. *Vol. II/190.*
Tomson, Peter J. and *Doris Lambers-Petry* (Ed.): The Image of the Judaeo-Christians in Ancient Jewish and Christian Literature. 2003. *Vol. 158.*
Toney, Carl N.: Paul's Inclusive Ethic. 2008. *Vol. II/252.*
Trebilco, Paul: The Early Christians in Ephesus from Paul to Ignatius. 2004. *Vol. 166.*
Treloar, Geoffrey R.: Lightfoot the Historian. 1998. *Vol. II/103.*
Troftgruben, Troy M.: A Conclusion Unhindered. 2010. *Vol. II/280.*
Tso, Marcus K.M.: Ethics in the Qumran Community. 2010. *Vol. II/292.*
Tsuji, Manabu: Glaube zwischen Vollkommenheit und Verweltlichung. 1997. *Vol. II/93.*
Twelftree, Graham H.: Jesus the Exorcist. 1993. *Vol. II/54.*
Ulrichs, Karl Friedrich: Christusglaube. 2007. *Vol. II/227.*
Urban, Christina: Das Menschenbild nach dem Johannesevangelium. 2001. *Vol. II/137.*
Vahrenhorst, Martin: Kultische Sprache in den Paulusbriefen. 2008. *Vol. 230.*
Vegge, Ivar: 2 Corinthians – a Letter about Reconciliation. 2008. *Vol. II/239.*
Verheyden, Joseph, Korinna Zamfir and *Tobias Nicklas* (Ed.): Prophets and Prophecy in Jewish and Early Christian Literature. 2010. *Vol. II/286.*
– see *Nicklas, Tobias*
Visotzky, Burton L.: Fathers of the World. 1995. *Vol. 80.*
Vollenweider, Samuel: Horizonte neutestamentlicher Christologie. 2002. *Vol. 144.*
Vos, Johan S.: Die Kunst der Argumentation bei Paulus. 2002. *Vol. 149.*
Waaler, Erik: The *Shema* and The First Commandment in First Corinthians. 2008. *Vol. II/253.*
Wagener, Ulrike: Die Ordnung des „Hauses Gottes". 1994. *Vol. II/65.*
Wagner, J. Ross: see *Wilk, Florian.*
Wahlen, Clinton: Jesus and the Impurity of Spirits in the Synoptic Gospels. 2004. *Vol. II/185.*
Walker, Donald D.: Paul's Offer of Leniency (2 Cor 10:1). 2002. *Vol. II/152.*

Walter, Nikolaus: Praeparatio Evangelica. Ed. von Wolfgang Kraus und Florian Wilk. 1997. *Vol. 98.*

Wander, Bernd: Gottesfürchtige und Sympathisanten. 1998. *Vol. 104.*

Wardle, Timothy: The Jerusalem Temple and Early Christian Identity. 2010. *Vol. II/291.*

Wasserman, Emma: The Death of the Soul in Romans 7. 2008. *Vol. 256.*

Waters, Guy: The End of Deuteronomy in the Epistles of Paul. 2006. *Vol. 221.*

Watt, Jan G. van der: see *Frey, Jörg*
– see *Zimmermann, Ruben*

Watts, Rikki: Isaiah's New Exodus and Mark. 1997. *Vol. II/88.*

Webb, Robert L.: see *Bock, Darrell L.*

Wedderburn, Alexander J.M.: Baptism and Resurrection. 1987. *Vol. 44.*
– Jesus and the Historians. 2010. *Vol. 269.*

Wegner, Uwe: Der Hauptmann von Kafarnaum. 1985. *Vol. II/14.*

Weiß, Hans-Friedrich: Frühes Christentum und Gnosis. 2008. *Vol. 225.*

Weissenrieder, Annette: Images of Illness in the Gospel of Luke. 2003. Vol. II/164.
–, and *Robert B. Coote* (Ed.): The Interface of Orality and Writing. 2010. *Vol. 260.*
–, *Friederike Wendt* and *Petra von Gemünden* (Ed.): Picturing the New Testament. 2005. *Vol. II/193.*

Welck, Christian: Erzählte ‚Zeichen'. 1994. *Vol. II/69.*

Wendt, Friederike (Ed.): see *Weissenrieder, Annette.*

Wiarda, Timothy: Peter in the Gospels. 2000. *Vol. II/127.*

Wifstrand, Albert: Epochs and Styles. 2005. *Vol. 179.*

Wilk, Florian and *J. Ross Wagner* (Ed.): Between Gospel and Election. 2010. *Vol. 257.*
– see *Walter, Nikolaus.*

Williams, Catrin H.: I am He. 2000. *Vol. II/113.*

Wilson, Todd A.: The Curse of the Law and the Crisis in Galatia. 2007. *Vol. II/225.*

Wilson, Walter T.: Love without Pretense. 1991. *Vol. II/46.*

Winn, Adam: The Purpose of Mark's Gospel. 2008. *Vol. II/245.*

Winninge, Mikael: see *Holmberg, Bengt.*

Wischmeyer, Oda: Von Ben Sira zu Paulus. 2004. *Vol. 173.*

Wisdom, Jeffrey: Blessing for the Nations and the Curse of the Law. 2001. *Vol. II/133.*

Witmer, Stephen E.: Divine Instruction in Early Christianity. 2008. *Vol. II/246.*

Wold, Benjamin G.: Women, Men, and Angels. 2005. *Vol. II/2001.*

Wolter, Michael: Theologie und Ethos im frühen Christentum. 2009. *Vol. 236.*
– see *Stuckenbruck, Loren T.*

Wright, Archie T.: The Origin of Evil Spirits. 2005. *Vol. II/198.*

Wucherpfennig, Ansgar: Heracleon Philologus. 2002. *Vol. 142.*

Yates, John W.: The Spirit and Creation in Paul. 2008. *Vol. II/251.*

Yeung, Maureen: Faith in Jesus and Paul. 2002. *Vol. II/147.*

Young, Stephen E.: Jesus Tradition in the Apostolic Fathers. 2011. *Vol. II/311.*

Zamfir, Corinna: see *Verheyden, Joseph*

Zangenberg, Jürgen, Harold W. Attridge and *Dale B. Martin* (Ed.): Religion, Ethnicity and Identity in Ancient Galilee. 2007. *Vol. 210.*

Zimmermann, Alfred E.: Die urchristlichen Lehrer. 1984, ²1988. *Vol. II/12.*

Zimmermann, Johannes: Messianische Texte aus Qumran. 1998. *Vol. II/104.*

Zimmermann, Ruben: Christologie der Bilder im Johannesevangelium. 2004. *Vol. 171.*
– Geschlechtermetaphorik und Gottesverhältnis. 2001. *Vol. II/122.*
– (Ed.): Hermeneutik der Gleichnisse Jesu. 2008. *Vol. 231.*
– and *Jan G. van der Watt* (Ed.): Moral Language in the New Testament. Vol. II. 2010. *Vol. II/296.*
– see *Frey, Jörg.*
– see *Horn, Friedrich Wilhelm.*

Zugmann, Michael: „Hellenisten" in der Apostelgeschichte. 2009. *Vol. II/264.*

Zumstein, Jean: see *Dettwiler, Andreas*

Zwiep, Arie W.: Christ, the Spirit and the Community of God. 2010. *Vol. II/293.*
– Judas and the Choice of Matthias. 2004. *Vol. II/187.*

For a complete catalogue please write to the publisher
Mohr Siebeck • P.O. Box 2030 • D–72010 Tübingen/Germany
Up-to-date information on the internet at www.mohr.de